Harvard Historical Studies · 149

Published under the auspices
of the Department of History
from the income of the
Paul Revere Frothingham Bequest
Robert Louis Stroock Fund
Henry Warren Torrey Fund

Oil Empire

*Visions of Prosperity
in Austrian Galicia*

Alison Fleig Frank

— social structure
+ legal policies
in Galicia helped
determine the fate
of its oil industry &
its potential to
produce
wealth

— (overproduction of oil was
seen as benefiting Galician
economy for more than
harming the environment
or causing a financial
crises though no control
of supply & demand

Harvard University Press
Cambridge, Massachusetts
London, England

First Harvard University Press paperback edition, 2007

Library of Congress Cataloging-in-Publication Data

Frank, Alison Fleig.
Oil empire : visions of prosperity in Austrian Galicia / Alison Fleig Frank.
p. cm.
Includes bibliographical references and index.
ISBN-13 978-0-674-01887-7 (cloth: alk. paper)
ISBN-10 0-674-01887-7 (cloth: alk. paper)
ISBN-13 978-0-674-02541-7 (pbk.)
ISBN-10 0-674-02541-5 (pbk.)
1. Petroleum industry and trade—Galicia (Poland and Ukraine)—History.
2. Galicia (Poland and Ukraine)—Economic conditions. 3. Galicia (Poland and
Ukraine)—Social conditions. I. Title.

HD9575.G35F73 2005
338.2'728'094386—dc22   2005046206

To the memory of my beloved mother,
Susan Findling Fleig
1941–2003

Contents

Illustrations

Maps

Photos

Figures

Acknowledgments

It is a pleasure to acknowledge some of the many individuals and institutions whose advice and support made the completion of this project possible. The research at the heart of this work began while I was a graduate student at Harvard University, and my first debt of gratitude is to my advisors there. Roman Szporluk's infectious suspicion of "ethnographic determinism" turned me down the path of transnational history. As any of his many professional progeny would readily attest, he is an inspirational scholar, outstanding teacher, and generous friend. David Blackbourn was willing to transcend German history and, taking me under his wing, taught me to value methodological innovation. Long before I met him, I knew he was a visionary scholar—he also has proven to be a kind and considerate counselor. Edward Keenan, Charles Maier, Terry Martin, Steven Ozment, and John Womack critically contributed to my training and to the initial conception of this project. My friends and graduate student colleagues, most particularly Ben Hett, Eric Lohr, and Jessica Elzinga, were also essential to my sanity, happiness, and focus. While at Harvard, my research was supported by generous grants from the Minda de Gunzburg Center for European Studies through its Program for the Study of Germany and Europe, the Harvard Ukrainian Research Institute, and the History Department, as well as by federal funding through FLAS and Javits fellowships.

This book matured during my tenure as an assistant professor at the University of Wisconsin–Madison, where I was blessed with many kind colleagues. Foremost among them is my adopted mentor, David McDonald, to whom I am indebted for his wisdom, wit, and generosity of spirit. I owe a special thanks to him, Rudy Koshar, and Lee Wandel for believing in me from the beginning. Brett Sheehan (who guided me through the revision process with logic and discipline), Fran Hirsch, and Karl Shoemaker have been dear friends and perfect role models. Bill Cronon, Suzanne Desan, and Mary Louise Roberts commented on early drafts of the manuscript. While at the University of Wisconsin–Madison, my research was funded by the Graduate School Research Council, the International Institute (including the Center for European Studies, the Center for Russia, East Europe and Central Asia, and the Center for German and European Studies), and the Border and Transcultural Studies Research Circle. Support of research, travel, and writing was also generously provided by the Austrian Fulbright Commission and the Austrian Cultural Forum in New York.

A number of other scholars have read portions of the manuscript in various stages, and offered useful comments and criticisms. I am particularly grateful to Emil Brix, Gary Cohen, Catherine Giustino, Mary Gluck, David Good, Yaroslav Hrytsak, Pieter Judson, Jeremy King, John McNeill, Jonathan Sperber, Nancy Wingfield, and Tara Zahra, whose suggestions have helped broaden my perspective on central European history. The many valuable comments made by Harvard University Press's readers, Thomas K. McCraw and Catherine Albrecht, have inestimably improved the text. I would like to thank editor Kathleen McDermott (who created all the chapter titles) for her guidance through every stage of the publication process, production editor Lewis Parker, and copy editor Charles Eberline for his careful reading and considerate correction of the text. Remaining imperfections and deficiencies are solely my responsibility.

My research abroad would not have been possible without the many scholars who expressed interest in my work and helped me navigate archives and libraries in Vienna, Cracow, Lviv, Paris, and London, including Moritz Csáky, Piotr Franaszek, Yaroslav Hrytsak, Jean-Marc Dreyfus, Andreas Kappeler, Lothar Höbelt, and Liliana Hentosh. In Vienna I was assisted by the friendly and capable staff of the Österreichische Nationalbibliothek and several archivists at the Österreichisches Staatsarchiv, in particular Helmut Karigl, Roman-Hans Gröger, Robert Rill, and Herbert Hutterer. Thanks to its congenial staff, the Internationales Forschungszentrum Kulturwissenschaften in Vienna provided not only a comfortable professional home, but also an incomparable intellectual climate in which to complete the manuscript. In Lviv, Myroslava Diadiuk and the staff of the Central State Historical Archives of Ukraine were enormously helpful. Oleh Mikulych acted as my guide and host in Boryslav, Droho-bych, and Skhidnytsia, and graciously shared some of his extensive col-lection of photographs and postcards of the oil region with me. In Paris, Roger Nougaret kindly made the archives of the Crédit Lyonnais acces-sible.

Marek Klara of the Muzeum Przemysłu Naftowego im. Ignacego Łuka-siewicza in Bóbrka, Liz Welsh (Chairperson of the Petrolia Heritage Com-mittee), and Anne Ashton of the Lambton Room were instrumental in tracking down portraits of Stanisław Szczepanowski and William Henry MacGarvey. Marieka Brouwer of the University of Wisconsin–Madison Cartographic Laboratory created the maps.

I am grateful to the faculty of Georgetown Day School in Washington, DC, and Green Acres School in Rockville, Maryland, for instilling an early love of reading and writing and an interest in foreign languages. On behalf of my entire family, I extend heartfelt thanks to our dear friends Janelle, Jim, Josie, Jack, and Karsyn Ulibarri.

Most especially and with a great deal of love, I express my gratitude to my family. Even in adulthood, my father, Albert Joseph Fleig, remains my intellectual hero. His commitment to science and the pursuit of truth has inspired me since he first put me to sleep with lectures on the libra-tion of a gravity-gradient-stabilized spacecraft in an eccentric orbit. My stepmother, Venus, has taught me the value of emotional intelligence. My uncle and aunt, Robert and Elizabeth Findling, remind me that our family is vibrant and strong even in its darkest hours. My brother, David, is living proof that our childhood was good. The Frank, Götzl, Rosenkranz, and Stabinger families make sure I always have a home. I thank my beautiful children, Alexander and Natalie-Susan, for every minute I was unable to work on this book. My husband, Holger, I thank for every minute I was able to work on it. He has given up his sleep, his job, his country, and his motorcycle to follow and support me as I have pursued my own career. Without his sacrifice, this book could never have been written, and it is his accomplishment as much as mine. He will, never-theless, understand that I have dedicated it to the memory of my beloved mother, Susan Findling Fleig, who would have burst with pride had she lived to see its completion.

Note on Translation

No history of Galicia is complete without an explanation of the principles of translation chosen by the author. German, Polish, Ukrainian, and Yiddish speakers each resided in the province, and each had their own appellations for places and for people, nicely represented by Alexander Granach's essay "I Come from Wierzbowce/Werbowitz/Werbiwzi." The province's capital was alternately known as Lemberg (German and Yiddish), Lwów (Polish), L'viv (Ukrainian), Lvov (Russian), and Leopol (French); the capital of the oil region as Drohobycz (Polish and German), Drohobych (Ukrainian), Drohobich (Yiddish), and Drogobych (Russian). Where modern English equivalents exist, as they do for most major cities, I have chosen to use them, hence Vienna, Cracow, Warsaw, and Lviv. For other cities, towns, and villages within Galicia, I have chosen to use the Polish names. The only exception to this general policy is made in quotations or titles translated from Ukrainian, in which I have maintained the transliterated Ukrainian spelling. The other logical alternative would be to use today's border between Poland and Ukraine as an approximation of the Polish-language area and the Ukrainian-language area during the time under consideration. Although using Ukrainian versions of place names to the east of this border would acknowledge that the majority of residents of many of these towns and all of these villages were Ukrainian speakers, it would be anachronistic. I have chosen not to attempt to remedy with my own terminology the wrongs done Ukrainian speakers in previous centuries, since distinguishing between Polish and Ukrainian Galicia would require projecting the current independence of Ukraine back into an earlier time in which an independent Ukrainian state was difficult to imagine. It would also imply a linguistic uniformity in each of the province's two halves that simply did not exist. In the nineteenth century, Poles and the Polish language were very much dominant in both eastern and western Galicia, even where they were numerically inferior. Using Polish names reflects the fact that, from the late 1860s, Polish was the official language of Galicia, and symbolizes my conviction that the province's political, social, and economic elites were themselves Polish speakers. Use of the word Borysław is thus in no way intended to carry irredentist implications that this area is naturally part of Poland.

I have honored the version of personal names that appears to have been preferred by the individual in question. So Szczepanowski, a self-declared Pole, is Stanisław Szczepanowski, not Stanislaus, although his name appears in both variations in contemporary sources.

The use of the term "Ruthenian" to describe the Ukrainian-speaking residents of the Austrian Empire in the first six chapters respects contemporary terminology. The people described as Ruthenians did not themselves object to this term in the nineteenth century. Only slowly over the course of the first two decades of the twentieth century did "Ukrainian" become the term of preference, intended to emphasize the connection between those Ukrainian speakers who were Austrian and those who were Russian subjects. (Symbolic of this transformation, the *Ruthenische Revue* became the *Ukrainische Rundschau* in 1906.) However, after the First World War, to refer to Ukrainian speakers west of the Zbruch River as Ruthenians was a political statement that denied them the status of a nation. By that time, the term had become offensive to politically aware Ukrainians. I have therefore chosen to use the word "Ukrainian" in my own references to all Ukrainian speakers in chapter 7, retaining "Ruthenian" only in translations of quotations that use that term.

I have tried to make this study accessible to readers unfamiliar with one or more of the various languages used in the sources on which it depends (German, Polish, Ukrainian, French, and Russian). This requires translating titles and offices, even where no clear English equivalent exists. At the top of the provincial executive government sat the viceroy (Statthalter, namiestnik, namisnyk), surrounded by the staff of the viceroy's office (Statthalterei, namiestnictwo, namisnytstwo). The viceroy's office oversaw eighty-five districts (Bezirkshauptmannschaft, powiat, povit), each presided over by a chief district magistrate (Bezirkshauptmann, starosta, starosta). The smallest unit of political organization was the local community (Gemeinde, gmina, hromada). Oversight of the oil industry fell under the jurisdiction of the Provincial Mining Office (Berghauptmannschaft), based in Cracow. The province was divided into four district mining offices (Revierbergämter), in Cracow, Jasło, Drohobycz, and Stanisławów. Other offices and titles that appear throughout the text are listed here:

District Court	Bezirksgericht/Okręg powiatowy
Exchequer	Hofkammer
Factory Inspector	Gewerbeinspektor
Fleet Commando	Flottenkommando
Front High Command	Etappenoberkommando
Imperial Parliament	Reichsrat
Mining Authority	Bergbehörde
Mining Commissioner	Bergkommissär
Mining Councillor	Bergrat
Mining Inspector	Berginspektor
Mining Police	Bergpolizei
Naval Section	Marinesektion
Polish Club	Koło Polskie
Polish People's Party	Polskie Stronnictwo Ludowe
President of the Provincial Diet	Marszałek
Prime Minister	Ministerpräsident
Provincial Diet	Landtag/Sejm
Viceregal Councilor	Statthaltereirat/Radca namiestnictwa
Viceregal Presidium	Statthalterei Präsidium/Prezydyum Namiestnictwa

The sources used for this book contain references to prices and valuations in numerous currencies. From 1867 to 1892, the basic unit of currency in Austria-Hungary was the silver florin (or gulden), which was equivalent to 100 kreuzer. In 1892, Austria-Hungary switched to the gold standard and introduced a new currency, the crown (*Kronen*). One crown equaled 0.5 florins and could be divided into 100 heller. The value of Austrian currency was not stable enough to be convertible until 1896 (see Marc Flandreau and John Komlos, "Core or Periphery? The Credibility of the Austro-Hungarian Currency 1867–1913," *Journal of European Economic History* [Italy] 2002 31, no. 2: 293–320). In order to make it easier for readers to get a sense of comparative values, I have provided equivalents of all other currencies in crowns wherever I was able to establish a reasonably accurate exchange rate.

All translations, unless otherwise indicated, are my own.

Abbreviations

A	Abend: Evening edition of a newspaper
AM	Ackerbauministerium: Ministry of Agriculture
AOK	Armeeoberkommando: Army High Command
BS	Bildersammlung: Picture Collection
CL	Archives historiques du Crédit Lyonnais
CPA	Commission for Polish Affairs
F.	Fach
f.	Fond
FM	Finanzministerium: Ministry of Finance
FO	Foreign Office
GLPV	Galizische Landespetroleum Verein: Galician Provincial Petroleum Association
HM	Handelsministerium: Ministry of Commerce
IAC	Inter-Allied Commission to Poland
IM	Innenministerium: Ministry of the Interior
k.k.	Kaiserlich königlich: Imperial royal (refers to the 'Austrian' half of the Austro-Hungarian Empire)
KM	Kriegsministerium: Ministry of War
KP(b)U	Communist Party (Bolshevik) of Ukraine
k.u.k.	Kaiserlich und königlich: Imperial and royal (refers to both halves of the Austro-Hungarian Empire)
LVRP	Landesverband der Rohöl-Produzenten: Provincial Association of Crude Oil Producers
M	Morgen: Morning edition of a newspaper
MföA	Ministerium für öffentliche Arbeiten: Ministry of Public Works
MS	Marinesektion: Naval Section
ÖHHSA	Österreichisches Haus-, Hof- und Staatsarchiv: Austrian Family, Court and State Archive

ÖSTA   Österreichisches Staatsarchiv: Austrian State Archive
PRO   Public Record Office
PSL   Polskie Stronnictwo Ludowe
SPA   Stenographische Protokolle über die Sitzungen des Hauses der
       Abgeordneten des Reichsrates: Stenographic protocol of the meet-
       ings of the House of Representatives of the imperial Parliament
TsDIAUL   Tsentral'nyi Derzhavnyi Istorychnyi Arkhiv Ukraïny, m. L'viv:
       Central State Historical Archives of Ukraine in Lviv
UNR   Ukraïnska Narodnia Respublika: Ukrainian People's Republic
ZUNR   Zachidno-Ukraïnska Narodnia Respublika: Western Ukrainian
       People's Republic

The Austro-Hungarian Empire, 1867–1914

Introduction

This study describes the human institutions, traditions, and preoccupations that helped shape the oil industry in the Austrian Empire and contributed as much to its fate as the geological features that created, five hundred million years ago or more, the oil that that industry began to exploit a mere century and a half ago. The lessons to be drawn from this story are widely applicable. Methodologically, they force us to reconsider our reliance on modern national boundaries for conceptualizing the organization of social, political, cultural, economic, and environmental change in the past. They contribute to an ongoing challenge to popular stories of modernization, of worker consciousness, of the redrawing of borders, and of the importance of diplomacy. These issues are not restricted to the Galician case or to the Austrian case. Nevertheless, one of this story's most important lessons is that the development of an oil industry—however international the politics and economics of oil may be—is also profoundly local. One must understand the local environment and, to borrow terminology from Fernand Braudel, its social, cultural, political, and economic landscapes[1] in all their complexity in order to understand why oil did or did not bring prosperity to those who attached their fates to it. In this particular case, that local environment was the oil basin that ran through the Austrian province of Galicia (and now is divided between the republics of Poland and Ukraine).

Human beings played no role in the actual creation of petroleum (literally, "rock oil"), nor were they present to witness its gradual formation. Nevertheless, geologists have been able to reconstruct what they believe to have been petroleum's origins. The explanation that is most popular today is the organic theory, which holds that oil was created over the

1

course of a great many years as millions of tiny sea creatures (plant and animal organisms, a sort of prehistoric plankton) died and their corpses sank one by one to the ocean floor. Over vast stretches of time, they were covered with layers of sediment and deprived of oxygen. The combination of immense pressure from sedimentary rock, the heat created by that pressure, and the activity of anaerobic bacteria transformed this biomass into petroleum. The necessary mixture of chemical and biological ingredients and geological conditions marked only the beginning of oil's activity, however. Once the petroleum had formed, it did not rest in its original nursery, peacefully awaiting discovery. Gases pushed oil from its primary slumbering places to secondary beds, bubbling and pressing against any weakness in its rocky cradle. Oil migrated along the path of least resistance from one geological layer to another, moving through porous rocks and sometimes even reaching the surface of the earth—or, in some cases, remaining locked beneath impermeable layers of rock in vast underground reservoirs often far distant from its place of origin.

Like most scientific theories that we now take to be self-evident, this one did not emerge without its share of controversy. In the pages of mining and petroleum trade journals throughout the nineteenth century, scholars and geologists debated whether the creation of oil under the earth's surface continued or had ceased entirely, whether it was of inorganic or organic origin, and in the second case, whether the biomass that led to oil's creation was primarily plant or animal matter.[2] Only oil's antiquity, which seemed to invite biblical imagery, was beyond question. The author of a 1925 monograph on petroleum described a world in which oil drills had replaced Gabriel's trumpet: "The poor souls of the living creatures that were once buried in the ocean floor certainly did not expect that they would experience the resurrection of their fats before Judgment Day. They have been all too rudely awoken from their peace."[3] It is with that awakening that a history of the oil industry can rightly begin.

For millions of years, human beings did not interfere in the process of petroleum's creation or in its movement. They did not add to or diminish it; they did not explore the depths of the earth in search of it, exploit its energy, or set it aflame for their own purposes. Even after the human discovery of the usefulness of petroleum, which sources suggest occurred in antiquity, humans' ability to collect it was limited for millennia to retrieving oil on or close to the earth's surface. Thus one cannot call this

a history of oil, or even of Galician oil. This story begins when the ac- *when this story begins*
tivities of men and women on the earth's surface began to affect hidden
sources of petroleum under it: that is, when the scale of human influence
on petroleum began to compete with geological givens in determining
how much oil there was, where and when it moved, and what was done
with it. This book is, then, a history of the Galician oil industry, of the
social, cultural, and political forces that shaped it, and of the new environment it created.

Before tanks replaced horses on the battlefields of Europe, before submarines and airplanes led to the mechanization of warfare, and long
before the two-car garage and the democratization of airplane travel, petroleum was essential—to European and North American consumers, industrialists, and military planners alike. Dependence on petroleum began *kerosene lamps*
when one of its by-products, kerosene, became a cheap and safe way to
illuminate homes, railway stations, and other public buildings after dark.
By the outbreak of the First World War, however, petroleum's use as a
source of energy to power machinery via the internal combustion engine *engines*
began to overtake its use as a source of light. "Hydrocarbon man," a
creature with whom we are all too familiar today, had emerged.[4] If we
were to find ourselves transported to the beginning of the twentieth century, much of what we would see on the pages of petroleum trade journals
would seem familiar. Then, as now, oil prices were carefully watched and
had the power to make or break personal fortunes and even national
economies. Many of the key players in the global oil game have remained
the same: the United States and Russia rank among the largest oil producers in the world today and headed up the list one hundred years ago
as well. The vast oil fields of the Middle East were unknown in 1900, but
were soon to be discovered. By 1925, Persia had become the world's sixth-
largest producer of oil over the entire period of the oil industry's existence.[5] Mexico and Venezuela were also major producers in the years
before the First World War, as they are today. Those who remember the
bombing of the Romanian oil fields during the Second World War would
not be surprised to learn that Romania was among the top five oil producers at the turn of the twentieth century.

Along with the familiar elements of the oil industry around 1900, however, we would also encounter surprising and even strange ones. Rounding

out the list of the world's top producers at the beginning of the twentieth century is one region that had no place in it at the century's end: the Austrian province of Galicia. Thanks to its Galician oil fields, Austria-Hungary was the third-largest oil-producing region in the world in 1909, accounting for 5 percent of world production. It ranked among the top five every year from the middle of the nineteenth century until 1910 and was not displaced from the top ten until after the end of the First World War. In 1920, only four countries had contributed more to the global production of oil over the entire course of the preceding seventy years than had Galicia.[6] The history of Galicia's oil production—like that of the province itself—is today a little-known curiosity. In 1909, however, Galicia sparkled like a gem on the tip of every oil driller's tongue, and its oil industry held the hopes for retirement in comfort of many a London waitress turned investor. Perhaps Galicia itself seemed as exotic then as it does today, but its oil industry was anything but unfamiliar. Newspapers in London, Paris, Brussels, Berlin, Vienna, and New York reported Galician oil production and price statistics that were studied with care by investors all over Europe and even in North America. One cannot understand Galicia, nor Austria, nor even Europe so long as this fact is obscured by the vagaries of politics and war (which destroyed Galicia) and the nostalgic insistence that Galicia was always a purely agricultural province.

Although petroleum runs like a black thread through this entire book, connecting each of its elements to all others, it is not this story's protagonist. Oil often appears to have agency, and humans' inability to control its behavior is a very important part of the history of its exploitation. But the story of oil in the absence of human involvement would not interest many readers. Oil achieved the monumental importance it now holds for human society only when people started first to exploit it and then to rely on it as a source of energy in the mid-nineteenth century. The very unpredictability that seems to make oil an actor in its own right only becomes apparent when people try to force it to behave as they wish and to serve their own agenda. In a story about the exploitation of oil—its production, chemical transformation, distribution, and consumption—oil itself can at best be the means that the protagonists use to achieve their goal or at worst be the antagonist—a force (whether human, animal, or, as in this case, natural) that hinders the protagonists.

Who, then, are the protagonists? They are all those people who hoped to use oil to achieve a certain goal—and they are legion. The task of this study is to understand those goals, whether or not they were achieved, and why. In the twenty-first century, oil is immediately linked in our minds to a very specific set of goals alluded to by Daniel Yergin in his masterful study of the international oil industry, *The Prize: The Epic Quest for Oil, Money, and Power*. The most famous story in the history of the oil industry is that of John D. Rockefeller, the founder of Standard Oil, who was phenomenally successful in his pursuit of the money and power that could be gained through the effective manipulation of people's increasing need for petroleum. Today we often feel that political and military actions of the greatest import can be explained with one word: oil. When we refer to oil in that context, we really mean the money to be made by selling it and the power that comes from controlling it.

Money and power are an important part of the story of oil exploitation in the Austrian Empire as well, but it is striking how often the goals motivating the protagonists were more complicated than the image of men and women inspired by greed and ambition would admit. It is a truism to say that oil represented different things to different people, yet this obvious and trite statement is the necessary beginning of an analysis of what motivated oil's exploitation in the days before life without the internal combustion engine was unimaginable. For the inventors of the first kerosene lamps, oil represented a challenge to the ingenuity of the scientist. For some of the hundreds of thousands of workers drawn to the oil fields, it held out the promise of freedom—whether temporary or permanent—from the oppressive routine of agricultural life and offered all the good times a few days' worth of money earned hard but fast could buy. Oil towns in Galicia, like oil towns in Pennsylvania or Texas, were decried as centers of licentiousness, lust, and liquor—a reputation that made them as appealing to some as it made them appalling to others. At the same time, a different cast of worker-peasants used a spell of hard labor in the oil fields to make extra money not to escape agricultural life, but to return to it empowered.

For some entrepreneurs, founding an oil empire meant attaining a degree of personal prestige attractive enough to draw them from across the Atlantic Ocean. But for other businessmen, the oil companies they founded and ran were a vehicle for the moral improvement of their workers, skilled and unskilled. They saw the benefit of oil extraction in the kind of industry that describes a person (industrious) rather than an economy (industrial). For still others, oil stood at the heart of an economic development seen as a proxy for (and eventually a bridge to) political independence. Oil exploitation was thus about national revival, independence, autonomy, and patriotism. The geologists, chemists, and engineers who made a living by applying their scholarship to the oil industry understood their contribution to their society as greater than the generation of profit. They argued that oil was the carrier of light and of progress, part of a civilizing mission that would illuminate Europe's darkest regions. For military planners, oil could be the key to winning war. For nationalists, it could finance (figuratively and literally) the realization of national identity and support arguments for historic continuity. In an era of fluid borders and transient states, oil could justify or belie individuals' and nations' claims to own or have rights to land.

Even though oil was a tool used to forge an independent nation, however, the oil industry was also the site of much pragmatic decision making, which undercuts historians' emphasis on the national above all else. The same oil industrialists who extolled the national-economic value of oil to Poland with one breath exploited their connection to Austrian consumers and the Austrian military with the other. As one prominent historian of the Austrian Empire has noted, "the responsibilities of the provincial, district, and communal governments" grew markedly throughout the empire in its last decades.[7] This does not mean, however, that the connection to Vienna weakened. The enthusiasm that local politicians in the oil basin and interest groups representing oil producers and refiners showed for assistance from Vienna when it suited their needs is a useful reminder that local autonomy and the unitary state, or at least the "decentralized unitary state," can be complementary phenomena.[8]

Methodologically, oil—or, for that matter, any natural resource that is the site of political, cultural, social, and economic controversy—provides the historian with the opportunity to avoid privileging one set of protagonists over others. By considering a single commodity, oil, one is able to ask questions that cut across the traditional boundaries of nation, state, and even class. What questions does oil—itself uninterested in administrative, linguistic, or social demarcations—demand be asked? What units of analysis are most useful in understanding it? The borders of the oil basin itself are determined geologically, but the social and political units that shape its exploitation are local, regional, national, continental, and global.

Studying an early oil industry helps us perceive more clearly our pre-conceptions about what is modern. The story of modernization is told as the story of the triumph of state building and nation building, of capitalism and industrialization, of class-based societies, of globalization, and of imperialism. The assumptions that we make about the intercon-nectedness of these various features—and about their creation of societies that we consider to be recognizably modern—increasingly have come under attack. In the case of the Galician oil industry, we see many of the markers of the modern world: industrial development, capital investment, legal structures supporting private property ownership, socialism, global economic networks, imperialism, and war, yet the sum of these modern innovations is a materially impoverished society characterized by outra-geous social hierarchies, intolerance, persecution, and ignorance. This story proves that the discovery of oil, however modern a resource it may be, does not set in motion a predetermined set of events or course of development. It reminds us, further, that there is nothing ineluctable about industrial development at all. The Galician oil industry followed a trajectory determined not by History or Progress, but rather by the social, cultural, political, and economic context of the specific time and the spe-cific place in which it rose and fell: that is, by its Galician, Austrian, and European environments.

The classic approach to writing about the Galician oil industry in the past has been to squeeze it into the paradigm of the national industry that promised, but sadly failed, to bring national prosperity—an industry peopled with national heroes and thwarted by foreign villains. It is not a comfortable fit. The industry's modern heroes—oil pioneers and entre-preneurs—are honored by no one. In some cases, their reputations were tarnished by criminal trials; in others, their corporate empires were dis-solved by new nations that needed to reconfigure in order to rebuild. Their biographies are left out of biographical dictionaries by compilers looking for national heroes, not for pragmatic businessmen willing to tolerate fluid national units. The industry's workers were carefree young men who whiled away their idle hours not by reading Marx, but with staggering alcohol consumption and rowdy behavior, and who, when they did go on strike, sought principally to undermine their own health in-surance. This "national" Austrian industry was financed by the French, British, and Belgians, legislated by Germans and Poles, inspired by North Americans and worked by men and women speaking primarily Ukrainian,

Polish, Yiddish, German, and English, but also a host of other languages. Its promise of wealth was as appealing in London and Brussels as it was in Lviv and Borysław, and its perils were as terrifying for investors in Berlin and bureaucrats in Vienna as for workers in the pits of the over 130 towns and villages where oil was extracted in Galicia.

Few enterprises demand as high a tolerance of risk as the attempt to earn a profit from oil. The greatest risk comes long before any possibility of reaping a pecuniary reward: exploration for and discovery of oil claim far more victims than they create victors. When crude oil is found, it must be extracted—the focus of Galicia's many producers. If producers are competing with one another for access to the same pool, the oil must be extracted quickly. Here the risk of catastrophe is great, either because of too little oil or too much. In the first case, producers suffer when wells fail to produce enough to cover the high costs of exploration and drilling. In the second case, success in finding oil turns into failure if it cannot be sold at a profit because of impossibly low prices caused by excessive supply in relation to current demand.

Producers have limited tools with which to protect themselves from these dangers. The two most effective are cooperation with other producers and vertical integration. Without the kind of cooperation made possible by cartels, it is nearly impossible to run a profitable operation based on production alone. In the words of one of the oil industry's most irresistibly witty analysts: "If industries, whose raw materials are in unlimited supply and in which exploitation methods do not necessarily imperil the future, elect to put their trust in day-to-day expediency reflected in the workings of a free market, that is their business. But if ever the case for co-ordination of interests has been made, it is on the producing side of the oil industry."[9] The problem, of course, is that such cooperation is difficult to establish and more difficult still to maintain. Cooperation in the form of price agreements or output quotas is attractive during periods of overproduction, when prices collapse, but when it solves the problem of oversupply and prices begin to rise, the temptation to abandon the agreement inevitably becomes irresistible to at least some of a cartel's members, making extended cooperation nearly impossible.[10]

More success has been achieved by companies that have turned to vertical integration, as did all of the major international oil corporations at the turn of the twentieth century, including Standard, Royal Dutch, Shell, and Anglo-Persian. This requires becoming involved in the other steps in the complicated process of bringing oil from wells to consumers. Extracted crude must first be transported to a refinery, where it is transformed into products ready for household or industrial consumption— from the heaviest tars and asphalts to the lightest products, including kerosene, diesel oil, and gasoline. Then those refined products must be distributed to wholesalers, who consolidate their inventories and sell products to retailers. Retailers must identify potential consumers, market their products, and sell them. Having access to local sources of crude oil provides an oil industry with an advantage only in the first steps of this process. But to succeed at delivery, refining, and distribution requires more than on-site production: it requires, above all else, economies of scale.

All of the large companies recognized the importance of upstream infrastructure: pipelines, refining facilities, and distribution networks. Only vertical integration enabled them to adjust activity at every stage to match upstream output and downstream capacity.[11] A vertically integrated company can monitor its crude oil production to match its refinery capacity (refineries are expensive to construct and, to maximize profit, must be run constantly and at capacity).[12] It can, in turn, limit its refining to what it feels the market will bear. Together these measures serve to adjust supply to demand, prevent price collapse, and provide stability. This sort of integration benefits not only individual companies, but the industry as a whole. In the words of one analyst: "If an entire industry consisted of only a few integrated companies behaving in this manner and if these companies refrained from price competition with each other in the market for end products . . . then for the industry as a whole, supply would be adjusted to demand very smoothly at the prevailing level of prices."[13]

Vertical integration enabled large companies to impose profit-driven discipline even where it was not provided by interventionist governments. Without careful management, there is no way to even out production flows from the beginning to the end of this process, and without the stability that even production flows provide, there is no way for oil companies to remain profitable. By coordinating every step along the way— not only production, but also transportation, refining, and distribution— and by indulging in other noncompetitive practices to secure dominance, companies like Standard were able to bring their prices down below those of almost all their potential competitors (revealing that Standard's goal was not stability for all, but rather profit for itself). Production alone was never these companies' focus: in 1918, Standard's own net crude production accounted for only 16 percent of the oil treated in its refineries.[14]

In a province like Galicia, where production was spread out among scores of different companies, this kind of coordination would have had to be provided by another source—an industrial association, a cartel, or a government body. At the very moment of the Galician oil industry's greatest success, its greatest weakness—the complete absence of any political or economic body able to take on the task of organizing the industry—was exposed. At no time was the oil industry run solely according to economic principles that argued in favor of consolidation, coordination, and centralized control. Instead, a bevy of external factors—social, cultural, and political—were allowed to shape the industry. Sometimes economic needs and political goals do not complement one another. National identity and self-determination mean more autonomy, but an oil industry requires central control, a renunciation of local autonomy in order to enable local industry to flourish. Even when Galician oil producers were forced to recognize that they needed Vienna's help, they were not willing to relinquish any of their own control.

Galicia's—and Austria's—political, social, and economic structure, reputation, culture, administration, and location in human terms shaped the fate of its oil. Concepts of remoteness and isolation are, of course, invested with meaning by human society. Social, economic, and political considerations—human decisions and patterns of behavior, not geological givens—determined how much oil would be left underground, how much would be laboriously unearthed, and how much would return to the soil, seeping into fields and streams. Conditions created by human society governed how much oil would be set ablaze in violent eruptions, and how much in the controlled environment of the petroleum lamp. The value of oil would be decided socially, not geologically, as men and women created new needs and new uses for a product that quickly moved from a luxury to a household necessity. Since, in this case, natural boundaries came close to following those arbitrary political boundaries created by men and women, the story begins not with the birth of oil, but with the birth of Galicia. Because of the importance of the Galician context for understanding the specific development of the Galician oil industry, the first task is to explore and explain the social structure and origins of Galicia itself.

At first glance, the Kingdom of Galicia does not appear to have been blessed by nature. Throughout the nineteenth century, the story goes, the crescent-shaped province marking the northeastern border of the Habsburg Empire was devoted exclusively to agriculture—and the land was not kind. Characterized by repeated crop failures, its agricultural yield even in the best years was the lowest of all Austrian provinces. Overpopulation, combined with primitive agricultural techniques, led to endemic famine, which contemporary critics and historians alike have believed to have caused an estimated fifty thousand deaths from malnutrition each year.[15] A wave of emigration that started in the 1880s carried over eight hundred thousand Galicians across the Atlantic Ocean by 1914, and still Galicia's population grew by 45 percent to approximately eight million between 1869 and 1910, making it the empire's most populous, as well as its largest, province (about the size of today's Austria).[16] It was a land that few could love. As for the unlucky inhabitants of this desolate landscape, government statistics suggested that the local Ruthenian peasants were as underdeveloped as the land they ploughed. In 1905, only 24 percent of male Ruthenian peasants aged twenty-four and older were literate, compared with 95 percent of the empire's Germans and Czechs.[17] Austrian officials considered the case of the undereducated and underfed Galician peasants, starving by the tens of thousands and emigrating by the hundreds of thousands, and shook their heads. Added to growing national tension between Polish landowners and Ruthenian peasants was resentment of the local Jewish population; Galicia knew neither prosperity nor peace. This is the image of Galicia that survives today and is summed up by one historian: "The reluctance of the large landowners in eastern Galicia to change the economic status quo (which assured them an unlimited supply of cheap labor) and the general Austrian policy that considered Galicia to be an agricultural zone and marketplace (a kind of 'internal colony') for products from the industrially advanced western provinces (Bohemia, Silesia, Lower Austria) are factors that caused the province to remain an economically underdeveloped territory."[18] While some historians have emphasized the political freedoms that its residents enjoyed as citizens of the constitutional Austrian Empire, most insist that the benefits of civil liberties were outweighed by the miseries associated with economic backwardness.

Given the overwhelming preponderance of agriculture and the centrality of village life, oil derricks and refineries, storage tanks, and pipelines have no place in our imagined landscape of Galicia—but they should. Galicia produced over two million tons of crude oil in 1909, accounting for 5 percent of world production. Observers lauded the Galician petroleum industry's great potential—there seemed to be no reason why the apparently unlimited supply of petroleum could not cover domestic demand (which it did from 1897) and even be exported—but it was equally evident that the actual state of the petroleum industry, like that of the province and its inhabitants, was lamentable. While phrases such as "Galician Hell," "Galician Mizrajim [Egypt]," and "Galician Sodom" complement modern accounts of malnutrition, illiteracy, and the "idiocy of rural life," the terms "Polish Baku," "Galician Golconda," "eastern European Pennsylvania," "Galician El Dorado," "Austrian Siberia," and "Galician California," along with comparisons to Australia and Alaska, more aptly reflect the enthusiasm of the late nineteenth and early twentieth centuries. What all of these appellations share is an invitation to comparison with foreign communities similarly characterized by the excitement of sudden booms and jolting progress upon the discovery of natural riches—be they in oil (Baku and Pennsylvania), diamonds (Golconda), silver (Siberia), or gold (El Dorado, California, Alaska, and Australia).

Oil, it was hoped, might be the salvation of Galicia, a province otherwise without much raw material from which to develop industry. Metaphors emphasizing the enlightenment to be expected from this new product, which was itself principally used for illumination, were plentiful. The central inspector of the Lviv-Czernowitz railway said in an 1884 lecture, "Petroleum is a lighting material—it is primarily destined to spread 'light.' "[19] The founder of the geology department at the Jagiellonian University in Cracow expressed even stronger optimism about the effects of petroleum on the morality and well-being of Galicians, writing in 1905, "Petroleum has played a prominent role in the history of the development of Galician industry over the past fifty years, in that inhospitable regions have become productive, significant capital could be fruitfully invested, and meaningful sums of money sprang forth from a mineral that, destined to radiate brightness, was able to bring light and wealth where there was only poverty."[20]

These comments echo a widely held conviction—often obscured by references to the general poverty of the province—that Galicia was indeed blessed by nature, and that human society was to blame for not taking full advantage of that blessing. Joseph Roth expressed the distinction most eloquently: "Die Erde ist reich, die Bewohner sind arm" (the earth is rich; the inhabitants are poor).[21] It was hoped that in oil, if in nothing else, Galicia's riches would prove boundless. Civil engineer Eduard Schmidt proudly proclaimed in 1865, "Austria possesses in Galicia immeasurable quantities of oil."[22]

The oil industry's advocates concluded that since Galicia's huge population simply could not be supported by agriculture alone, the only way to improve the lives of the Galician population was through industrial development. In the words of August Ritter von Gorayski, president of the Galician Provincial Petroleum Association, "our country [Galicia], even given the greatest advances [in agriculture], must always lag behind if it fails to create for itself any industry, through which, without doubt, the entire civilized world is morally and economically improved."[23] Economist (and oil entrepreneur) Stanisław Szczepanowski argued that the conversion from a traditional agricultural economy to a modern industrial economy was a prerequisite for national survival: "For nations not waiting for providential deliverance, but desiring to rise from misery by their own exertion, there is only one path—the path of simultaneous economic, social, and intellectual transformation."[24] At the same time, however, Galicia's entire social structure was built on the old agrarian order, in which prestige and privilege derived directly from landowning. At the top of that social order were Polish magnates who owned huge properties, were exempt from most taxes and other communal obligations, and were endowed with privileges reminiscent of the preemancipation era. Forty percent of all territory in the province belonged to the latifundia.[25] Large landowners controlled over 50 percent of the seats in the Provincial Diet, although they represented only .4 percent of those eligible to vote. These landowners were notoriously disinterested in industrial development in Galicia. According to Ukrainian radical populist Ivan Franko (1856–1916), the Polish nobility had "always carried a disdain for industry, trade, and commerce."[26]

In Galicia, then, professors, engineers, geologists, and economists who had identified a promising raw material on which to base a new industry that, they argued, could save Galicians from the malnutrition, disease, and emigration that would otherwise remain their lot coexisted alongside a politically and socially dominant conservative agrarian elite. This would appear to be the perfect backdrop for disagreement about whether or not to extract oil in the first place. One can imagine battles between land-owners fearful of oil spills and industrialists indifferent to their plight—between progressive defenders of modernization and industrialization and conservative defenders of the aesthetic and social benefits of tradition. As the next pages will make clear, there were many opportunities for such conflicts to erupt, in particular after the repeated natural disasters that occur wherever oil is exploited. There were indeed disagreements about who was to blame for the severity of their effects on the physical and social environment in the oil basin, but there was little conflict in eastern Galicia about whether or not to extract oil in the first place. Instead, conflict centered on who should control that oil, who should profit from it, and who should decide how much it was worth.

The effects of Galicia's social structure on the development of its in-dustry were grounded in its evolving political relationship with Vienna. Initially, Vienna sought to include the province within the centralized empire as closely as possible by standardizing administration, laws, and education. In the aftermath of the Austro-Hungarian *Ausgleich* (compro-mise) of 1867, however, Vienna turned the province's fate over to its own elites as part of a mini-Ausgleich intended to secure critical support for the central government from powerful Polish magnates. A series of con-cessions made in the latter third of the nineteenth century won for Galicia a degree of autonomy unique within the Austrian lands of the empire and unheard of in the Polish territories of the Russian Empire and Prussia. Of course, not all Galicians benefited equally from this autonomy. Socially and economically privileged Poles enjoyed their favored status in provincial government, educational, and cultural institutions. Szczepa-nowski could rightly brag of "the invaluable privilege of free civic activity, a privilege without which even the wealth of El Dorado would be loath-some."[27] In contrast, Ukrainian-speaking Galicians found that the more autonomy the province's elites were granted, the less control they could expect over their own cultural and social development.[28] A growing body of historical literature has demonstrated that Ukrainian nationalists and social reformers themselves viewed the main obstacle to the development of the peasant population not in some sort of colonial administration in Vienna, but rather in the Polish landlords that dominated their own prov-ince.[29] These landlords, according to Ivan Franko, "unscrupulously consider all sense of justice to be not obligatory for themselves and suppress with the tenacity characteristic of all parasites any stirrings of independent thought and occupation in the popular soul—including that of their own people. That is the greatest Galician misery."[30]

The economic and political structure of constitutional Austria and the peculiarities of Polish elites' control of the province combined to create a land that was neither Austrian nor Polish, but distinctively Galician. Hence Galician history simultaneously belongs to Austrian, Polish, and Ukrainian history, but fits fully within none of those categories. The acquisition of Galicia greatly affected the course of Austro-Hungarian history, adding a huge number of Slavs to the empire's population and making German speakers statistically a minority. The Galician oil industry provided a valuable resource to the empire's economy, supporting refineries outside of the province itself (many of them in the area surrounding Vienna). Polish elites held important positions within the power structure of the imperial capital. At the same time that Galicia contributed to the course of Austrian history, the Austrian constitution fundamentally affected the political and civic experiences of Galicians, guaranteeing civil liberties such as freedom of association, assembly, speech, and the press. As Mykhailo Drahomanov, a Ukrainian socialist and leader of the Ukrainian radical nationalist movement in the Russian Empire, took care to point out, such constitutional rights were all but unknown to the millions of Poles and Ukrainians living in the Russian Empire.[31] This has led historians to explore the ways in which Galicia served as both a Polish and a Ukrainian Piedmont.

Despite constitutional rights and privileges, despite the legal organization of socialist societies, despite access to imperial schools and training facilities, banks and insurance companies, and despite the energy and hope of dozens of committed oilmen, the Galician oil industry failed to bring lasting wealth or significant improvements in the quality of life of the vast majority of those touched by it. Contemporaries agreed that the actual benefits brought by oil to Galicia fell far short of its potential. Who was to blame for the difficulty in capitalizing on Galicia's rich natural resources? This question afforded Polish landowners, Ruthenian socialists, and imperial bureaucrats the opportunity to reflect on Galicia's proper place within the duchies, kingdoms, and margravates that made up the Austrian Empire. A mining and metallurgical engineer offered one possible explanation, calling Galicia a land "itself actually quite rich, but stripped of capital and intelligence."[32] Often, blame was placed on the shoulders of the province's Jewish businessmen, to whom was attributed responsibility for the industry's "oriental" flavor.[33] Austrian officials themselves thought that their own influence could only improve the condition of the region, arguing that the more closely the government monitored the petroleum industry, the better for workers, landowners, and tax collectors alike. The author of a description of Galicia's mineral resources, in a section on a small village that had earned notoriety as the center of oil production, optimistically predicted a continuing improvement derived from government influence:

> Borysław has long been made a notorious spectacle by ruthless exploitation, many thousands of life-threatening shafts all sunk on a relatively small surface, a heterogeneous working population, the hardly praiseworthy management style of most of its businessmen, and numerous accidents. It is the scene of a petroleum and paraffin fever reminiscent of Californian or Australian conditions. Only slowly has the beneficent influence of progressive culture and the Mining Authority been able to blaze a trail through the region.[34]

On the other hand, Szczepanowski did not see Vienna's interference as either benevolent or necessary. He claimed that Galicia's oil producers and refiners had been hamstrung by Viennese centralism. "Much more damage has been done indirectly, in that the general opinion has been willfully fostered in our imperial capital—the seat of the banking and railway administrations that govern our land—that absolutely nothing can be accomplished in Galicia, and that every Galician project is from the very start not even worthy of consideration. Thus, in Vienna, no one has any idea of the rich sources of aid lying fallow in the province."[35] As long as Viennese politicians and bureaucrats, personally unfamiliar with Galicia and maintaining opinions about the province based on rumor and prejudice, were responsible for making laws affecting its fate, he argued, no good could be expected for the local economy.

   The social and economic conditions that help to explain how the legal status of Galician oil was determined are examined in detail in chapter 1. Chapter 2 concludes that the timing of oil's discovery influenced the formulation of the legal framework that guided the distribution of mineral rights to petroleum. Unlike many other valuable minerals that could only be exploited under government concessions, oil was repeatedly designated private property over the course of a protracted struggle between representatives of provincial landowners and imperial engineers. This policy distinguished Galician oil not only from other precious minerals in the empire, but also from oil in almost all other countries, with the notable exception of the United States. The owner of a plot of land could lay claim to any oil that he could cause to emerge from the earth with an exit point lying on his own property. In Galicia, the battle over the rights of the landowners to subterranean bitumina was presented in terms of provincial autonomy versus Viennese centralism. During these early years, the typical oilman was not a wealthy industrialist, but rather a foul-smelling young bachelor, blackened by grease, whose tools of the trade were a shovel and a bucket. Ruthenian and Jewish peasants with small landholdings in the oil basin teamed together with large Polish estate owners to defend the principle of the vertical indivisibility of property.

The benefits and costs of private property versus state control were the subject of intense debates held in the chambers of the provincial and imperial legislatures and on the pages of newspapers and trade journals over the entire seventy-year life span of the Austrian oil industry. In the minds of many contemporary engineers, this legal framework had devastating effects on the Galician oil industry. Some argued that in Austria, and in particular in Galicia, the state needed to act as the instigator and organizer of industrial development in the absence of private investors who could fill that role. According to the mining commissioner, it was absurd to leave control over such a valuable substance to the caprice of landholding patterns. He promised myriad benefits that would "emerge from submitting bitumina to the authority of the government." Among those benefits were "extensive mining, which develops this valuable treasure and entrusts it to the public," and "freer competition." Government control would guarantee "an orderly construction" that would in turn save "both human life, as well as the surface of the land," from destruction. By eliminating unsafe and unsustainable enterprises, the industry would be left to "large companies and establishments," which would lead to "cheaper production, which goes to the common good, as a consequence of that, a quicker and more general turnover of capital, and thus a fresher and freer movement and prosperity of the population connected to this natural product." What stood in the way of all these beneficial developments was simply "the purely accidental property boundaries" of private property.[36] The mining commissioner proposed, in effect, that

industry did not consolidate

rational economic development could not be left to "accident"—that the common good overrode the demands of private property. This rhetoric led to heated conflict with Galician landowners.

In the early decades of its development, representatives of the petroleum industry rejected government assistance or guidance and the interference that it would bring in tow. In consequence, the industry did not consolidate. Every person with access to enough capital to secure a lease of mineral rights to a diminutive plot of land had the chance to be an oilman. This fragmentation may have given local peasants a feeling of empowerment and made large landowners feel more secure about their own property rights, but it also cost oil producers for decades all the advantages associated with coordinated production—in marked contrast to their competitors elsewhere.[37] In Texas and Oklahoma, for example, none of the rhetoric of free trade and unhindered entrepreneurial spirit prevented state agencies (the Railroad Commission in Texas and the Commerce Commission in Oklahoma) from managing oil production, both by mandating limits on extraction and by enforcing those mandates with frequent inspections.[38] The small scale and uncertain profitability of petroleum production in the mid-nineteenth century help explain the government's initial laissez-faire attitude to its extraction—an attitude it would come to regret later, and one that stood in marked contrast to its behavior in the late nineteenth and early twentieth centuries.

Nevertheless, there were soon attempts to transform Galician oil production into an industry run on an international scale. Starting in the 1880s, the oil industry entered a new period of rapid maturation and exponential growth, the subject of chapter 3. Initially, oil pioneers had been adventurous chemists who invented a commodity out of what had been little more than a curiosity. Now these men were replaced by a growing cadre of industrial pioneers who introduced new technologies and new business practices to "backward" Galicia. Prominent among them were the Canadian driller William Henry MacGarvey and the Polish economist Stanisław Szczepanowski. These men were educated in the West and relied on importing Western skills and techniques to achieve two complementary goals. First, they hoped to find in oil a vehicle for the creation of vast personal fortunes. Second, they sought to revive the lagging economy of the province (part of a greater national movement for a rejuvenation of Poland not dependent on political revolution). More was at stake than the acquisition of personal wealth: this was a program to reinvent Galicia as more than a miserably backward agricultural province. Oil pioneers recruited all the resources at their disposal, technological, human, and natural. They were willing to reshape their entire environment in an effort to improve its utility. With the onset of oil production on a grander scale, the oil industry began to transform Galicia's physical landscape. But the oil industry proved to be both fickle and dangerous to those who entrusted it with their fortunes. For every hopeful industrialist able to build up a petroleum empire, there was another whose money and reputation were sacrificed to the whims of geology.

While some were dreaming of glory for the province and the Polish nation, others were wasting away in dark and dangerous mines and in fume-filled refineries. At the same time that investors and drillers were drawn from the farthest reaches of Europe and North America to take their position at the top of the petroleum industry, a new social group emerged to fill out its bottom. Workers, like industrialists, were drawn to the oil basin by optimism and hopes for a better life. They are the focus of chapter 4. Workers became the targets of socialist agitation, aimed at awakening in them a proletarian consciousness and encouraging them to improve their lives and their working conditions via collective action. Socialist intellectuals began to hope for a restructuring of Galician society with what they perceived to be an emergent oil proletariat as the primary agent of change.[39] The oil industry's workforce, however, did not respond to socialism with the enthusiasm that agitators hoped for and employers and imperial officials feared. Like migrant villagers turning to industrial centers elsewhere in eastern Europe, these worker-peasants had no intention of breaking off ties to their village communities.[40] Worker-peasants formed a labor force as unpredictable and volatile as oil itself, showing up for work when it suited them and staying only as long as they pleased. Ultimately, oil workers were more easily divided along religious lines than they were united along class lines. Violent expressions of religious tensions, exacerbated by workers' widespread abuse of alcohol and the carefree culture of communities dominated by single men, were more typical of collective action in the oil basin than were explicitly politically or economically motivated activities. Both the industrialists' and the socialists' programs were ambitious—all the more so because industrialists and socialists were always a minority in Galicia. But while they enjoyed occasional successes (especially in the realm of personal fortune), these proved to be short-lived.

The apex of the Galician oil industry came in the period 1895 to 1909

APEX of oil industry 1898-1909

and is examined in chapter 5. Years of unprecedented drilling success revealed to producers and consumers alike that the richness of the soil could bring as much financial ruin as prosperity. Borysław, which had had fewer than five hundred residents in the 1860s, had swollen to twelve thousand by 1898. No description of the region could fail to mention the oil production that had become its most notorious trademark. In the words of one geological treatise: "The numerous occurrences of petroleum are too peculiar and too characteristic of the Carpathian sandstone for us to pass them by unheeded. After all, oil derricks have already practically become a characteristic attribute of the Galician-Carpathian landscape."[41] But increased profits did not automatically accompany increased attention. In fact, too much interest on the part of too many discrete producers, investors, and speculators, combined with a dramatically augmented power to discover and extract previously inaccessible oil deposits, led to disaster. In the early twentieth century, oilmen paid a hefty price for their lack of organization. Overproduction showed to what great extent producers acting alone could cause one another to suffer, underbidding their competitors and causing a devastating price collapse. In 1905, the oil industry entered a period of intense crisis. After the unexpected discovery of vast new oil deposits, production grew by approximately 50 percent in one year and nearly trebled in three years. Many of the new wells were gushers whose rates of production could not be reined in at will. The prospectors' victory over chance revealed itself to be Pyrrhic when unprecedented overproduction led directly to an unprecedented price collapse. The ensuing crisis brought attention to the fundamental weakness of the oil industry's infrastructure.

Amid this crisis, local politicians and interest groups—having long claimed to desire nothing more than complete autonomy—quickly learned how critical an ally the central government could be. They had lobbied the government for tariff protections in the nineteenth century, but had been equally concerned to protect their industry from too much imperial interference. Now the government was called on to become a major consumer of the oil that could be neither profitably sold nor safely stored in the quantities in which it was exploding out of the ground. At the same time, the imperial administration offered military support to quash the oil workers' strikes that, with remarkably bad timing, began in a period in which producers were more than happy to find an excuse to halt production. The assistance provided by the central government, although enough to stymie any strike activity, proved to be too little, too

late. A preoccupation common to all the Empire's provinces with nationality and language issues stood in the way of Galicia's closer economic
integration with the rest of Austria and thus hampered attempts to
smooth oil's pathway from Galicia into those portions of the empire that
had a stronger consumer base. Only a few years later, Austria's producers
and consumers were confronted with a very different problem. Although
it had seemed unthinkable during its proverbial seven years of bounty,
the Austrian oil industry found that it had entered seven years of famine
completely unprepared.

After reaching its peak in 1909, Galician production suddenly and in-
explicably began to drop. From 1910 to 1918, rates of production declined
steadily year after year, while consumption increased to unanticipated
levels, propelled in part by the mechanization of warfare that came with
the First World War. Chapter 6 assesses the role oil played in Austria-
Hungary's wartime strategy. Galicia was the only domestic source of petroleum for the Central Powers, particularly important in periods when
access to Romania's oil fields was uncertain or outright impossible. Desperate to keep the industry afloat, the government made it a high priority
after the end of a brief but traumatic Russian occupation of the oil basin
from September 1914 to May 1915. Oil workers were exempt from military duty, which made the profession more attractive than ever before.
Confronted with a drawn-out European conflict that did not meet their
expectations for quick victory over Serbia, Austria's military leaders were
incapacitated by a shortage of the very fuel whose excess supply had
plagued the empire's economy only a few years earlier. During the years
of overabundance, no one had thought to improve the lines of transportation that could move oil from Galicia, where it served little purpose, to
the naval base on the Adriatic, where it was desperately needed. Nor had
they bothered to build up the necessary reserves to fuel the military
during a protracted conflict. At the same time that Austria's army and
navy, like the armed forces of both its allies and its enemies, had become
more dependent on petroleum than ever before, their foreign supply was
cut off, and their domestic supply was running dry. In this case, decisions
made on the basis of political needs and social priorities exacerbated
rather than mediated a natural decline in production. Even during the
conflict itself, the belief that too much centralization would prove politically fatal led to the complete failure to control oil extraction and distribution effectively.

Although oil supplies had become critically low during the war, few thought that the golden years of the Galician oil industry had come to an end. Only with hindsight does the gulf between foreign expectations for the future of the Polish oil industry and its actual performance in the 1920s become clear. The Galician oil fields continued to be important in the international arena after the end of the First World War, as is explained in chapter 7. The hopes of politicians, industrialists, and investors alike rested on a period of reconstruction and continued investment that they expected to follow the cessation of conflict. But conflict continued in Galicia and on its oil fields long after the belligerents had signed the armistices that ended the First World War. For residents of Eastern Galicia, 1919 and 1920 were years of continued warfare—only now, the belligerents were Galicians themselves. For Poles, this was a civil war fought between Polish-speaking and Ukrainian-speaking residents of the new Polish Republic. For Ukrainians, it was a war of liberation fought to repel Polish troops from land occupied by a largely Ukrainian population, in the hopes of carving out an autonomous—if not a fully independent—Ukrainian republic. The Polish-Ukrainian War was fought throughout the territory of Eastern Galicia, but concentrated on two objects of particular value: the regional capital city of Lviv and the oil fields of the Borysław-Drohobycz basin. Control of these two objects would guarantee control of Eastern Galicia's most valuable assets and seal the fate of the fledgling Western Ukrainian People's Republic.

The Polish-Ukrainian War provided the backdrop for negotiations over Poland's boundaries held among the Allies in Paris. Although oil played a significant role in these discussions, the Allies were not prepared to allow financial interests to interfere with their principled resolution of Poland's border question—at least not openly. But the Allies had less control over the determination of Eastern Galicia's final borders than some might expect. The border was decided as much on the battlefields of Eastern Galicia as in the conference rooms of Paris. Nevertheless, the Poles were able to convince the Allies that a novice Ukrainian government would not know how to manage the oil industry, endangering Western investments and reversing decades of steady progress under the aegis of Polish control. This succeeded in making the French delegation, if no one else, even more sympathetic to continued Polish belligerence than it would otherwise have been. It was the Allies' decision not to punish Polish military incursions into Eastern Galicia that enabled the Poles to regain physical control of the region and present its inclusion within the

Polish Republic as a fait accompli. The French were rewarded for their steady support of the Polish cause in Eastern Galicia with special treatment of French businesses and investors after Polish control of the region had been secured.

The book closes with a portrayal of Galicia after the decline of its oil industry. Its landscape bore the scars of decades of extraction, marred by cavities large enough to swallow a passerby. Long after these holes were filled in the interest of public safety, traces of the industry remained. Some of these traces are linguistic: town names such as Ropica Polska, Ropica Ruska, Ropa (Poland), Ropa (Ukraine), Ropienka, and Ropianka derive from *ropa* (oil in both Polish and Ukrainian). Some of these traces are literary: Ukrainian authors like Ivan Franko immortalized the oil industry in fiction, and authors better known in the West, such as Joseph Roth and Robert Musil, incorporated this industry into their nostalgic portrayals of the former empire. Physical traces of the oil industry can be seen in the landscape itself in the form of monuments to oil pioneers scattered across Polish and Ukrainian Galicia and in an occasional lonely pump standing in the small gardens of Borysław (now Boryslav) or on the pastures of neighboring Schodnica (now Skhidnytsia).

The Austrian Empire's oil industry—once the third largest in the world—is now preserved only in archives and historical documents. As international demand for oil exploded in the years after the First World War, production in the Galician oil basin (by then, part of the Second Polish Republic) imploded. The story of the Austrian oil industry is thus not a story of success, of unimpeded progress and the accumulation of immeasurable fortunes. It is, however, a failure that deserves and has not yet received its due measure of recognition. For over seventy years, the petroleum industry influenced the cultural, social, and physical environments of workers, peasants, and princes in Galicia, and affected engineers, bureaucrats, and legislators in Vienna, and consumers and investors throughout Europe. Polish-, Ukrainian-, and German-speaking Austrians, Belgian, French, and British investors, and even Canadian drillers all placed their hopes and fortunes at the mercy of Galician oil. Their motives, their successes, and their failures are the subject of this book.

— 1 —

The Land Where Salt and Oil Flowed

Austrian Galicia

Emperor's 1880 visit

In early 1880, the staff of the Austrian emperor Francis Joseph meticulously planned a late summer tour of the province of Galicia as part of a four-week trip that traversed the northern and eastern parts of his realm. The seating arrangement at each banquet underwent revision upon revision to ensure that the importance of individuals was properly reflected in their proximity to the emperor and his distinguished hosts (who were willing to go into debt in order to welcome the emperor lavishly).[1] Likewise, the significance of each place visited was measured by the length of the imperial stay and the number of imperial meals taken in it. Not surprisingly, the emperor's schedule was filled with reviews of military exercises and visits to charitable institutions. Amid the schools, shooting ranges, cathedrals, and museums that drew his attention, his advisors had placed only one industrial site: the "most interesting" petroleum and wax mines in Borysław. Here his imperial highness spent all of ninety minutes.[2] Later, during the ceremony to celebrate his visit to Sambor, he was greeted with a cantata composed specifically for the purpose:

> Welcome to the land where salt and oil flow,
> Welcome here where there is naught but forest![3]

The emperor was notoriously disinterested in economics and has often been criticized by historians for his failure to appreciate the connection between "the economic potential of the country and its military power."[4] Francis Joseph's visit to Borysław indicated that by the third decade of its existence, the oil industry had achieved a level of notoriety that suggested that it deserved imperial attention, although industrial development was hardly a pet project of the emperor's.

An imperial visit was a momentous occasion for locals, both elites and those of modest station. The Société Française pour l'Exploitation de Cire Minérale et Pétrole (the French society for mineral wax and petroleum) decked out its mines with wreaths, flowers, flags, and decorative arches bearing the inscription *Viribus unitis* (with united strength).[5] The Society of Petroleum Producers erected a triumphal gate. To soften the emperor's introduction to the dark and unseemly world of underground oil and wax exploitation, it commissioned the construction of a miniature wax mine, set up at the foot of the pavilion from which the emperor viewed the expanse of wells and mines that were scattered throughout Borysław. Only after familiarizing himself with the vision of a "typical" wax mine in miniature was the emperor ushered to the next step in his indoctrination: a full-scale reproduction of an underground gallery re-created aboveground, "just as if below the earth, to demonstrate the subterranean constructions."[6]

This was the emperor's first visit to Galicia in three decades. He had last set foot in the province in 1851, during a tour in which his reception among elites was considerably less enthusiastic. Given the importance of imperial inspection tours for creating direct connections between the emperor and those of his subjects who lived far from his center of power, the infrequency with which Francis Joseph graced Galicia with his presence may be revealing.[7] But what exactly does it mean? That the province was of little interest to the emperor, and by extension to the imperial government in Vienna, beyond the possibility of exploiting its raw materials? This is the position taken by many historians, particularly those who treat Galician history as part of Polish history. Or could it reflect Francis Joseph's admission that Galicia was somehow a land apart—not really part of the empire's core? Or could it possibly indicate that relations between Vienna and Galician power structures were so satisfactory from the perspective of the former that little persuasion was necessary? This was certainly not the case during the emperor's first visit, but much had changed in Galicia between 1851 and 1880 beyond the appearance of a blossoming oil industry. The local political climate and the web of relations between Galician towns, the provincial capital, and Vienna form the backdrop against which the oil industry developed and therefore deserve thorough consideration.

Galicia graced the map of Europe for nearly 150 years—far more than the Republic of Austria has accumulated to date. Nevertheless, it has often been dismissed as a political artifice, a meaningless construction that should never have been created, and whose eventual destruction was inevitable. Modern historians have shared many contemporaries' general disdain for this province, created by the juxtaposition of optimistic enlightened philosophy and the cold, calculating cynicism of absolutist rule in the eighteenth century. Galicia arose out of the first partition of the Polish-Lithuanian Commonwealth, finalized in meetings between Maria Theresa of Austria, Frederick the Great of Prussia, and Catherine the Great of Russia in 1772. After Polish-Lithuanian reformers at the Great Diet of 1788–1792 transformed the commonwealth into a constitutional monarchy, a second partition, in which only Russia and Prussia participated, further reduced Poland's external boundary in 1793. Tadeusz Kościuszko, a veteran of the American Revolution and honorary citizen of France, led an uprising against Russian occupying forces in 1794 that again rallied the partitioning absolutists around a common (though unfounded) fear of Jacobinism in their midst. In 1795, the remaining Polish

The Société Française pour l'Exploitation de Cire Minérale et Pétrole (French Society for Mineral Wax and Petroleum) festively decorated its wax mine "Franz Joseph" in honor of the emperor's 1880 visit. (Reproduced by permission of the Österreichische Nationalbibliothek, Vienna.)

WEIRD GEOGRAPHY

territory, a sort of nascent rump republic, was absorbed by the partitioning powers, effectively wiping the name of Poland off the official map of Europe.[8]

The lands that came under Austrian control in 1772 were not united by nominal, historic, or administrative tradition. In an attempt to create some modicum of historical legitimacy for its annexation of the new province, the Habsburg imperial government baptized it the Kingdom of Galicia and Lodomeria, a name derived from latinized versions of the medieval dynastic territories Halych and Volyn, to which the Habsburgs resurrected an ancient claim as kings of Hungary.

The province that now marked the northeastern border of the Austrian Empire was a terra incognita to the empire's rulers and administrators. Their lack of familiarity with its territory was such that they chose a river that had been drawn on a 1772 map, but that did not actually exist, as the border between the Austrian and Russian partitions.[9] Neither Maria Theresa nor her son and successor Joseph II was enthusiastic at the acquisition of this distant property. So far were they from imagining its incorporation into the core lands of the empire that Austrian chancellor Anton von Kaunitz was charged with the hopeless task of trying to negotiate a trade with Prussia by which Austria would regain the much more attractive territory of Silesia, lost by Austria during the Seven Years' War. Despite the artificiality of Galicia's creation, this temporary acquisition survived as an administrative and political unit until the dismantling of the Austrian Empire itself in 1918.

Galicia was the largest of the empire's crownlands, or provinces. It stretched over 81,900 square kilometers (31,600 square miles), representing roughly one quarter of the territory of the Austrian half of the empire after its borders were settled in 1867.[10] Galicia had few so-called natural boundaries, aside from the Carpathian Mountains, which loomed along its southern edge, dividing it from the Hungarian plains. The largest river that coursed through the province was the Dniestr, which ran to the southeast through the Ukrainian territory of the Russian Empire before ending in the Black Sea. Most of the province's waterways, running north-south in the direction of Poland, rather than east-west toward the rest of Austria, did not favor trade and commerce with the rest of the empire. To get to Vienna from Galicia by water, one had to travel down the Dniestr to the Black Sea and then back up the Danube through Romania and Hungary. Even by land, Galicia was only tenuously connected

distant property

artificially created by partition

most waterways run N/S to Poland, rather than E/W than rest of Austria to the rest of the Austrian Empire; its border with Moravia was fifty kilometers long, that with Silesia another forty kilometers.[11] Indeed, the physical character of the Austrian northeast served as a proverbial point of contrast to the sunnier regions of southern Austria.

Although the Carpathians were geologically considered an extension of the Alps, guidebooks to the region stressed their remoteness, rather than this connection.[12] The "wildly romantic wooded" Carpathians were the province's most distinctive landmark, their dark peaks and cold lakes forming the stuff of folktales and featuring prominently in travelers' accounts.[13] The author of numerous studies of Poland written for German readers described the western portion of the Carpathian mountain range thus: "Narrow crests, serrated rocky cliffs, dreadfully mysterious mountain lakes, yawning abysses, and strangely beautiful valleys of rivers flowing out of terrible caves, steeped in legend, together lend the Tatra Mountains an unusual appeal. A different world."[14]

Less dramatic, but more characteristic of the province were the vast plains that stretched north of the Carpathians and provided the majority of Galicians with their livelihood. Galicia was known for its rich, black earth. In 1869, 96 percent of its surface area was considered productive: 46 percent farmland, over 25 percent forest, and almost 25 percent grassland (pasture and meadow).[15] Half a century later, these figures had barely changed. Galicia's ample forests and rich fields provided grains, cattle, wood, honey, and wax for export. Nature's bounty bubbled up out of the soil in the form of hot springs and mineral baths, making Galicia a popular destination for Polish-speakers from the Russian Empire.[16] Animal husbandry was common in the province, particularly in the rolling hills and mountain pastures of the south. In addition to salt, western Galicia also had some coal deposits, albeit of poorer quality than those found in Moravia and Bohemia. Despite the presence of these mineral riches, the Galician economy remained almost exclusively dependent on agricultural production. In 1900, more than 80 percent of the Galician population derived its livelihood directly from agriculture.[17] One contemporary social critic and economist estimated that distilleries, mills, and breweries accounted for one-third of Galician factories.[18] Although alcohol production was one of the province's largest trades, it was hardly considered industrial. Distilling, viewed as a "secondary line of business of agricultural production" whose primary goal was to "promote agriculture," did not fall under the purview of the factory inspector.[19]

Even where fertility of the land can bring wealth, too much fertility in its population can bring great poverty. The Galician economy was burdened with a population growing at rates higher than those in any other Austrian province.[20] From the time of the empire's reorganization in 1867, Galicia was the largest province not only in surface area but also in population, accounting for approximately one-quarter of Austria's total residents. Galicia's population growth was rapid and outstripped its impressive rates of emigration; its population was 4.5 million in 1843, grew to 7.3 million by 1900, and surpassed 8 million by the outbreak of the First World War.[21] Despite the relative weakness of cities, Galicia was one of the most thickly populated provinces in the empire. By 1869, 65 percent of all Galician districts had a population density above the Austro-Hungarian average.[22] Szczepanowski calculated that Galicia's population density was only surpassed by England, Italy, Belgium, Holland, and Germany. If one considered only the rural population, it was surpassed by none.[23]

The population's diversity put as great a strain on Galicia's social structure as its size put on the province's economy. In the later nineteenth century, as national or language-based identity became the norm, the province's residents were divided into four groups: Poles, Ruthenians, Jews, and Germans. Each of these terms requires some explanation. In the nineteenth century, residents of the Austrian Empire who spoke a language one would now call Ukrainian were called Ruthenians. At that time, a Ukrainian was a resident of the southwestern region of the Russian Empire. While "Ruthenian" was largely a linguistically-defined category, it also had a religious component: most Ruthenians were Greek Catholic.[24] Jews were recognized as a religious group, but not as a nationality, by the Austrian government. Therefore, in any census figures or other official statistics broken down by nationality, Galician Jews were categorized generally as Poles or, less frequently, Ruthenians (depending on the language they claimed to speak with greater fluency). Germans, in the Galician context, were citizens of the Austrian Empire whose native language was German and are not to be confused with citizens of the neighboring German Empire, founded in 1871.

The meaning of the term "Pole" evolved considerably from the late eighteenth to the late nineteenth century. The Polish-Lithuanian Commonwealth had been a society of estates, with a political structure that had reflected the status of the nobility as the bearers of Polish nationality and political voice. Historian Andrzej Walicki has called the common-wealth a "multiethnic, multireligious, federal republic of the gentry." This does not mean that the nobility was consciously tolerant of ethnic diversity, however. Walicki argues that the binding element that pulled the nobility together was belief in its members' common ancestry, that is, that they were all "descendants of the ancient, powerful, and famous Sarmatians" and hence not ethnically diverse at all.[25] Nevertheless, by modern standards, in the eighteenth century, Poles were a very diverse group indeed. A Pole might have spoken Lithuanian, Belorussian, Ukrainian, or German at home. Although the vast majority of Poles were Roman Catholic, some were Greek Catholic, and a smaller number still were either Lutheran or Calvinist. Historian Roman Szporluk has defined Poles in the early postpartition state as all "those possessing a political awareness, a national consciousness, regardless of their ethnic/religious back-ground."[26] In one matter, however, Poles were completely homogeneous. Regardless of the language they spoke or the religion they professed, in the eighteenth century, all Poles were noble, and only nobles were Poles. According to Jerzy Lukowski, the Polish nobility, or *szlachta*, accounted for between 6 and 7 percent of the Polish-Lithuanian Commonwealth's twelve million inhabitants, suggesting that there were an estimated 120,000 adult male nobles. Only about one-third of those nobles actually owned land, although all nobles, landed and landless alike, were entitled to the same legal privileges.[27]

Once Galicia became part of the Austrian Empire, it was the land-owning Polish nobles who provided the province's social and political elites. Tilling their fields and mending their roads were millions of peasants to whom they felt little or no connection whatsoever. In the western half of the province, these were overwhelmingly people who later were considered Poles, but at the time were often referred to as Mazurians.[28] In the eastern half of the province, they were Ruthenians. Residing mostly in the cities and towns of the province were several hundred thousand Jews.[29]

For a long time, speaking Polish did not bring Polish peasants any closer to their noble landlords than were their Ruthenian colleagues to the east. Rousseau quipped in his *Considérations sur le gouvernement de Pologne (1791)*, "The Polish nation consists of three estates: the nobles who are everything, the townsmen who are nothing, and the peasants who are less than nothing."[30] That changed over the course of the nineteenth century as Mazurian peasants were gradually embraced within the Polish nation. The main impetus compelling the more politically aware nobility to take this step was the failure of the February 1846 uprising led by revolutionary democrats in Cracow.[31] Instead of rallying to the democrats' cause, peasants in western Galicia started a jacquerie, revolting against their Polish landlords and forcing them to acknowledge, in the words of social critic and poet Ivan Franko (1856–1916), "Had lords like you / But looked upon your serfs as men, / They never would have tried to do / You harm, but would have helped you then."[32] Commenting on the Cracow uprising, Karl Marx approved of the peasants' display of animosity toward their lords.[33] What he would not have been as pleased to acknowledge was that over the course of the nineteenth century, Polish peasants, given the choice between national and class allegiance, more and more consistently chose nationalism. The experience of Ivan Franko (too socialist for Ukrainian nationalists, too Ukrainian for Polish socialists) reveals just how shallow overtures to Polish-Ruthenian solidarity were. Although Franko was attracted to Polish socialism in the 1870s and 1880s, he was driven out of that camp by his realization that even Polish socialists cherished the dream of restoring Poland to its old boundaries (that is, denying any kind of autonomy to Ukrainian-speaking peasants in eastern Galicia). In the mid-1880s, he turned to the nationalist Ruthenian populists.[34]

The legacy of the Polish-Lithuanian Commonwealth made its mark on Galicia. Although this may have been a new territory to the Austrian authorities charged with administering it, it was by no means a tabula rasa. Austrians struggled to balance their vision of what their empire should become with an admission that this territory was, somehow, more Polish than Austrian. For the first half of the nineteenth century, relations between Vienna and its newest acquisition were characterized by the juxtaposition of the principles of centralism and absolutism (which initially made German the official language of government and of education), on the one hand, and an almost laissez-faire attitude of relative disinterest in the province, on the other. French Jesuit Balthasar Hacquet, one of the first scientists to travel through the new province, did not blame Galicians themselves for the province's problems, but rather the Austrian administration's lack of familiarity with local culture and landscape.[35] The only hope for the province, he argued, was assimilation into German culture.

This attitude continued to characterize German visitors into the early nineteenth century. Johann Georg Kohl published an account of his trip to Galicia in 1841 that reflected the contemporary conviction that civilization regressed as one moved from west to east. Kohl saw great prospects for Galicia in its exposure to German culture: the rule of law applied equally to every man, the order imposed by the police, paved roads, a better postal system, forest management, more rational exploitation of the wealth in salt and minerals, and the introduction of German language and culture were all bound to bring about an improvement that even the Poles, still smarting from the theft of their independence, would be forced to acknowledge.[36] This attitude seems to have been shared by the Austrian government, at least initially.

The first Austrian governor of Galicia, Count Johann Baptist Anton von Pergen, filled his reports on the province with complaints that the nobles displayed "groundless conceit, insatiable pride, boundless arrogance, abysmal ignorance, unlimited greed, and a disposition to drunkenness."[37] He held further that the "slavish" Ruthenian peasants were

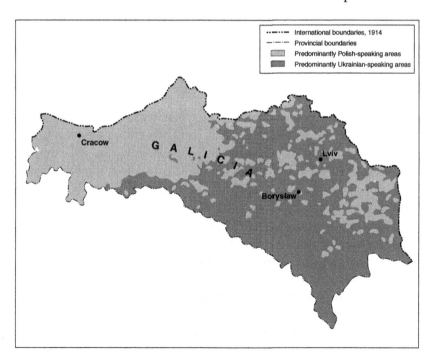

Galician language areas, 1914

W — E

Polish ⟷ Ukrainian

LANGUAGE

"impoverished, poorly housed, poorly clothed, given to drunkenness, lazy, and indifferent . . . living more an animal than a human existence." The priests were drunken and ignorant, the craftsmen were "clumsy, lazy, expensive, deceitful, and drunken," and the towns were filthy, lacking in the sanitary, medical, and hospitable amenities associated with civilization. In short, Pergen's reports leave the impression that exploitation was the key to all social interaction in Galicia—not to mention that every single resident of the province, whether noble, peasant, craftsman or priest, was drunk. Pergen suggested that only the introduction of far-reaching social reforms could transform Galicians into "citizens" worthy of the name.[38]

During the first century of Austrian rule, measures were taken to incorporate the province into the empire as closely as possible. In 1786, Austrian codes replaced Polish laws, and Austrian bureaucracy was imposed on the province.[39] From the highest executive authority (the governor of the province) down to the civil servants staffing Galicia's eighteen county administrations, all positions of authority were staffed by German speakers from the core of the monarchy.[40] The province was also immediately filled with Austrian soldiers, stationed in Cracow, Przemyśl, and Lviv.[41]

Around the middle of the nineteenth century, this policy of Germanization and centralization underwent a dramatic change that was felt more strongly in Galicia than anywhere else in the empire outside of Hungary. Already reeling from its myriad blunders during the Crimean War, Austria suffered a defeat at the hands of Piedmont-Sardinia in the Italian wars of 1859 that led to a massive loss of territory in northern Italy and the institution of various attempts at constitutional government and internal reform. With the October Diploma of 1860, Francis Joseph made overtures in the direction of greater federalism and signaled the beginning of the Constitutional Era. Although the February Patent of 1861 withdrew somewhat from the greater federalism allowed by the October Diploma, it nevertheless established a bicameral system and led to constitutional rule. Robert Kann has described the February Patent as "a poor representative constitution in which, to quote Orwell, everybody was equal but some more equal than others, but . . . a representative constitution of sorts nevertheless."[42] Also in 1861, Galicia's Provincial Diet became an active legislative organ with rights and responsibilities that remained largely unaltered until the First World War.[43] At the same time, the failure

of the 1863 uprising in Russian Poland shocked the Polish elite into re-
considering the appropriate strategy for the pursuit of national renewal.
A new conservative school based in Cracow cautioned against quixotic
political revolution and advocated the concessions and favors that loyalty
to the Habsburg ruling house would procure.[44]

True to the conservatives' hopes, the favors did come. After Austria's
humiliating defeat by Prussia in 1866, it became clear that Austria's future
depended on reaching a workable compromise between the German,
Slavic, and Hungarian lands. Agonizing negotiations produced the ill-
fated Austro-Hungarian *Ausgleich*, or Compromise, which created the du-
alist Austro-Hungarian Empire in 1867. The two halves of the monarchy
were connected only by the personal union of the monarch, a joint foreign policy, defense, and financing of the common government. Simultaneously, the Fundamental Laws of 1867 set up a new constitutional
system for the Austrian half of the empire, now officially called "the
kingdoms and lands represented in the Parliament," but known to its
residents simply as Austria, or Cisleithania. The extent to which the Fundamental Laws truly did, in practice, establish a functional constitutional
regime in Austria has been the matter of some debate. A. J. P. Taylor's
claim that "the Austrian citizen after 1867 had more civic security than
the German and was in the hands of more honest and more capable
officials than in France or Italy" would not be endorsed by most historians.[45] Nevertheless, the Fundamental Laws guaranteed all citizens
equality before the law, abolished every relation of vassalage, and guaranteed liberty of person, along with the rights of petition, assembly, and
free expression. Article 19 specified that all the nations of the empire
should have equal rights, including the right to equality of the various
languages in schools, public offices, and public life. At the same time,
Jews were emancipated and given full rights to own property. Although
the importance of these advances to the development of civil society in
Galicia should not be underestimated, events over the next few years
showed that it was unquestionably the Poles, and more specifically the
Polish aristocratic elites, who benefited most from the new arrangement.

The terms of the Austro-Hungarian Compromise could be passed only
with the approval of the newly empowered Parliament, which required
the acquiescence of Polish delegates grouped together in the powerful
Polish Club. Their endorsement of the Compromise marked the beginning of decades of cooperation between the Austrian Crown and repre-

sentatives of Galician (i.e., Polish) elites. The Polish Club was rewarded with a series of measures granting Poles special privileges within Galicia that together came to be known as the "mini-*Ausgleich*."[46] While the Poles did not receive official political autonomy, as the Hungarians did, for all practical purposes, control over Galicia was turned over to the Polish upper class. Polish elites' eagerness to cooperate with Vienna in 1867 has been condemned by historians who see in it a sycophantic abandonment of Polish national rights, quoting one phrase from the address prepared by the Provincial Diet for the emperor on 10 December 1866: "That we stand by you and will stand by you, most merciful Highness." But this avowal of loyalty must be understood in context. The entire sentence read as follows: "Without fear of having to turn away from the national idea, believing in the mission of Austria and trusting in the endurance of the changes that your imperial word has announced as an unalterable intention, we declare from the bottom of our hearts that we stand by you and will stand by you, most merciful Highness."[47] Far from representing a rejection of Polish national politics, this statement, in its entirety, is evidence of the Polish nobility's recognition that under the current circumstances, Austria offered the best forum for the creation of an autonomous Polish political entity.[48] After all, it was the Polish nobility that dominated the Galician Provincial Diet. With freedom of speech, freedom of the press, and the right to sing the Polish national anthem and "discuss the reconstruction of Poland and run around the streets in Polish clothing,"[49] Galicia could serve as a Polish Piedmont, providing the core of a future independent Polish state.[50]

The chairman of the Polish Club, Kazimierz Grocholski, looked on the constitution with great satisfaction, declaring before the Parliament on 19 January 1870, "The essence of our constitution is: Unity of the state with greatest possible autonomy for the individual kingdoms and crownlands."[51] He was right to be pleased, for in no Austrian crownland was that autonomy as far-reaching as it was in Galicia. Although Galician viceroys were imperial appointees, from 1866 until martial law was instituted during the First World War, they were all Poles. In 1867, a Polish school board was founded that made Polish the language of school instruction; in 1868, Polish became the language of the courts; and in 1869, Polish was made the official language of the province, resulting in an exodus of German-speaking civil servants and making it virtually impossible for Ukrainian speakers to serve in schools, courts, or public offices.

From 1867 to 1871, the universities in Cracow and Lviv were polonized, and the Academy of Arts and Sciences was founded in 1872.[52] From 1871, a minister for Galicia (without portfolio), was appointed to the Austrian cabinet, a privilege that was granted nowhere else outside Bohemia. The importance of these concessions may be hard to appreciate today, but should not be underestimated. Language and hence education were "the central battleground in nationality struggles in countries like the Habsburg monarchy" and had far more than symbolic importance. In historian Roman Szporluk's assessment, "the struggle for language of instruction in school was not a diversion from the real issues such as suffrage or wages or land reform . . . but a fundamental struggle about the kind of persons that were being made—and thus about the limits of political units."[53] In Galicia, provincial laws made it much easier to make Poles than to make Ukrainians.

In comparison with the Polish residents of the other partitioned territories, Galician Poles had reason to celebrate. In Prussia, Bismarck launched the *Kulturkampf*, or clash of civilizations, in 1872. A program that united the state and liberals against the kingdom's Catholics, who, in their eyes, "stood for 'backwardness' in all its forms: economic, social and intellectual,"[54] the *Kulturkampf* demanded that all Prussians take part in an overtly German public culture. The attack on Catholicism was simultaneously an attack on Polish culture. Bismarck himself claimed that "at the beginning of the Kulturkampf, its Polish aspect was decisive for me."[55] German became the exclusive language of schools (where Polish priests were removed from teaching posts and replaced by Prussian state officials) in 1872 and of the administration and courts in 1876. Place names and even family names were Germanized.[56] Even when the *Kulturkampf* itself abated, enforced Germanization continued: in 1887, Polish was officially abolished as a subject taught in schools.

In Russian Poland, retribution against Poles in the wake of the January Insurrection of 1863 endangered the continued existence of any separate Polish political entity. The estates of Polish insurrectionaries were confiscated and given to Russian officials. The name of the territory, which had been Congress Poland, was changed to the more innocuous Vistula Land. Vistula Land was administered by Russians; its official language was Russian; schools were Russified; here, too, the Catholic Church was persecuted (this time, in favor of Orthodoxy).[57]

Compared both with other nationalities within the Austrian Empire and with Polish subjects of the German and Russian empires, the rights and privileges secured by Poles both in the Austrian central administration and in the province of Galicia itself stood out. Austria's favorable Polish policy was a matter of some consternation for Bismarck, who feared the effects it might have on Polish demands in Prussia.[58] Starting in 1866 and continuing over the course of the following decades, Polish elites built up a powerful presence in Vienna, in particular in Parliament, where they were well represented in both the House of Lords and the House of Representatives. The Polish Club was able to enforce strict solidarity across party lines (at least until the first Polish socialist delegates were elected in 1897).[59] The Viennese newspaper *Die Zeit* concluded in 1894, "The Polish Club is at present the decisive power in the Austrian Parliament, and the tightly closed ranks of the Polish delegates exercise enormous influence on the inner life of all Austria."[60] According to their non-Polish colleagues in Parliament, the Poles "pursue their own politics, rarely make deals with other parties or factions of the House . . . They have only one goal in mind: the defense of their national interests."[61] Polish elites featured prominently in the emperor's cabinet: Poles served as prime ministers, Austrian ministers of agriculture, finance, religion and education, railways, defense, and the interior, as well as Austro-Hungarian ministers of foreign affairs and finance.[62] In sum, with its own Provincial Diet and a powerful lobby in the central government in Vienna, Galicia continued to enjoy relative political autonomy from 1867 to 1918.

Of course, the autonomy of Poles in Galicia was really the autonomy of Polish noblemen, whose power was underwritten by the Galician Provincial Diet. All matters not expressly reserved for the Parliament became the responsibility of the Provincial Diet.[63] The more responsibility was given to the Provincial Diet, the more secure Polish elites were from unwanted interference from below. This security was a luxury not enjoyed by the empire's elites as a whole. On the contrary, in the later years of the nineteenth century and the first decade of the twentieth, electoral reforms in the Austrian half of the empire continued to widen the franchise. Delegates to the imperial Parliament were designated by the provincial diets until 1873 and were then elected by four curiae until 1895, when a fifth curia was added to represent all male voters.[64] In 1907, universal manhood suffrage was introduced throughout the Austrian Empire for elections to the imperial Parliament.[65] None of these reforms affected the electoral laws that produced the delegates to the Galician

Provincial Diet, however. Long after universal suffrage had introduced populists and socialists into the hallowed halls of the Austrian Parliament, the Galician Provincial Diet continued to be elected by estate. Representatives of the Catholic Church were guaranteed seats, as were university rectors from Cracow and Lviv and the presidents of the Academy of Sciences and the Lviv Polytechnical College. The approximately two thousand large estate owners qualified to be members of the first curia were represented by forty-four delegates. The second curia represented Galicia's three chambers of commerce and hence the interests of trade and industry. The third curia, with twenty delegates, represented the crownland's large cities. The fourth and final curia represented the provincial communities, organized into seventy-four voting districts. This was not, however, a universal curia. According to one Polish historian, it is reasonable to estimate that only 10 percent of Galician adults actually qualified for the vote. Large landowners, representing 0.4 percent of voters, were directly entitled to around 28 percent of the seats. Together with the church and university representatives and delegates from cities and chambers of commerce, provincial elites could claim 54 percent of the seats in the Diet.[66]

The power of the fourth curia was further reduced because its eligible voters often elected (intentionally or unintentionally) members of the gentry representing the interests of the landlords. This was a source of much irritation for representatives of the populist Polish People's Party (Polskie Stronnictwo Ludowe), including its cofounder, Jan Stapiński. In a speech given to a group of peasants and oil workers in 1904, Stapiński railed against the practice of electing nobles to fourth-curia seats:

> We peasants, farmers, and workers should have our own representatives, not the lords'. To choose a lord as a representative would be like chickens choosing a fox for their guardian. I've always said, and I'll say it again: Peasants! You are the foundation of society, you should be on top. The common people feed the world and therefore have the right to leadership. I always say that, and that's why the lords hate me. Gentlemen! I don't wish you ill. I do not want, however, that you should decide about our finances.[67]

Leaving aside perennial complaints of corruption and manipulation of ballots that rendered the results of the provincial elections notoriously distorted, the fourth curia was undeniably underrepresented in the Provincial Diet. Although peasant representation in the Provincial Diet had been relatively high when it was first convened in 1861, from 1877 to 1889 there was not a single peasant deputy in the Provincial Diet.[68] Meaningful reform was not proposed until 1914, and its implementation was prevented by the outbreak of the First World War.[69]

With a near monopoly on political power in the province, Polish nobles were able to secure continued privileges even after the emancipation of peasants in 1848. Relics of feudalism lingered in Galicia through the nineteenth century. Nobles retained rights to 90 percent of private forests. They held a monopoly on the production and distribution of alcohol, represented by *Propination,* the right to distill spirits, and *Schankrecht,* the right to control the sale of alcohol in taverns. Nobles also had the right to nominate priests for vacant parishes.[70] The Road Maintenance Act forced the communes to bear the costs and the burden of road maintenance. The Game Act required the communes to lease hunting rights in the village to the local noble, thereby losing those rights themselves. Peasants were unable to defend their gardens against rabbits, deer, or wild boars. In 1866, the Provincial Diet voted to remove the manorial area from the commune. This meant that the manors were exempt from all communal taxes and, after the passage of the Popular Schools Act, were not required to pay for village education.[71]

In Galicia and Bukovina, the only crownlands where this exception existed, there were between five and six thousand manorial estates that were separated from the autonomous village communities. The landlord's right to act as a "hereditary mayor"[72] on his own estate, neglecting the needs of the local village, was lamented by contemporary peasant advocates. Father Andrzej Gołda pointed to the devastating effects of separating manors from the village communities, thereby denying villages any access to the wealth generated by the large estates, which he claimed was one of the most important causes of peasant poverty.[73] The effect that the shortage of funds for educational purposes had on the villages cannot be stressed highly enough: a survey conducted in 1887 revealed that 86 percent of members of village community councils were illiterate.[74]

Even when they were willing to let go of traditional privileges, as in the case of the 1874 abolition of the feudal monopoly in alcohol production, nobles knew how to ensure that this was done to their advantage. Having decided to sell their Propination rights to the province, landowners retained exclusive rights to lease the inns that sold alcohol from the province, effectively prolonging their monopoly for decades. Only in 1910 did the sale of concessions for taverns become available to the general public.[75] Some of the landlords' rights were remnants of traditional seigneurial privilege that outlived their actual juridical relevance. Long after peasants had officially won the right to own firearms, for example, they were unable in practice to obtain weapons' licenses, which gave the nobles a de facto (if not a legal) monopoly on hunting.[76]

Nowhere did the chasm separating legal and actual rights gape as wide as among the Ruthenian peasants of eastern Galicia, despite attempts to reconcile the simultaneously national and social conflicts that divided Ruthenians and Poles in Galicia. When the metropolitan of the Greek Catholic Church died in 1898, Polish ruling circles were relieved to find in the person of Count Andrei Sheptyts'kyi (1865–1944) a candidate they believed would represent their own interests. The youthful Sheptyts'kyi was appointed bishop of Stanisławów in 1899, in a clear signal that he was being groomed for the position of metropolitan. When Sheptyts'kyi's appointment to the office of metropolitan followed in 1900, he had been a practitioner of the Greek rite for only twelve years.[77] The son of polonized Roman Catholics who spoke French at home, Sheptyts'kyi was initially not popular among Ruthenians, who likewise expected him to represent the interests of Polish elites.[78] Sheptyts'kyi was to surprise both camps by his tactful but consistent support of the Ruthenian cause. Although he was opposed to socialism, which he called a "theory of exaggerated freedom and absolute equality," Sheptyts'kyi recognized that the plight of his Ruthenian parishioners was simultaneously national and social. Within limits, he was prepared to support the democratic movement, which he wrote was "not foreign to the Church, but, on the contrary, is favoured by priests of all countries, for the spirit of Christ's Gospel is also democratic through and through."[79] When Sheptyts'kyi looked for the social causes of injustice in Galicia, he pointed not to the inherent evils of Ruthenians or Poles, but rather to the horrible miscarriages of justice that plagued every provincial and imperial election in the crownland. "The least injustice in the social order," he wrote in a 1913 pastoral, "by its very nature causes dissatisfaction and becomes an occasion for electoral abuses, which only corrupt people and feed the flames of fratricidal hatred, that veritable plague of Christian life."[80] In this conviction he was not alone.

Like Sheptyts'kyi, Ivan Franko saw a connection between social injustice and electoral abuse. Franko sought to bring the Ruthenians' plight to the public's attention in dozens of articles published in Ukrainian, as well as Viennese, journals. According to Franko, Ruthenian voters were kept forcibly away from voting stations unless they were willing to vote for the reigning establishment. Ruthenian candidates found their electorates' votes purchased for vodka and bread by their wealthier opponents.[81] Electoral abuses prevented Ruthenians from enjoying the political rights they had been granted by the emperor and thwarted Franko's own bid for election in 1895.[82] In 1895, elections to the Provincial Diet produced only seventeen Ruthenian deputies.[83] Even those who did get elected found themselves bullied and browbeaten by the Polish majority in the Provincial Diet.[84]

Ruthenians faced graver danger than electoral chicanery. During the "bloody elections" to the imperial Parliament in 1897, eight people were killed, twenty-three wounded, and over eight hundred arrested in eastern Galicia.[85] During agitation for general suffrage that took place in Galicia in 1906, four Ruthenians were killed and nine wounded; similar protests occurred in 1907 with similar results.[86] Not only did Polish manipulation lead to the disproportionately low number of Ruthenian mandates, but the Polish viceroy of Galicia, Count Andrzej Potocki, was accused of knowingly permitting the most flagrant abuses of the electoral process: the falsification of voter lists, the suppression of information announcing places and dates of voting, and the overruling and ignoring of protests lodged by local mayors.[87] When Potocki was assassinated by a Ukrainian student on Palm Sunday, 1908, this was viewed by some nationalist Ukrainians as just retribution for Potocki's sanctioning of electoral abuses directed against Ruthenian voters and candidates.[88]

Franko's list of abuses was not limited to those occurring before and during elections. Ruthenians, he claimed, were mistreated by Polish administrators at every level of provincial government.[89] Ukrainian speakers found their demands for equal treatment of the Ukrainian language, as mandated by Article 19 of the Fundamental Laws, effectively blocked by the Polish majority in the Provincial Diet. In 1898, Ruthenian delegate Anatol' Vakhnianyn (1841–1908) requested that the equality between Ukrainian and Polish be recognized in eastern Galicia in those areas where Ruthenians and Poles lived together, meaning that correspondence between government officials and the public would be accepted and written in both Polish and Ukrainian. In response, the Diet approved a

[handwritten margin note top: UNEQUAL DISTRIBUTION OF POLITICAL POWER]

[handwritten margin note: UNEVEN SOCIAL STRUCTURE]

law calling on the government "to respect the rights of the Ruthenian language in accordance with existing laws and regulations, just as up to now," indicating that nothing would change at all.[90]

Even this admission was apparently too generous for some delegates, who found its symbolic weight of ill portent. According to Ruthenian delegate Teofil Okunevs'kyi (1858–1937), Polish delegate Mieczysław Onyszkiewicz had warned his colleagues of the danger of setting a new precedent. "Do not forget, Ruthenian delegates," Onyszkiewicz admonished, "that the Viennese ministers may have granted some language rights for the Ruthenians, but that the Galician Diet has never recognized them. In the Galician Provincial Diet's request to the government that it respect the ministerial decrees in favor of the Ruthenian language lies the recognition of these decrees on the part of the Galician Provincial Diet."[91] The Polish stranglehold over political participation at the imperial level was recognized by contemporaries, who argued that "only the constitutional central government can protect [Ruthenians] from complete subjugation to the rule of the Polish element," and that, therefore, Ruthenians should "hold fast to the constitution and fight every attempt at a federal arrangement of the state."[92] But while Viennese politicians hoped to rely on the loyalty of the Ruthenian masses, the inability of the central government to enforce its guarantees within Galicia itself threatened to make its assistance moot. Franko, for one, concluded that imperial protections amounted to little more than empty phrases; Ruthenians were at the mercy of their Polish oppressors.[93]

[handwritten margin note: centralized Vienna wanted to help but was unable to enforce its guarantees w/i Galicia]

This unequal distribution of political power meant that the pressing issue of land reform could not be effectively addressed. Despite the fertility of the soil, Galician peasants were vulnerable year after year to crop failures, malnutrition, and famine. Hunger was such that some dubbed the province "Golicja i Głodomeria" (*goły* and *głodny* are Polish for "naked" and "hungry," respectively).[94] Critics, politicians, and scholars alike recognized that the problem lay with Galicia's social structure. Josephinian attempts to strengthen the peasants' rights to the soil they worked were no more successful in Galicia than elsewhere.[95] All land had been divided into two categories: the lords' land was called "dominical" or "manorial" and the peasants' "rustical." Lands could not be transferred from one category to another at will, which meant that while no individual peasant was guaranteed possession of any plot of land, the sum total of peasant possessions would remain stable and was not vulnerable

[handwritten note bottom: 1. dominical 2. rustical]

to encroachments by the lords.[96] In addition to limiting the growth of dominical holdings, this legislation also guaranteed that when the peasants were finally freed from their service obligations in 1848, they were not kicked off their landholdings, in contrast to peasants in Prussia. So, perhaps surprisingly, the large class of landless peasants that characterized postreform Prussia did not develop in Galicia.[97]

The province's noble landowners, whose income was based on the agricultural production of their vast estates, could not survive without an adequate supply of cheap labor. That they would approve of peasant emancipation was out of the question. In the midst of revolution across Europe, Galician governor Franz Stadion, afraid of being upstaged by revolutionary Poles, proclaimed the end of all labor duties by order of the emperor on 22 April 1848 (although the emperor had made no such decree and only ratified Stadion's decision after the fact).[98] The promise of the 1848 revolution led quickly to disappointment. When the imperial emancipation decree was ratified by the revolutionary Parliament on 7 September, noblemen demanded compensation for their loss—at a minimum, the suppression of so-called servitudes (traditional peasant rights to use forests and meadows for fuel, timber, and pasture) and indemnification for their lost dues. The Parliament agreed that the Provincial Diet should make an indemnification payment. Although peasants did not have to compensate the lords for their land or lost labor directly, as taxpayers they bore the brunt of the financial burden of indemnification.

Although the 1848 laws had upheld the peasants' rights to pastures and forests, servitudes were not to last for long. Noble landlords, who already owned 43 percent of arable land and 90 percent of forests, were eager to extend their property as a compensation for their lost labor.[99] The exact regulations settling the question of servitudes were passed in 1858, when the fear of revolution had subsided and the desire to court noble support was great in Vienna. Although servitudes were not officially abolished, peasant claims to these rights were to be evaluated on a case-by-case basis by a special commission, which was itself dominated by the gentry.[100] Of 32,000 servitude trials held over the course of the following half century, 30,000 ended in a loss for the peasant. Although nearly every Galician peasant could proudly point to a plot of land that was his own, peasants had ultimately lost access to forests and pastures and had been burdened by indemnification payments.[101] One could argue that even the benefits they did derive from emancipation were deceptive. As the laments of social critics and economists over the next seventy years showed, the peasants had been saddled with plots of land that they would not abandon, but could not make self-sufficient.

The loss of access to pastures and forests was made worse for the peasants because of the woeful inadequacy of their own landholdings. The evil of parcellation became the slogan of politicians and socialists demanding land reform. The tradition of dividing land among all one's children only worsened the condition of peasants with already minimal properties. From 1848 to 1890, the amount of arable land owned by peasants increased by less than 7 percent, but the total number of hold- ings nearly doubled by 1900.[102] According to Ivan Franko, in 1897 the average landholding of Galician peasants was a mere 4 *Joch* (2.3 hec- tares).[103] Even this average, however, implies a stability that did not exist. The size of most peasant holdings became smaller and smaller with each passing generation; by 1882, more than half of Galician peasants owned less than 2 Joch (1.15 hectares) of land.[104] To make matters worse, most peasants' landholdings were divided across several noncontiguous plots. In 1859, there were fifteen million separately registered lots in Galicia, which suggests an average of twenty separate plots per peasant owner.[105] Not only were the plots themselves getting smaller, but the income that their owners could derive from them got smaller as well. Szczepanowski suggested that compared with norms set by other European countries, every resident of Galicia "does one-quarter of a man's work and eats one- half of a man's food."[106] Wilhelm Feldman tried to measure the poverty of Galicians by comparing the taxes they paid with those paid by people in other crownlands. In 1898, the minimum taxable income was 600 florins a year, and 7.29 percent of citizens of Cisleithanian Austria were eligible to pay it. In Galicia, however, such prosperity was rare: only 0.78 percent of Galicians were deemed taxable.[107]

While the percentage of Galicians engaged in agriculture did decrease over the course of the nineteenth century, the extent of the change was modest in comparison with other crownlands. The number of agricultural workers in Lower Austria dropped by 64.5 percent from 1850 to 1910, and in Bohemia by 40.6 percent. The drop in Galicia was only 16.4 per- cent—the lowest in all the provinces of the Austrian half of the monarchy, with the exception of Dalmatia.[108] Galicia had 25 percent of the land area in the Austrian part of the monarchy, but only 9.3 percent of the indus- trial enterprises.[109] Galicians were also paid considerably less than their equivalents in other provinces. If wages in Lower Austria are indexed at 100, then wages in Lviv grew from 47.4 in 1895 to 62.4 in 1913. While economic historian David Good sees in this increase an indication of diminishing regional disparity throughout the empire, the figures also show dramatically how impoverished Galicia's workers were.[110]

Advocates of Galician peasants tried desperately to publicize their plight. Wilhelm Feldman's interpretation of the statistics from the Ministry of Agriculture produced a bleak picture indeed: in 1857, for every landowner there were 13.4 hectares producing an income of 59.18 crowns; by 1896, these figures had declined to only 0.92 hectares with an income of 26 crowns.[111] Ivan Franko tried to give depth to similar statistics by pointing out that if over 80 percent of all peasant holdings in Galicia were registered with an annual profit of less than 40 crowns, then the total possessions of those families were worth between 200 and 1,000 crowns.[112] To put these figures in context, in 1900, the average civil servant in Austria earned 400 crowns a month,[113] and the director of the Galician Savings Bank earned 18,000 crowns a year.[114] For Franko, the statistics documenting parcellation could not have provided a clearer sign of impending doom for Galician farmers. "It is evident," he wrote, "that Galicia is dominated by small village holdings, which include over three-fifths of all the properties in the country, and that . . . 350,000 families, that is, 1.75 million people, find themselves in a situation that—should the harvest turn out bad or potatoes refuse to grow—they are exposed to die of hunger."[115] Try as they might, year after year, thousands of peasants were forced to conclude that they could not make ends meet on the land that they had. According to historian Stefan Kieniewicz, 23,649 peasant holdings were forcibly sold at auction between 1875 and 1884 (a period of agricultural depression throughout the empire), often over debts of less than forty crowns, which he claims was the equivalent of ten bushels of wheat.[116]

As Franko predicted, too many people trying to squeeze a living out of too little land led to endemic famine, making Szczepanowski's infamous claim of fifty thousand deaths from malnutrition plausible.[117] There were famines in Galicia in 1847, 1849, 1855, 1865, 1876, and 1889.[118] Peasant children had little prospect of moving up the social ladder; according to government statistics for the 1870s, only fifteen of every one hundred Galician children of school age actually attended school.[119] Attempts to address the Galician misery were often stymied by the fact that the conflict in Galicia occurred on two levels. First, it was a national conflict, between Polish speakers and Ukrainian speakers. Second, it was a social conflict, between peasants and landlords. In the minds of some Ruthenians, Polish peasants should have been their natural allies in a common battle against the hegemony of the landlords.

In Galicia, only 6 percent of Ukrainian speakers engaged in nonagricultural occupations, as opposed to 33 percent of Poles.[120] This social disparity and the control Polish elites had over the crownland help explain why the principal enemy of the Ruthenian national movement was never perceived by Ruthenians to be Austria, but rather Poland. Regardless of the location of the central government and the identity of the ruler who claimed the loyalty of Galicians as his due, control over Galicia lay in the hands of the Polish landlords. It was Polish landlords who retained control over forests and meadows (and hence over sources of fuel and building materials) and blocked any reforms put forward in the imperial Parliament intended to improve the social or economic status of Austria's disenfranchised peasant population. Indeed, if the emperor could grant rights that were worthless as long as the Polish nobility prevented their exercise, what good was the emperor? Francis Joseph, even if benevolent, was rarely viewed as the best vehicle for the social changes that leaders of Ruthenian political parties considered to be in their own interest.[121]

Ultimately, contemporary social critics decided that there was no need to try to distinguish the Polish ruling elite in Galicia from the imperial ruling elite in Vienna. According to Ivan Franko, the blame for Galician misery should be shared between the Polish nobility, "who have always carried a sovereign disdain for industry, trade, and commerce and in former Poland prevented the development of cities with all of the means of their class superiority," and the Austrian government, "which consciously or unconsciously has followed a politics of not allowing any industry or factories to come into Galicia for over one hundred years."[122]

Historians have generally agreed with Franko's analysis that it was the lack of industry that kept Galicia backward and Galicians poor and undernourished and have repeatedly echoed contemporary Galicians' claims that their quasi-colonial status was to blame for their poverty without conclusively demonstrating that it is appropriate to refer to Galicia as a colony in the first place. Raphael Mahler has argued that it is difficult to separate the interests of the central government and those of the Polish landowning nobility: "Austria deliberately and consistently promoted a

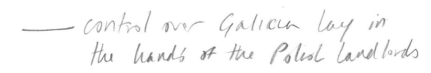

— control over Galicia lay in the hands of the Polish landlords

system of 'colonial policy.' Galicia was set aside as a market for the products—chiefly the so-called 'inferior' goods for the 'use of Galicia'—that
the industrial areas in the monarchy produced. In this respect the interests
of the Austrian government coincided with those of the large Polish landowners."[123] Krzysztof Dunin-Wąsowicz assents, "Any change in the economic structure of Galicia was neither in the interest of the central authorities nor in that of the Galician large landlords. One considered it
inadvisable to invest capital in this poor country; Austrian economic
policy treated Galicia like a colony, a source of raw materials and a market
for the products of its more strongly industrialized provinces."[124] Paul
Robert Magocsi has a similar formulation, calling Galicia an "internal
colony" that remained "economically underdeveloped" because of "Austrian policy."[125] But was Galician poverty really beneficial to Viennese
policy makers? Why would Vienna, eager to promote industrialization
and catch up to its economically more vibrant western neighbors, be
content to let the Galician economy rot? Recent research has shown the
extent to which Austria-Hungary's economy was much more vital than
historians had previously allowed, but this vitality did not extend to Galicia.[126] That this failure to thrive was caused by a poorly defined colonial
policy, however, has not yet been proven.

The real source of Galician poverty puzzled contemporaries. How
could a land so rich in natural resources be so terribly poor? Some went
so far as to call it a land blessed by God: "So, as you see, dear readers,
God is always just and compassionate, and if he disadvantaged us in one
respect, he lavishly recompensed us in another. You must be told that as
far as mineral resources in salt and oil, Galicia is the richest in all of
Europe. And to whom are we indebted for that, if not our beautiful
mountains and their foothills?!"[127] If fertile earth, abundant salt, and the
liquid gold flowing in its petroleum beds made Galicia a naturally rich
land, then its poverty was an injustice—the result of mismanagement,
imperial exploitation, or some other cause attributable to man, not to
God or nature. In the chapters that follow, we will examine the extent to
which men (and a very few women) attempted to take advantage of
Galicia's natural gifts to remedy its social ills.

— 2 —

Galician California

Battles for Land and Mineral Rights

Comparison to U.S.

OIL AS PVT PROPERTY

In the nineteenth century, engineers, social critics, and literati often referred to the Galician oil basin as an "eastern European Pennsylvania." The comparison was apt—serious exploitation of the oil fields of Pennsylvania and Galicia began at about the same time, and the material and social conditions of Galicia's oil towns were reminiscent of Titusville or Oil City.[1] In the early twentieth century, nearly concurrent new discoveries in Galicia and Texas led anew to the former's comparison to the United States. But the most common, most fashionable, and most lasting comparison was not to another oil field at all, but rather to the goldfields of California that had created such a stir in the 1840s and 1850s.[2] The flurry of activity that characterized the many boomtowns in this Galician California was reminiscent of those gold rush years. But in its infancy, the oil industry developed very differently from the typical boom and bust cycle of excited speculation that followed the discovery of California gold.

Unlike gold rushes, which are caused by the discovery of a product first cherished and then deliberately sought out, the chronology of the oil boom in Galicia was reversed. The attribution of value to petroleum came long after its discovery. This delay had profound effects on the legal framework that defined control over mineral rights to oil, which in turn shaped the nature of the oil industry in its early years. This chapter will examine the factors that led to the peculiar Galician formulation of a petroleum mineral rights policy that at first glance appears progressive (even American), but that most contemporary Austrian observers thought was backward. It will then consider the evolution of legal standards to regulate the oil industry and the effects that this legal framework had on the shape of the industry in its turn.

PA

like the U.S. gold rush

delayed realization in oil's value in Galicia

48

ANTHROPOCENE
del.

Understanding the oil industry's development in the nineteenth century requires forgetting much of what one knows about oil, oil exploration, and oil consumption today. In today's petroleum-driven society, allusions to oil evoke thoughts of what Daniel Yergin has called "the epic quest for oil, money, and power." But oil was not highly prized in Austria-Hungary in the early nineteenth century; on the contrary, it was initially a peripheral product, produced literally on the periphery of the empire. The general lack of contemporary interest in the politics and prestige of oil should not be interpreted as complacency or indifference regarding all sources of energy. In 1855, Austrians were urgently concerned about energy, and rightly so.

While neighboring Prussia steadily converted its factories to use coke, Austrian industry continued to rely heavily on lumber for fuel.[3] In 1858, Jakob Scheließnigg, the manager of a factory in the Austrian province of Carinthia, gave a lecture before the metallurgy section of the Mining Engineers' Society in Vienna in which he warned of the danger of fuel shortages throughout the empire as forests were depleted:

> Our blast furnaces and iron-smelting factories consume a great deal of wood and charcoal; production ought to increase still in order to satisfy the multiplying demands created by the railroads, machine shops, and heightened cultivation of the soil. At the same time, locomotives and traditional consumers (such as crafts, households, limeworks, brickworks, agricultural industry, etc.) storm the forests. Thus have we reached the point where use of new forest growth is insufficient, and we have been consuming the capital for years.

The solution to this crisis, he suggested, lay in alternative sources of energy—and, in particular, those that lay deep within the belly of the Earth: "It is necessary to use wood and fossil coal only for those purposes where it is absolutely indispensable, and to base the refining of iron on a fuel surrogate. We should see that this fuel surrogate also gains entry into common life, and in general seek in the depths of the earth that which its surface from year to year increasingly denies us."[4] The alternative fuel from the "depths of the earth" that Scheließnigg had in mind was peat moss.

At the time of Scheließnigg's lecture, oil was but a curiosity. There was no shortage of it in Galicia. It floated on puddles after rainfall and bubbled up in natural and man-made depressions in the ground. Yet, with the exception of half a dozen men over the course of the century's first fifty years, no one had thought to link oil and profit, or oil and industry, or oil and power (either metaphorical or material). One must keep in mind throughout the study of the early oil industry that oil pioneers did not intend to challenge the supremacy of coal. Oil was associated with lamps and light, not engines and furnaces. It was the extension of light into the evening and nighttime hours, not an explosion of industrial activity, that meant that oil would improve living standards.[5] An oilman was more likely to be a chemist or a peddler than a businessman or a factory manager. In 1853, Galicia officially stepped into the oil era, but it was the age of the mad scientist, not of the wealthy industrialist.

Identifying the first oilmen is as difficult as placing an age on the industry—a task complicated by the immense age of the product itself. A history of oil would begin long before humans began to wonder how they could make machines driven by energy other than their own work for them, how they could lengthen the day with artificial light, or how they could propel themselves forward at speeds with which no living legs would ever carry them. A history of oil would begin long before humans even wandered the earth. Indeed, as one commentator put it, "In the first few minutes of a drilling operation, the fishtail bit has often penetrated antiquity more remote than recorded human history."[6] Even the human discovery of oil, although falling perhaps within the realm of the historical, certainly took place in antiquity. Noah waterproofed his ark with pitch,[7] Herodotus described petroleum springs in Zacynthus, and Plutarch depicted a burning lake at Ekbatana.[8] The nineteenth-century German and Polish terms for petroleum, *naphta* and *nafta*, respectively, both derived from the ancient Persian word *naphtha*. Nineteenth-century authors who described the earliest years of the European oil industry agreed that peasants in all localities where oil was discovered had known of it for centuries, using it to lubricate their wagon wheels or as a medicine for their livestock. From as early as the thirteenth century through the first half of the nineteenth, oil was casually collected by peasants who dug shallow pits in the ground, waited for oil to seep in, and scooped it off the surface of puddles with ladles or small brooms made of twigs.

In the eighteenth and early nineteenth centuries, oil was gathered by digging a small ditch and lining it with branches. The ditch gradually filled with water mixed with oil. Peasants plaited long strands of grass or horse tails and swished them through the puddles. The oil that stuck to these makeshift brooms was then squeezed out by hand into another container. This process was repeated until there was no water left in the mixture.[9] Men and boys who earned their bread in this fashion were called *lubaki* (skimmers). To bring the oil to consumers on market days, the skimmers thickened it with the addition of clay, peat, or cattle manure, which contributed to its terrible odor. These skimmers, many of whom were impoverished Jews, lived on the edge of society, shiftless and landless; in contemporary literature they were portrayed as "black and foul-smelling."[10] They rarely had families and entertained no prospects of earning a fortune from their labor. They spent their days laboriously gathering small quantities of oil and their evenings making the long trek back to the market in the regional capital of Drohobycz, their wares suspended from a yoke across their shoulders.

The peripheral status of oil in its early years is central to any explanation of the specific course of development that the oil industry followed. The Austrian imperial government's policy toward oil was originally formulated during a period in which no one thought that oil was of much value. This, along with political considerations shaping the relationship between Vienna and the provincial capital, contributed to the nature of early laws covering access to mineral rights to petroleum. The mineral rights policy that emerged was fundamental to the development of the oil industry, as it has proved to be elsewhere.

The world can be divided into those states in which the Crown or central government controls mineral rights, including those to oil, and those in which those rights remain in the hands of the owners of lands suspected of bearing valuable minerals. In the first case, the sovereign power grants privileges, or concessions, to individuals or corporations in return for considerable royalties. The term "royalty" itself derives from a British law that designated gold and silver mines the property of the Crown and required payments in exchange for mineral extraction. The exploitation of these rights is generally well organized and concentrated in the hands of a few large corporations that have the capital necessary to purchase them in bulk. Centralized control limits the number of producers and offers them the advantages that come with unhampered control of supply: prevention of overproduction and the ensuing ability to drive prices up and keep them stable. It also allows for governmental supervision of and influence on the mining industry. This supervision tends to increase the prevalence of safety measures and to encourage a slow, calculated rate of exploitation.[11]

A stylized image of a *lubak*, the typical oil collector of the 1860s. (Author's collection.)

In the second case, property ownership is considered inviolable, and mineral rights remain in private hands. Here, ownership of oil was subject to a legal principle derived from English game laws and known as the "rule of capture." According to this principle, the owner of oil was the person who could capture it by causing it to appear on the surface of his or her own land. This system offers the advantage of respecting land-owners' property claims (assuming that respect of private property is considered an advantage) and broadening the market for oil exploration. Only a relatively modest amount of capital is needed to begin exploring for oil, since a would-be producer need only convince one single land-owner to lease the mineral rights to a portion of his or her land. This allows investments on a much smaller scale and encourages a proliferation of smaller, low-capital firms. On the other hand, it exacerbates all the usual disadvantages associated with oil production, most significantly, the apparent futility of any attempts to organize producers to defend their economic interests by limiting production. Overproduction inevitably lowers the price at the expense of the producers themselves.

The second pattern is the one that famously prevailed in America's early oil industry and remains familiar today. According to proud Texan wildcatters and academic champions of their unique spirit of enterprise, this is a peculiarity of American history. They claim that in all other countries, the state or its sovereign controls these rights.[12] For Texas oilmen at the turn of the twentieth century, the private ownership of mineral rights embodied the American dream, encouraged the spirit of free enterprise, and supported small producers, or "independents." The opportunity to make a fortune based on a combination of gumption and good luck was often seen to distinguish America from the Old World.

Even if the encouragement of private industry and independent explo-ration was symptomatic of a commitment to freedom and private prop-erty, it was not uniquely American. In fact, the Austro-Hungarian Empire also left mineral rights to petroleum products in the hands of private landowners. This may come as a surprise to students of nineteenth-century central Europe, since the political demise of the Austro-Hungarian Empire in 1918 has often been linked to a perceived failure to modernize its economy. Austria-Hungary has been described as suf-fering from low levels of industrialization, uneven economic develop-ment, a lack of interregional integration, increasing backwardness relative to other European powers and the German Empire in particular,[13] and a high degree of protectionism.

In the 1960s and 1970s, historians began to redeem the Austro-Hungarian economy—in particular, industrialized regions such as Bohemia and Lower Austria.[14] They have largely supplanted the traditional view, which holds a relatively stagnant economy at least partially responsible for the empire's dissolution. Aspects of the Galician oil industry belie the image of Austria's economy as unabashedly statist and inhospitable to new ventures. In the case of the oil industry, the empire followed the American pattern and demonstrated considerable respect for private property by allowing each individual landowner to decide how to exploit, or refuse to exploit, mineral rights to his or her land. The empire's mineral rights policy for petroleum infuriated protectionists and those who favored the formation of cartels and monopolies as well as engineers and advocates of rational exploitation. Why, they asked, should Austria deny itself the advantages so many other states had secured through public control of mineral rights? Even today, the privatization of petroleum ownership remains the exception, not the rule.

The question of control over mineral rights to petroleum was a major theme in trade journals, parliamentary debates, and meetings of industrial clubs and mining societies throughout the second half of the nineteenth century. Many contemporary Austrians were surprised that the state chose private over Crown control. Most mineral rights, including those to gold, silver, platinum, copper, iron, coal, zinc, tin, lead, mercury, alum, and salt, were controlled by the state.[15] It was not obvious why the same should not be true for *Erdharze*—the family of solid, semisolid, and liquid mixtures of hydrocarbons that includes liquid petroleum, asphalt, and ozokerite (a paraffin-like member of the bitumina family, also known as earth wax, mountain wax, and mineral wax), known in the nineteenth century as "bitumina." In 1854, Robert Doms, a Prussian industrialist with a factory in Lviv, developed an interest in founding a company to produce petroleum and ozokerite in Galicia.[16] At the time, Doms was more interested in ozokerite than in liquid petroleum. Ozokerite was a promising material with many possible applications, including—most profitably—candle production, but also medicines (such as lip balms). Like any sensible entrepreneur considering a new venture, Doms had several questions whose answers would determine how willing he was to invest time and money in this new enterprise. There was, after all, little precedent for investment in the oil industry, which had not existed as such until 1853. What and where was he allowed to mine? From whom should he lease the mineral rights? What exactly would these rights allow him to extract and sell? Another mining expert had dismissed his questions as functionally irrelevant, since "bitumina appearing in the Austrian monarchy . . . are mineralogical rarities."[17] This attitude may have been historically justified in 1854, but it was on the verge of obsolescence, thanks to Doms and others who would follow him. That Doms was unable to find satisfactory answers to his questions in any legal reference work is understandable, given the multiplicity of laws that had already been passed, repealed, and amended by the imperial government at that time.

The declaration of the Imperial Mining Prerogative, defined as "that sovereign right according to which certain minerals, appearing in their natural beds, are reserved for the exclusive disposal of the all-highest sovereign,"[18] had been explicitly extended to oil in the kingdom of Galicia in 1804. At that time, an imperial patent announced that control over all metals and minerals in Galicia found in ravines, galleries, deposits, and seams (with the exception of peat and bogs, which remained private) was reserved by the imperial government. The exploitation of these minerals would henceforth require the acquisition of a royal concession, in keeping with mineral policies elsewhere in the empire. To the extent that the exploitation of oil or wax interfered with normal agricultural activities, the discovery of oil would come at no benefit and considerable expense to the landowners. In 1810, this decision was modified: while solid bitumina continued to be considered imperial property, just like coal, liquid petroleum remained the property of landowners.[19] As far as the government was concerned, there was no reason to anger landowners with challenges to their property rights over a peripheral good such as oil. After all, until the middle of the nineteenth century, there was no profitable use for bituminous products. No lamp would burn oil safely, and the odor emitted by a petroleum lamp was, by all accounts, unbearably rancid.[20] Oil was, at best, useful as a lubricant to grease wagon wheels and as a primitive veterinary medicine for the skin diseases that plagued livestock.

The curiosity and creativity of a few men resulted in early attempts to profit from this strange substance. In 1817, Josef Hecker explored the feasibility of connecting the rural supply of oil to an urban demand and was able to secure a contract from the magistrate of Prague for three thousand tons of oil at 340 florins per metric ton. Unfortunately for

Hecker, transportation problems, leaky barrels, and transportation costs equivalent to nearly two-thirds of the price of the oil forced him to breach his contract, prematurely ending his Rockefellerian experiment in distribution.[21] Given the limited appeal of putrid-smelling, highly combustible oil lamps, this was perhaps fortunate for Prague, since the use of oil was extremely dangerous throughout this period.

Hecker's failure did not prevent others from trying their luck, however. There were twenty oil pits dug in Borysław in 1835,[22] and oil began to look as if it might be profitable, if only to those with a large tolerance for personal risk and fiscal adventure. Indications of oil's eventual utility as a source of illumination suggested that the government's decision to concede the right to royalties might have been foolish and premature. Consequently, the Exchequer reconsidered its earlier decision and announced its new policy in October 1835: all bitumina, including those in liquid form, were to be subject to the Imperial Mining Prerogative and thus fell under imperial jurisdiction. Privileges would be distributed by the Ministry of Finance, as they were to Josef Micewski in 1838 and the Drohobycz Chamber of Commerce in 1841.[23] In 1840, the Exchequer announced that a mining tithe of 10 percent would be collected on all bitumina, and that, in general, possessors of land containing bitumina would be treated according to the same mining laws that applied to other enfeoffable minerals. But this soon changed. The Exchequer responded to local pressure in December 1841 by again removing liquid bitumina that did not appear in conjunction with coal or solid bitumina from the Imperial Mining Prerogative.[24]

The real boost to interest in oil came with the 1853 invention of a new lamp that would burn petroleum odorlessly and safely, the result of many years of research. Several young men were involved in the various stages of both sides of experimentation: purification of oil and lamp design and construction. Most of them were connected in one way or another to a prominent pharmacy near the Lviv city center, Piotr Mikolasch's Pod Gwiazdą (Under the Star). Among them was Jan Zeh (1817–1897). Zeh's first exposure to oil came in 1830 while an apprentice in a pharmacy in Sambor. He heard that a local peasant, known only by the name Bajtał, had invented a means of distilling crude oil using a contraption he had constructed from an iron pot and the barrel of an old rifle. Zeh described Bajtał's distillate as "colorless, volatile, with an unbearable odor, and extremely flammable."[25] Bajtał wandered through Galicia with his wares strapped to his back, selling his distillate as a medicine for sheep. Try as he might, Zeh was never able to discover Bajtał's real name, how or when he began distilling oil, or where his primitive refinery was located. Zeh lost all trace of Bajtał in 1840 and claimed that he simply disappeared from the face of the earth.

Years later, in 1852, Zeh was employed as a laboratory assistant for Mikolasch when Abraham Schreiner and his partner Leib Stierman brought in a few hundredweights of oil that they had subjected to a primitive purification process—the same pungent material Zeh remembered from the days of Bajtał's peddling. Now Zeh was in a better position to indulge his curiosity about the material, and he devoted himself to the task of classifying and purifying it. In order to make the product useful, Zeh would have to both separate the most volatile fractions (which make oil explosive) through distilling and remove impurities (which cause its noxious odor) through purification. Zeh's search came at a cost: since his days were devoted to his pharmaceutical duties, he labored all night long without suitable equipment, suffering from persistent headaches and dizziness caused by the stinking, toxic gases. His clothes, hair, and skin were so saturated with the stench of burning oil that he was hardly able to appear in public. Zeh later reminisced that people avoided him, suspecting that he was insane; he even claimed that old ladies whispered and pointed at him when he walked down the street. The price he paid for his discovery was beyond measure: he later lost his wife and sister-in-law in an explosion set off when a match ignited petroleum gases near their store.[26]

Finally, Zeh was able to come up with a purified material he claimed was "relatively odorless." He proudly applied for and received an imperial patent for his purification process from the viceroy's office in Lviv and founded a distillation factory, employing four workers and running two stills. As promising as his new lighting material was, and as carefully as he explained how to use it, it did not catch on. Servants and cooks in Lviv households who experimented with the new product cursed his invention.[27] Only the subsequent creation of a suitable petroleum lamp made the whole enterprise possible. Zeh's junior colleague at the pharmacy, Ignacy Łukasiewicz (1822–1882), assisted him in this process, as did a local tinsmith, who developed a new lamp to burn petroleum safely in 1853.[28] They immediately sent a sample of two thousand kilograms of their purified product and the new lamps that would burn it to the Lviv

General Hospital.[29] The hospital's management was duly impressed, and on 31 July the Lviv General Hospital could proudly claim to be the first public building in the world to be lit solely by petroleum-burning lamps. A few months later, one of continental Europe's oldest railroad lines, the Emperor Ferdinand Northern Railway, began to experiment with replacing tallow candles with the new lamps in a few of its larger train stations as part of a general overhaul of its station buildings from 1859 to 1865. In the winter of 1858–1859 the railway converted entirely to petroleum lighting.[30] By the end of the decade, the Lviv Chamber of Trade and Commerce could declare that the use of lighting oil, "due to its beautiful and intense light and its comparatively low cost," was spreading rapidly.[31] Łukasiewicz quickly realized that the real profit lay in refining oil and worked together with Moritz Baron Brunicki and Eugen Zieliński to build a refinery in Klęczany.[32] After leasing a pharmacy in Gorlice, through which he hoped to make his living, he built a refinery in Gorlice in 1854 and subsequently built refineries in Jasło, Polanka, and Ułaszowice.[33]

While Łukasiewicz built up a small refining empire, others became interested in profiting from the supply of this new commodity. As one contemporary described the early stages of exploration, "a lively interest in the treasures slumbering in our native soil" developed, and "one began, though with undeniable mistrust, to set to work on rock oil production."[34] This brings us back to the Prussian entrepreneur Robert Doms, who recognized in the early 1850s that ozokerite promised to offer a cheap alternative to beeswax candles if a method of purifying it enough to transform it into an attractive household commodity could be found. As mentioned earlier, his interest in ozokerite led him to apply in 1854 for a clarification of Galician mineral rights possession laws. The final status of those laws, after so many reversals, was obscure indeed.

Contemporary observers noted that the government's interest waxed and waned with the current level of business interest in oil itself, so it is not surprising that Doms's request elicited a considered response from the Ministry of Finance. The ministry decided that in accordance with the General Mining Law of 23 May 1854, petroleum and mineral wax were in fact imperial property, along with "all minerals whose usefulness derives from their content of metals, sulfur, alum, vitriol, or common salt, furthermore, cement waters, graphite, and bitumina, finally all forms of black and brown coal."[35] Thus the imperial government allowed itself to distribute concessions without consulting the wishes of the landowners. In keeping with this decision, Doms was given a concession by the imperial government, which encouraged his exploitation of ozokerite with the provision that he regularly report on his progress and findings.[36]

While the General Mining Law declared that all bitumina were subject to the Imperial Mining Prerogative, it failed to elucidate exactly which products were actually considered bitumina, leaving the door open for further disputes. A few years later, in November 1860, the government explicitly insisted that liquid petroleum belonged to the bitumina family, but the Galician Provincial Diet would hear nothing of this. One of the Provincial Diet's earliest demands, after being reconstituted by Francis Joseph's February Patent in 1861, was to respond to a petition sent by the provincial Agricultural Club by announcing in April that the finance minister's 1860 Resolution did not apply to Galicia. In January 1862, the imperial authorities recognized Galicia's claim to liquid petroleum and, in February 1865, to ozokerite. To qualify for the exemption, both products had to be used exclusively for the purposes of illumination, a nearly meaningless caveat, since lighting was oil's only profitable use at that time.[37]

This admission had monumental consequences for the Galician oil industry and its dependence on local versus imperial decision making. It meant that determining the legal connection between ownership of surface land and subterranean goods, introducing guidelines for maintaining worker safety, writing regulations to protect farmland and waterways from oleaginous pollution, constructing housing and hospitals for oil workers, and arranging for transportation of goods and people into and out of the oil basin, as well as providing mortgages for investors, technical schools for oil engineers and drilling experts, and health and life insurance for workers, all were left to the discretion of the landowners who controlled the Galician Diet.

So, in the early 1860s, even before the extension of comprehensive political autonomy to Galicia in 1867 in the wake of the Austro-Hungarian Compromise, Galician landowners had successfully asserted their claim to any mineral rights pertaining to the extraction of oil on their land. In principle, legal conditions remained unaltered for two decades, a critical period in the history of the Galician oil industry. On the basis of these laws, hundreds of contracts were drawn up, control of the land changed hands even where its ownership remained constant, and, perhaps most significant, the land itself was fundamentally reorganized and reshaped. The parcellation that had plagued Galicia since the 1848 emancipation of the peasants continued to present a major problem. Because of the specific nature of the emancipation and because of laws regarding land categorization that dated back to the reign of Maria Theresa, Galicia was characterized by a large class of petty landowners with plots of land too small to support their families.[38] These landowners saw an opportunity finally to derive profit from their dwarf holdings. In order to maximize the number of contracts a landowner could turn to profit, and in order to keep the purchase price attractively low, ever smaller plots of already small peasant holdings were leased on an individual basis. Peasants became speculators, only to see their plots sublet at even higher rates. Small plots of land suited the needs of small-scale operators, whose investment in oil exploration was very low. All that was needed to become a wildcatter in the early days of the oil industry was a ladder, a windlass, a pickax, a shovel, a rope, and a pail.[39]

Despite the ease of entry into the industry, optimism about oil's profitability, and the conviction that the amount of oil was limitless, big capital and large companies largely steered clear of Galician oil in the 1860s and 1870s. By 1870, only one joint-stock company for the extraction of Galician oil, the Boryslawer Petroleum Gesellschaft, was in place.[40] A few brave foreign capitalists did attempt to enter the industry despite the specter of what one factory director described as "a foreign country punished by political confusion, poor in capital and trust, completely devoid of any popular education or a serviceable working class."[41] Under these circumstances, however, capital was not enough to ensure success. The Hamburg-Galizische Petroleum-Actien-Gesellschaft moved into Kłęczany (in western Galicia) and equipped itself with the best modern tools available—drills, steam engines, and all the necessary materials for purification and refining. All its investments notwithstanding, it was still driven to bankruptcy by the "deplorable conditions of the oil industry" in Galicia. Its ruin was blamed in particular on competition from a plethora of small local companies.[42]

Operators interested in entering the Galician oil industry were faced with a number of structural difficulties directly related to the empire's mineral rights policies. First, they were generally unable to convince locals to sell their land outright, since even in those cases where landownership was clearly established by land title registers, peasants were reluctant to relinquish hard-earned control.[43] The vast majority of landowners, however, fell into the rustical rather than the dominical category.[44] This meant that until the very end of the nineteenth century, their landholdings were not even included in land title registers, which made the sale and purchase of their land nearly impossible.[45]

This factor contributed to the second problem: big business was scared off by the ambiguity of provincial property law, which affected what was or was not specifically outlined in the typical contract between landowner and operator. Landowners were free to enter into leases with operators who would then acquire extraction rights, usually for a period of roughly twenty years, in exchange for an annual rent payment as long as no oil was discovered. Once oil production had commenced, the landowners collected a percentage (usually between 10 and 20 percent) of revenues (not profits). However, since ownership of the mineral rights was bound to ownership of the land, it was unclear what would happen if the land was sold. Although land sales were rare, they were possible, a source of disquiet for operators with long-term plans for large-scale investments. A new landowner was not explicitly obliged to honor any contracts for mineral rights made by his or her predecessor, because these obligations did not appear in the land title registers recording landownership.[46]

Finally, parcellation meant that these problems were multiplied over dozens of contracts drawn up with dozens of landowners. Since plots of land were very small, gaining control over a large tract of land required successfully cobbling together scores of parcels all held by different owners.[47] The need for large plots was not based only on the desire of larger firms to dominate the industry; it had a pragmatic origin based on the nature of the targeted material itself. The oil industry was and is very risky. Only when a prospector could sink multiple wells did the odds of finding oil in at least one of them become favorable. The rule of capture exacerbated this problem still further. Like a deer that wanders from one manorial estate to another, ignoring the niceties of human property and poaching laws, subterranean oil was notoriously inconsiderate of dearly purchased rights to its extraction. It flowed from one underground cavity to another in search of areas of relatively low pressure. Since pressure was released through drilling, the first prospector to tap into an underground cavity caused oil to rush to the surface, often far from where it had peacefully slumbered for ages. Unable to demonstrate whence the oil came, although often suspecting that it came from right under his nose, a prospector who had struck oil was forced to watch despondently as his neighbors quickly responded to any successful wells they saw on his land by digging wells of their own. The neighbors' goal was to sink wells as close to the boundary between the two plots as they could manage. According to law, the minimum distance between two wells was a mere ten fathoms, or about nineteen meters.[48] If competitors were promptly able to dig a pit deeper than the original one, the chances were good that the oil would rush into their wells and out into their storage barrels. This problem was so widespread that the battle between spiteful neighbors formed a literary trope in stories and newspaper articles about Borysław. A classic example of the former is Ivan Franko's story "The Bonus," in which one oilman's rage after his neighbor steals his oil leads to his premature death.[49]

The infamous rapaciousness of neighbors made it strategically important to oil prospectors that the perimeter of their land be as far as possible from any successful wells, granting them some measure of protection from neighbors. This, too, made small parcels of land unattractive to serious investors. To make matters worse, landowners did not lease their parcels in their entirety to a single bidder, but rather divided them further into sections, each large enough for a single shaft, so that thirty to forty different oil operators could find themselves sharing access to less than six thousand square meters of land.[50] According to one proponent of Crown control, this proximity exacerbated tensions: "in a short period of time shafts cropped up thickly upon one another, so that it was inevitable that competing companies would bump into each other, and the feverish activity of the mostly uneducated businessmen on such a crowded territory could not help but lead to the reciprocal infliction of coarse injuries and even to the law of the jungle."[51] This was no happy village of locals taking a common stand against the threat of foreign exploitation.

The oil industry did not appear to thrive under the aegis of private property. Consequently, the imperial government did not happily leave control over the oil industry to the provincial government and Galician landowners. Nor did everyone agree that it should have. Mining inspectors who were sent to report on whether local government officials seemed to be up to the job of regulating the industry and guaranteeing safety inevitably reported that they were not. The ministries of agriculture and the interior urgently dispatched memoranda reminding the viceroy of Galicia of his duty to report to the central government, evidence both of continuing concern in Vienna and of local inattention to mandated communication with the imperial capital.[52] Nor were landowners themselves unequivocally happy about the new situation. The courts were filled with contractual disputes and angry lawsuits between landowners and operators, neither of whom were given any legal protection or administrative guidance in understanding their respective privileges and obligations.[53] By 1870, the Drohobycz District Court was notoriously overburdened by the highest per capita caseload of any court district in the empire. Local landowners complained that the settlement of even the most urgent civil disputes took several years. By the First World War, the Drohobycz District Court, the largest in Austria, boasted thirty judicial officials.[54] The region's reputation for excessively litigious tendencies was recorded in József Rogosz's semiautobiographical novel *In Galician Hell*, in which he claimed that the Ruthenian villagers of the oil basin drove themselves to ruin with protracted legal battles: "Indeed, people litigate a cause sometimes for an entire year all for nothing and in so doing lose their possessions. Nevertheless, with very few exceptions, they do this only because they seek justice."[55]

Engineers and industry observers from Vienna submitted a barrage of complaints and horrified reports to newspapers, trade journals, and government officials about the hazardous nature of the oil industry. They lamented the workers' peril, the abuse and misuse of the land, and the generally miserable conduct of all parties involved. A devastating fire that ravaged Borysław in September 1874, destroying two hundred shafts and innumerable outbuildings and costing several workers their lives, drew renewed attention to the inadequacy of local conditions. The fire, which started when a worker foolishly tossed a match he had used to light an illicit cigarette into a bucket of oil, revealed the lack of any kind of fire prevention measures, fire-fighting abilities, or safety precautions in the oil industry. The chief district magistrate concluded that the enormous piles of extracted ozokerite left to accumulate near the mines had blocked passage through the terrain and inhibited attempts to gain control over the spreading fire.[56] The minister of agriculture, in a report to the minister of the interior, lamented the fact that the oil industry, excluded as it was from the Imperial Mining Prerogative, no longer fell under his jurisdiction. He was more determined than ever to support passage of a bill he was working on at the time to bring all bitumina back under the government's care. This disaster revealed to him, however, the necessity of reforming the industry before such a measure was taken. Not to do so, he warned, would mean burdening the government with an industry that had already been "condemned to eternal ruin."[57]

After the fire, inspectors sent by the Ministry of Agriculture in 1875 submitted very similar reports on the industry's problems: the land parcels were too small, and industrial conditions endangered workers, were terribly inefficient, and did not observe any of the rules of rational, professional, scientific mining. Their complaints centered on the wax industry in particular, since the paraffin candles that were produced from ozokerite were much more profitable than petroleum for lamps throughout the 1860s and 1870s.[58] They pointed out the danger that the prevalent style of wax mining posed to the environment. The activities of men below the ground were changing the land's outward appearance. The pockmarked surface of the earth warned of the dangers of unhampered mining, and even the industry's most ardent supporters believed that mining for oil products "makes greater demands on the earth's surface than any other form of mining, making [the land] unusable for any other purpose."[59] Too many holes in the earth dug too close together and with insufficient internal reinforcements had led to a mass movement of earth: "This mass movement expresses itself through the collapse of shaft reinforcements, the formation of wide clefts reaching to the surface, and the sinking of public streets and houses."[60] There were no land title registers for rustical properties, so it was difficult to record who actually owned the land. Contracts between landowners and leaseholders would be canceled if and when the land was sold, which made entering into contracts dubious and dangerous for serious long-term investors. The government, they concluded, must distribute, regulate, and control mineral rights. If it failed to do so, advocates of Crown control warned, "in a short period of time the entire wax terrain of Borysław will be lost to production, and a catastrophe will occur costing hundreds of lives."[61]

The bulk of the dissatisfied were mining entrepreneurs, major industrialists, and professional engineers. The difference between celebration and dismay over the current laws mirrored the difference between the small independents and those who had a reason to believe that they could successfully request a royal commission under the Imperial Mining Prerogative. The latter wanted to create big businesses by making large investments and reaping large gains. The landlords, on the other hand, were willing to lease to anyone, in complete disregard of the lessor's ability to finance professional production. Dividing land into small plots had the natural effect of making it generally affordable, which meant that cost considerations did not weed out small, incompetent competitors. Critics noted that producers failed to take advantage of the rising price of oil during the 1870s and blamed the decline in production not on the depression that started in 1873, but rather on mismanagement and a system of overexploitation or "predatory mining," which made it impossible to effectively extract even oil and ozokerite that had already been discovered.[62]

The government's inspectors and commissioners sent to investigate Galician conditions throughout the 1870s had no shortage of recommendations on how to improve them. All unanimously advocated a return to the Imperial Mining Prerogative and couched their arguments in terms of securing a more democratic distribution of mineral rights access, although many rightly suspected that the application of the Imperial Mining Prerogative would have the opposite effect. Galician advocates for the Imperial Mining Prerogative tried to argue that government control would give mineral rights to anyone who applied for them and could

Rapacious digging under the ground caused the collapse of poorly constructed wooden dwellings in Borysław. (Author's collection.)

demonstrate the ability to make use of them: "Since the state only reserves the right to exploit subterranean mineral treasures for itself in order to grant it to the first suitable applicant, mining is in fact made independent of the conditions of surface ownership and placed under the protection of the entire community to the benefit of both parties."[63] Leaving mineral rights in private hands, however, meant abandoning them to the mercy of landlords who operated according to motives that were not open to public scrutiny.[64]

There was no expectation that large landlords themselves might want to take advantage of these rights. Early observers claimed that landowners who directly entered the oil industry were few and far between, reflecting the widespread aristocratic contempt for developing industry. Chief Mining Commissioner H. Wachtel claimed in 1860 that "the landowners themselves have not taken advantage of the favorably developing industrial opportunities, and—one must sadly admit—hardly ever will."[65] On the other hand, some argued, the Galician oil industry was living proof of the validity of the old proverb "Wie gewonnen so zerronnen" (Easy come, easy go): peasant landowners who had suddenly found themselves heirs to unimagined sources of wealth simply let it ooze through their fingers.[66] Why should this precious commodity be left in the hands of those who either lacked the will or the means to take advantage of their hidden riches?

Some argued that the landowners themselves suffered from the twin evils of parcellation and land speculation. In the 1870s, no one knew how to determine accurately what land would hold oil. As soon as anyone in a particular village stumbled upon any underground repositories of oil, everyone's land for miles around was considered suspect, land prices soared, and speculation took off. A contemporary described the process thus:

> If a prospector sank a shaft maybe 8–10 fathoms [ca. 15–19 meters] deep and found oil, or a landowner suspected with confidence that he had oil in his field, then he would have nothing more pressing to do than to divide the entire field into small segments 1 fathom wide and 2 feet deep, about 2–3 fathoms from one another, without any regular order or succession, and to sell the ensuing divisions, called *zakopi*, to individual operators. According to the probability of success, *zakopi* cost 15, 50, 100 or 200 florins, in addition to one-fourth of the production. ... These *zakopi* are traded like stocks on the exchange.[67]

Borysław notoriously offered the starkest picture of the parcellation of land that followed its division into ever smaller lots for sale. In 1881 there were 204 different companies engaged in the search for and extraction of bitumina in Borysław and in the villages immediately surrounding it.[68] Together these enterprises controlled 1,462.74 hectares. The average plot size per organization or individual would thus appear to be approximately 7.17 hectares. However, the Prince Günther Schwarzburg Sondershausen Company in Schodnica controlled 1,351 hectares of this land. If we exclude this one property, we are left with a mere 111.74 hectares for 203 companies, for an average of .55 hectares, or 5,500 square meters, per company—approximately the size of a regulation American football field.[69] But even that average is misleading: 184 (90 percent) of these 203 companies controlled less than 1 hectare, and 132 (65 percent) of them owned less than .1 hectare, that is, one-fifth of a regulation football field. While the Schwarzburg Sondershausen Company sank only 5 wells on its vast tract of land, the other companies together accounted for 547 wells under construction and 1,232 wells in operation, along with 1,548 that had already been abandoned. There was, thus, a total of 3,327 large holes in the ground spread out over a space of 111.74 hectares, for an average of 29 holes per hectare, or 1 every 336 square meters. Taken together, these statistics paint a clear picture of a terrain crowded with pits, mines, shacks, derricks, and great expectations.

Hardly a year went by in which proposals for reform were not made. In January 1874, the Galician Provincial Diet debated the merits of an imperial government motion to return all bitumina to the Imperial Mining Prerogative over a three-year transition period. The Provincial Diet had the right to approve any laws pertaining to oil, in accordance with the law of 1861 that granted it jurisdiction over all matters not specifically reserved for the imperial government.[70] Its debate deserves closer examination, because within its polemics we find hidden clues about the nature of the controversy and the adversaries' motives. When the imperial Viennese government proposed to claim control over local industry and the Provincial Diet refused to grant the government that control, rhetoric quickly became infused with references to the colonial status of the periphery versus centralized imperial power. Throughout the oil industry's development, self-defined Poles such as Stanisław Szczepanowski claimed that the Galician oil industry suffered precisely because it was in Galicia rather than in Bohemia or Lower Austria.[71] The debate over mineral rights did not, however, emerge as a nationalist conflict

— complicated web of overlapping
and competing concerns

between defenders of Polish interest and propagators of German and Jewish interest masked as imperial justice. In a political context rife with national and nationalist conflicts, the absence of ethnicized rhetoric in the debate over the oil industry stands out. At issue here were questions of landownership, private property, and local control. At the heart of the matter lay a web of overlapping and competing concerns: first, conservative agricultural landowners against landowners who were interested in the technological and industrial potential of their properties; second, landowners in general against capitalist investors; third, small business against big business. The process of disentangling these various conflicts is complicated by the facts that small capital often lined up with local capital and that large business and foreign capital (including Viennese capital) were nearly synonymous. But the major difference between the two camps lay in the kind of industry that would be created and its relative prominence vis-à-vis agriculture, not the language its administrators would speak.

The interests of each side were reflected in the 1874 Provincial Diet debate and represented by the two alternate proposals that emerged from a subcommittee established to review the government motion. Both proposals accepted the government's claim that more supervision was needed to regulate the industry. The first proposal, however, insisted that ownership of mineral rights must remain exclusively in the hands of landowners. Although landowners would need government permission to explore their land for oil and to set up production on their land, they could not be forced either to explore themselves or to allow anyone else to do so without their permission. This would provide for regulations on the conduct of oil production operations without permitting regulations that constricted the rights of agrarian landowners or endangered the value of their property. Here the first priority would be to respect the rights of landowners to decide the extent to which they wished to exploit the mineral wealth hidden beneath the surface of their property. The promotion of oil production and the development of industry were of secondary concern.

The second proposal put forward by the subcommittee and favored by three of its five members went much further. While it stopped short of returning mineral rights to the Imperial Mining Prerogative, it accepted the supervision of minerals' exploitation as a government concern. The proposal's premise was that the government had the right to encourage and oversee oil production with or without the support of the land-owners. In the final analysis, industrial development was as important as the sovereignty of landowners—if not more so. Landowners would have the right of first refusal: that is, no one would be allowed to apply for a concession to explore for oil on someone else's land unless the landowner had first declared an unwillingness or an inability to explore. A declaration of intent to explore did not guarantee that the landowners would be protected from external interference, however. Each landowner who wished to take advantage of his or her land's subterranean wealth would have a limited time to do so (the proposal suggested six months). If a landowner chose not to pursue his or her claim within that time, the government would be free to grant a concession to any applicant. In this case, extracting oil from the ground and making it available to the empire's consumers was the first priority; landowners' rights were respected only as long as they did not inhibit this primary goal.

Some of the men who voted for the first proposal spoke Polish, some Ukrainian. Some of the men who voted for the second proposal spoke Polish, some Ukrainian. Not one of them argued that Vienna was the natural seat of decision making in Galician affairs. Edward Dzwonkowski, who spoke in favor of the second, further-reaching proposal, was just as ardent as representatives of the more moderate proposal in his opposition to returning mineral rights to the Imperial Mining Prerogative. He argued that doing so would mean the end of the small companies and the demise of scores of local entrepreneurs, chased out by big business:

> Entrepreneurs who had earned significant amounts before but whose wells produced only a few barrels [would] lose their mines, because they would not be able to survive the competition. This is what awaits our businessmen if large capital concentrates. Our country [Galicia] will produce, companies will grow, but what will our country profit from that? . . . If significant foreign capital enters the picture, then our country will indeed produce truly great quantities, but the profits will not stay with us; they will go to Vienna, to Berlin, or to London.[72]

While the danger of foreign interference in local business was a popular theme in the Galician Provincial Diet, the familiar juxtaposition of us (Poles) versus them (everyone else) masked an equally significant difference between large businessmen, small businessmen, and large landowners. The mineral rights issue created a bond between a trinity of unlikely bedfellows. The first group was made up of small, predominantly Jewish producers whose inefficient and risky enterprises would be threatened by competition from large, capital-rich corporations. These small producers were joined by the Ruthenian peasants who leased their strips of land, or *zakopi*, to them. Finally, they found allies in large Polish estate owners who dreaded the prospect of foreigners converting their fields into strips of muddy black earth poisoned by the putrid stench of petroleum gases. They feared that the presence of influential businesses in Galicia might interfere with the hegemony of the large landowners.

Polish-speaking gentry with large land holdings and Ukrainian-speaking peasants in eastern Galicia with small plots had little in common, but they did share an interest in protecting their sovereignty on their own land, regardless of its size. For Polish landowners, this meant securing the right to refuse to explore for oil; for Ruthenians it meant protecting the small landowners' rights both to explore themselves and to be protected from the ruthless competition of more competent parties.

One of the few Ruthenian delegates to the Provincial Diet, lawyer Vasyl' Koval's'kyi (1826–1911), argued that all landowners were equally threatened by the rapaciousness of external business interests: "Now, is it right to change decisions about the characteristics of these products [that is, whether or not they fall under the Imperial Mining Prerogative] because a few nonlandowners, casting an envious gaze on others' property, suddenly wanted to make profits?" Landowners were the only group who could be trusted with the care of Galicia's natural wealth, he continued. "American entrepreneurs and other foreigners will begin exploration, acquire land and bring in real engineers to dig wells and change the land, but they will not produce oil in our country, but will convey their American oil over here and sell it to us! Such cases have already occurred."[73] Oil offered poor Ruthenian peasants a unique opportunity to enrich themselves—to their benefit and also to the benefit of the state, which enjoyed higher returns on its tax claims. Denying them access to their own good fortune, however, would reduce them to the abject poverty from which they had only recently been rescued. In the words of another Ruthenian deputy, history teacher Mykola Antonevych, "Our country would be left like a squeezed lemon, and the landowners would come to poverty and misery."[74] Appealing simultaneously to a localized sense of identity and a broad fear of challenges to landownership, advocates of the minority motion presented themselves as the champions of the province's entire landowning population, that is, as friends of wealthy and poor landowners alike.

The proponents of the second proposal, however, refused to defend their position as one that asserted the rights of outsiders or imperial authority. They insisted that the real issue was whether uneducated laypersons in political offices should retain oversight over mining affairs, or if responsibility would be better invested in the hands of trained mining professionals. The question did not pit Vienna against Lviv, they argued, but rather the modern, rational, technological scientist against the backward, agriculturally oriented politician, easily confused by the intricacies of industrial development. At the same time, it revealed the different motives and interests of serious miners and investors who wanted to pursue oil exploration and production over the long term against the petty businesses that deputy Ferdynand Weigel called "small, haphazard *Raubwirtschaften* [predatory and exploitative mining companies], without any significance—on the contrary, actually harmful with their backward methods of production." These small producers threatened to ruin the industry beyond repair: "Anyone who has observed our style of production in person has realized that owners together with a mass of petty entrepreneurs, lessees, and sub-lessees tempted by the lure of even insignificant profits, extract oil so unprofessionally, so out of step with the rules of rational mining, that it is a horror."[75] Weigel went on to compare the effects of these small businesses to those of moles, who in digging their holes destroy the land and render it useless without providing any benefit in exchange.

In the end, the Provincial Diet elected to pass the more conservative minority proposal, retaining the landowners' exclusive right to determine in what manner and to what purpose their land should be used. In the absence of extensive new government regulations, the landowners' attendant obligation to abide by such regulations was of little import. Discussion continued over how best to administer and regulate the reform of the industry. Chief Mining Commissioner Edward Windakiewicz, having abandoned all hope of returning control over petroleum extraction to the Imperial Mining Prerogative, suggested establishing a mining police to supervise the industry. Petitions were submitted to the District Mining Office from both sides of the conflict: landowners predictably demanded that their rights be respected, and miners and industrialists insisted that the reckless mining style of dilettante producers had led to a dramatic decline in production. Borysław's face was marred by 8,000 abandoned shafts; in Galicia only 4,000 shafts were still in operation out of 20,000 dug. Small producers did not know how to efficiently run a well and were therefore more likely to abandon prematurely the oil left in dug pits without exhausting the supply.[76]

The controversy led the Galician Society for the Improvement of the Oil Industry to submit a bill before the Provincial Diet in 1881.[77] This motion eventually led to the passage in 1884 of a definitive new mining law, the Imperial Petroleum Law, intended to eliminate remaining uncertainty surrounding the Imperial Mining Prerogative and mineral rights once and for all. The law was approved by both the imperial Parliament (in May) and the Galician provincial diet (in December). In keeping with years of indecision, the new law attempted to incorporate both the benefits of state supervision and those of private control.

The first sentence of §1 confirmed that all bitumina, in particular petroleum and ozokerite, were at the disposal of the landowner, a clear victory for the latter. The very next sentence, however, announced that the extraction of these minerals was subject to the supervision of the Mining Authority, a concession to the demands of the mining professionals and industrialists.[78] In this fashion, the law immediately created an intermediate status for mineral rights between the two poles of landowners' absolute sovereignty and outright Crown control. The law's second substantive change involved the creation of a new ownership category: "oil fields." Ownership of an oil field referred to the right to exploit oil, not to the ownership of the field that held it. This meant that mineral rights were henceforth held separately from the land itself and could thus be leased independently of changing landownership. As a consequence of the new law, the minister of justice decreed, with the approval of the Galician Provincial Diet, that control over the oil fields would be recorded in oil registers, just as control over land was recorded in the land title registers.[79] Maintaining a clear record of mineral rights ownership would serve to alleviate the lessee's insecurity in a case where the landowner sold the land itself.

The delicate balance struck by the new mining law restricted the rights of landowners and increased their responsibilities without diminishing their ultimate ownership of their land and all its resources—animal, vegetable, or mineral. Landowners were not free to deny operators access to their lands under all circumstances: operators were guaranteed the right to compensate neighboring landowners for the purposes of erecting out-buildings, removing water from their mines, and building roads or rail-road lines to the extent required by their mining operation. Provisions were made to ease the acquisition of mortgages to finance prospecting and production, and the government promised to oversee the negotiation and management of those mortgages. Although oil fields could be leased at the landowners' will, they had to meet certain requirements set by the imperial government: they could be no smaller than one hectare and no larger than thirty-six. The upward limit was designed to prevent specu-lators from purchasing rights to large tracts of land and profiting from their subsequent subletting. The law also established a mining police and created regulations intended to monitor and control working conditions. Further legislation began the process of protecting workers' rights by ban-ning children and women from subterranean labor, limiting the length of shifts to twelve hours, and forbidding work on Sundays.[80]

In recognition of the considerable autonomy of Galicia's landowners, many of whom were also the province's leading political figures, the new law envisioned a restricted role for the imperial government in the de-velopment of any further rules and regulations relating to the daily man-agement of the oil industry. In §13, jurisdiction over further legal deci-sions concerning extraction rights to bitumina was placed in the hands of provincial lawmakers. Provincial legislation would have to decide how to monitor "the operation and administration, the mining police and the conduct of the Mining Authority, and finally the penal power of the Mining Authority."[81] While mining activity in general remained the re-sponsibility of the Ministry of Agriculture, which continued to oversee matters relating to the industry as a whole until the Ministry of Public Works took over supervision of the petroleum industry after its creation in 1908, detailed supervision over the legal framework of the industry clearly devolved to provincial authorities.

In the context of an empire often posthumously derided for its inability to create "institutionalized channels that allow for regularized forms of participation on the part of the populace in order to enhance the legiti-macy of government,"[82] the entire debate about the property regime best suited to oil—and which governmental authority had the right to deter-mine what that property regime was—takes on a particular significance. The oil industry was and is fundamentally unfair—there is no justice in the distribution of wealth and success among its participants. In that sense, one cannot begin to talk about a democratic distribution of power, or of oil as empowering the little man. Peasants and "little men" in general were as poorly represented in the provincial government as in the imperial government, if not more poorly still. Nevertheless, this debate represents an occasion on which local politicians and local interest groups were able to hold their own against the central government and its official and unofficial agents. As historian Gary Cohen would have suspected, since the middle of the nineteenth century, the site for discussions of "social welfare, crime, public health, primary education, and economic development"[83]—at least as far as they related to the oil industry—was thus clearly not Vienna, but Lviv.

These new regulations and restrictions may seem modest in scope and did not change the fundamental nature of the oil industry overnight. They did, however, create a legal framework for the gradual entry of foreign capital into the industry, even while maintaining local supervision. By introducing extensive government regulation of the industry without claiming state ownership of oil and wax, Vienna was able to indirectly interfere with the industry's organization, design, and management. Although landowners had exclusive rights to the profits derived from their subterranean property, the government retained the position of arbiter, mediator, and negotiator between conflicting parties—whether landowner and operator, producer and refiner, or employer and employee. Over the next two decades, large businesses, most of them set up with foreign capital, began to take hold of the Galician oil industry. Once their position was secure, they used economic tools to accomplish privately what the government had been unable to do by fiat. They slowly squeezed out local producers, established economies of scale, and created and recreated cartels and cooperatives to share the costs of pipelines and storage facilities. But in the 1860s and 1870s, organization and modernization were concepts for the future. The oil industry awaited the coming of leaders who would make it viable in a world of international competition. In the 1880s, they would appear.

p. 59

pp. 49-51, 55

peripheral
status of
petroleum

p. 56 -- 1853 - invention of new lamp,
        increased int. in petroleum

60-64 - small-time character of
    oil digging created env. problem

unlikely bedfellows in Galicia all feared
    foreign, ext. business interests extracting profits

— 3 —

Petroleum Fever

Foreign Entrepreneurs
and a New National Industry

The story of the oil industry's economic maturation is not a simple one of industrialists forging ahead with a project of modernization and development. Galician oil entrepreneurs' political battles and social status reveal that the Galician oil industry was the site of disputes with more than merely economic consequences. At no point in the course of its development were decisions relating to oil production, refining, and trade made solely on the basis of economic interests or reasoning. Political debates within Galicia, as well as those between Lviv and Vienna, were colored by competing visions of Galicia's proper place in the Austrian Empire (or in a reconstructed Poland). External participation in Galician industry was accompanied by overt and hidden attempts to "civilize" the province and its inhabitants, or, conversely, to develop appropriate strategies for dealing with the lack of civilization in Europe's own "Siberia."[1] At the same time, Galicia became the site of attempts to create a mini-Polish state in the absence of the "historic" Polish-Lithuanian Commonwealth, taking advantage of the political privileges that came with widespread autonomy and the economic opportunities offered by what appeared to be immense natural wealth. Although oil producers of the 1860s and 1870s were grouped together in the contemporary imagination under the rubric of selfish, ignorant, and shortsighted peasants, the oil producers of the 1880s and 1890s would earn themselves the respect and admiration of engineers for decades to come. This was a period in which reputations and fortunes were established by a group of pioneering young men who chose Galicia as the site of a grand experiment in national and personal improvement. Their individual stories cannot be divided from the story of the maturation of the Galician oil industry.

75

Traveling to Borysław in the early 1880s was an onerous task not to be undertaken lightly. Although it was connected to the Austrian railroad network via an extension of the Dniesterbahn in 1872, travel remained arduous. First, the visitor would be subjected to the discomforts and hazards of Galician train travel, immortalized by General Stumm's complaint in Robert Musil's 1930 novel *The Man without Qualities:* "But do you know what it's like?! It's like traveling second class in Galicia and picking up crab lice! I've never felt so filthy helpless!"[2] After arriving in Borysław's train station, which was itself two kilometers from the town, the hapless visitor would struggle to find a hackney carriage to take him the remaining distance along a dirt road that was impossible for a pedestrian with city shoes to navigate.[3] Once there, he would find none of the amenities that ease the weary traveler. An illustrated guidebook to Galicia written for tourists and business travelers reported little that would recommend Borysław to the accidental tourist. This "Petroleum California of Galicia" offered the spectator a "valley filled with thousands of mines and shafts, piles of clay and slate, numerous barracks, buildings, and warehouses," but although it had delivered "over 20 million [*sic*] wax, oil, and oil products," one saw "no prosperity in this village of 10,000 souls. . . . The workers are demoralized by alcoholism. Although a Mining Office has its seat here and the influx of foreigners is considerable, one finds no hotels—only crude inns and a few miserable *traiteurs.*" Visitors to the nearest metropolis, Drohobycz (which boasted 18,225 residents in 1882), fared little better. Despite the presence of three hotels, two restaurants, and a café, Drohobycz was derided as a "rich but unclean city." As a symbol of the city's unusual wealth, the authors noted that an asphalt sidewalk (a rarity in the small towns of Galicia) ran along the main boulevard that was lined by the beautiful houses and gardens of the "petroleum kings."[4] Commenting on its filth, another visitor lamented that this same sidewalk was frequented by petroleum peddlers, "covered with petroleum from head to toe," who "brush against pedestrians whose clothes they besmirch." To place this outrageous behavior in context, he added: "in other towns, these peddlers have their designated places of sales, and they are not permitted to use the sidewalks."[5]

But despite these obstacles, over the next few decades more and more prominent personalities and humble vagrants chose to travel to the oil basin. In addition to Emperor Francis Joseph, whose 1880 trip represented a calculated desire to demonstrate support for the province's newest and most promising industry, the oil basin drew thousands of other, more characteristic, new faces. From 1882 to 1914, Drohobycz's population rose from just over 18,000 to around 38,000 residents. Borysław and Tustanowice, two villages that had grown together into one sprawling town, together housed 28,000 (up from a modest 7,613 in 1872).[6] Even these numbers are deceptive, however, since not everyone who came to the region was counted in official censuses. Many lived in neighboring villages and hoped to supplement their income with casual day labor in one of the wax mines or oil pits. These drew the attention of locals who saw in the booming population of newcomers, itinerants, and passers-through opportunities to make money from the provision of lodging, food, and drink. A few optimistic socialists sought progressive, modern men and women in the local workers. Then there were entrepreneurs, most of them exogenous, with visions of future fortunes that justified the present personal sacrifices required in a move from the civilized West to the Galician hinterland.

While migrant and temporary workers had characterized the villages and towns of the oil basin since the beginning of the industry, as had the innkeepers and tavern keepers who lived off those workers' need for shelter and entertainment, only in the 1880s did the oil region begin to attract significant numbers of serious entrepreneurs and the skilled workers who were required by technologically modern production methods. In the decade that began with the introduction of the new mining law in 1884 and ended with the opening of the particularly rich oil fields of Schodnica in 1895, Galicia saw a transformation in the technology used to extract oil, a concomitant explosion in production, and the emergence of a powerful lobby of large-scale producers who made it clear that they had linked their personal fortunes to those of the oil industry. At the turn of the twentieth century, the companies founded by those entrepreneurs were joined by a plethora of new joint-stock companies backed by banks and conglomerates from outside Galicia, including some of Vienna's most prominent financial institutions. Their proprietors and governing boards were prepared to defend their interests against those of landowners, of small business operators, of central Viennese authorities, and of refiners. At the middle of the nineteenth century, oil was a curiosity, and its extraction and exploitation were the realm of scientists and adventurers. By the beginning of the twentieth century, oilmen represented a powerful social and economic force that helped define the course of Galician politics.

Starting in 1884, the methods of financing and executing oil production and refining in Galicia matured. New technologies that promised to raise the Galician oil industry to standards set by the United States were introduced. At the same time, a group of large, capital-rich companies, often with foreign backing, slowly tried to drive smaller, more haphazard companies out of business, a process that continued until the outbreak of the First World War. Neither of these developments were complete metamorphoses, however. Digging and hand drilling continued side by side with machine drilling. Small-scale companies with a handful of employees and no capital investment held on to their precarious existence for decades more.

Interest in oil had been slow to materialize among larger companies. A list of 205 oil and wax production companies active in 1881 reveals that almost all companies were run by individual Galicians, most of them Jewish. The only exceptions were two large wax companies: the Galician Credit Bank and the Société Française pour l'Exploitation de Cire Minérale et Pétrole, commonly refered to as "the French Company."[7] The Galician trade inspector reported in 1884: "it is a well-known fact that, with the exception of the city of Biała, there is not a single so-called industrial city in all of Galicia, and that the few factories lie like oases scattered in a desert."[8] There were several explanations for this: one Viennese mining commissioner suggested that it was in part the fault of the "stranglehold of taxation" (a remark that aroused the immediate objection of the Ministry of Finance) and in part the fault of still underdeveloped consumer markets.[9] In addition, the weakness of the domestic (that is, Galician) market was such that high-quality oil made for export could not be sold there, leading to the production of two different grades of oil, described in a government report as "one white, high grade, identical to American [oil] for the cities, the wealthiest rural residents, and for export, and one yellow, mixed with gasoline to raise its illuminating power and its quality, for the rural poor." A subsequent comment in this report revealed that the difference was not just cosmetic: "This lesser type, although called 'explosive', poses no threat when one knows how to handle it and has won, due to its *much* cheaper price, a large market."[10] But exports remained low: in 1891, Galicia produced 87,700 tons of oil, of which only 2,630 tons (less than 3 percent) were exported.[11] The high costs of production and shipping made Austrian oil incapable of competing with American oil outside of the empire, and little had been done to lower those costs.

In the early 1880s, a series of developments made the industry more promising to entrepreneurs. First, an 1881 law ensured that foreign joint-stock companies could legally run mining operations in Austria.[12] Second, the construction in 1883 of the Transversalbahn, which ran through the entire oil basin, connected production regions with the rest of the empire. Third, the 1884 Mining Law, which introduced registries for landownership and mineral rights control, brought about greater regulation of the oil industry. Fourth, the introduction of higher tariffs for crude and refined oils in 1882 provided some price protection from imports.[13] These developments did not themselves cause the explosion in production and investment that characterized the oil industry in the last years of the nineteenth century, but they did create a more promising market. That promise drew the attention of several inspired individuals whose actions did indeed directly contribute to the oil industry's unprecedented growth.

Two men took the lead in taking advantage of this improving situation: Stanisław Antoni Prus Szczepanowski (1846–1900) and William Henry MacGarvey (1843–1914). Neither was born in Galicia. MacGarvey was a native of Canada; Szczepanowski was born in the Duchy of Posen (Poznań). Nor did they represent the type of great and prominent figures who are memorialized in biographical dictionaries of Galicia. Neither was noble, neither was invested with particular artistic talents, and neither participated in any of the numerous nineteenth-century uprisings that created popular Polish heroes. But both were symptomatic of a new breed of Galician citizen; as Ivan Franko put it, such entrepreneurial spirits were still without "stable foundations" in Galician culture,[14] but they were increasingly to be found. Szczepanowski and MacGarvey were fully committed to the Galician oil industry; their personal fortunes would rise and fall with oil production and prices. Not connected to Galicia by birth or breeding, they chose to settle in the province and make it their permanent home. Pioneers, innovators, and self-made men both, they set an example of the great potential and the great peril of the oil industry and left that industry transformed.

Both Szczepanowski and MacGarvey turned their attention to Galicia around 1880 (Szczepanowski in 1879 and MacGarvey in 1882) amid news of impending legal reform. What they found when they got there was an industry that had stagnated, in particular in the years after the depression of 1873. Mining was carried out largely in the same primitive fashion that had characterized the previous decade. The quarter century of technological progress that had made advanced drilling commonplace in the oil fields of Pennsylvania and Ontario had not brought great change to exploitation techniques in Galicia. As early as 1865, the sinking of wells in Pennsylvania was powered exclusively by engines.[15] By 1873 in North America, percussion drilling had replaced older methods that used spring poles and grasshopper walking beams.[16] At that same time in Galicia, nearly all shafts were dug, rather than drilled, and steam engines were an unknown luxury: in 1885, there was one steam engine with sixteen horsepower in use in the entire Galician oil production industry.[17] The widespread absence of drills can be explained by three factors. First, wax could only be retrieved from wells that had been dug. As long as wax was more profitable than oil, as it was throughout the 1870s and 1880s, this made operators anxious to protect any possible wax deposits.[18] Second, although attempts to drill rather than dig had been made as early as 1862, no drilling method had been found that exactly suited the geological conditions of the Carpathian foothills.[19] Third, the plethora of small, low-capital companies could not afford the initial investment required to purchase drills and pay skilled drillers. That the lack of capital was at the heart of the problem is demonstrated by similarly weak figures in refining: in 1876, Galicia's forty-seven refineries had only seven steam engines with a total of thirty-eight horsepower.[20]

When a new oil field was discovered in Galicia, it immediately became the scene of a flurry of activity. After acquiring a plot typically thirteen to twenty square meters in size [sic], a prospector would dig a round hole about one meter in diameter. He would then sink poles about two to three inches thick vertically around the perimeter of the hole. These would be plaited with hazelnut twigs like a basket. Then the hole would be sunk further and reinforced with more basket weaving. Two poles about six inches thick and forked at the top would be hammered into the ground on either side of the hole to serve as supports for the windlass, made from a crooked piece of wood with a naturally formed winding handle. A hemp rope wrapped around the windlass was attached by a simple knot to the belt of the pit worker who would be lowered into the pit. (Pit workers were invariably men, for although women were employed in the oil industry, they were never allowed to work underground.) Standing at the pit's bottom, the pit worker would dig deeper and deeper, shoveling the earth he removed into a wooden bucket now suspended from the same rope that would later pull him out of the pit.[21] Workers aboveground would lift up the bucket and empty it, forming huge mounds of earth, which were left to stand next to the pits and became obstacles in times of fire. When the pit had been sunk to a depth at which gases became dangerous, workers (sometimes female) aboveground would turn a ventilator that was supposed to circulate fresh air into the shaft. This continued until the pit worker reached a point where he could smell or see oil bubbling up at the bottom of the well. At that point, he would be pulled out of the well, which would be covered with wooden boards overnight. The well's anxious owner and his employees would wait for the pressure of the oil to push through the thin layer of earth between it and the air. Usually, when the wooden planks were removed the following morning, the well would be filled with oil, which would then be removed by the bucket.[22] Not surprisingly, digging proceeded slowly, and rates of oil production were low. In the 1860s and 1870s, Galician prospectors could expect to make no more than twenty centimeters of downward progress on a typical day. A government inspector in the 1870s called the production of a mine that produced 3.1 tons of oil a day for several days in a row "marvelous."[23]

In addition to being incredibly inefficient, this style of extraction was a safety hazard. The workers were often victims of collapsing shafts, the primitive cribbing provided by hazelnut twigs notwithstanding. According to one engineer, "a shaft sunk in this fashion cannot resist the underground water or the pressure of the earth for long. Already several lives have been lost because of the collapse of shafts or falling stones caused by this irrational, unprofessional manipulation."[24] The noxious gases that filled these pits often knocked workers unconscious; if workers lost consciousness while they were being lowered into or lifted out of the pit, they could (and often did) fall to their deaths. If they became unconscious while working at the pit's bottom and this went unnoticed by their colleagues aboveground, they would continue to inhale the poison until they suffocated to death. In addition, a pit worker was in constant danger of being caught unexpectedly by sudden eruptions of oil that turned out to be closer than he anticipated. Even those pit workers who were able to avoid all underground accidents could be (and frequently were) killed by a stone accidentally dropped into the shaft from above or by a fire started when gases were ignited by even the smallest spark.[25]

Despite accident rates more reminiscent of factory than farm life, there was little that seemed modern about the oil industry. Many small operators seemed satisfied with the risks and rewards offered by the status quo; their inertia and resistance to change frustrated early attempts at reform. Contemporaries were quick to blame these small operators, most of whom were Jewish, for the deplorable condition of the industry. Few Jewish producers were able to overcome prejudice and establish reputations as men of skill and conscience. One such man was Efroim Hersch Schreier (1844–1898). A long-standing member of the Galician Provincial Petroleum Association (GLPV), he successfully transformed a small company founded in the earliest days of oil exploitation into one of Galicia's few successfully integrated companies, Gartenberg and Schreier, with a refinery in Kołomyja, built in 1882 and another near Jasło, built in 1890. Upon his death, a contemporary, Stanisław Olszewski, called him "one of those citizens of the Mosaic faith who know how to bring his own interest into harmony with that of the country."[26] Such words of praise for Borysław's earliest entrepreneurs were exceedingly rare, however, and no one expected that reform would come at the hands of producers themselves.

Nevertheless, when Szczepanowski and MacGarvey looked at the oil industry, they saw the potential to transform it into a mining branch organized along the model of industries in Canada, England, Germany, and northern Italy. They saw industrialists, not landowners, taking the lead: entrepreneurs who spurned slow industrial development that was subordinated to the needs of agriculture in favor of rapid change that was driven by the importation of new technologies and new ideas.

Szczepanowski was among the first men deliberately to choose Galicia as the site of a grand experiment in industrialization. He was born in December 1846 in the Duchy of Posen and was thus a subject of the king of Prussia. As a youth, he worked with his father, a railway engineer, building bridges, culverts, embankments, and junctions in Hungary before moving to Vienna to attend the Polytechnic High School.[27] After graduating in 1867, he left Austria to travel through western Europe.[28] This trip, a bourgeois version of the grand tour, occupied the next thirteen years of his life. After a brief stay in Strasbourg, he moved on to northern Italy, where he visited textile mills, a progressive dairy factory, and various other industrial sites. Almost two years spent in Piedmont left him with great admiration for the architect of Italian unification; years later he wrote, "My dream was to become a Polish Cavour."[29] Eventually, however, he found the pull of Europe's greatest economic power irresistible.[30] In March 1869, at the age of twenty-two, he arrived in London, where he remained with only few interruptions for over a decade. He served as secretary to John Forbes Watson, the director of the department of trade and industry in the British 'India Office in 1870, a position he held for the following nine years. While working in that office, Szczepa-nowski conducted economic studies of India, with an emphasis on sta-tistical analysis.[31]

During his long residence in the West, Szczepanowski returned to Austria-Hungary only once. In 1873, at the age of twenty-six, he made his first trip to Galicia, visiting his ailing father, who had moved to Lviv to work for the Archduke Albrecht Railway.[32] His father's poor health did

Stanisław Szczepanowski. (Courtesy of the Ignacy Łukasiewicz Memorial Museum of the Oil Industry in Bóbrka.)

not induce the ambitious Szczepanowski to stay, nor did he return upon his father's death in 1875. Back in London, he decided to accept British citizenship in 1877.[33] At this point, all evidence suggested that he intended to make London his permanent home, and yet within two years he changed his mind and left England for good. Szczepanowski later claimed that the Prince of Wales, the future Edward VII, asked him in 1879 to participate in an expedition to India to investigate the effects of the famine of 1876–1878 as his "expert on Indian economic affairs." His refusal to do so amounted to a withdrawal from British society and necessitated his resignation and departure from England.[34] In December 1879, Szczepanowski returned to Galicia to visit his mother, who had remained in Lviv. In the spring of 1880, he took a course at the Geological Institute in Vienna and then returned to the Carpathian Mountains to conduct geological investigations, practicing the empiricism that was central to his positivist outlook by traveling the width and breadth of the province on foot. It was during this tour that he first visited Galicia's petroleum springs.

Szczepanowski's ultimate goal was to convert what he had learned as an economist and a scientist into practical assistance for the land of his birth. His writings make clear that in his mind, his homeland was Poland—a country that, although not represented by an independent state, nevertheless continued to exist in the hearts of Polish patriots. Experiences gained in England convinced him that Poland's salvation lay in the resuscitation, organization, and industrialization of its economy, not along the path of political revolution. Only with economic revitalization, he argued, "can we make a nation where today one finds only the raw materials of a nation."[35]

Szczepanowski was not alone in stressing economic and social modernization. After the disastrous January Insurrection of 1863 in the Congress Kingdom (Russian Poland), many Poles turned further away from what seemed to be suicidal attempts at political revolution, stressing instead other sources of national regeneration.[36] According to historian Andrzej Walicki, this strand of "positivism" or "organic work," which "concentrated on the problems of the economic and social modernization of the country and took for granted that this meant development on the Western model," was especially strong in Posen, the province of Szczepanowski's birth and early education.[37] Szczepanowski was critical of a focus on economic development to the detriment of moral and spiritual development. According to Szczepanowski, popular opinion held that "it is easy to make a hero out of a Pole, but hard to turn him into a decent person." This had led to attempts to create "decent Poles" who would look like "a breed of Polish-speaking Germans and Englishmen"—attempts that inevitably ended in disaster. What was needed was a class of Poles who were simultaneously "decent" and "heroic": "In every Pole, from peasant to nobleman, there is a spark of heroism." Instead of imitating contemporary Germans, hampered by their "bureaucratic straitjacket," Poles should look to an earlier generation of Germans, characterized by Johann Heinrich Pestalozzi's school reforms, Friedrich Ludwig Jahn's foundation of nationalist gymnastic clubs, and the creation of a network of musical societies. In sum, Poles should strive to create a "steady and harmonious cultivation of all physical and spiritual powers on the model of ancient Greece."[38] Although Szczepanowski was himself an economist and an industrialist, his writings reveal that his inspiration lay not in personal wealth, but rather in the pursuit of a simultaneously economic and spiritual rebirth of the Polish nation. He demanded a revolution in every aspect of Galician society. Without a cultural transformation, there could be no economic transformation; without an economic transformation, there could be no political transformation.[39]

During Szczepanowski's 1880 geological tour, he concluded that oil would be the key to reviving the Galician economy. Szczepanowski immediately set about organizing the Galician oil industry. After collecting 900,000 florins (1.8 million crowns), he quickly set up an oil company in Słoboda Rungurska, a sleepy sheepherding village in the Kołomyja district, and promptly struck oil in October 1880.[40] Always seeking the most modern means of production, he became only the second oilman in the region to make use of a drill powered by a steam engine. In 1889, the company he founded, S. Szczepanowski and Company, became the First Galician Petroleum Industry Corporation.[41]

None of his previous experiences in industry had prepared Szczepanowski for the success that greeted him in February 1881 with the tapping of the oil well Wanda. According to widely varying accounts, Wanda was dug manually to a depth of between 90 and 150 meters and in the first period of exploitation produced between 10 and 70 tons of crude oil a day (the disparity in figures is a feature of the widespread rumors of Szczepanowski's success).[42] Wanda made Szczepanowski a household name; along with his fame came increased attention to the promise of oil, intense competition, and skyrocketing land prices. Success revealed new ways in which the process of building up an oil company was fraught with obstacles. Sudden increases in production caused by hyperproductive wells like Wanda brought with them harried attempts to conjure up storage tanks, pipelines, and barrels to contain and transport the oil that would otherwise be lost as it ran into the ground and spilled into waterways.

Five years later, experience forced Szczepanowski to answer his own rhetorical question, "For is not flowing oil the same as flowing gold?" in the negative. "Oil and gold," he explained, "but before that transformation takes place you must get that oil into barrels and reservoirs, which costs money. Barrels leak, so you either squander oil or spend more money on a cooper's workshop. Oil flows—there are no barrels and here there are no buyers . . . so you need to build distilleries, that is, once again spend money and buy yourself new hopes and new troubles." Speaking generally about the oilman's challenges, Szczepanowski also aired his own vexation at the tribulations wedded to success: "My God, your neighbors are so greedy for this oil that you cannot sell, leaking out of thousands of barrels, that every day, every hour, you hear about new intentions to sink ever more wells close to your 'Eldorado' and take away your treasure. So then you have to sink new wells yourself under the worst conditions, quickly, quickest! Spend more money! Spend money on engines, tools, fuel, and people. Spend money to build roads, for rail transport. . . . Flowing oil and flowing gold! Yes, only it is not oil that is transformed into gold, but rather the other way around." It took much more than a lucky strike to make a fortune from oil.[43]

Realizing that the highest profits were gained by refining the crude oil extracted from wells, Szczepanowski opened a refinery in Peczeniżyn in 1882. His refinery was intended to provide a ready consumer of the excess crude oil his wells produced by fabricating lighting oil for transport to Bohemia and Moravia, but his plans were continually frustrated by high transportation costs. Since he owned no land of his own, he was forced to lease mineral rights from landowners who were now all too aware of the value of their land. In extreme cases, he paid up to 65 percent of his profits for the privilege. Nevertheless, he remained optimistic, continued to expand his enterprise, and was rewarded with high profits from wells like those in Kucow, which produced 600,000 to 700,000 florins (1.2 to 1.4 million crowns) in pure profits a year. Szczepanowski's dramatic story ignited a petroleum fever throughout Galicia. Here was a man with no prior entrepreneurial experience who had quickly built up a veritable fortune through clever investments in an industry in which it appeared that one could not lose. Investors snapped up any and every opportunity to get involved in oil, often without closely examining the financial solubility or technical expertise of the recipients of their credits. Szczepanowski himself benefited from creditors' excessive good faith: he was "able to get a 75,000 florin [150,000 crown] advance within a few hours" and in Vienna, a loan of over 150,000 florins [300,000 crowns] "after a conversation of only a few minutes."[44] He was easily able to acquire 25,000 florins (50,000 crowns) each from the Galician Savings Bank (Galizische Sparkasse), the Galician Mortgage Bank (Galizische Hypothekenbank), and the Lviv branch of the great Viennese bank, the Creditanstalt für Handel und Gewerbe. He later recalled that "the petroleum business had at that time hypnotized everyone, even cold calculators like the Lviv financiers, such that all it took was one word in order to acquire relatively high credit."[45]

A tireless advocate of oil as a vehicle for the improvement of Galician social conditions, Szczepanowski used every means at his disposal to defend the industry. He was a member of the Trade Society and an arbiter in the GLPV. His first experiences as a publicist came in England, where he later claimed to have published articles in the financial gazette, *The British Economist*,[46] while his friends said that he had worked for the *Times*.[47] In Austria, he became a regular contributor to a number of newspapers, including the Kołomyja biweekly *Pomoc własna* (Self-help), which he founded in 1889,[48] and *Ekonomista polski*, which was founded in 1890 to serve as an organ for Szczepanowski's "new economic program."[49] He also sat on the editorial board of *Naphta/Nafta* (the newspaper organ of the GLPV, published in separate German and Polish editions) and edited the newspaper *Słowo Polskie* (the Polish word). In 1888, Szczepanowski gained widespread notoriety with the publication of *The Poverty of Galicia in Figures and a Program for the Energetic Development of the Economy of the Country,* the product of twenty years of research.[50] In this work, he compared the quality of life in Galicia with that of Russian Poland, Hungary, Italy, Germany, Belgium, France, and England and concluded: "if there is a country anywhere where the fault for miserable conditions lies more with its people than with its institutions, then that country is Galicia." On every level of governance, whether local, district, or provincial, he claimed that "at every step we meet examples of the rights and privileges of titled people who either are unable or unwilling to make use of them." The means, he argued, were as important as the material ends: "We in Galicia ... have a miraculous and rich nature. We have lacked until now the people who were able to make use of it, but we possess the invaluable privileges of free civic activity, privileges without which even the wealth of El Dorado would be loathsome."[51] These privileges included not only the rights of assembly and expression, but also political powers that enabled Poles to defend their interests and those of their province when the central authorities were not interested in doing so. For example, when Szczepanowski publicized massive smuggling of a Russian *falsifikate* (a refined oil that was discolored with heavy oils that were easy to remove in order to be carried across the Austrian border as "crude oil" at much lower tariffs), discovered by his friend and colleague Schreier, he was able to expose the laxity of border controls. Their agitation made the combating of the Russian product a key topic in the decennial negotiations to renew the *Ausgleich* between Austria and Hungary (which set tariffs on imports to both halves of the empire).[52]

Szczepanowski's involvement in the oil industry served as a clarion call to talented young Poles looking for a vocation that would serve equally as career and calling. These included bank director Franciszek Zima and aspiring engineers Wacław Wolski and Kazimierz Odrzywolski, who later became his most faithful financial benefactors. Szczepanowski inspired the confidence and loyalty of dozens of men who viewed him as something of a Polish messiah. From among his immediate circle of friends and acquaintances, and from a larger group of Poles who were generally characterized as "democratically leaning," Szczepanowski was able to raise truly impressive amounts of capital, generating a swell of investment in the industry led by his own example. By January 1899, his debts, all of them guaranteed by friends and colleagues, ran to over eleven million crowns (at a time when the director of the Galician Savings Bank, who approved most of these loans, earned eighteen thousand crowns a year), indicating an enormous growth in the scale of investment.[53] Without reservation, Szczepanowski poured all of these funds into the development of Galician industry; even his enemies never thought to accuse him of pursuing personal gain or a luxurious lifestyle.

Szczepanowski initially eschewed political activity, consistent with his belief in the primacy of economic improvements. Nevertheless, when he was elected as a representative to the Imperial Parliament in Vienna in 1886 and a few years later to the Galician Provincial Diet in Lviv—in both cases, he proudly insisted, without having campaigned for the position—he did agree to serve. Even when he was a prominent politician and a member of the Polish Club, Szczepanowski's primary identification was with the oil industry. In the introduction to *The Poverty of Galicia,* he claimed that he had only been elected on the basis of the "fame [he] had won from petroleum affairs" before he had even had the "opportunity to reveal briefly [his] views on public affairs." This led him to conclude that his election was symptomatic of a growing recognition of the ineffectiveness of "complicated political calculations" in the absence of the successful generation of provincial wealth. Political channels offered only secondary paths to his stated goal, a vibrant Galician economy. He believed that "it was high time to lead the economic politics of the country from the area of worthless parliamentary debates to the region of positive, profit-bringing work." Szczepanowski always insisted that his political activity was intended only as a means of furthering his economic program. In turn, his economic program was a means of helping Polish Galicians "make our society equal to the civilized nations and graft onto it the embryo of independent spiritual and economic development that characterizes modern civilization."[54] In short, Szczepanowski saw in oil an opportunity to rescue Poland.

Others saw in Galicia's "black gold" an opportunity to make a name and a fortune. Foreigners from beyond the reaches of greater Poland and the Austrian Empire were not inspired by patriotic considerations. Rather, they were lured by a province described as an industrial wasteland, in which an ambitious and inspired entrepreneur could quickly make his mark. John Simeon Bergheim, for example, was an English engineer whose talent and ambition led him to search for oil in Hanover, Bavaria, Romania, Galicia, southern Russia, Mexico, and Nigeria (where, with diplomacy and perseverance, he was able to convince officials of the Colonial Office to grant him a near monopoly over prospecting rights).[55] At the time of his death in an automobile accident in 1912, he was chairman of International Maikop, the Nigerian Bitumen Corporation, the Anglo-Mexican Oilfields, the Cuban Petroleum Company, Tampico Oil, and the Société Française de Pétrole. Long before he became one of the international oil industry's "best-known supporters,"[56] however, Bergheim was indirectly responsible for one of the greatest events in the history of

Galician oil: the arrival of the young Canadian driller, William Henry MacGarvey.

MacGarvey had begun his career in the oil industry in Petrolia, Canada, sometime around 1862.[57] He rose to prominence as local mayor and owner of eighteen producing oil wells, in addition to a store.[58] In 1881, he was recruited by Bergheim to try their luck in Ölheim, Hanover.[59] In 1882, MacGarvey moved to Galicia and offered his services as a drilling operator. In 1883, the two men joined forces again, founding the petroleum company Bergheim and MacGarvey.[60] Principally a drilling expert during his first years in Galicia, MacGarvey introduced the Canadian cable drilling system to Galicia in 1884, a moment that marked Galicia's entry into the world of modern petroleum mining.[61]

Although there had been some drilling before MacGarvey arrived, it had remained rare because of the limitations of local technology. Once the shallow beds that could be reached by digging or hand drilling were tapped and exhausted, operators had to assume that there was no more oil to be had, since they could no longer search for it. The Canadian drilling system, with which MacGarvey had first become familiar while working in Enniskillen, Canada, in 1866,[62] allowed exploration at previously unheard-of depths and unimaginable speeds. Instead of the 20 centimeters that had been the local norm, drillers could now delve 24 meters into the earth in twenty-four hours and easily reached depths of over 1,000 meters where 150 meters had been the limit only a few years before.[63] This not only sped up exploration in new oil fields, but also reopened old ones long thought dry. MacGarvey imported dozens of Canadian drillers in addition to new equipment[64] and, after adapting the technique to suit local geological conditions, led a technological revolution in the Galician oil basin.

Borysław, which later became synonymous with the oil industry, was of little interest to oilmen at the time MacGarvey first came to Galicia. The entire region had been thoroughly explored in the search for ozokerite. Using MacGarvey's techniques, drillers discovered that there was an entire bed of oil approximately 150–200 meters underneath the old wax mines.[65] This territory had initially been unavailable to exploration for oil because it had been controlled by large wax extraction companies such as the Compagnie Commerciale Française (which had taken over the mines of the defunct Société Française pour l'Exploitation de Cire Minerale et Pétrole) and the Galician Credit Bank, which viewed oil ex-

William Henry MacGarvey. (Courtesy of the Lambton Room, County of Lambton [Ontario] Libraries, Museums, and Cultural Services Department.)

traction unfavorably.[66] As the first person to discover this second stratum of oil deposits in Borysław, MacGarvey was thus responsible for an unprecedented increase in Galician production. In 1894, the year he first started drilling for oil, total Galician production was 132,000 tons; only ten years later, Borysław's production alone accounted for 560,000 tons, making Borysław far and away the most significant source of petroleum in the empire. In the first ten years after his arrival in Galicia, MacGarvey drilled 370 boreholes with a total depth of 100,000 meters.[67] But MacGarvey was not satisfied as a drilling operator.

MacGarvey understood the oil industry in a way that few of his colleagues in Galicia could match: his is a rare example of vertical integration, the key to his unparalleled success. MacGarvey continued to invest in production itself, but in addition to overseeing and carrying out exploration and drillings, he also acquired control of extraction rights and built and maintained refineries and factories for the manufacture and repair of drills, engines, and various tools needed for the oil industry. He also produced barrels and storage containers, set up pipelines, and stored petroleum produced by his competitors in exchange for hefty storage fees.[68] Forging ahead was not always easy for MacGarvey. He had to fight with landowners to get his fancy machinery in place. Even with the new mining laws, it was not always clear who held title to properties and their mineral rights, and occasions arose on which MacGarvey's right to use land for which he held a contract was challenged. MacGarvey's determination was not lessened by these obstacles. When his access was denied, he sued. When he lost a suit, he appealed without concern for the power and prestige of his opponents. He did not hesitate, for example, to appeal to the Ministry of the Interior for protection against the Roman Catholic bishop, Dr. Łukasz Ostoja Solecki, when the latter challenged MacGarvey's right to set up a steam engine and a steam boiler on his estate.[69] He later said that the oilman's best motto was one derived from Rockefeller's philosophy: "Do unto others as they would like to do to you, but do it first."[70]

Throughout the 1890s, MacGarvey's company acquired mineral rights all over the province. Multiple contracts were drawn up with lessors ranging from the Galician Credit Bank to individual villages.[71] By 1901, the cost of mineral rights to a plot of land in a part of Borysław considered certain to return oil ranged from 3,000 to 4,000 crowns, in addition to 20 percent of the extracted crude gross. Away from the anticline, where success was most likely, rights to a plot of the same size in regions where oil was less certain would sell for 600 crowns and 12 percent of the gross.[72] High prices did not deter MacGarvey, who also purchased exploration rights from other companies that had chosen not to make use of them or had been unable to do so profitably. In one case, he purchased the rights to explore for "naphtha, oil, mineral wax, and all other minerals not reserved under the Imperial Mining Prerogative" from competitors for the astonishing sum of 2,083,200 crowns.[73]

Like Szczepanowski, MacGarvey was quickly acknowledged to be a leader in the oil industry. He, too, was an arbiter in the GLPV and a powerful figure who took part in all meetings and conferences relating to oil production in the province. The GLPV's print organ, *Naphta*, was used to publicize the benefits of MacGarvey's patented products. Purported news stories reporting on the benefits of Canadian drilling techniques served to convert even MacGarvey's competitors for drilling contracts into customers of his patented machines and drilling tools.[74]

After a decade of steady growth, on 4 July 1895, MacGarvey and Bergheim transformed their private firm into a joint-stock company that became one of the leading corporations in the Galician oil industry: the Galizische Karpathen-Petroleum Actien-Gesellschaft vormals Bergheim & MacGarvey (the Galician Carpathian Petroleum Joint-Stock Company, henceforth the Carpathian Company). The company's headquarters were in Vienna, its machine shops and foundry were in Glinik Maryampolski, a village near Gorlice in western Galicia, and it had branch works in Borysław and Tustanowice.[75] The Carpathian Company was founded with a capital of 10 million crowns and ran with equipment and tools and on property that had been purchased for 8 million crowns.[76] In its first year of existence, the new joint-stock company produced nearly 35 million kilograms of crude oil, 17.5 million of which were refined in its own refinery in Glinik Maryampolski.[77] By the early twentieth century, the Carpathian Company employed 2,400 workers, owned steam engines and water power in the strength of 2,800 horsepower, and produced crude oil, refined petroleum, gasoline, lubricating oils, paraffin, steam drilling engines, drilling rigs, boilers, pumps, core drills, winding machines, portable electric cranes, and eccentric drilling bits that had been patented by MacGarvey himself.[78] The Carpathian Company offered investors 15 percent dividends in 1900.[79]

Canadian journalist Gary May has devoted an entire chapter of a book on Canadian oil workers abroad to MacGarvey, whom he calls the "Petroleum King of Austria." MacGarvey's exploits were popular fodder for local newspapers in Petrolia, Canada, where his daughter's marriage in 1895 to the nephew of the German count Ferdinand von Zeppelin caused an explosion of pride. Although at age sixty-seven, after nearly three decades in Galicia. MacGarvey still described himself as "a Canadian and a citizen of the Great [British] Empire" he clearly had committed himself and his family to a life in Austria. By bringing his family with him to Europe, he did what few of Canada's "hard oilers" chose to do and signaled that Austria was his new home.[80]

An abundance of other drillers and investors followed MacGarvey's lead. By 1886, the factory inspector could claim that "the petroleum industry is and will remain absolutely the most important industry in the country"—beating out other Galician industries, including the production of metals, engines, tools and machines, glass, clay, wood, leather, textiles, paper, and foodstuffs (including liquor), chemistry, and construction.[81] In 1900, there were 1,722 different petroleum companies exploring, drilling, and extracting in ninety-seven different towns and villages in Galicia. Of those, only 120 had actually extracted oil, 34 had begun drilling, and 16 had given up their business.[82] Active companies produced 347 million kilograms of crude oil in 1900.[83] More oil production meant more oil to be refined. In 1900, Austrian and Hungarian refineries treated 390 million kilograms of crude, 84 percent of which originated in Galicia.[84] As rates of production increased, so did the founding of oil refineries. From 1872 to 1901, fifteen new petroleum-refining joint-stock companies were created with a combined total of 33.7 million crowns of founding capital. These companies offered astonishing rates of return: the Floridsdorf refinery offered dividends of 25 percent in 1896 and an annual average of 20 percent from 1897 to 1902.[85]

Although technological innovation laid the groundwork for a new period in oil exploration, it was not publicly inaugurated until the opening of the Anglo-Österreichische Bank's well Jakób in Schodnica in 1895. Like many Austrian and foreign banks, the Anglo-Österreichische Bank, or Anglobank, became directly involved in the Galician oil industry. It created the "Schodnica" Actiengesellschaft für Petroleum-Industrie in 1894, which owned Jakób, an explosive gusher that proved that great successes could be equally great calamities. After it had been drilled to 304 meters, Jakób initially produced 1,000 tons of oil a day (fourteen times as much

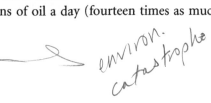

as the highest estimates for Wanda). Internationally recognized because of its productivity and the local environmental catastrophe caused by the sudden gusher that flooded a territory half a kilometer in diameter in oil, Jakób was Galicia's most famous and most productive well to date.[86] Together with its neighboring well, Cäcilia, it produced 8,000 tons of oil in 1896, but it had the potential to have produced much more. No one could calculate how many tons had been lost when, in the initial outburst, oil had streamed into the Stryj River. Geology professor Władysław Szajnocha called the loss of so much oil a "tragedy" for the producers.[87] But the petroleum lake Jakób created also distressed local farmers, women who used the Stryj's water for cooking, drinking, and laundry, as well as fishermen, and, presumably, many fish.

Beyond that, the film of petroleum that covered water and land created a considerable danger of uncontrollable fires, making everyone in the region vulnerable to loss of life or property. The factory inspector described the cause for concern: "At the beginning of the eruption, before the drill hole could be plugged, the oil poured into streams, gutters, onto streets, etc., and in this manner came into proximity with various fires (steam boilers, smithies, private houses, etc.) so that there was constant fear of the outbreak of a general fire in Schodnica. Before the drill hole could be successfully covered, all possible measures were taken to collect the flowing petroleum; among others, sixty provisional oil reservoirs were dug a few meters deep and wide." Attempts to collect the petroleum into reservoirs notwithstanding, the factory inspector feared that human activity tended to increase, rather than decrease, the risk. "The poor population scooped the oil out of the gutters, brought it home, and in this way turned every residence into a dangerous oil depot; it came to the point where lighting a fire in many private houses had to be forbidden. The drill hole had hardly been blocked and the oil from the same directed into an iron reservoir when the gas pressure that collected in the reservoir tore its roof and lifted it into the air."[88]

The factory inspector's report represents a catalog of the many ways oil production threatened the lives and property of those in its immediate environment. First, by covering the land (and the vegetation growing on it) for hundreds of yards in all directions with a blanket of oil, a gusher made agriculture in its immediate proximity hazardous. Second, by flowing into rivers and streams, the oil not only killed fish in those waterways but also polluted the fields and meadows that they irrigated during periodic floods. Third, oil "run wild" posed the threat of fires that started quickly and burned long and threatened both human life and property. The risk of fire was ubiquitous. It could be the result of lightning, considered a "natural catastrophe," or the product of human interference. Humans could cause fires either unintentionally because of ignorance, carelessness, or both, as the factory inspector feared, or because of arson, a perennial fear during recurrent worker disturbances. Fourth, the effort to contain gases in man-made vessels was rarely successful for long and regularly led to explosions. A fifth category of damage not mentioned by the factory inspector in the context of the Jakób disaster, but appearing in his reports elsewhere, was the effect of the hundreds and at times thousands of holes dug in the ground throughout the oil basin. "Thousands of uncovered shafts are the cause of many accidents. Even if an owner is so conscientious as to cover his shaft, the [wooden] cover is simply stolen overnight and not replaced."[89] Abandoned pits, left unguarded and uncovered, posed a danger to unwary pedestrians and were the cause of numerous drownings when they filled with water (leading to the development of a new genre of popular literature in which murdered corpses were routinely hidden in them).[90]

Research conducted in the 1970s and 1980s has demonstrated that oil acts as a herbicide and reduces soil fertility when spilled on land, fatally damages marine ecosystems when spilled into water and contributes to acid rain when burned.[91] Today these considerations may suggest to some that the oil industry was not always a boon to the physical and social landscape of Galicia. The connection between oil and environmental disaster seems natural and universal. Calamity has accompanied the human interaction with petroleum at every historical stage of the development of the oil industry, from the ancient military use of pitch set aflame to oil spills that routinely made headlines at the turn of the twenty-first century. Then and now, catastrophes occur at every stage in oil's extraction, distribution, and consumption, from oil set ablaze at the point of production to famous spills, explosions at the point of sale, and fires set off in the living rooms of kerosene's first consumers. So it might seem obvious that wherever oil extraction begins, those around it should object—if not in the interests of nature, then in the interests of their own safety and economic security.

The historical record furnishes ample proof that the "illumination" and "enlightenment" offered by oil came at a heavy price in Galicia. The production and distribution of oil led directly to pollution, property damage, injury, and death. Yet nary a voice was raised against the oil industry. Disasters inspired outrage and protest, but it was not directed against the industry as such. When the phrase "natural disaster" was employed, it referred to an unfortunate conflation of natural phenomena and human action that caused loss of life, limb, or property—that is, disasters caused by man's inability to control natural phenomena fully. The idea that the environment was itself a victim of economic development simply does not appear in any of the debates about the Galician oil industry. On the contrary, every catastrophic explosion, every widely publicized spill, and every fire caused by too much oil spurred another rush of interest in Galicia's magnificent new source of wealth. The hopes of Galicia's many oil investors were justified; suspicions that the wealth of Galician soil had been underestimated and in reality was boundless seemed confirmed. Even territories that had been given up as exhausted seemed to hold new promise of endless riches—a promise that tantalized ambitious young men far and wide.

In the mid-1880s, MacGarvey desperately sought help from Canada by advertising for drillers in local papers and sending his brother back to Petrolia to recruit them.[92] A good number of the men behind this explosion in investment and production did come from Canada, although it is not always possible to ascertain if they came at MacGarvey's request. MacGarvey's brothers, Albert and James, joined him, as did Alvin Townsend, Neil Sinclair, Elgin Scott, George MacIntosh, his son, Carl, and their relatives, George, Cyrus, and Jacob Perkins.[93] Jacob Perkins was a contemporary of MacGarvey's, born in Canada in 1855. He moved to Galicia in 1885 and took a position in MacGarvey's Carpathain Company. His sons Herbert and Carl (born in Krosno) followed their father into the oil business. Robert Waldeck (1856–1901) and Albert Fauck were both Germans who went to the United States for training before settling in Galicia. Waldeck was drawn to Galicia to work with MacGarvey in 1884.[94] Fauck was born in Danzig in 1842 and emigrated to the United States during the Civil War. He acquired U.S. citizenship, but after learning the drilling trade in Pennsylvania, he moved to Galicia in 1867, where he became the first to use a steam engine for drilling.[95] But by the mid-1890s, the Galician oil industry could boast two generations of modern oilmen, and most of the younger engineers and entrepreneurs (including Szczepanowski's own son and namesake, Stanisław Wiktor Szczepanowski) were

Poles who had been handpicked by more established oilmen like MacGarvey and Szczepanowski. Whereas other industrialists were reputed to employ the cheapest possible labor, even in managerial positions, government inspectors credited Szczepanowski with insisting on well-trained overseers and offering employment to many young engineers and chemists.[96] These men received their training under his wing, became skilled drillers and in some cases investors in their own right, and offered Szczepanowski unwavering loyalty.

Representative of the new generation were Kazimierz Odrzywolski (1860–1900) and his brother-in-law, Wacław Wolski (1865–ca. 1919). Odrzywolski was born in Congress Poland, but when his father's participation in the January Insurrection of 1863 forced the family to emigrate, they moved to Galicia. Young Odrzywolski studied chemistry in Cracow, graduated from the Technical Institute in 1885, and then worked as a chemist in Szczepanowski's refinery in Peczeniżyn. Later he worked as a drilling engineer in Szczepanowski's oil fields in Słoboda Rungurska. From 1886 to 1893, he joined a petroleum-seeking expedition to Argentina led by Dr. Rudolf Zuber and financed by an Argentine company that chose to bring all its technical experts from Galicia. Upon his return, he and Wolski founded a company, Wolski and Odrzywolski Mining and Industrial Works, based in Schodnica. They soon engaged in oil exploration and production in Borysław and Tustanowice, as well as in other towns in Galicia and even Romania.[97] Wolski, who was described by a contemporary as a "noble man and an ingenious young engineer,"[98] studied mechanical engineering in Vienna and then joined the Austro-Hungarian navy. Before becoming Odrzywolski's business partner, he worked for Szczepanowski. An accomplished inventor, he took out several patents, including one for a hydraulic percussion drill that was used in Galicia, Russia, Silesia, Westphalia, and the United States.

Oil in its liquid form was not the only target of investor attention. The attraction of investment in the wax industry was heightened by advances in the treatment and refining of ozokerite that occurred in the late 1870s. It was the wax industry that first attracted large-scale foreign businesses. Borysław's ozokerite deposits were the largest in the world and promised to provide cheap mineral-wax candles at great profit to their producers, especially given the great expense of alternative sources of wax. With certain rewards came equally certain perils. Mining for wax was the most irrational and troubling element of the petroleum industry, at least to outside observers. The wax industry, as it was organized before the 1880s, was hazardous to workers and destructive of the environment. A plethora of small producers, most of whom were reported to be Jewish, controlled small plots of land, which they scoured for any wax deposits. They expanded their mines with poorly monitored use of dynamite and crisscrossed under one another's territory and under public roads and buildings, leading to "the sinking of public roads and houses."[99]

Careless exploitation only exacerbated the dangers inherent to wax and oil; the deeper one dug and the richer the terrain, the greater the risk. A particularly unstable section of Borysław optimistically called "the New World" (Nowy Świat) housed enormous nests of wax. Chief mining commissioner Heinrich Walter described the problem, "Often shafts suddenly hurl out wax from a depth of 160–180 meters all the way to the surface with such violence that workers have no time to flee and are only pulled out after months of excavation." Mining experts agreed that what was needed were large companies that would be capable of overcoming the technical obstacles posed by such dangerous terrain. Thus Walter welcomed large-scale foreign investment. "Mining technology will doubtless find means of overcoming the difficulties of excavation in Borysław, and then Borysław will become a mining object unique in its type. Recently the Galician [Credit] Bank acquired the greater part of the New World and it has begun to renovate mining in a completely rational fashion, just as Wolanka is now mined properly and profitably by the French Company."[100]

The Galician Credit Bank and the Compagnie Commerciale Française (formerly the Société Française pour l'Exploitation de Cire Minérale et Pétrole) were the first two major companies to move into the Borysław basin to exploit wax. They promised to revolutionize the way wax was extracted, introducing a central-shaft system, in which only one vertical shaft was dug, and galleries radiated outward from its core.

The arrival of more serious wax and oil production companies brought with it advantages for the towns and villages in which they made their homes. Some of these were by-products of the need for developments in infrastructure that accompany industry: new railroad lines were built to convey oil from producers to refiners and consumers, but could also be used to transport workers and visitors, socialists and soldiers. The local railroad connecting Kołomyja and Słoboda Rungurska, for example, was built explicitly to respond to the sudden opening of oil fields in Słoboda

by connecting them to refineries.[101] One of the first complaints of professional mining engineers who moved to a new exploration and production region was the absence of a convenient railroad station, and this
was one of the first insufficiencies they lobbied to fix.[102] Because the absence of a local rail station could significantly diminish the value of oil-
bearing property, landowners who had never been concerned about railways before became eager to see stations placed near their holdings.[103]
When the Carpathian Company built a refinery in Glinik Maryampolski,
it also built a train station on the Gorlice–Zagorzany line and a post office
(both opened in 1898) and installed telephone service.[104]

Even the backwardness of some enterprises bestowed lucrative employment upon locals. Pani Straszewska, the owner of an estate in Lipinki,
allowed both production and refining to take place on her property. She
did not, however, allow the construction of a pipeline connecting the
mines to the refinery, but preferred instead to have crude oil delivered
by horse and carriage, "for in this fashion the manor horses and coach-
man found employment."[105]

For great Polish patriots like Szczepanowski and his disciples, Wolski
and Odrzywolski, providing employment was not enough to create a new
breed of noble and morally elevated Poles. Szczepanowski believed that
his duties as an industrialist extended beyond profits and economic expansion. In keeping with his vision of his ethical responsibilities, he established his refinery in Peczeniżyn as a model of modern factory in-
stallation and management, demonstrating that modernization was good
for both business and workers. According to the factory inspector, it was
a "large petroleum factory that can be counted among the best-equipped
not only here [in Galicia], but, I am justified in assuming, in all of Europe." Szczepanowski's own skills were credited for the laudable condition
of his refinery: "It is equipped according to the newest advances in technology by its owner, himself a capable technical expert; he has taken
particular care to protect the workers as much as possible from harmful
influences."[106] Szczepanowski also looked after workers' health more directly. At a time when few employers had any interest in doing so, even
when they were directly ordered by the factory inspector, he set up a
health insurance association for his factory workers, built a hospital, and
kept a doctor on staff, bearing one third of the expenses of the doctor's
room and board from his personal funds. He also established a library
and a reading room for his employees next to the factory,[107] as well as
promoting elementary education.[108]

When Wolski and Odrzywolski founded a factory to produce drilling engines in Schodnica, they also founded two schools and financed a Roman Catholic church, created a health insurance cooperative, and organized an agricultural cooperative. They purchased the newspaper *Słowo Polskie* and had plans to found a large educational institution and several orphanages.[109] The Galician Credit Bank sponsored the opening of a private mining school in October 1888 in Borysław, which had the goal of "educating the more intelligent and educated mining workers and their children to create capable overseers and managers for the mining of bituminous minerals."[110] There was another school to train drillers in the Canadian method in Wietrzno (in western Galicia), subsidized by the Galician Provincial Committee. Mine owner Victor von Klobassa provided free housing and lighting in the neighboring villages of Bóbrka and Równe for students enrolled in the school.[111] These and other improvements fit into a greater trend to engage in paternalistic techniques of managing the relationship between employers and their workers. Providing for the religious and secular education of local children (i.e., future employees) was not simply a selfless act of community improvement, but rather a rational policy, in that these children were thus raised to adopt the values held by the employers themselves.[112]

Of course, industrialization, even when it was successful for businesses, did not bring only benefits to the common folk who were touched by it. Contemporaries were aware that the oil industry put great strains on local peasants even when it appeared to offer them great opportunities. For many, a life spent working in the wax mines and oil pits was no life at all. Their working conditions were dark and dangerous, their pay was meager, and government officials were surprised that the workers did not take to more radical protests of their lot.

If the oil mines brought tangible peril to the men who worked in them, they could also be treacherous to those who ran them and financed them from above the ground. No one, however popular, was immune to the damage bad luck could inflict on those who made the speculative investments that characterized the oil industry. In the midst of a decade of unprecedented investment, a prominent case of failure reminded all involved of the potential cost of trying to make one's fortune in oil. In 1899, Szczepanowski, that paragon of Polish national virtue, was involved in the Austrian oil industry's greatest scandal. On 14 January 1899, the shareholders of the Galician Savings Bank broke into a panic when rumors of the bank's insolvency abounded and caused a devastating run on the bank. News had leaked that the bank had lent exorbitant amounts of money on credit to businesses threatened with bankruptcy—a clear violation of the depositors' trust. The rumor got started when the bank's board, having noticed that a significant portion of its reserves were mortgaged and that the debts accrued by Stanisław Szczepanowski had reached appalling levels, ordered a "restoration to profitability." By 1895, Szczepanowski's debts had reached nearly 2.4 million florins (4.8 million crowns).[113]

Even under these circumstances, Szczepanowski's reputation as a leader of Polish industry enthralled the Galician Savings Bank's director, Franciszek Zima, who continued to lend him money in the hope that Szczepanowski could thus save his enterprise. Zima seemed willing to take any risks necessary to protect Szczepanowski, who represented to him Poland's salvation. Himself a Polish nationalist patriot, Zima had participated in the January Insurrection of 1863 and was a member of the secret Liga Polska. He had met Szczepanowski during the latter's residence in England. One Szczepanowski scholar has speculated that Zima "considered the risk of illegally granting him [Szczepanowski] credit as almost a patriotic conspiracy against the servile conservative mood of Galicia's administration, a conspiracy with the goal of preserving the oil industry in Polish hands."[114] Because of Zima's generosity and Szczepanowski's inability to capitalize on it profitably, by 31 December 1898, Szczepanowski owed the bank nearly 5.5 million florins (11 million crowns).[115] As Szczepanowski slipped further into debt, Zima took steps to protect himself and Szczepanowski from the ruin that would have struck them both if Szczepanowski's debt and Zima's foolish lending had been revealed. He created fictional accounts without the knowledge of the bank's board in order to hide the scope of Szczepanowski's loans. Further evidence of Szczepanowski's charisma came when the news of his debts broke, and Wolski and Odrzywolski put up 7 million crowns on his behalf.[116]

When the story broke, Zima was accused of fraud and embezzlement (for falsifying the bank's books and for convincing Wolski and Odrzywolski to give a security under false pretenses). Szczepanowski was accused of complicity in fraud for encouraging Zima to falsify the books. The scandal that followed the revelation of the extent of his loans to Szczepanowski destroyed Zima's reputation and precipitated his death even before the trial began. The press latched on to his attachment, at age seventy-two, to a young woman named Marie Stephanie Fuhrmann.

Fuhrmann, who had been a pauper a few years earlier, had mysteriously acquired a house worth 40,000 florins (80,000 crowns) and an account with the Galizische Landesbank worth another 45,000 florins (90,000 crowns) by the time of the scandal. Zima died in prison on 4 August 1899 under circumstances that led to speculation that he had poisoned himself. The coroner claimed that he had died of a heart attack.[117]

All of the monarchy's major newspapers covered the trial, which ran from 1 October to 9 November 1899, in all its harrowing detail. The liberal Viennese daily *Neue Freie Presse* published daily reports throughout the trial's six-week duration, including long transcripts of particularly interesting testimony. For the first few weeks of the trial, readers were kept informed by two updates a day: both the morning and evening editions reported on the latest news received by telegram from Lviv. The Lviv paper *Słowo Polskie* (owned by Wolski and Odrzywolski and favorable to Szczepanowski) and the Cracow paper *Czas* (a conservative organ of the Stańczyks,[118] decidedly hostile to Szczepanowski) also reported on the trial daily. The negative publicity cast a shadow over the whole industry. Comparisons were made between Szczepanowski and Ferdinand de Lesseps, and the epithet "Polish Panama" replaced "Polish California" in the press.[119]

The trial revealed the extent to which chaos had come to characterize Szczepanowski's personal finances. He had already been threatened with bankruptcy in 1893. His friends Wolski and Odrzywolski, wanting to rescue him from ruin, turned over the management of his business to Bolesław Łodziński, the director of the Handelsgesellschaft in Gorlice. Łodziński recommended that Szczepanowski declare bankruptcy immediately, even before he learned of his debt. Łodziński was convinced that Szczepanowski's businesses were being run by untrustworthy characters who misinformed him (politics kept him in the capital and away from the day-to-day oversight of his companies) and led him to believe that drillings had better prospects than they did.[120] Wolski and Odrzywolski were anxious to spare him from the scandal that bankruptcy would cause and offered to take responsibility for his debt. In early 1896, Zima convinced them to put up a security of 550,000 florins (1.1 million crowns).[121] But not even the unflinching loyalty of his supporters could save Szczepanowski from impending ruin.

If there is an element of the tragic in Szczepanowski's story, it lies in a decision he made in 1894. Under enormous pressure from Count Kazimierz Badeni to repay a portion of his debts, he sold his petroleum shafts in Schodnica, an unexplored but promising oil field near Borysław, to the Anglobank for 1 million florins (2 million crowns; 40 percent in stocks and 60 percent in cash) only two years before the explosive discovery of Jakób.[122] In 1893, 10,000 tons of crude oil were produced in Schodnica; in 1894, 21,000 tons; in 1895, almost 84,000 tons; and in 1896, 189,360 tons.[123] By 1899, these shafts had come to be worth 15 million florins (30 million crowns), more than enough to cover Szczepanowski's entire debt.[124] To make matters worse, Szczepanowski sold the oil fields in order to protect his investment in coal mines in Myszyna and Dzurowa, which never produced any profit. In his trial, he explained his decision: "I was mistaken regarding the value of the coal mines and preferred to get rid of Schodnica rather than the coal mines." But by the time his debt was exposed, his "seventy-eight shares in Galician coal mines" were considered "absolutely worthless."[125] One of oil's greatest champions thus was driven to ruin when he lost faith in his own product.

Although his advocacy of rejuvenation through industrialization and modernization required that he become involved in business, Szczepanowski's character seemed ill suited to the task. Believing that modernization was possible only if it was built upon the foundations of a moral revival of the nation, he combined a call for rapid industrialization with what one historian has called a "strong anticapitalist bias."[126] Thus his emphasis on investment, infrastructure, and industry was combined with contempt for some of the values that they required. During the trial, Szczepanowski portrayed himself as the hapless victim of his own ignorance rather than a conniving embezzler. According to his testimony:

> When he returned to Galicia, he got involved in trade for the first time. . . . In the practice of this new profession, he was truly met with good fortune initially. A new California arose in Galicia. One constantly found new, very productive petroleum sources. However, there were great technical obstacles one had to overcome. The oil fever that prevailed throughout Galicia attracted numerous foreigners and caused the defendant to undertake geological investigations, deep drilling, and investments that turned out to be a great loss of capital. Now, since his funds did not suffice, he tried to get advances. . . . He did not understand how to protect his own interests.

Szczepanowski testified that fate had played against him. Just when it looked as if he was going to start making some money, he was unfairly

hampered by competition from smuggled Russian distillates. All his attempts and those of his fellow oilmen to get the government to protect
them were in vain. In the midst of this mess, "The defendant, as he claims,
was elected to the imperial Parliament without having run for office.
There he took the interests of the petroleum industry, and thus also his
own, under his wing and stood up against customs abuses. His parliamentary career, however, led to a change in his relationship with his
former colleagues (Biedermann and Company). Politics and business did
not allow themselves to be mixed."[127] Szczepanowski explained that however valuable his political activity may have been in the long term, it kept
him away from his oil business. He spent six months of the year in
Vienna, another month and a half in the Galician Provincial Diet, and
one month in the delegations, thus spending nearly three-quarters of the
year on activities not directly related to running his business.[128]

To make matters worse, Szczepanowski's luck began to run out. After
a few early lucky guesses, which gave him the feeling that he could practically smell oil, misplaced hopes in oil deposits invisible deep below the
Earth's surface proved that he was no diviner. Szczepanowski had to acknowledge that "when it comes to discovering oil territory, the rule is, as
it turned out, that there are no rules. In the tremendous petroleum com-
motion of the early years, which brought Englishmen, Americans,
Frenchmen, Spaniards, and Germans to Galicia, he dared—against his
earlier resolution—to found a company on a large scale,"[129] although he
had no experience in running such an enterprise. He and his family invested 90,000 florins (180,000 crowns), but, given the high cost of land
leases, he soon found that he needed ten times that much capital.

After thirty-three days in court, a jury of Szczepanowski's peers (merchants, businessmen, and civil servants) acquitted him unanimously on
all counts. But Szczepanowski was a broken man; he died less than a year
later, a month before his fifty-fourth birthday.[130]

During the trial and in its aftermath, defenders and opponents of
Szczepanowski alike linked his fall to greater issues. In his memoirs, oil
engineer Stefan Bartoszewicz recalled, "At that time, we all felt that the
honor of the oil industry was engaged in the proceedings of the trial."[131]
This was not merely a question of fiscal incompetence, greed, or the
whims of fortune. Rather, Szczepanowski's rise and fall were tied to questions of Polish patriotism in an age of fragile reconciliation to autonomy
within a partitioned Poland and of social reform and the economic revolution that accompanied it. Szczepanowski's defenders included celeb-

rities from Russian Poland, such as the renowned author Bolesław Prus and Władysław Rabski, who referred to him as a "tragic hero." A young associate compared him to Job.[132] His friends argued that he was a man of greatness brought down by the mediocrity of the world around him, the "greatest of contemporary Poles."[133] Wolski claimed that Szczepanowski's *Nędza Galicyi* had been the inspiration for a generation of democratically inclined industrialists. Odrzywolski attributed his downfall to his failure to account for the baseness of other people.[134] At his funeral, he was lauded as a man with the will and the ability to return Poland to the center of Europe: "We waited for him as a hungry worker awaits the arrival of the innkeeper, for the specter of misery or earning a daily wage from foreigners had already begun to sneer at us. He came—he appeared." His fall was caused not by his own weakness, but by the greed of outsiders, indifferent to Poland's fate: "Foreign capitalists block[ed] his path, paralyzing and truly wishing to destroy in the bud and annihilate that which Szczepanowski created and took such pains to cultivate: the children of his spirit and his creativity."[135]

But it was not only foreigners who stood in Szczepanowski's way. Although he did not mention them directly, Szczepanowski's eulogist did not fail to point the finger at Galicia's conservative elites, who favored agriculture over industry and whose refusal to support the growth of industry kept their province in a state of wretched poverty. Agriculture, he argued, was no longer sufficient to support life: "Today agricultural conditions are so difficult, the expenses so enormous, that if a farm is not supported by an industrial branch's exploitation of the soil, then it can only vegetate from day to day, never blossom."[136] From the vocabulary of enlightenment and education, the industry's defenders now turned to the vocabulary of the agriculture they hoped to replace. Szczepanowski's mines, his vision of derricks, steam engines, and pipelines crisscrossing the Polish landscape—this is what would allow the land to "blossom."

Szczepanowski's opponents also allowed Szczepanowski's trial to become the forum for a debate on the merits of democracy and socioeconomic change. Not even they seriously accused him of embezzlement for the purpose of personal gain. Szczepanowski was incompetent, his penchant for democracy led him, predictably, in the mind of conservatives, to exercise bad judgment. While claiming to represent morality and the best interests of Poland, he had proven himself to be at best amoral, if

embezzlement

not immoral, in his financial dealings. They emphasized the damage that Szczepanowski had done to Poland's reputation and to the national pride of Poles. No less could be expected from such a "democrat." According to the commentary of Ludwik Straszewicz, courting Galician conservatives in the Cracow journal *Kraj,* it was the fault of Szczepanowski's sort that so much of Polish industry had fallen into foreign hands in the first place. Given his recklessness, gullibility, and excessive belief in the word of the people, "it [was] very likely lucky for Galicia that Szczepanowski broke his wings as an industrialist."[137] Conservatives tried to prove that Galician Savings Bank funds had been used to finance the Polish Democratic Party and the publications of its press organ, *Słowo Polskie,* and the leader of the conservative Stańczyks, Stanisław Tarnowski, claimed that Szczepanowski's acquittal was further proof of the worthlessness of jury trials. The *Ruch Katolicki* called Szczepanowski "an apostle of the corrupted morals of great capital."[138]

Conservatives' criticism of Szczepanowski did not soften after his demise. In the obituary published in the conservative newspaper *Czas,* he was described as "a brilliant representative of political and economic romanticism, who in contact with cold reality had to surrender to sad defeat. In him were strangely combined a thorough knowledge and an unparalleled impracticality in the field of technical enterprises, which was in him the usual result of blazing fantasy, not resting on real foundations. This was the origin of the mistakes and errors committed in this field, and this led him to the final catastrophe."[139]

Both sides seemed to agree that Szczepanowski's trial represented more than his own individual fate. Nevertheless, while they were willing to explore broader questions relating to Galicia, Poland, honor, and prestige, neither newspapers, eulogists, friends, nor foes questioned the reasons why Szczepanowski had to supplement the funds he raised legally with others secured through connections, personal charisma, and the patriotism of like-minded Poles. Whether Szczepanowski was to be commended as too good for this world or condemned as foolish and "romantic," all agreed that the problem lay with Szczepanowski himself. And while the normative value they attributed to his character differed widely, there was surprising agreement on what that basic character was. Long before the outbreak of the scandal, the author of a book of sketches of parliamentary delegates foreshadowed descriptions of Szczepanowski made after his death. In a tone that was simultaneously affectionate and condescending, Szczepanowski was described was well-meaning, naïve, and misguided. "[He] has learned and observed much, but does not know how to reconcile the observed with the learned"—this was, after all a man who was both an experienced economist and an incompetent businessman. "He uninterruptedly founds companies that earn money for others. He allows careerists, who like to hide their own lack of character in the shadow of his naïve honesty, to exploit his indestructible drive to work and his wealth of knowledge. . . . [He is] an educated, hardworking, altruistic man, but at the same time confused in his ideas and goals like no other. A man of progress who cluelessly pulls forward like a workhorse without noticing that he is hitched to the cart of reaction."[140]

Like MacGarvey, Szczepanowski invested in refining, as well as production, a fact that indicates some appreciation for the benefits of vertical integration (it was his investments in exploration and production, not refining, that were his downfall). But unlike MacGarvey, Szczepanowski did not focus exclusively on the business of running a business. MacGarvey was an oilman first and a Canadian second. Szczepanowski thought that he could force oil to do his bidding, but was forced to recognize that this was beyond his power. Nevertheless, the rhetoric of oil as a tool of national regeneration that Szczepanowski employed to such great effect outlasted his own personal disaster. Throughout the next decades, Galician producers (including MacGarvey) warned of the danger of too much foreign involvement in Galicia and thus in Polish industry. Although Austrian officials might laud the improvements brought by foreign investors and managers (as did the factory inspector in his reports on the wax industry), Poles were wary lest profits derived from their soil fill foreign coffers. As foreign investment increased and international tensions sharpened, even government representatives began to view the nationality of those who controlled the industry with concern. In an era of overproduction and brutal competition for international markets, the battle over what was good for Galicia became a battle between those who advocated what was good for the empire, what was good for Poland, and what was good for business. At the same time, the dissonance between what was good for elites and what was good for those at the very bottom of the pyramid became starker than ever before.

— 4 —

The Boys Don't Sleep at Home

*Workers' Dreams of Wealth
and Independence*

While the vision and risk tolerance of oil entrepreneurs are essential in jump-starting an industry, entrepreneurs are powerless to realize their dreams without the assistance of the skilled and unskilled workers who make their companies run. The oil and wax industry officially employed 11,944 workers in 1897,[1] but this number did not include any of the thousands of workers who came to the oil fields for a day or two at a time without ever appearing on employers' rolls. How did these workers fit into Galician society? What were their motivations and interests? Describing the men and women who worked in the Galician oil industry today is as difficult as understanding them was for government officials and socialist agitators at the turn of the twentieth century. The difficulty stems from the dizzying diversity of this group, which makes speaking of workers as a coherent collective well-nigh impossible. Here were Ukrainian, Polish, and Yiddish speakers, local peasants and travelers from afar, destitute Jews picking wax from piles of rock and highly trained master drillers from technical colleges in the Austrian Empire and abroad, registered workers listed on payrolls and casual day laborers who appear in no statistical compilations.

One thing is clear: oil workers did not act as Galicia's revolutionary class. Skilled workers, including drillers, stokers, smiths, and boilermakers, were well paid and well respected. Unskilled workers were neither, but nevertheless were resistant to socialist rhetoric. This was not a cadre of peasants who had abandoned their farms to devote themselves to industrial work, but rather a huge number of workers who filtered in to oil towns seasonally, when they needed a little extra cash, or when there was less work back on the farm. Unskilled workers in the oil pits and wax mines of Galicia seemed to think and act more like peasants moonlighting in oil towns than industrial workers. At the same time that master drillers could demand 10 to 12 crowns per shift, unskilled workers (aboveground) were paid no more than 3 to 4 crowns and sometimes as little as 0.8 crowns per shift.[2]

Peasants who trekked to the oil basin in search of temporary work to relieve their debts, ease their hunger, or provide a longer-term escape from the "idiocy of rural life" were greeted by long hours, low pay, and the companionship of thousands of other villagers sharing their daily routine, most of them young men either single or temporarily rendered so by distance. The plight of the unskilled workers in the Galician oil basin drew attention from civil servants and social critics throughout the empire, many of whom argued that their misery had to be unique. The Galician factory inspector, Arnulf Nawratil, lamented that "the situation of the Borysław and Wolanka mine workers . . . is in every way so peculiar that there cannot be workers existing under similar conditions anywhere in Austria or anywhere in Europe."[3] Nawratil's claim, however well intentioned, was absurd. Any of the features that characterized the oil workers—unhealthy and unpleasant working conditions, cultural and religious divisions and tensions, ambiguous relations with socialist agitators, lingering connections to village life, and the dream of retiring as well-to-do peasants—could be found among working populations from the oil fields of Baku to the ore mines of the Donbass-Dnieper region, the factories and mills of Friuli, and the coal mines of the Ruhr Valley.

In the late nineteenth century, the ranks of the proletariat increased across Europe. In Galicia, as in other European regions where traditional agricultural techniques proved incapable of supporting ballooning peasant populations, rumors of employment opportunities at mines and in factories drew thousands of unskilled laborers.[4] In the industrial centers of Britain, Germany, Belgium, France, the Netherlands, Italy, Scandinavia, and Russia, they began to form mass parties to represent their interests—now seen as distinct from those of the villages they had left behind. People from all social strata took note of the growing numbers of laborers with either alarm or ecstatic optimism.[5] Politicians hurried to take action, using the imagined threat of socialist-led revolts to justify extensive police surveillance in the Austrian Empire, political oppression in Germany, and concerned attention throughout Europe.

While socialist organizations and publications remained legal in Austria, they were not greeted enthusiastically by the government or its representatives. Austrian officials envisioned a network of spies, cells, secret meetings, assassination conspiracies, inflammatory speeches, and sabotage organized by a nebulous combination of anarchists and socialists and infecting the minds of the impressionable, but otherwise generally loyal, masses. Austrian socialists took full advantage of all the legal forms of protest available to them: ballots, parades, and vitriolic articles in the (relatively) free press. What if they should turn to illegal measures? Galician elites, in particular, were all too aware of the activities of Russian radicals on their eastern border. Russian socialists did not enjoy the constitutional freedoms guaranteed by Austria's Fundamental Laws. In Russia, the terror caused by socialist and anarchist activities (the two were inseparable in the minds of the authorities) reached its highest level in the twenty years before the Russian Revolutions of 1917. The governor of St. Petersburg was assassinated in 1878. Subsequently, two provincial governors were killed, and six failed attempts were made on the life of Tsar Alexander II before he was assassinated in March 1881. One historian has estimated that "17,000 people were killed or wounded by terrorists during the last decades of the tsarist regime."[6] News of assassinations and homemade bombs traveled quickly across the Russian-Austrian border.

Socialism, however, was easier to fear than to stop. The Antisocialist Law of 1878 outlawed the socialist party organization and press in the neighboring German Empire and empowered the state to abolish any organizations with perceived socialist tendencies and to break up any socialist meetings or assemblies. Imperial German trade unions were also abolished, and suspected socialists were subjected to unprecedented harassment in the courts.[7] Despite these measures, socialist parties provided not only a political agenda, but also clubs, institutions, and social events that came to shape their members' lives outside of work.[8] Emerging slowly in the 1870s and 1880s, socialists in Galicia benefited from the constitutional guarantees provided by the Austrian Rechtsstaat and the legality of social democracy in the Austrian Empire. From 1896, when the franchise was extended to all adult males, socialists were well represented in the Austrian Imperial Parliament. Even the most utopian socialist, however, had to recognize that many obstacles hindered the wielding of any real political power. Galician socialists faced a myriad of challenges, the foremost of which were the conflicting ties of national versus class solidarity and the complete domination of agriculture over industry in the province.

Despite the insistence of internationalists (citing Karl Marx) that "the working men have no country," and their hope that "national differences, and antagonisms between peoples, are daily more and more vanishing," the attraction of national identity was acknowledged by the Austrian Social Democratic Party's decision to declare itself a federal organization at the party congress of 1897. At this congress, the party became, in effect, an umbrella organization composed of six different nationalities (German, Czech, Polish, Ruthenian, Italian, and Slovenian) that would cooperate in the imperial Parliament, but retain autonomy in local administration.[9] While all socialist parties came to accept (or at least claimed to accept) the existence of nationalities in the Second International, what was exceptional about Austrian socialists was their acceptance of the Habsburg monarchy (earning their movement the derisive nickname "k. und k. Sozialdemokratie"). The desire to balance class solidarity and national identity found different expression in the development of Austro-Marxism. The two Austro-Marxist thinkers who most prominently turned their attention to the nationalities question, Otto Bauer and Karl Renner, reflected the paradox of Austro-Marxism in their attempts to coordinate the needs of the empire's many nationalities without sacrificing the implicit leadership of Vienna. It was Bauer's hope that nationalism and socialism would prove to be complementary, not contradictory. In a chapter titled "The Realization of National Cultural Community through Socialism" [sic!], Bauer wrote, "Incorporation of the entire people into a national cultural community, achievement of total self-determination through the nation, rising spiritual differentiation of nations—this is the meaning of socialism," a formulation that presumably would have astonished Marx.[10]

Galician socialists were equally vulnerable to the siren call of nationalism, even as they advocated class solidarity. Polish socialists, led by Ignacy Daszyński (1866–1936), stressed that their ultimate goal was Polish independence (a giant step beyond regional autonomy and federalism).[11] With that in mind, Polish socialists in Galicia were more inclined to work with socialists in other partitioned lands of the Polish-Lithuanian Commonwealth than with socialists in the other provinces of the Austrian Empire. Internationalists, led by Rosa Luxemburg, were adamantly opposed to the pursuit of Polish independence, reflecting Marx's insistence that "if the Russian autocrat were to be replaced by Polish aristocrats, then despotism would merely have taken out naturalization papers." But another strain of Polish socialist thought, represented by Kazimierz Kelles-Krauz, argued that the nation-state was itself fundamental to the development of socialism, since workers tend to achieve national and class consciousness simultaneously.[12] As nationalist sentiment became more widespread, internal divisions between Polish and Ruthenian socialists deepened, since for many Ruthenians the words "Pole" and "landlord" were synonymous. Ruthenian socialists knew that the platform of their Polish comrades included re-creation of a Polish state in its prepartition borders—a proposition that they believed guaranteed continued Ruthenian cultural subjugation. The conviction that Polish landlords, not distant Austrian imperialists, were the true persecutors of the Ruthenian peasantry led to self-defined Ukrainian intellectuals' most resentful complaints about the Habsburg monarchy: "the failure of the Austrian government to protect the Ukrainian peasant from the abuses and exploitation suffered at the hands of the Polish *szlachta* [nobility]."[13] Jewish socialists, too, argued that their interests could not be represented by Poles: "There is an erroneous opinion here in Galicia that one can unite all nations and languages—i.e., the Polish, the Ruthenian, and the Jewish—under the Polish flag . . . [but] in order to propagandize the great masses of Jewish, Ruthenian, and Polish workers it is essential to take and enlighten each linguistic group, each people, separately."[14]

Nationalism did not provide the only ideological challenge to socialism. In a province so heavily dominated by peasants, it was natural that a strong populist trend overshadowed the development of socialism. The program of the Polish Populist Party (founded in 1895) called for the "national, political, economic, and cultural advancement of the people." As social underdogs, populists were radical like socialists (with whom they were often conflated by conservatives), but, as representatives of landowning peasants, they could be economically conservative. The relationship between populism and socialism was fraught with difficulty and disagreement over issues like socialization of land. Sometimes the two were uneasily combined in the person of one individual, such as Ivan Franko. Populism had the advantage of widespread appeal, but the decided disadvantage (from a socialist perspective) of ineradicable ties to the socially conservative clergy. In this sense, Galician socialists suffered from the same shortcoming as their comrades in the Russian Empire: the notorious absence of an industrial workforce among which to spread their message. Even in Germany and France, where only 36 and 43 percent of the population, respectively, lived by agriculture, compared with 80 percent in Galicia, socialists recognized the necessity of broadening their appeal to encompass rural farmers. If this was a challenge in western Europe, it was more difficult still in the East.[15]

Historians of Galicia have generalized that it was the nearly total lack of industry in the province that provided the main obstacle.[16] In describing Galicia as a completely agricultural province, they follow not only official statistics, but also contemporary commentators who lamented the fate of a province that modernity seemed to be passing by. The Galician factory inspector reported in 1884, "It is a well-known fact that, with the exception of the city of Biała, there is not a single so-called industrial city in all of Galicia, and that the few factories lie like oases scattered in a desert."[17] To whom could socialists direct their attention in the absence of an urban industrial proletariat? For some, the burgeoning oil industry provided the most obvious answer.

But even in those cases where oil and wax workers cooperated with socialists, their actions lacked the commitment and conviction necessary for true and lasting success. As in Russia and eastern Ukraine, where workers maintained ties to their village communities even after they left them for employment in industry,[18] Galician oil workers' continued identification of themselves as landowners, peasants, and villagers diminished their need to throw in their lot with strike leaders. This phenomenon was not, of course, unique to the Galician oil basin. Throughout Europe, the formation of a class of worker-peasants, described by anthropologist Douglas Holmes as "sojourners who traverse regional and national frontiers as easily as they trespass the conceptual boundaries fabricated by social scientists," characterized the early stages of industrial development.[19] Worker-peasantries are most likely to develop in areas plagued by endemic unemployment, where capital is concentrated, and where society is dominated by the land-poor rather than the landless.[20] High population density and decreasing plot size due to inheritance practices based on splitting parental land also contribute. Extenuating circumstances notwithstanding, studies of biemployment (industrial and agricultural) confirm that from west to east, it was only the poorest peasants who chose to supplement their rural income with work in factories or workshops.[21]

The rapid growth of industrial activity, combined with increasing rural poverty throughout Europe in the late nineteenth century, encouraged unskilled agricultural laborers to turn, long- or short-term, to mines and factories for work. Mine owners actively recruited agricultural laborers to fill unskilled positions—often turning to workers from different regions, practicing different religions, and speaking different languages than locals.[22] In Germany in 1893, 14 percent of the total workforce in the Ruhr coal region had moved there from Polish-speaking communities in eastern Prussia; by 1908, migrants from eastern Prussia, most of them unskilled agricultural workers, represented 37.9 percent of the workforce.[23] At the turn of the twentieth century, 72.6 percent of the population in the Baku oil region had been born elsewhere.[24] Charters Wynn's study of the industrial workers in the Donbass-Dnieper Bend coal and iron region, one of Russia's largest industrial areas, reveals striking parallels between the conditions and activities of workers there and those in the Galician oil basin. Donbass workers, although viewed by Russian socialists as the perfect targets for agitation, were called "nomads alternating between industry and agriculture" by the French consul in 1893.[25]

Unlike the French consul, Galician socialists could not comprehend the liminality of worker-peasants caught between the world of the village and that of the mine. They expected the oil basin to be fruitful terrain for worker solidarity against capitalist oppression. The conditions in which oil workers lived and worked were notoriously hazardous to life and limb. By the first years of the twentieth century, the oil fields around Baku had lent the city a reputation for continual socialist agitation, which historian Ronald Suny attributes to their "miserable physical conditions . . . conditions in which it seemed as if nature itself had conspired to deprive men of simple pleasures such as trees or fresh air."[26] In Galicia, although a new mining law introduced in 1884 mandated regular inspections of oil production and refining companies, heightened government attention did not immediately bring safe working conditions. The effectiveness of the hundreds of fines levied annually against mine owners and operators appears to have been negligible: many firms were assessed fines for the same transgressions year after year, judging the payment of penalties to be less expensive than the structural changes that would have been necessary to meet new safety requirements.

Nawratil noted a general absence of any safety precautions among petroleum distilleries and refineries, "where in addition to the danger of fires, the danger of explosions is very great, and thus the absence of care taken at the construction of such factories is most regrettable." The combination of flammable wooden buildings and frequent explosions was a fatal one and led in several instances to cases where "these establishments simply flew into the air." Refineries were generally filthy and overcrowded with machines; they suffered from a general lack of fans or ventilation of any kind and from excessive temperatures of up to 35°C (95°F). Any windows that did exist were sealed shut, which meant that the stale, hot air was contaminated by distillation vapors, gasoline-tainted steam, and sulfur dioxide. Refineries had insufficient lighting, a lack of potable water, no sanitary facilities, running water, or washrooms, and no coatrooms or common kitchens. As for the workers' living quarters, the inspector found them in deplorable condition:

> In one petroleum production company I found a cave-like, overheated sleeping room for the workers, thickly settled with foul-smelling beds. In response to my remark that these facilities did not meet human requirements, I was told that the residents of these rooms were very satisfied. This they themselves actually confirmed with the comment that their comrades at other companies did not have any kind of sleeping quarters, that they lived miles away, that they seldom were in a condition to go home, and that they were offered no other kind of lodging.[27]

Year after year, in his annual report as Galician factory inspector, Nawratil wrote that unskilled workers in Galicia were generally miserable and that overpopulation was leading to inflation and living costs that soared even as wages stagnated. Nowhere was this more noticeable than in Borysław, the center of the empire's petroleum industry. A decade later, the superintendent of mines painted an equally harrowing picture of work conditions:

> The work conditions in Borysław are extremely unfavorable. The workers are mostly itinerant, or peasants who flow in from time to time in order to make a little money in Borysław and work for a few isolated shifts. In comparison, there are very few stable workers. Most workers are on a very low cultural level, can read and write only in the rarest cases, have no housing of their own, and are satisfied to spend the nights in the highly deficient taverns, in which an inordinate number of people find shelter.[28]

Only the lucky few could even avail themselves of the substandard conditions in local inns and the aptly named worker "barracks." According to the director of the Carpathian Company, Commercial Councilor Otto Brunner, most slept outside, irrespective of the weather: "They don't go home, because they have no home. They don't go to the barracks, because they have nothing with which to pay. They aren't afraid of rain, they don't try to avoid swamps, because they work all day in wet mud." When winter conditions made sleeping outside suicidal, workers would gather on the floors of taverns by the scores: "They drink vodka, talk, curse their torturers. One by one they drowse off, some sitting, others lying in the corners or under benches. And thus lie twenty to seventy people, men, women, and children, so close together that it is impossible to roll over."[29]

In 1896, Labor-Zionist Saul Raphael Landau undertook an expedition to Galicia and Russia to observe the conditions of the Jewish proletariat on assignment for the London-based the *Jewish World* and the Viennese *Die Welt*. Borysław was one of the seven towns he chose to describe, since, according to Landau's own figures, two-thirds of its wax workers were Jews. The Borysław wax workers who "collected here by the

Worker pumping overflowing oil out of a ditch. The original caption of this propaganda photo from the First World War read: "Pumping off overflowing oil diverted into a ditch. The newly eruptive oil source now delivers 400 tons a day, compared to 200 tons a month before." (Reproduced by permission of the Österreichisches Staatsarchiv, Kriegsarchiv.)

thousands from all regions, in order to carry out this work and through their labor to create new objects of value, [did] not share in any of its fruits." Only two buildings in the entire village were made of stone, and the remaining wooden buildings sank below the level of the street because of the sinking of the earth they were built on. The whole village resembled a morass of yellowish muck.[30]

It was not only oil and wax workers, of course, whose work conditions were bad. The inspector noted that the proverbial Galician misery was worsened in large towns and cities where massive immigration from the land continued to bring wages down. There was thus nothing surprising to him in the frequency of strikes that plagued the province throughout the 1880s and 1890s. Each year he reported on several strikes among the province's artisans, who, as John-Paul Himka has argued, took the place of an industrial proletariat in leading the socialist movement in the province.[31] In the last decade of the nineteenth century, for example, the factory inspector noted strikes among tailors, tinsmiths, tile-oven setters, printers, bakers, brush makers, smiths, the employees of a wagon factory, coopers in various breweries, shoemakers, steam carpenters, workers in a horsehair factory, porcelain painters, and tallith weavers, all of whom demanded that their wages go up and the length of their shifts go down. Doubt that worker complacency would last in the face of worsening conditions was shared by the superintendent of mines, who declared in 1892, "If perhaps in one regard an improvement [in work conditions] begins to appear, then it would be only insofar as one is able to find individual workers who slowly become conscious that they can complain about the occurrence of abuses."[32]

If skilled artisans were so eager to strike, one might have expected that the oil workers, whose shifts were also long and whose wages were also low, would strike as well. After all, oil workers seemed to represent the ideal protagonists in a progressive workers' movement to demand greater rights. In addition, their working conditions had reached a level of misery that made the moment seem ripe for action. According to one left-leaning law student in Vienna, conditions for workers had only worsened as the industry matured. If the oil industry in its infancy had offered a life of adventure to wild young men with nothing better to do, in the years of its development it had turned into a classic playground for exploitative imperialists. The operators of the new companies, he wrote, were "men of no conscience speculating with money and land, as well as eccentric characters whose past is vividly reminiscent of the adventurers of California, and whose present is reminiscent of the slave drivers of ancient Rome."[33]

The young Ruthenian socialist and writer Ivan Franko was among those who placed great faith in the progressive nature of the Borysław workers. Franko was born in 1856 in Nahujowice, a small village not far from Borysław. When he was nine years old, his widowed mother married Hryn Havrylyk, a local oil worker.[34] In his childhood, he was treated to "wonderful and dreadful stories about Borysław and the oil mines there."[35] He studied classical philology and Ukrainian language and literature at the university that would later bear his name in Lviv, where he supported himself by writing short stories and essays that supplemented the modest stipendium he received from the Provincial Fund. His studies were abruptly interrupted in his fourth semester when he was identified as a socialist by the Austrian authorities and subjected to numerous arrests, prison sentences, and postacquittal harassment.[36] One can speculate on the effect his exposure to the Borysław workers had on his proclivity for socialism: the prominent Polish socialist Ignacy Daszyński suggested that familiarity with the oil and wax workers' lot was enough to turn anyone's blood red. Daszyński himself had been moved by it: "The atmosphere of Drohobycz incited me to revolt. The brutality of the sinister blackguards who made their careers in Drohobycz at that time was so clear and public that it was not necessary to truly be a socialist in order to hate this criminal 'production,' based on the natural treasures of mother Earth and on the boundless exploitation of several thousand Ruthenian peasants, digging wax in Borysław."[37]

It was during a visit to Drohobycz that Daszyński first met Franko, who he claimed was responsible for the development of a socialist movement in the region.[38] Regardless of the cause of Franko's attraction to socialism, heightened government concern about socialism's spread led in 1877 to his first arrest on charges of propagating socialist ideas. These charges resulted in eight months' detention awaiting trial and six weeks' imprisonment after his conviction. During his university studies, which he resumed after his release from prison, he became the close friend and collaborator of another Ruthenian socialist, Mykhailo Pavlyk, with whom he founded the first of many new Ukrainian-language periodicals, the monthly *Hromads'ski Druh* (Communal Friend). Franko soon turned his literary attention to the oil workers. A series of stories called his Borysław cycle was among the first that he published (including the novellas *Boa Constrictor* in 1878 and *Boryslav smiiet'sia* [Boryslav Is Laughing] in 1881).[39] In a letter to Pavlyk that he wrote in November 1882, Franko suggested that they establish the new center of their socialist activity in Drohobycz, specifically in order to be closer to Borysław than they had been in their earlier headquarters, Kołomyja. He advised Pavlyk to "take note of the proximity of Borysław, the large number of Jews, many of whom are progressive, and even socialist elements among the youth," concluding that "all of this would push our activity in Drohobycz toward an interethnic-federal basis."[40] Franko submitted a letter to the socialist newspaper *Praca* (Work) in October 1880 in which he derided Galician socialists for their preoccupation with artisans and consequent neglect of oil workers.[41] While Franko periodically worked for the Polish socialist newspaper *Przyjaciel Ludu* (Friend of the People), his primary loyalty was to the Ruthenian masses. Perhaps this contributed to his desire to see heroes in Borysław's oil workers, many of whom were Ruthenian, rather than urban artisans, who were predominantly Polish.[42]

Progressive elements notwithstanding, the hopes of socialists who expected dramatic strike activity in the Borysław oil basin were disappointed. There were no strikes before 1900, despite intense agitation on the part of socialists.[43] May Day celebrations remained peaceful; workers spent the "holiday" singing and lounging about in the fresh air. Not even local government officials were alarmed, despite the participation of up to one-third of the workers in celebrations.[44] Inspector Nawratil speculated that the unskilled workers themselves were not as disturbed by their working conditions as he would have expected. "The peasant worker is agreeable, obedient, satisfied with extremely modest nourishment, views his employer as a benefactor, takes on his hard-earned pay with real gratitude, and, when well treated, allows himself to be used to any purpose. Unfortunately, the peasant worker is very uneducated, most often unable to read or write, and has neither any real sense of the laws nor of the favors that those laws secure for him. He has, namely, no idea what his rights are."[45] In addition, he noted that workers were themselves little inclined to observe regulations designed to protect them. They showed no understanding of or interest in safety precautions and were more likely to consider them a nuisance than a protection: "The indolence of the workers and their apathy and insensitivity to the greatest dangers is unparalleled. Most of them see any kind of protective measures with scaled eyes and would prefer to eliminate them entirely, as they will not recognize their utility."[46]

Nawratil's claim is supported by thousands of files detailing fines levied against workers for disobeying rules designed to prevent their injury and death. Although workers regularly objected to their fines, they were almost universally upheld by the courts. Worker violations most frequently fell into one of three categories: allowing stones to fall down shafts where their colleagues were working, carrying lamps in the vicinity of oil wells (where the slightest spark sufficed to ignite petroleum gases and cause an explosion), or smoking cigars or cigarettes in the wooden barracks or near the oil pits.[47] There was no question that the work was exceedingly dangerous: according to the Ministry of Agriculture's official statistics, 261 oil and wax workers were killed and 596 seriously wounded in mine accidents between 1886 and 1900.[48] In one particularly horrible incident, 80 miners suffocated to death in a wax mine when a boiler explosion at the surface made it impossible for men to work the ventilation apparatus.[49] Government sources admitted that their statistics did not represent the full extent of the danger. According to the factory inspector, only a small portion of accidents were ever reported to official sources.[50]

Despite the widespread conviction among outsiders that unskilled workers were stupid and carefree, the absence of concerted demands for higher wages and shorter hours cannot be ascribed to worker satisfaction with the status quo. Misery and poverty alone did not suffice to inspire collective action, nor could they have been expected to do so. As Marx himself cautioned, the objective situation of a class—the conditions that linked individuals as members of the proletariat—was not the same as those workers' subjective awareness of those links.[51] In *The Poverty of Philosophy*, Marx explained the importance of the workers' realization of their common interests: "The combination of capital has created for this mass a common situation, common interests. This mass is thus already a class as against capital, but not yet for itself. In the struggle . . . this mass becomes united, and constitutes itself as a class for itself. The interests it defends become class interests."[52] The key to a successful strike, as socialists knew and tried to communicate, was sustained action on the part of a united body of workers, made possible in the industrial age by "the ever expanding union of the workers."[53] A sense of class solidarity that transcended individual companies and villages would in turn rouse the solidarity of the surrounding population, who would refuse to act as scabs during the work stoppage. But solidarity was not a characteristic of relations between workers in the oil basin in the late nineteenth century.

Part of the problem was the ease with which unskilled oil workers (those who dug the pits of the smaller companies, turned the windlass, or worked in the wax mines) could be replaced. Employers complained that it was easier to hire new workers each week than to convince the old workers to stay. One company reported that it employed an average of 50 workers at any given time, but that the total number of workers it had employed over the course of 1896 exceeded 760.[54]

Ivan Franko anticipated the problem that would be caused by the ready availability of substitutes from surrounding villages in case of a strike. He took steps to avert it by providing the oil workers with a strikers' textbook, a sort of manual on how to act collectively and effectively, written in the form of his novella, *Boryslav Is Laughing*. The story features Bened'o, a mason who moves to Borysław after having learned the techniques of a successful strike in western Galicia. He teaches his new friends to work together to plan an organized strike instead of relying on a sense of vigilante justice that is satisfied by beating up brutal or unjust overseers in the shadows of the workers' barracks at night. Bened'o cautions that a critical step is recruiting the assistance of young men in neighboring villages and explaining to them how important it is that they stay clear of the oil wells for the duration of the strike. An early example of socialist realism (first published in 1881, it predated Zola's *Germinal* by four years), *Boryslav Is Laughing* was written as if it documented real events. Franko himself appears to have later come to believe that the story was true: in a history of Ukrainian literature that he wrote years later, Franko described *Boryslav Is Laughing* as "an attempt to portray the original workers' strike of the Boryslav workers, which ended with the great fire of 1873."[55] This strike has become the starting point for Soviet-era histories of the rising working class in Galicia.[56]

But there was no workers' strike in 1873.[57] There was a devastating fire that ravaged Borysław in September 1874, destroying two hundred shafts and innumerable outbuildings and costing several workers their lives, but there was no strike associated with that fire. An extensive investigation revealed that the fire had started when a worker foolishly tossed a match he had used to light an illicit cigarette into a bucket of oil. The fire was scandalous because it revealed the lack of any kind of fire prevention measures, fire-fighting abilities, or safety precautions in the oil industry.

But none of the sources on the fire—government reports, parliamentary debates, investigatory commission findings, court cases, penalties levied, and petitions calling for reform—mentioned any unrest.[58]

Franko's tale of workers committed to cooperation against their foremen and bosses may have been realistic, but it was not real. There was little unity among the workers, and no signs at any point in the nineteenth century that they were interested in class-oriented action. There are three reasons for this. First, the unskilled workforce was made up predominantly of peasants who occasionally and temporarily turned to the oil fields to supplement, but not to replace, their earnings at home. Second, oil workers were divided into national and confessional groups that, even when they did not come into conflict with one another, were little inclined to cooperate. Third, the Jewish wax workers, in particular, found no appeal in socialists' call to action. According to Saul Landau, their problems were too deeply rooted in "racial animosity" to be solved by united class action: "Jewish workers have more pressing concerns than class struggle, the eight-hour day, and universal suffrage. First they want out—out of the Galician Mizrajim [Egypt]."[59] And fourth, skilled and unskilled workers labored under conditions and with prospects whose vast difference precluded common interests.

Historians have long recognized that the actual divisions between workers and peasants in nineteenth- and early twentieth-century Europe were not as impermeable as Marxist theory might imply. Terminologically convenient distinctions between the peasants who made up most of Galicia's population and the workers who were employed in the oil basin must be disaggregated to be understood. Most unskilled oil and wax workers fit into the category of worker-peasants—wage laborers by necessity who retained cultural and psychological connections to the villages whence they came. Paying closer attention to the nature of the workforce helps explain why it is so difficult to determine exactly how many oil workers there were in Galicia or what language they spoke. Employers submitted annual official reports on the number of their employees, which suggested that the workforce fluctuated from eight to ten thousand oil and wax workers in eastern Galicia (over six thousand of whom found employment in the Borysław basin).[60] These reports, however, were dismissed by contemporaries (and even government officials themselves) as highly unreliable.[61] On the one hand, employers underreported their employees in order to avoid paying higher insurance fees.[62] On the other hand, even an employer eager to provide accurate figures would find estimating the number of employees to be a task of astonishing complexity. Villagers and "traveling people flowing in from various countries" who were interested in a day's work would gather in the town square in Drohobycz early in the morning.[63] Foremen of local companies would come to this so-called slave market,[64] choose the workers they needed, and pay them in advance for one shift. After finishing a shift, these casual day laborers had the choice of moving on or finding a place to sleep and going through the same process the next day.

Ruthenian peasants from surrounding villages were drawn to the oil fields whenever they needed an escape from work on their farms. In 1897, a male peasant who could expect to earn 30 to 50 kreuzer (0.6 to 1 crown) a day during the harvest and a mere 15 to 25 kreuzer (0.3 to 0.5 crowns) a day during the long winter months working as a day laborer on a large plantation could expect to earn 50 to 70 kreuzer (1 to 1.40 crowns) a day as an unskilled laborer in the oil and wax mines of eastern Galicia.[65] According to the mining authorities, landowning peasants who were interested in working would "only come to Borysław when there is no field work to be done at their farms." Not surprisingly, oil production generally reached its peak in the winter because of greater availability of labor. Whether in winter or in summer, most of the unskilled oil workers, recruited from neighboring villages, were not interested in permanent or even steady careers in the oil fields.[66] While the factory inspector and mining inspector both treated the mobility of the oil workers as a unique and troubling characteristic, over the past twenty-five years, historians have shown that migration was a ubiquitous element in the life of European workers, "rootless masses of labouring people," in the nineteenth century.[67]

Given the harrowing descriptions of conditions in which oil and wax workers spent their waking and sleeping hours, it is hard to imagine that anything but the most abject poverty would draw villagers to the oil fields. There is evidence, however, to suggest that the freedom associated with daily wage labor in Borysław held a certain appeal. The mythological promise of a few days of hard work, followed by a few days of hard drinking, followed by wealth back in one's native village, was preserved in Ruthenian folk songs. Many of these songs, recorded by Ivan Franko in one of his ethnographic articles, simply promised wealth and luxury to those willing to endure the privations of mining work:

> Whoever wants to make some money and smoke cigars
> Let him go to Boryslav and turn the windlass.
> Whoever wants to make some money and eat sweet cake
> Let him go to Boryslav and crawl around in the pits.

Others referred specifically to the enhanced social status back in the village that would come to those who had earned the money to pay their debts and run their own farms:

> I'll go down to Boryslavka and earn myself a fortune,
> When I return from Boryslavka I'll be my own master.

Of course, not everyone celebrated the new source of employment found in the oil fields. The seasonal disappearance of village bachelors was noted in a popular Ruthenian women's folk song:

> Ever since they started working in the pits in Boryslav
> Since that day the handsome boys don't sleep at home.[68]

Not all women stayed at home and sang songs lamenting their lost suitors. A good number of women were themselves employed in Borysław, although few of them were the wives of the male workers. According to the mining inspector, "the moral conditions of the Borysław working population are deplorable. The married workers come to Borysław without their wives and live in sin here with wenches. The indecency is promoted by the fact that it is mostly women who are employed at the ventilators day and night."[69] Another Ruthenian folk song celebrated the attraction of these women: "If there were no forest, if there were no forest, if there were no hazelnut tree / I wouldn't have gone to Boryslav if there were no young lady."[70] Tales of loose women and plentiful liquor may have held a certain appeal, but villagers expecting that life in the oil fields would be all fun and games were sorely disappointed.

Franko, despite his hopes for the Borysław workers, knew that they were peasants at heart. Even after he gave up on the oil workers, Franko sought to teach lessons in organized action via his Borysław stories. But now the stories were designed to keep peasants away from the mines rather than to shape their actions once they were there. The hero of Franko's story "The Shepherd" spends his mining shifts in Borysław's wax pits dreaming of the pastures and livestock he will be able to buy with his earnings.[71] Franko's Borysław cycle of short stories does not advise the move to Borysław that he recommended to his fellow socialist agitator Pavlyk. Instead, each story warns of murder, premature death, greed and loss of loved ones, all fates awaiting peasants who, perhaps inspired by folk songs, turned to Borysław. Although songs promised wealth to peasants who came to Borysław as workers, conventional wisdom noted that more often peasant landowners were turned into paupers by the oil industry. According to Chief Mining Inspector Johann Holobek, "tidings of successful oil excavation enticed hordes of 'entrepreneurs,' who knew how to make themselves masters of the terrain and to turn the former landlords and property owners—although they sold their land at the highest prices—into workers literally vegetating in the most miserable conditions."[72]

Franko hoped that peasants could learn more from Borysław than merely the fear of life in the mines. In 1894, he published the tale of an Irishman, John, who found employment as a driller at an oil well in eastern Galicia, in the Ukrainian journal *Hromads'kyi holos,* the organ of the Ukrainain Radical Party. Keeping the company of Ruthenian peasants, John learned rudimentary Ukrainian. When alcoholism cost him his job, his newfound peasant friends collected enough money to pay his fare back to his own homeland. Not expecting to hear of John or to see their money ever again, the peasants were surprised later to receive from John by post not only their money, but also a much greater treasure: a letter "in which John acquainted the Ruthenian peasants with the Irish boycott and strike system in satiric form." It was as a model for a peasant strike, not an oil workers' strike, that this information was to be used. Franko claimed that this letter found great popularity, running through three thousand copies in only two months, passing from hand to hand, and eventually contributing to the outbreak of peasant strikes in eastern Galicia in 1900.[73]

The second obstacle to unified strike activity derived from the diversity of the workforce and the primacy of allegiances not based on class. Galician workers appear to have felt the pull of national or religious identities more strongly than those of class identities. The working population was mixed among two "nationalities," Ruthenian and Polish, and three confessions, Jewish, Roman Catholic, and Greek Catholic. In the industry's infancy, they had all performed similar tasks. After MacGarvey introduced the Canadian drilling system into the province in the early 1880s, however, sophisticated modern drilling operations gradually began to displace and replace older operations based on digging and hand drilling. This new form of oil exploration and exploitation required a bevy of skilled and unskilled workers. Drillers and stokers were the most central, but their work was impossible without tool dressers, machinists, carpenters, smiths, boilermakers, coopers, iron lathe operators, boiler attendants, welders, fitters, and metalworkers—all at the level of masters and of journeymen. Derricks had to be constructed, boilers built and attended, pipelines erected and maintained, pits drilled and reinforced, and machinery installed and repaired. After a short period in which many of these positions were held by North Americans, Galicia was able to supply its own skilled workers. According to the superintendent of mines, the majority of men who were trained to take these skilled positions were Polish-speaking Roman Catholics (references to west Galician workers and east Galician workers being thinly veiled references to the differences between the skilled Polish worker and his unskilled Ruthenian counterpart): "For drilling they use almost without exception west Galician workers, namely from the area surrounding Jasło, Krosno and Gorlice, while the local Ruthenian workers only find employment as common day laborers." He attributed this preference to the "unreliability of the local workers in terms of showing up for their shifts," exacerbated by the fact that Ruthenians' observance of numerous Greek Catholic holidays would force the drilling work to suffer from many unwarranted delays.[74] The prejudice of employers, most of whom were Polish speakers, may have also contributed to this favoritism. Jews found employment as the tremendously unpopular overseers and foremen and also as unskilled laborers in the wax industry. Impoverished Jews worked as wax washers (who washed the waxy earth in cold water by stirring it with long pieces of wood and then collected the wax pieces as they floated up to the water's surface), wax sifters (mostly women and children, who picked the wax apart from the stones and chunks of earth in which it was embedded), stone carriers (who carried away the discarded rock after any last remnants of wax had been removed by the wax sifters), and other unskilled positions on the surface.[75] Some Jews worked belowground in the wax mines, but they were outnumbered by a larger minority of Roman Catholic workers and a majority of Greek Catholic workers. Unskilled Ruthenians worked in the mines as face workers and aboveground at the windlass.[76]

Contemporary stereotypes of Jewish, Polish and Ruthenian workers were ruthlessly consistent. The existence of Jewish laborers was rarely acknowledged in contemporary sources that presented a stereotypical image of Jews as foremen, small business owners, and tavern-keepers. While the chief mining inspector, Johann Holobek, described skilled Poles as "diligent and sober," he called unskilled Ruthenians disrespectful, unreliable, lazy and "boundlessly unstable." He complained, "The east Galician [Ruthenian] worker is undisciplined and comes to work when it pleases him. Indeed, there are cases when he will ride down into the pit, work half a shift, and then go away: he has earned the necessary pocket money for his tobacco and thus satisfied his needs for a week." The mining inspector believed that he knew what caused this lack of ambition: "The main cause of this phenomenon lies in the worker's lack of material needs. When a worker is accustomed to eating meat, then he works more diligently and comes to work more regularly." This same reasoning, he continued, had led one Galician industrialist to try to accustom his workers to eating meat: "he provided them with meat at a loss, but the result of this action was nothing more than a complaint by the local priest, who accused the mine manager of demoralization because the peasants no longer observed the strict fast days. Ruthenian peasants are namely not permitted to eat meat for at least twenty weeks out of the year, not including Sundays and holidays." To the mining inspector, this was no joke. The absence of meat in the Ruthenian peasants' diet had pernicious effects: "Naturally a diet composed primarily from potatoes is insufficient and the peasant lacks the strength required for strenuous work. This partially explains the laziness of Ruthenian workers, who work only intermittently because they have no strength for intensive, continuous work and seek fortification in schnapps, but not in strengthening foodstuffs."[77] There was little expectation that these peasants would find much common cause with the highly skilled and highly paid Roman Catholic workers from the west.

The absence of organized strike activity did not mean the absence of what contemporary officials liked to call "excesses," although these looked nothing like the model described in Franko's *Boryslav Is Laughing*. There were fights, skirmishes, and pogroms, all of which led to work stoppages, but none of which had class-oriented, or even work-oriented, motives. Instead, these conflicts revealed deep confessional divisions. The most notorious cases were the "Borysław wars" of the summer of 1884 and the Schodnica pogrom at Pentecost in 1897. These excesses show that like the coal and iron workers of the Donbass-Dnieper basin, where "worker anti-Semitism played a major role in the evolution of the labor movement,"[78] oil workers were more than willing to engage in violent collective action against "outsiders" deemed to be their enemies.

The so-called Borysław wars of July 1884 were marked by anti-Semitism rather than any articulated economic concerns. At the time, wax extraction in Borysław was dominated by two companies, the Compagnie Commerciale Française in Wolanka and the mines owned by the Galician Credit Bank, which had started to buy up the properties of smaller companies in the early 1880s, in Borysław proper. But there were still scores of smaller wax companies, most of them owned by Jews. While most companies were managed by Jews, the French company stood alone in employing mostly Christian workers. Jewish overseers were responsible for distributing workers' wages; to make extra money, they were also often involved in the provision (at a profit) of food and drink. This led to a complicated network of debts and loans that caused frequent skirmishes on payday. Such a skirmish could lead to broader conflict, as it did in the summer of 1884. In the late evening of 19 July, a fight broke out between a Jewish overseer and a Ruthenian wax miner who refused to pay a debt that he owed. When the Ruthenian's colleagues from the French company joined in, the fight escalated, and only police interference was able to restore order. The following day, the French company's wax workers attacked Jewish homes in Wolanka (a Borysław suburb), broke down doors, destroyed furniture, and attacked the local Jewish synagogue. Police arrived on the scene, only to find several thousand Jewish workers retaliating with an attack on the barracks of the Christian workers.[79] There is little chance that the conflict was caused by a displacement of occupational or class-based tensions, because neither group contained tavern keepers, landlords, or overseers; everyone involved was a wax worker. These wax workers' allegiances did not manifest themselves in class categories. Rather, their principal identity, and the one they were willing to defend with violence, was religious.

In John-Paul Himka's has subtle interpretation, the 1884 Borysław wars reveal that workers were motivated not only by "ethnic/religious" identities, but also by a sense of "corporate allegiance," which he argues was demonstrated by the undercurrent of competition between the Jewish and Ruthenian workers' employers.[80] But the "corporations" were themselves ascribed "national" identities. The Compagnie Commerciale Française, which employed the Christian workers in Wolanka, and the Galician Credit Bank were both relative newcomers to the wax industry, and their more modern enterprises threatened to drive the smaller, largely Jewish-run companies that preceded them out of business.[81] The Compagnie Commerciale Française and the Galician Credit Bank were both praised by inspectors for introducing more modern mining techniques, paying their wax workers reliably and regularly, and building barracks to house those workers whose homes were too distant to allow a daily commute. They were lauded by government inspectors for their fair treatment of laborers, who worked underground shifts of eight hours each (compared with the industry standard of twelve), followed by a minimum of two shifts' rest.[82] Smaller companies could not afford to take any of these measures. Larger companies' greater capital meant that they could run their businesses more efficiently, to the benefit of the land, workers, and the industry in general. Although Polish industrialists and politicians lamented the excessive influence of foreign capital, the Catholic workers themselves seemed to feel more common cause with a French company identified as Catholic than with a Jewish neighbor. An analysis of the types of victims targeted during the riots suggests that it was primarily the religious identities of the workers that defined the conflict.

A second and more serious conflict had an equally overt religious basis. After the discovery of the gusher Jakób, the number of oil workers in the sleepy village of Schodnica quickly jumped to over three thousand. Most of them were young bachelors who had recently moved to the east from western Galicia, where oil fields were gradually becoming exhausted. If work was readily available in Schodnica, many of life's basic necessities were not. Although employment was available in Schodnica and wages for skilled workers were generous, workers were faced with a dramatic housing shortage and outrageous food prices. Interest in drilling in Schodnica was so high that the entire region had been leased to oil prospectors, leaving no room for the construction of private housing for incoming workers employed by smaller companies without barracks. When a riot broke out in May 1897, socialists believed that it had been caused by worker frustration with exploitative food prices on the part of the mostly Jewish innkeepers, who, it was argued, were the relatives and cronies of the employers in Schodnica.[83] This is further evidence that Jews in Galicia, as elsewhere in Austria, found themselves victims of both capitalism and its critics. In an age in which "the Capitalist" was a universally reviled figure, Jews of all economic backgrounds and occupations could not shake their association in the popular imagination with capital. That anti-Semitism, mixed with resentment of the economic role played by small Jewish businessmen, was pervasive throughout the empire is beyond dispute; as Robert Wistrich has commented, "the combination of delayed modernization, an anachronistic class structure, the dynamism of Jewish capital and the bewildering whirlpool of nationality conflicts was to give it [anti-Semitism] deadly effect."[84] In the words of another historian, popular Viennese anti-Semitism combined "economic protest and racial hatred, rationalist opportunism and irrationalist anxiety."[85]

While socialists considered anti-Semitism abhorrent, they, too, maintained an inconsistent attitude toward Austria's "Jewish problem." At the same time that they defended Jews against attacks from Karl Lueger's Christian Social Party, they attacked the latter and the "Christian capitalists" that made up its constituency as "Judaized."[86] According to Victor Adler, "The workers of Austria want neither 'Jewish' nor 'Christian' exploitation and will not allow themselves to be used as a battering-ram either for or against the Jews."[87] Austrian socialists were unwilling or unable to distinguish between an attack on Jews as Semites and one on Jews as agents of worker exploitation. Thus, instead of condemning the attack on Jews in Schodnica, they condemned the Jewish role as middlemen, repeating generalizations about *Schutzjuden* who served the interest of the ruling class by exploiting the workers: "As agents of the Schlachta, who sublet their rights as leaseholders of the liquor monopoly to Jewish innkeepers, the latter were inevitably among the first targets of popular wrath and bitterness."[88]

At first glance, it would appear plausible that religious and economic tensions overlapped in the case of Christian violence directed against Jews. In 1900, there were 811,371 Jews in Galicia (approximately 11 percent of the total population), according to the official census.[89] Many of those Jews (29.4 percent) were indeed merchants, dealers, shopkeepers, and brokers. If innkeepers (in 1900 there were over 22,981 Jewish tavern keepers in Galicia, and another 50,000 Jews whose living depended on them) and other small businessmen listed under industry and trade are added, the total rises to 37 percent.[90] Nevertheless, socialists' claims that Jews were targeted only by occupation rather than by religion are not convincing. While innkeepers in Germany were disproportionately represented in the membership polls of the Social Democratic Party (accounting for 5.5 percent of party members in Munich in 1906 and half of all nonproletarian members of the Hamburg SDP, for example),[91] in Galicia they were reviled as the workers' bitter enemy—not because they sold liquor, but because they were Jews. As the Borysław wars of 1884 revealed, even Jews who were themselves workers were not immune to attacks and were associated with the hated foremen, middlemen and innkeepers, not with the Christian workers. Whatever their motives were, oil workers expressed their dissatisfaction in a manner that made all Jews, regardless of occupation, age, or sex, victims of their anger.

The May 1897 riot in Schodnica passed largely without incident, but the oil workers' anger continued to fester. At Pentecost (two weeks after the original incident), that anger led to a pogrom in which a mob of over six hundred oil workers beat up a Jewish tavern keeper, attacked Jewish homes, broke window panes and doors, destroyed furniture (smashing chairs and tables, breaking mirrors, and removing pillars from beds), sliced through pillows and featherbeds, scattering the feathers on the street, and terrorized Jewish residents of the town, who either "ran into the woods or hid in their cellars and attics." In the pogrom's vilest moment, a young mother was hit so violently that she broke her arm and dropped her baby, who subsequently died from the injury. Five other Jews were wounded during the plundering, thirty houses were destroyed, and property damages were estimated at 3,300 florins (6,600 crowns). One of the rioters, Stanisław Kokulski, was killed by gendarmes in an attempt to gain control over the situation; forty-two other workers were arrested.[92]

After the riot was over, socialists feebly attempted to defend the workers who had shown themselves in such an unfavorable light. Accusations that several of the employers had incited their workers to attack Jews were published in the *Arbeiterzeitung* and subsequently investigated by the authorities, who did not, however, give them any credence.[93] In this case, it was government officials, not liberals or socialists, who defended the Jewish victims of the pogrom. In his report on the pogrom to the Galician viceroy, Drohobycz Chief District Magistrate Napadiewicz noted that there were frequent skirmishes between young Jewish men and the oil workers, most of whom were Polish speakers filled with "racial hatred" of Jews. This could not be explained by exploitation of the workers by the Jews, however, for there was none.[94] He asserted that every worker was housed by his employer and took his food either from acquaintances or in one of the Catholic snack bars. Although workers did come into contact with Jews when they were buying wares from local stores, the prices were fixed, standard, and reasonable. Drawing on his own impression as well as information given to him by his colleague, Schodnica's Magistrate Switalski, Napadiewiz concluded that oil workers, young men without the stability offered by wives or families, were naturally aggressive and prone to fights, especially when they were agitated by alcohol. Their favorable economic situation was an additional irritant: "the workers are generally very well paid and lack anything else to do on Sundays and holidays besides visiting bars, as there is a particular lack of religious observance (although the church has already been constructed, no priest has been engaged yet)."[95] All of these factors, Napadiewicz continued, made workers vulnerable to certain local agitators, who could easily transform a drunken crowd into a belligerent, anti-Semitic mob. To the extent that the workers did indeed believe that the Jewish shop owners and innkeepers were exploiting them as a class, one could claim that there was an economic element to this disturbance. Nevertheless, to describe it as a strike rather than as a pogrom would be wrong.

That the pogroms and disturbances of the nineteenth century existed on a continuum with the more overtly economically oriented strikes of the early twentieth century is demonstrated by a transitional event that occurred in 1900. That was the first year in which the superintendent of mines noted what he chose to call a "strike" among oil workers.[96] This strike still bore the hallmarks of the earlier pogroms; its precipitating cause was not economic in nature, but rather a limit imposed on the consumption of spirits.[97] As the mining inspector, the factory inspector, and numerous visitors to the oil basin had noted, alcohol formed a central component of the daily caloric intake of most oil and wax workers. In reports on the 1897 strike, their drunkenness was blamed for their propensity to violence. Ivan Franko's short stories blame alcohol consumption for the inability of even the best-intentioned miners to save the money they earned in the mines, making a return to their villages less and less likely as they fell further into debt.[98] The shortage of housing, which drove many workers and their families to seek nightly refuge on or under benches in local taverns, can only have exacerbated the tendency to turn to drink. Alcoholism among workers was also a perennial complaint of well-minded reformers in the Donbass mining region and led to unsuccessful attempts to set up temperance societies and limit the sales of alcohol. But in neither region did the workers themselves see alcohol as their enemy. When socialists in the Donbass region attempted to close liquor stores during a general strike in October 1905 in order to focus worker attention on political and economic demands and to prevent counterproductive violence, they were surprised to find that "most of the workers at the depot were hostile" toward them.[99] Likewise, workers in Borysław were quick to defend their right to drink and get drunk without extending their protests to any other demands. In the case of the 1900 "strike," the work stoppage lasted two days before the workers returned to the mines unconditionally. The superintendent of mines himself concluded that the strike was actually nothing more than a demonstration in support of the right to drink.[100] Nevertheless, workers had explicitly chosen a work stoppage instead of a riot or pogrom to express their dissatisfaction.

In 1901, wax workers went on strike on three different occasions. The first and third strikes lasted only a few days, but a strike that started on 7 June 1901 became more serious. Tadeusz Bobrzyński, the chief district magistrate for the Drohobycz district (which included Borysław), was greeted at nine in the morning with a telegram from Borysław notifying him that 500 workers from the Joint-Stock Company for the Oil and Wax Industry in Borysław (a subsidiary of the Viennese Länderbank) had gone on strike. By half past five that evening, workers from the wax mines of the Galician Credit Bank had joined in, and the number of striking workers had exploded to 1,626. At first there was general confusion about what the striking workers' demands were; rumors spread about motives and causes, all of which were discounted by Bobrzyński, who said that they were unsubstantiated. As far as he could tell, the workers had no legitimate grounds for a strike, but were merely responding to socialist agitation from the notorious social democrat Semyon Vityk.[101]

By Sunday, 9 June 1901, the workers were already getting restless and ready to return to work. A week later, on Sunday, 16 June, Ignacy Daszyński, the leader of the Polish socialists in the imperial Parliament, was able to convince the Länderbank to receive a workers' delegation sent to its offices in Vienna. Daszyński's involvement reveals the high profile of the strike. He was the undisputed leader of Polish socialism in Austria, was known to be an exceptionally gifted orator, and had many demands on his time and attention, because his interpolation was requested by Poles in Prussian and Russian Poland as well as those in Galicia.[102] Although the Länderbank refused to raise wages, it was willing to meet the workers' other demands: it would speed up the process of transporting the workers from the pits to the surface at the beginning and end of their shifts, thus lowering the shift length; it would pay the workers every week; it would cease automatically deducting from workers' pay a mandatory contribution to the construction of a local church; it would build apartments for the workers; and it would grant all strikers an amnesty and agree to rehire them once an agreement had been finalized. Subsequently, the management of the Galician Credit Bank's mines assented to the same conditions, and on Monday, 17 June, the workers returned to the mines.[103]

When everything was said and done, work had stopped for eight days, one water pump had been attacked, leaving a turbine and the pipes leading from the turbine to the mines damaged, several alleged strike-breakers had been beaten, and a handful of workers had been arrested.[104] Any serious or irreparable damage had been averted, along with any immediate or substantial reform. The wax workers' strike had remained local, spreading neither beyond Borysław nor even to local oil workers. But this strike was merely a prelude to the period of tension between workers and employers that was just beginning. Strikes became a frequent part of the annual schedule—occurring almost always in the summertime, when labor was relatively scarce[105]—throughout the last decade before the First World War.

What had changed? Conditions had improved in some respects and worsened in others. Improvements came from individual companies, mostly large companies with foreign backing, that instituted policies that were in line with government regulations: they built housing for their workers and heightened safety precautions. But despite better conditions for some, the numbers of workers enduring miserable conditions continued to rise. This was caused in part by a dramatic increase in the number of oil companies in Borysław and the surrounding area after MacGarvey introduced serious oil exploration to the region in the mid-1890s. At the same time that the local oil industry found new life, the wax industry was finally forced to undergo a massive reconfiguration. After years of mounting pressure from mining experts, the Ministry of Agriculture pushed through new regulations mandating that wax companies use a central-shaft system instead of the multiple-shaft system that had been characteristic of the region, a change only feasible for the largest

extraction companies. In only two years after the government's an-
nouncement of the new law in 1898, the number of operating wax mines
in Borysław dropped from thirty to five. Accompanying the smaller companies' forced closure was an equally dramatic reduction in the number
of workers employed in the wax industry. In 1898, there were 4,894 wax
workers in Borysław, but in 1900 only 1,924, a drop that appears to have
left the workforce trim, committed to industry over agriculture, and rad-
icalized.

Knowing that the forced company closures would mean massive layoffs
and anticipating that those layoffs would create a large body of disgruntled and idle young men, a committee of Borysław entrepreneurs and
government officials met in September 1899 to determine how to remove
any danger these workers might pose to public order (and, presumably,
company profits). Under the presidency of Prince Adam Sapieha,[106] they
determined to set up a labor office to find new jobs for those former
miners who had worked full-time in the wax industry and to pay for
their relocation.[107] Funding for this venture would be provided by the
two largest wax companies in Borysław, the Compagnie Commerciale
Française and the Galician Credit Bank, as well as institutions and offices
representing every level of authority within the empire, from the most
local through the highest provincial authority, and both regional and national representatives of the imperial state itself (the poor fund of the
local community council, the District Court in Drohobycz, the Provincial
Sejm, the Galician Viceroy's office, and the Imperial Ministry of Agriculture).[108]

For the employers, these layoffs provided a golden opportunity. They
could choose which workers they would let go, and according to the
mining inspector, the majority of those laid off were "unreliable workers
who engage in mining work only as a side job and include those elements
known in Borysław for their disinclination to work and a tendency toward
alcohol, and whose removal has always served in the interest of the successful development of the wax mining industry, as well as the economic
and moral improvement of the workforce."[109] To further demonstrate that
the absence of the fired wax workers would bring regularity and discipline
to Borysław, the mining inspector pointed out that of all the workers
employed by the Galician Credit Bank in one week, only 5 percent worked
the full six shifts permissible by law, 12 percent worked five shifts, 13
percent worked four shifts, 12 percent worked three shifts, 19 percent

worked two shifts, and 39 percent worked only one shift. At the smaller companies, the ratio of regular to casual workers was even less favorable.[110] As for the fates of these workers once they were fired, the majority returned to their hometowns, "in which they most often possessed small properties," or were otherwise employed as agricultural day laborers. The willingness with which workers took advantage of free rail passage to other towns and villages resulted in a worker shortage in Borysław by the summer of 1899 as rumors of impending layoffs spread. Over 500 workers and 300 dependents were placed in other jobs, and over 350 families of Jewish foremen and workers were sent by ship to America, sponsored by a local committee and external Jewish Support Societies.[111]

Weeding out the unreliable and inconstant workers was considered a great victory by employers and local officials alike, but it also appears to have had unintended consequences. In the years from 1901 to 1911, the majority of strikes in the oil basin were started not by skilled oil workers, but by wax workers, the same group that had formerly been considered so indolent. Three wax strikes in 1901, two wax strikes in 1902, two wax strikes in 1904, two wax strikes in 1906, one wax strike in 1907, three wax strikes in 1909, three wax strikes in 1910, and one wax strike in 1911 added up to a total of seventeen wax strikes, compared with only five among oil workers (two in 1904, two in 1907, and one in 1910).[112] It is possible that the reshaping of the wax industry's workforce removed one of the main obstacles to strike activity: an absence of commitment to mining as the miners' main source of income. With those workers who had alternate sources of income gone, Borysław was left with wax workers who, though unskilled, were absolutely dependent on earning a living in the wax mines. These workers could be relied on to show up for six shifts a week because they had nowhere else to go. Indeed, during work stoppages throughout the first decade of the twentieth century, most workers stayed in town and tried to interfere with the continued operation of their mines, rather than abandoning Borysław for some other home.

Calculating the total number of workers in Galicia can only mislead historians hoping to explain the long absence of strikes and then their general lack of success. To understand the nature of Galician social structure and the importance of a proletariat within it, one cannot merely divide the number of workers in industry by the number of adults in the province. On the one hand, as we have seen, official figures underestimated the numbers of workers. On the other, workers' behavior and identities did not always reflect their official occupational categories. Understanding or predicting the behavior of Galicia's oil workers without considering the effects of internal migration and the liminal quality of their identities is as impossible for historians today as it was for socialists then. We have already seen that for decades, Galicia's so-called industrial workforce was less likely to engage in strikes or proletarian behavior than artisans and peasants. Even when socialist agitators were able to rally support for strikes (after decades of propaganda falling on deaf ears), their interests were not always those of the men whom they claimed to represent. The workers themselves wanted clean housing, cheap food, and liberation from the oppressively expensive and worthless fraternal associations that they loathed. Socialists clamored for the eight-hour workday, higher wages, and universal manhood suffrage.[113] Neither group seemed to make much progress in forcing the employers' hand.

Nevertheless, conservative or apathetic workers do not provide the only explanation for the initial absence of strikes and their failure when they did occur. On the contrary, external conditions that had nothing to do with worker consciousness or lack thereof made the chances of successful strike activity slim indeed. Some of these related to forces outside human control: fluctuations in oil production, oil prices, and therefore the very desirability (from the employers' perspective) of quickly ending a work stoppage. Others testify to the power of Galician elites to rally the provincial and imperial government to their assistance. Many who had Poland's interests at heart were convinced that it was the victim of Austria's pseudocolonial aspirations. Ignacy Daszyński insisted that the province was "treated by the Austrian government like a colony that provided raw materials and food and was forced to buy manufactured products of the Austrian western provinces."[114] This was not just the self-interested opinion of Galicians; Kelles-Krauz thought that suppressing Galician industry was fundamental to the very essence of the Habsburg monarchy: "Multinational empires do not in practice seek to 'organically incorporate' their various national regions. The dominant nationality will develop its industry at the expense of others. Industry in the Congress Kingdom is discriminated against within the Russian Empire; Galicia is kept in a state of backwardness by Vienna. These regions will remain vulnerable so long as they lack a national government to protect them and a national market to serve."[115] Regardless of the fundamental obstacles laid by the economic policy of the Austro-Hungarian Empire, the imperial government believed that by strongly supporting oil industrialists' attempts to put down strikes it was providing critical assistance to the industry itself.

Elite responses to strikes showed the strained loyalties of company owners, managers, inspectors, local government officials, and parliamentarians. That Galicians wrestled with different national, religious, and state-oriented identities is well known. But how did these different private identities mesh with their occupational identities? By examining responses to strikes, various conferences, committees, and associations formed to deal with the crisis of overproduction and price collapse, one can uncover some of the positions that characterized this period.

— Biggest challenge to Galician socialists was that
tues were often more national than they were
(126) class-based
    ↳ peasant, unskilled workers were a very
        diverse bunch, speaking a # of diff. languages
    German, Czech, Polish, Ruthenian, Italian, Slovenian,
            — Jewish —
— Populism, w/ its ties to the conservative clergy, and
the significant # of rural peasants, also posed
challenge to socialism
— many peasants lived a liminal lifestyle, only working in
mines or factories part-time, while maintaing strong agric.
ties to their rural village
$) 120-21 – unskilled workers were clearly impoverished, but lacked a
    sense of unity, class solidarity – no class consc.,
    only national, linguistic, + religious differences
    ↳ p.123 – 4 reasons for lack of class solidarity

— 5 —

Oil City

The Epidemic of Overproduction

APEX OF OIL INDUSTRY   p. 20
1895 – 1909

From the 1870s to the middle of the 1890s, Galician producers' greatest problem had been discerning where oil could be found. Landowners with the means to do so paid geologists and scouts to improve their chances of choosing the most promising locations for their slow and expensive downward exploration. After the initial opening of the oil fields of Borysław in 1894, the explosion of Jakób onto the fields of eastern Galicia and the newspapers of Europe in 1895, and then, in 1906 and 1907, the discovery of eruptive new wells such as Wilno and Oil City in the Borysław suburb of Tustanowice, all this changed.

Galicia's most famous well, Oil City, produced over one hundred thousand tons of oil in 1908.[1] The Borysław basin was so rich in oil that it quickly became responsible for almost all of the province's impressive growth in production. In 1904, Borysław alone accounted for two-thirds of total Galician production and surpassed the entire demand of the Austro-Hungarian Empire, leading one geology professor to proclaim, "A veritable flood of petroleum pours out of local oil wells."[2] With the opening of these new oil fields, the challenge facing producers collectively was no longer to increase production, but rather to find new consumers for the sudden wealth of crude oil exploding onto the market. Domestic demand, far behind German rates, could not keep up with burgeoning supply. From 1901 to 1909, Austrian consumption rose modestly from 4.9 to 5.9 kilograms per capita annually, whereas it had already reached 18 kilograms per capita in neighboring Germany.[3] The principal use for petroleum was still as kerosene, and although it remained the only lighting source for most Europeans, the gradual spread of electric lighting in Europe's larger cities presented a new problem. True, gas and electricity

140

were still considered "luxury lighting," reserved for the very wealthy, but how long could that situation be expected to last? Forward-looking producers recognized that the potential for growth in the demand for kerosene was limited, and that this outlet for oil might even dry up.[4] Given the anticipated impossibility of wooing more domestic consumers of their traditional product, whom could producers convince to use (and pay for) this oil? And at what price could this now bountiful commodity be sold? In the face of a devastating price collapse, producers recognized the need to gain foreign markets in addition to securing sole control over the domestic (imperial) market. Over the two decades from 1895 to the outbreak of the First World War, Galicia's producers adapted to their new circumstances quickly and adeptly, recruiting in the process a powerful ally—the imperial government.

Overproduction was very much a result of human decisions. For decades, oilmen's challenge had been the deciphering of mysterious natural laws governing the creation and concealment of oil deposits. Even the most experienced oilmen were forced to admit, along with the ill-fated Szczepanowski, that the earlier belief that "one could predict a success in deep drilling" was "only an illusion," since "when it comes to discovering oil territory, the rule is, as it turned out, there are no rules."[5] Geologists who thought that they could designate drilling points "so precisely marked by nature that . . . there can be no possibility of the prospecting's failure" had to concede that "in questions of geology, one cannot rule out the possibility of mistake."[6] No amount of inspection by expert geologists, carefully examining the earth for signs of Oligocene and Eocene deposits—proven by the experience of Schodnica to be the most productive sources of petroleum in the Carpathian region—could ensure that oil would be found below any particular spot on the surface.

Nature did not bestow its gift of oil evenly, and human effort expended to find it was not reliably rewarded.[7] As Wolski explained, one of the defining characteristics of the oil industry was that "it is not possible to reduce or increase production arbitrarily; rather, a series of circumstances of legal, economic, and technical nature combine to give production the stamp of an elemental force."[8] These circumstances made investing in oil no different than gambling—and the stakes were very high. The danger was well known to the province's political elites, who recognized the perils of financial volatility inherent in the industry. Michał Bobrzyński (Galician viceroy from 1908 to 1913), even as he called petroleum a "great source of our country's wealth," noted in his memoirs the risks involved: "the capital laxly invested in petroleum production was like a sort of game, in which a lucky few became rich, while the majority lost its savings. Every trend in the market, every stock speculation whose subject was oil, was reflected in the petroleum industry and affected its participants."[9] Whether one man found oil or not was a matter of chance; whether oil was to be reached below a particular search point had been determined long before humans could affect the environment around them.

Nevertheless, while the discovery of of oil may have been based on luck at an individual level and did indeed lead to many personal disasters and company bankruptcies (Szczepanowski being, again, a case in point), on a larger scale, human influence played a more decisive role. If we are concerned not with who extracted the oil, but rather how much oil was extracted and how quickly, the story is different. Total rates of extraction and overall Galician production were very much determined by human influence. Overproduction (and early depletion) can be prevented by evenly spacing wells and by drilling slowly and at a regular rate—that is, by measures directly opposed to the unrestrained development that characterized the Galician (and the Pennsylvanian) oil industries. The "series of circumstances" to which Wolski referred—law, technology, and economy—are all factors determined by human society. The legal debate over ownership of mineral rights was won by those who favored dispersed control by landowners, thereby ensuring that production would be spread out over many small businesses. Technological advances were imported by a few ambitious individuals from as far away as Canada and gradually (with adaptations to local geological conditions that were themselves made possible by human ingenuity) came to predominate in native industry. As for the economy, poor Galicia lacked the infrastructure to ease overproduction (e.g., storage facilities in the province or pipelines out of it) because men had not chosen to erect it; and it was politicians who created the freight costs that hindered export.[10]

Although one industry expert, estimating that Galicia had produced over six million tons of petroleum between 1855 and 1904, argued that there was good cause to believe that the wealth of oil that remained in Galicia was truly limitless,[11] overproduction was not caused by an uncontrollable increase in the amount of oil forcing itself to the surface. On the contrary, it was caused by factors that reflected the structure of Ga-

lician, Austrian, and European society, politics, and economics and had
little to do with natural "givens." Too many companies too concerned
with their own immediate gain were working with tools too efficient and
productive to unearth as much oil as they could, flooding the market (as
well as local rivers) and causing a price collapse that threatened the livelihood of all. In a conference called to discuss the "crisis in the mineral
oil industry" in the Vienna Chamber of Commerce in November 1910,
the empire's leading oil experts (including Galician producers and Viennese refiners) met to discuss its causes and remedies. They did not blame
nature for this crisis: they knew very well that its causes lay with their
own practices (or at least those of their selfish neighbors).

What had caused the problem of overproduction? First, new technologies made it possible to reach oil at previously unreachable depths and
record speeds. Second, the increasing number of companies involved stymied attempts to organize producers in a cartel with effectively enforced
price controls. Rockefeller was a household name, oil was a household
item, and investing in it came to be a common gamble for Europeans far
beyond Galicia's borders. These eager investors provided all the funding
necessary to support a plethora of small, speculative companies in addition to an increasing number of larger companies. Unlike the U.S. oil
industry, which was controlled by a Standard Oil monopoly, and the
Russian industry, where Nobel and the Rothschilds had a firm grip on
production, refining, marketing, and export,[12] neither monopolies nor
cartels could be successfully established in Galicia. The Galician refining
branch was hardly more organized than that of production. In 1910, there
were forty-nine petroleum refineries in Galicia, sixteen of which produced
less than one hundred tons of refined petroleum a year and thirteen of
which produced over one thousand tons of refined petroleum a year.[13]
Before the First World War, 45 percent of Galician crude was refined in
Galicia, but 32 percent was refined in other Austrian provinces and another 20 percent in Hungary.[14] Repeated attempts to form cartels both
among oil producers and refiners in Austria-Hungary met with no lasting
success. On the contrary, the Galician oil industry was characterized by
the participation of dozens of large companies and scores of small ones.
Viceregal Councilor Piwocki estimated in 1904 that there were twenty-
four large production companies and seventy small companies in
Borysław alone.[15]

Small local companies tried to solicit foreign investment with promises

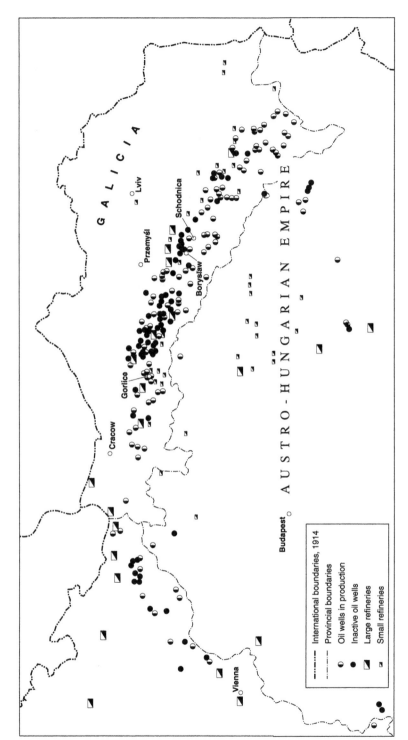

Oil wells and refineries in Austria-Hungary, 1914

Legend:

- - - International boundaries, 1914
— Provincial boundaries
◕ Oil wells in production
● Inactive oil wells
◪ Large refineries
◩ Small refineries

G A L I C I A

AUSTRO-HUNGARIAN EMPIRE

Cracow
Gorlice
Przemyśl
Lviv
Schodnica
Borysław
Budapest
Vienna

of immense riches and comparisons to the now world-famous fields of
Borysław. The Crédit Lyonnais, for example, was repeatedly approached
with requests to fund new companies that would acquire petroleum holdings in Galicia.[16] The bank's analysts demonstrated that because of the
high price of Galician refined petroleum in export markets, it was not in
their interest to invest in Galician oil. Smaller investors, however, were
often willing to take greater risks and were the principal target of start-
up companies' fundraising attempts. Notices advertising available stock
in new companies appeared regularly in foreign newspapers like the
Times, and new companies typically produced promotional materials. Immediately after founding the new joint-stock company Niebyłów in 1904,
for example, its board published a publicity brochure in German, Polish,
and English in order to attract interest in this "prominent new petroleum
and ozokerit [*sic*] district in Eastern Galicia," complete with an expert
opinion provided by Professor Dr. Rudolf Zuber (a well-known petroleum expert) and certificates from the president of the Imperial-Royal
State Board of Mines. Dr. Zuber's recommendation asserted that since
Niebyłów "*showes in every respect a complete analogy with the rich Oilfields
of Borysław . . . I must declare it to be specialy adapted for petroleum deep-
borings and excedingly promising.*"[17] Comparisons with Borysław had by
that time become commonplace and reflected the authors' hope that their
Niebyłów property would prove to be not only as rich in oil, but also as
popular among investors as Borysław itself. As MacGarvey pointed out
during the 1910 oil crisis conference, there had been an influx of foreign
capital into the Borysław basin: "Money flowed into the business from
all sides, from waiters, laundry maids, civil servants and various other
people. A few were lucky, but many lost their money, and it is again a
misfortune that foreign money came into an industry from people who
understood nothing about it."[18] Foreign interest had led to an increase
in the number of companies speculating in oil, companies that, when
they did get lucky, could not be convinced to limit their own production
for the general benefit of all. Despite the attempts of large companies
to buy out their competitors, the number of oil companies in Galicia
continued to grow throughout this period, from 95 in 1898 to 310 in
1909.[19]

While they may have primarily been concerned with the sheer number
of competitors, older Galician companies preferred to express their distress in national terms, lamenting the influence of foreign capital. (It is

critical to remember that in this context, "foreign" meant "not Galician"; companies with headquarters in Vienna were considered—by Galicians, but not by the imperial authorities—just as foreign as those in London or Brussels.) Despite the concerns of Galician oilmen, in the absence of significant sources of Galician capital interested in the oil industry, nothing could be done to prevent the influx of foreign capital. Those who favored Polish control had to admit that not enough domestic elites were interested in investing in industry to the required degree. This reproach was not unique to the oil industry. One commentator on the gentry's spending habits pointed to the effects of the provincial government's purchase in 1889 of the rights to distill and distribute alcohol (so-called propination), previously a noble privilege. The government compensated the province's nobility for these rights with 124 million Austrian crowns, but in the hands of the nobility, this money did not trickle down to the province's other residents: "In every other country such sudden wealth would be used to establish new railroads and industrial enterprises. Not so in Galicia. The millions that had snowed in on us disappeared in a few years, without bringing the country the desired advantages. . . . What was not simply squandered was used to buy new property."[20]

There were, of course, exceptions. The Lubomirski family, one of Poland's finest, for example, showed an early interest in petroleum. Count Andrzej Lubomirski (1862–1935) acquired new properties specifically in order to use them for oil exploitation, most profitably in Iwonicz, and encouraged his friends in Galicia and in Paris to do the same.[21] Lubomirski was perhaps unusual in the degree of his political and economic engagement: he was a member of the Austrian House of Lords, a representative in the Galician Sejm, a delegate to the Austrian Parliament, the curator of the Ossolineum in Lviv, and the president of the Polish Industrial Aid League. Because he was one of the leading members of the social and political elite, his investments served to demonstrate that oil investments were not always below the attention of the province's nobility. In addition, many noblemen and noblewomen profited from percentages of gross profits to which they were contractually entitled when they allowed oilmen to extract on their land. Most of the province's prominent families, including the Sheptyts'kyis, Potockis, Gorayskis, Zamoyskis, and many others, were involved in the oil industry. In most cases, however, the nobility's principal interest remained tied to their agricultural exploits, and they did not invest large sums of money in the oil industry. Thus the most significant source of large capital appeared to be foreign investors.

Not everyone agreed that foreign investment was pernicious. Wolski, whose patriotism was beyond reproach, claimed that it was not the passport of the investor, but the size of the investment that mattered. If foreign investment in Galician oil had brought no good, then it was "not because the capital is foreign, but rather because it is small."[22] Many small investments led to uncontrollable land speculation, speculative drillings, and parcellation. "It is exactly because we are capital-poor that we have drilled so insanely. We drilled because we had to drill, because it is a necessary consequence of small capital. If large Austrian capital does not want to come to us, if it restricts itself singularly to the refineries and represents their needs, then we must turn to foreign capital."[23]

In a province as poor as Galicia, few could deny that increased investment, whatever the source, would be beneficial. Even so, there were attempts to distinguish between good companies and bad companies, and the subject of debate became where to draw the line between the two. The natural and man-made disasters that characterized the industry were blamed on small producers and small companies that did not have the capital to invest in modern equipment, efficient extraction methods, or adequate housing and facilities for their employees. Large companies (such as the Compagnie Commerciale Française in Borysław) and the reforms they could afford to introduce had been welcomed in the early years of oil and wax extraction. From 1892 to 1896, for example, the Compagnie Commerciale Française and the Galician Credit Bank had a fatality rate of 1.82 per 100 workers, while their smaller competitors' rate was 4.16 fatal accidents per 100 workers.[24] It was the size of these companies that attracted attention, not the nationalities of the members of their boards.

At the turn of the century, however, the debate began to change. Attracting capital was no longer enough. There was plenty of investor interest, but what kind of influence would these new investors have? Producers and government officials alike worried that it would not be purely beneficial. At the same time that large foreign companies were commended for the advantages they brought, there were concerns lest Galician industry come to be dominated by foreigners. By the beginning of the twentieth century, references to foreign control of Galician oil had become commonplace. The newspaper organ of the GLPV warned in

1901 that "most of the companies [in Borysław] are foreign: German, English, American, Belgian, Dutch, Hungarian, and French. There are only four domestic companies; this is in any case a sad sign of the lack of entrepreneurial spirit, capital, or good will among us at home."[25] For all their differences, Polish magnate Count Andrzej Potocki and Polish socialist Wilhelm Feldman shared the widespread conviction that the wealth generated by the petroleum industry had nothing to do with Galicia.[26] The oil industry was controlled by foreign companies, so its profits went into foreign coffers.

To make matters worse, as MacGarvey claimed, without any commitment to the benefit of the industry as a whole, outsiders were more likely to drive prices down by foolishly flooding the market as soon as they struck oil instead of holding it in reservoirs until the market could bear it. For example, he argued, after having invested as much as thirty million marks in Galician oil, German investors with no interest in Galicia's economic development naturally wanted to see some oil sold and impatiently awaited their dividends.

MacGarvey's fears were shared by other members of the GLPV. Week after week, the producers' paper warned of the dangers of uninformed investments. The inability of distant, inexperienced, and indiscriminate investors to distinguish between promising and worthless terrain led to investment catastrophes that damaged the reputation of the whole industry. Allowing foolish investments today would make attracting investors tomorrow impossible: "Belgians have, with various dizzying foundations, gained truly pathetic experiences with Galician oil terrains. Cases have arisen where such terrains, worth no more than 400,000–600,000 crowns, have been financed with four to five million francs in Belgium. This is why Galician oil terrains have such a terrible reputation, not just in Belgium, but everywhere abroad."[27] The English were no better: "English [oil company] founders, who view the oil industry as the best-suited means of exploiting human stupidity and naïveté, are not picky in their methods of bringing worthless petroleum objects on the market for prices in the millions as often as the opportunity presents itself. These [millions] then disappear into the pockets of the founders themselves." The editors of the weekly Drohobycz journal *Oleum* launched a campaign to expose the doings of Bruno Maisel, "a sort of English-Galician Rockefeller in miniature," whom they considered to be the worst perpetrator of such speculative ventures.[28] Despite his Canadian origins, MacGarvey himself became an outspoken opponent of foreign interference, apparently viewing himself as a Galician industrialist after nearly thirty years of working in the province. At the oil crisis conference of 1910, MacGarvey complained of the bad influence of too many foreign companies: "I tell you, foreign money means misfortune for our petroleum industry."[29] When his Polish colleague Wolski pointed out the apparent irony of a Canadian holding such a position, MacGarvey replied, "I came with foreign knowledge, but not with foreign capital."[30] MacGarvey's position suggests that some of the "nationalist" rhetoric advocating provincial control of the province stemmed from specific business interests rather than from nationalist aims.

It was easy to blame the need for foreign investment on conservative landowners' contempt for industrial advance. But calls for restraint did not come only from expected quarters, such as large landowners and parish priests. Government officials who insisted that industrialization was desirable and who lamented Galicia's relative backwardness warned of the dangers inherent in a blind focus on profits: "The conscientious factory owner, who is not only concerned with profits, but also with the well-being and woe of his workers, does not neglect to set up operations such that the workers employed in the factory are under no danger of harm to life or limb. The factory owner, however, who concerns himself mostly with profit and nothing else, builds his factory in the most careless fashion. . . . His operations therefore entail much lower outlays, and he offers the real industrialist dangerous competition."[31] From the factory inspector's perspective, it was large companies, whether foreign or not, that needed protection from unscrupulous small producers, whose lower costs allowed for lower prices. In the absence of this protection, how could the "conscientious factory owner" possibly compete with the factory owner who cared only for profit, and not for his employees' safety and well-being? The question of where one's loyalties should lie (with Poland, Austria, or Galicia; with local producers, Christian producers, or professional producers; with workers, with compatriots, or with coreligionists) continued to plague Galicians throughout the decade before the First World War.

Whether or not foreign investors or small companies were to blame for overproduction, no one could deny that overproduction was the greatest problem facing the oil industry's producers from 1895 to 1909. By 1907, Galician production had surpassed one million tons, and the

next year it was over two million.[32] Insufficient infrastructure only worsened the disaster: in June 1908, only 49,710 tons worth of space remained
available in all the storage tanks and reservoirs in Borysław, Tustanowice,
Hubicze, and Popiele, which together had a total capacity of 810,302
tons.[33] Sufficient storage facilities could have alleviated (if not overcome)
the crisis by eliminating the need to sell oil stocks at rock-bottom prices.
Learning from the Jakób miracle-turned-disaster in Schodnica, where
there had been "no reservoirs to store the excess of liquid gold,"[34] industrialists tried to compensate with the construction of new reservoirs
and the creation of a Storage Society, which stored crude oil (for a price)
on behalf of companies with insufficient storage capacity.[35]

Storing oil presented its own problems, however. Oil that had been
comfortably cached deep within the earth for millions of years was much
more difficult to store once it reached the earth's surface. Signs of producers' desperate attempts to find someplace to put it scarred the landscape, a phenomenon described by economist, socialist, and parliamentary representative Hermann Diamand (1860–1930): "One sees in the
valley of Boryslaw itself groups of iron reservoirs left over from earlier
times; there are, I think, about one hundred of them. Today, they build
earthen reservoirs on the hills toward whose feet the oil-rich arteries are
drawn. A stranger would suppose the grass-covered earthen banks were
military fortifications. These earthen reservoirs grow out of the ground
like mushrooms; they dominate the entire region." Diamand was not
worried about the aesthetics of the Galician landscape; rather, he feared
the dangers inherent in storing thousands of tons of a highly combustible
material within yards of human dwellings. Oil producers were engaging
in a high-risk enterprise, and villagers were paying the price. Diamand
argued that anyone who thought that oil and gas could be safely contained
for an extended period of time was simply naïve. "Oil," he explained, "is
not a peaceful inhabitant of these holes in the ground. Light, volatile oils
demand free passage for their evaporation. They penetrate through the
chimney-like wooden ventilators, but also find their way through the embankments, as even heavy, viscous oils push their way through the earthen
walls. Such an earthen reservoir is surrounded by a strong gasoline
haze."[36] Visitors found the sight curious and the odors disturbing. Residents of the surrounding villages perceived in the ominously prolific reservoirs portents of disaster.

This perception was not without cause: if there was one constant from the earliest years of Galician oil extraction through the First World War, it was the ever-present threat and periodic outbreak of fire. In 1908, for example, twenty-two oil derricks along with outbuildings, six boiler rooms, and three other buildings were destroyed by fire.[37] Most fires were small in scale, claimed no human lives, and could be contained within hours (although damages could easily reach twenty thousand crowns, as in the case of the fire that struck the oil wells of David Fanto and Company in 1909).[38] Such small fires caught the attention of few outside the oil basin, with the exception of the Viennese insurance companies that paid for the damages. Periodically, however, a more dramatic fire broke out. In November 1902, for example, a fire erupted in Borysław that could not be put out until January 1903. According to Diamand, another Borysław fire in September 1909 captured the imagination of Galicia's entire literate public:

> All Galicia experienced a day of excitement shared by the entire public interested in the Galician oil region. In Lviv, posters on street corners announced the appearance of extra editions of newspapers that would contain special reports from the region of the fire catastrophe in Borysław. Special reports carried horrifying news. A great number of oil reservoirs were on fire, burning oil was pouring into neighboring villages, even the relatively distant city of Drohobycz was in danger of being destroyed by flames, many human lives and countless millions in property fell victim to fire.[39]

Media attention was frenzied, but the fire itself was limited and had not reached anything close to the predicted dimensions. Diamand argued that the journalists had done nothing more than describe the possible—although such a disaster had been avoided on that particular occasion, all its necessary ingredients were in place.

Readers were ready to believe such horror stories because of an earlier catastrophe that not only had made the Galician news, but had been described throughout Austria and abroad.[40] On 4 July 1908, Galicia's most productive well, Oil City, was struck by lightning and burst into flames.[41] The lightning was perfectly timed to maximize its effect: only three weeks earlier, Oil City had been drilled down to 1,016 meters, where it produced first one thousand tons and then two thousand tons of crude oil daily. On the day of the disaster, over six thousand tons of crude were stored in the immediate vicinity of the well. These were all set ablaze. The surface area set on fire reached fifty thousand square meters (about twelve acres). The blaze lasted for four months, during which "the fire and column of smoke resembled a volcano."[42] Had the oil been able to shoot straight from the well into the air unhindered, it would have burned in a "tall column of oil in the air," a lesser disaster from the perspective of those trying to limit the damages. Instead, shafts and struts at the point where the pipe lining the well connected to the derrick above it "scattered the oil in all directions," which meant that "only a part of the [oil] burned, while the rest poured into ditches as a burning mass."[43]

Despite (or perhaps because of) smoke-filled air and oil-filled water, the Oil City blaze became a tourist attraction. Photographs of the burning well (in which all one can actually see is a sky full of billowing smoke and hundreds of people loitering around beneath it), sometimes touched up with brightly colored paints for enhanced dramatic effect, were manufactured as popular postcards, examples of which can still be found in flea markets and private collections in western Ukraine today. Even years later, tourists still hoped to be fortunate enough to catch a glimpse of a burning well. One guidebook to the province advised its readers: "Of particular interest is the sight of an eruption of crude oil bursting forth as an oil bed is tapped—or equally the not uncommon sight of drilling derricks and boreholes that have burst into flames, and blazing streams of crude oil (usually the result of lightning)."[44]

Although fires were the most dramatic catastrophes, they were not the villagers' only problem. After the opening of Oil City, Galician viceroy Michał Bobrzyński received so many "alarming complaints from the rural population in the region of Tustanowice about immense damages caused by the flowing of petroleum into the Tyśmienica River" that he personally visited the village to inspect the situation himself in June 1908. His conclusion:

> Unfortunately, an inspection taught me that these complaints are all too grounded. . . . The crude oil flowing into the Tyśmienica River is carried for miles by this river, which is itself, in addition, constantly polluted by waste and sewage from the refineries. It is deposited onto the fields by periodically occurring floods. These deposits have as an inevitable consequence the lasting deterioration—if not the destruction—of meadows and fields for miles, throughout the entire riparian region of the Tyśmienica River, and in the farther reaches of the Dniestr.[45]

Damage to rivers and waterways from petroleum-related pollution was nothing new, of course. In the early 1890s, the viceroy's office had been approached with complaints about oil pollution from individual farmers, as well as from the Provincial Fishing Society, leading the Mining Authorities to order the cleansing of ponds "emitting suffocating odors" and the removal of oil and drilling grime from rivers.[46]

If concern for the environment was not enough to motivate the government to take action, perhaps concern for its own reputation would. Bobrzyński warned the imperial cabinet in Vienna that the failure to manage the oil region's environment properly was damaging the image of the Austrian authorities and straining the imperial budget:

> These conditions give rise to a sharp criticism of the public administration. This criticism is all the more embarrassing for me because it is made by foreigners, who stay in Drohobycz for longer or shorter periods in large numbers, and who are inclined to judge the Austrian administration according to what they see there. To these criticisms are joined the loud complaints of the rural population, who must watch as their fertile meadows and fields are destroyed in stretches miles wide, which in turn requires emergency aid on the part of the state.[47]

"Oil City: The Largest Oil Well in Flames." Contemporary postcard depicts proud witnesses of the spectacular 1908 blaze. (Author's collection.)

In his memoirs, Bobrzyński referred to the situation in the Borysław oil basin as a "natural disaster."[48] In using such strong language, his concern was not with maintaining a picturesque pastoral landscape, but rather with protecting those men and women whose livelihood depended on clean earth and water.

While Bobrzyński's report seems to pit farmers against oilmen, it should be remembered that oilmen suffered from overproduction, spills, and fires as well; in fact, their complaints were the loudest and the most frequent. They, too, perceived a connection between threats to nature, to the economy, and to human life. In their minds, and in the minds of inspectors, engineers, local politicians, and newspapermen, the interests of nature, society, and the economy did not compete with one another, but rather shared a common need for investment, infrastructure, and further development. It was more industry that would protect the Galician environment and those who lived in it, not less. Oilmen would not concede that agriculture suffered in order that industry might prosper (since, they asserted, neither was prospering). Oil industrialists, too, demanded reform and restructuring. The best measure to prevent oil from polluting the Galician landscape, they argued, was to remove it as quickly, safely, and efficiently as possible. This would necessitate a major investment in transportation technology and a restructuring of freight fees. The unusually high production costs in Galicia made competition for foreign markets well-nigh impossible and even that for domestic markets difficult. The expense of overland versus overseas transport meant that despite the proximity of neighboring Germany, Galician producers could not sell their oil in Germany at prices lower than those offered by Standard Oil. Economists employed by the Crédit Lyonnais noted that in 1898, the price of Galician petroleum in Germany amounted to as much as 19.80 francs, while the sale price of U.S. refined oil in Hamburg was only 16 francs. They argued, "It would thus be imprudent to conclude that the German market will be open to Austrian petroleum unless the price of crude falls below four crowns, and even in this case the Austrian refineries will only make an insignificant profit."[49] Because of this price difference, the Crédit Lyonnais went so far as to discourage its clients from investing in Galician oil production. Given insufficient domestic demand, a bleak outlook for export, and a lack of sufficient storage facilities, overproduction led to price collapse as naturally as it led to pollution. It was this price collapse that concerned producers most.

Prices reached an all-time low in June 1909 at 0.80 crowns for 100 kilograms, stirring painful memories of the "golden years" of oil prices: in 1867, the market price for kerosene had been 15 florins, or 30 crowns, and in 1863, it had reached 25–30 florins or 60 crowns.[50] Nor could producers be consoled by drops in the costs of exploration. On the contrary, the new dependence on steam engines and drilling technology made exploration more expensive than ever before, as did the increasing depths at which oil could be found. Whereas in 1870, the deepest shafts reached 150 meters below the earth's surface, by 1908, companies were forced to drill down to between 1,000 and 1,100 meters to find the rich beds of the Eocene layer.[51] In the final analysis, it was this price collapse, rather than overproduction per se, that forced Galicia's producers to change their priorities. They now had a threefold goal: to eliminate competition by driving out smaller companies, to create some degree of cooperation between remaining producers that could keep prices stable, and to find new consumers. These new strategies helped define the producers' response to a series of strikes that broke out between 1904 and 1910.

The oil workers' strikes were poorly timed to be successful. In an era in which overflowing storage tanks led to forced sales and plummeting prices, major producers actually found that an occasional strike could be used to their advantage. Thus there was no real need to bend to worker demands—at least not for the large companies with reservoirs that could hold the oil they could not contain within their wells. This belief was put to the test by the first major oil workers' strike, which took place in the summer of 1904.

On 9 June 1904, 900 wax workers walked off the job, objecting to obligations to pay additional fees to the Fraternal Association on behalf of their wives and children. Fraternal associations, established by paternalistic company founders to protect their workers in case of disability or death, were very unpopular among the workers themselves, who were required to give up approximately 25 percent of their weekly wages in fees. Although these were supposed to be returned to the workers upon retirement or to their families in the event of their untimely death, few expected to remain in the industry long enough to collect. The striking wax workers expected their colleagues in the liquid oil industry to join them at any moment. Nevertheless, weeks passed in which tension mounted, but work continued unabated. During this period, local officials sent dozens of telegrams and memos to their superiors in Lviv and Vienna. They tried to explain the urgency of the situation and the need to take measures to guarantee peace and order in the increasingly likely event of an oil strike. Chief District Magistrate Tadeusz Bobrzyński (not to be confused with the Galician viceroy) insisted on adding twenty gendarmes to the six he had on staff. He estimated that there were 2,200 wax workers and 5,000 oil workers in Borysław and the surrounding villages and feared that over 7,000 workers without occupation could be expected to cause a great deal of trouble.[52] Bobrzyński hoped that a strike could be averted by encouraging the workers and employers to discuss their demands in advance. The producers whom he was presumably trying to protect did not, however, appear to share his concern. From the outset, the employers' cavalier attitude doomed Bobrzyński's efforts at mediation.

Both before and during the strike, government representatives struggled to forge some sort of compromise. But the larger producers were never interested in compromise, nor did they have any reason to be. Of course, they did not admit openly that the strike was in their best interest, instead arguing that they were unable to negotiate with workers on principle. Over the next few months, the employers came up with a litany of excuses justifying their refusal to negotiate, including claims that the workers' demands were unreasonable, would lead to financial ruin for the employers, and were not in the workers' best interests, and that the workers' committee was made up of terrorists. The employers' committee suggested that the workers were inspired by the terrorism of the socialist revolutionaries in Russia, who had recently assassinated Viacheslav Plehve, the Russian minister of the interior, on 15 July 1904. It was clear to them that the local socialists' habit of constructing amateur bombs out of boxes filled with gunpowder was in imitation of their Russian counterparts.[53]

On 22 June, the largest employers held a meeting in which they discussed their united stance vis-à-vis the strikers' demands. According to the employers, led by Wacław Wolski, the conclusions they reached were inspired by fiscal responsibility and necessity tempered by a moral commitment to helping their workers. They would reject unconditionally the demand for an eight-hour day, but in its place, they would offer the workers improved living quarters, the supply of clean water for drinking and bathrooms, and the introduction of a branch of the district health insurance agency in Borysław. For their long-term benefit, the employers also planned to build a reading room for the workers, which they hoped would draw them away from the club Górnik (Miner), which was controlled by socialists.[54]

The employers' offer was summarily rejected. Far from disappointing the employers, the intransigence of the socialist leaders of the strike provided the employers with an excuse to allow the workers' threatened strike to go ahead. Within twenty-four hours of the outbreak of the oil workers' strike on 8 July, an estimated 7,300 Borysław workers had ceased work.[55] The strike quickly spread to the western Galician oilfields in Krosno, Równo and Potok.

The oil producers may have believed that the strike was in their best interest—a sudden drop in production would have the side effect of raising the price of oil—but the imperial government was considerably less enthusiastic at the prospect of thousands of idle hands and angry heads. Vienna took the position that an agreement should be reached immediately. Annoyed by constant complaints of chaos and disorder, the minister of the interior asked Galician viceroy Count Andrzej Potocki (holder of this position from 1903 to 1908) why the provincial government could not provide the necessary mediation.[56] Even as his underlings struggled to find a solution that would do justice to workers and employers alike, Potocki, himself the owner of an oil refinery in Trzebinia, made his sympathy with the producers clear from the outset. In the orders that he issued to his subordinates on the scene several times a day from Karlsbad (where he was vacationing at the time), he insisted that the provincial government's first priority was to maintain order and to protect those workers who were willing to work with as much military assistance as was required. Potocki's position was rather to sustain the safety of the companies than to bring the strike to a close. He repeatedly advised against making any concessions to strikers, insisting that it was better to wait the strike out than to meet any of the workers' demands.[57] Perhaps Potocki's position should come as no surprise, given that he was appointed viceroy after Count Leon Piniński was forced out of office by eastern Galician magnates for having been too lenient on striking peasants in 1902.[58] Nevertheless, his unwavering support of the employers put him at odds with both the imperial government and local authorities. Prime Minister and Minister of the Interior Ernest von Koerber personally pleaded with Potocki to act as a mediator and facilitate peaceful negotiations.[59] Although the Austrian government had proven itself willing to suppress workers' strikes by military force in the past, Koerber had already revealed his distaste for firing upon workers.[60] During a coal miners' strike in 1900, he set the precedent of government-sponsored negotiations, a course he appears to have been eager to follow during the 1904 oil workers' strike as well. In Galicia, the imperial government had even acquired the reputation for being something of a socialists' watchdog, demanding explanations from Lviv when socialists were unfairly arrested or denied permits for gatherings.

Ignoring Potocki's clear sympathy for the employers, his provincial and local subordinates did everything within their power to prevent the strike and then bring it to a peaceful and prompt resolution. Not relying on the skills of the local chief district magistrate, the day after the strike began, the viceroy's office in Lviv dispatched a viceregal councilor, Piwocki, to Borysław to oversee negotiations personally, coordinate government action, and report regularly on the local situation back to Lviv, as well as to Potocki in Karlsbad. In the first three days of the strike, over fifty telegrams were sent back and forth between the viceregal presidium, Chief District Magistrate Bobrzyński, Viceregal Councilor Piwocki, Viceroy Potocki, Minister of the Interior Koerber, the provincial gendarmerie headquarters in Lviv, and the Tenth Corps Commando in Przemyśl.[61] In contrast to the flurried actions of the various government authorities, the employers remained steady in their refusal to discuss the workers' terms. Instead, they published emotional pleas for sympathy in *Słowo Polskie* and distributed polemical literature in which they insisted that "this is not the normal battle of labor against capital, this is a continuation of the centuries-old battle of good against evil."[62]

Despite tremendous pressure from the Ministry of the Interior, Piwocki was unable to sway the employers. Twelve days after the strike began, he had already given up hope and begged to be allowed to return to Lviv. In his opinion, any further attempts to reach an agreement were futile, given the companies' intransigence, and his continuing presence was an unnecessary punishment: "It would be a waste of my time and health to wait here until work is resumed," he lamented in one of numerous requests to be relieved of his onerous duty.[63] The workers, he explained, were ready to come back to work, "forced by hunger and poverty," if only some resolution protecting them from more radical elements could be reached. Piwocki had his own theory on the cause of the employers' inflexibility, and it had little to do with the noble motives they professed. The cause of their intransigence, he explained,

> must be sought . . . in the hyperproduction of crude oil and the enormous multiplication of small companies, [which are] inconvenient for a few large companies. These large companies cannot, despite the control of large capital, buy out the small companies, and strive for their elimination by other means, and the current strike offers them the opportunity to do so. I do not contend that these companies started the strike intentionally. . . . That said, they use the work stoppage for their own purposes, and for that reason reaching an agreement remains simply impossible.[64]

The large—and principally foreign—companies, he continued, were happy to see a work stoppage drive prices up by limiting production, since they all had huge oil reserves. He predicted that they would only try to negotiate when they had sold their oil reserves and wanted to continue drilling. He expected the small companies, on the other hand, to go under before the strike was finished and to be forced to sell their mines at the lowest imaginable prices. Piwocki reported that the general director of the Anglo-Galician Company, Julius Priester, had confirmed that this was indeed the strategy of the larger companies. Piwocki suggested that the large companies' ultimate goal was to provoke an amendment of the oil laws along the lines of the recently passed changes in the wax industry, which had introduced regulations that all but mandated the shutting down of small companies. Piwocki claimed that after only eight days on strike, the workers were already running out of food and money and could no longer support themselves. "Worker apathy and discouragement regarding the strike are increasingly widespread," he wrote, concluding that any overtures from the employers would be greeted enthusiastically. He predicted that eventually the workers would simply agree to resume work without having reached an agreement— assuming that the employers were unable to find enough strikebreakers first.[65]

The companies' unwillingness to negotiate should not imply that they were indifferent to the course of the strike or relaxed throughout its duration. As Piwocki himself made clear, there was no threat to the large companies as long as their oil stocks and equipment were protected. But they were powerless to protect their expensive equipment, pipelines, turbines, engines, and reservoirs from thousands of angry workers (who knew as well as they did that this valuable property was the producers' Achilles' heel). From the employers' perspective, the most important task was to continue to pump the crude oil into cisterns to prevent it from flowing out of the wells and creating a fire hazard. This could only be accomplished with military assistance.[66]

The strike leaders made it clear from the outset that their principal targets would be technical installations and oil reservoirs (the secondary target would be scabs recruited to maintain basic daily operations). They immediately attacked telegraph lines and destroyed operating pumps, which meant that oil ran into local streams, increasing the risk of widespread fires. To maintain order (and protect property), the employers immediately turned to the Austrian government for support; their requests for protection, echoed by Bobrzyński and Piwocki, went to provincial authorities in Lviv, military authorities in Przemyśl, and imperial authorities in Vienna. The Ministry of the Interior was bombarded by direct petitions from the employers in Borysław with urgent pleas for assistance that combined references to every kind of danger oil could pose—to human life, to the environment, to property: "situation most serious, 1,600 soldiers absolutely necessary, lives threatened, pumping of crude oil prevented with violence, all streams flowing with petroleum, request most urgently intervention from minister of the interior." In addition, the Interior Ministry heard from diplomats representing foreign company interests and even insurance companies that threatened to cancel fire insurance coverage because of the increased danger. On behalf of the employers, Bobrzyński requested that four companies of infantry and one company of cavalry be sent immediately to protect the large terrain, adding that the employers promised to cover any costs of the troops' dispatch, including the costs of special trains. However reluctant they were to meet the workers' demands, the employers would spare no expense to protect their equipment and stores of oil from potential arsonists. The employers' thirst for military presence was insatiable: even after three companies of infantry had arrived, Piwocki insisted that three more companies of infantry, along with some cavalry, were necessary.[67]

The employers' protests that local authorities gave their plight too little attention were unfair. The truth was that the incredibly large areas to be protected—the village of Borysław alone covered an area approximately eight times as large as the Vatican—combined with the challenges posed by a terrain pitted by holes in the ground, crisscrossed by wire fences, and littered with other obstacles to equestrian travel, made the region particularly difficult to defend and the implementation of cavalry impractical.[68] Within a few days of the strike's outbreak, the military presence in Borysław had become quite impressive and included two generals with regimental staff, seven battalions of infantry, and one platoon of pioneers. On the basis of the average size of battalions in the Austro-Hungarian army, this would mean that approximately seven thousand soldiers were stationed in Borysław to watch over approximately eight thousand striking workers.

The task facing those soldiers upon arrival was unenviable. Twenty-two children were arrested for attacking the mines of Dr. Stephan Freund's petroleum company; "mobs of women" damaged pumping equipment and could not be removed despite the attempts of three-quarters of a company to stop them.[69] Defending not people, but objects (pumps, pipelines, turbines) against neither enemy troops nor armed civilians, but rather women and children, was not a task in which the soldiers took any pride.[70]

Although endemic overproduction made the large companies feel financially secure in the face of an extended work stoppage, they knew that the threat of environmental catastrophe was very real. At that time (and in that place), an "environmental catastrophe" was not understood as a threat to local flora and fauna, but rather as a threat to human safety. So much crude oil had broken out of wells that there was great danger of fire. After a monthlong impasse, a band of skilled workers (along with a member of the strike committee), eager to provoke a more urgent desire to negotiate among the employers, resorted to arson.[71] Their campaign lasted for six weeks (extending beyond the official cessation of the strike) and included burning down derricks and setting drill holes ablaze, detonating handmade mines in offices and barracks and under pumps, and setting fire to oil reservoirs.[72] With oil flowing into streams, fires raging, and idle workers patrolling the streets, Borysław was safe for neither fish nor people. Arrests for violence became routine, but the crimes that provoked them reveal that more was on the workers' minds than politics. In the night of 18 July, for example, two workers were arrested—one for threatening strikebreakers, one for poaching. Another threw a makeshift bomb made of gunpowder and a rope soaked in cart grease into one of the wells of the Storage Society. Another four wax workers were arrested for beating up scabs. A stoker working for the Anglo-Galician Company was attacked, seriously injured, and robbed of a silver watch and fourteen crowns, an incident that led to five arrests.[73]

The 1904 strike proved that emotional and economic ties to village life were not the only obstacles to an effective strike. Arrests for poaching and petty theft of lunchboxes indicate that the striking workers quickly ran out of food. Unskilled workers, in particular, lived on subsistence wages and had no savings on which to draw during a period of unemployment. On 12 July, about fifteen hundred workers were forced by hunger to leave Borysław. There was little possibility of creating a sense of solidarity between unskilled workers nearing starvation and skilled workers carrying silver watches. When Galicia's most prominent socialist, Ignacy Daszyński, visited Borysław, his arrival was greeted by only a few hundred workers, although thousands were idle. The prominence of socialist leaders on the national level did not guarantee them any more leverage locally. According to Piwocki, Daszyński's influence was limited and much less weighty than was commonly believed. Piwocki was informed by an acquaintance among the employers that the latter's own workers had confided in him that local socialist agitators Wohlfeld and Górski did not take Daszyński's advice, but on the contrary resisted his wishes. It appeared that the behavior of the workers was even embarrassing to Daszyński, who had argued in his 12 July speech that the leaders of the country had provided so much military force that workers could not be successful in a fight. By that time, many of the workers seemed to share his pessimism; according to Piwocki's report, "Other workers gave restrained speeches—only one of the women gave a heated speech interspersed with phrases used by the social democrats about the exploitation of the working people, about revenge against the lords, etc."[74]

When provincial authorities closed down the workers' club Górnik, 100 workers marched in protest, only a small portion of the seven thousand to eight thousand that had initially participated in the strike. The majority of the workers, however, seemed desperate to find harmless amusement after four weeks off the job. Perhaps in an attempt to gain publicity for their cause (or perhaps out of boredom or the not uncommon desire of the troublemaker to discomfort the well-to-do), on 2 August, a portion of the striking workers set off for Truskawiec, a nearby spa town, where they marched down the promenade singing workers' songs. This, according to Potocki (himself a frequenter of spas), "gave rise to the consternation of the spa guests" and resulted in the intervention of the gendarmerie. At the same time, the employers themselves increased the level of their own propaganda, cursing the constitution behind which the so-called terrorists hid from justice and requesting the imposition of martial law: "Your Excellency! We understand the whole importance of the constitutional law that today the strikers exploit. But still even we, too, have the right to protection and defense on the part of the state. After all, we represent the country's greatest industry and form an important member of the community economically and socially." While many workers were tired, hungry, and ready to return to work, a small minority was committed to continuing at all costs. The more radical attacks, initially directed only at objects, were increasingly aimed at former colleagues: those who returned to work were beaten, pelted with stones, and doused in crude oil.[75]

Despite the increased violence, the employers' calculations seemed to pay off. As the strike wore on and the workers ran out of money and food, large employers suffered little.[76] MacGarvey's Carpathian Company, for example, produced 97,423 tons of crude oil in its fiscal year 1904–1905, made 1,622,000 crowns in net profit, and paid its shareholders a 12 percent dividend of 9,000 crowns per share. Under the protection of the military, and with the assistance of stokers imported from Hungary and Vienna, MacGarvey was able to continue pumping as necessary.[77] Piwocki reported on 14 July that "regular well work can be halted without greater damage to the interests of the entrepreneurs even for a longer period of time. Only a few smaller businesses and contract workers are worried."[78] Recognizing their precarious situation, several small Jewish producers reached agreements with their workers (both parties being equally desperate to see the strike end). The large firms did not try to stop them, since they had agreed that every individual employer had the right to take back workers under previously existing conditions as long as no concessions were granted. On 6 August 1904, the workers' assembly voted to resume work, although they had achieved nothing. Many of those who had left Borysław did not immediately return even when the strike ended, leading to a slight worker shortage. On 14 August, there were 1,891 oil workers in 191 shafts, and another 102 shafts lay idle because of lack of workers.[79]

The strike highlighted the different needs and interests of large producers and small producers and revealed that references to "employers"
as a homogeneous category are misleading. Discussions of their differing
needs demonstrated how confusing the issue of loyalty and progress could
be. Shortly after the outbreak of the strike, Piwocki correctly anticipated
the diverging interests of the various producers:

> the exploitation of terrains rich in oil in Borysław would be more ra-
> tional if it were carried out by a few powerful companies, and not as it
> is today, where along with twenty-four large companies there are also
> around seventy small ones. The only circumstance unfavorable to our
> country [Galicia] is that the most powerful companies work with foreign
> capital, while the small entrepreneurs destined to be exterminated are
> predominantly personages who are our local countrymen, who, having
> invested only a relatively small capital, have used an enterprising spirit
> and an acquaintance with local conditions to reach relative affluence.[80]

The owners of these small companies were, according to all other sources,
predominantly Jewish, although Piwocki did not specifically mention any
confession in his letter. Piwocki's comments on the motivations of the
larger companies and the drawback that this would have (forcing small
local companies to close) betrayed confusion regarding how to balance
the apparently incompatible goals of creating a more effective industry,
on the one hand, and encouraging "national" (preferably Polish and
Catholic, but at the very least Galician) investment, on the other.

Fear of the effects of overproduction on the Galician industry and fear
of the excessive influence of foreigners united the producers and the imperial government. Here their interests were shared, and the government
became the producers' best ally in both instances. The next round of
strikes revealed that providing military assistance was not the limit of the
government's support. Worker demands during strikes in 1909 and 1910
mirrored those of 1904 closely. Little had been done to improve the
workers' quality of life in the intervening five years. A law required that
employers provide living quarters for workers who lived more than five
kilometers from the wells where they worked, which did result in an
increase in worker housing. By November 1909, twenty-eight companies
had their own barracks, but housing remained insufficient in quantity
and quality. Only long-term employees were housed; day laborers were
forced either to pay most of their wages for bunks in overcrowded inns

or to sleep outside. There was still too little attention paid to providing drinking water or bathing facilities.[81] Wax workers continued to resent mandatory payments to the fraternal associations, particularly those made on behalf of their spouses.[82] This time around, however, the government's intervention successfully averted a protracted work stoppage. In December 1910, the employers demanded from the government a series of measures designed to alleviate the overproduction crisis. Producers had finally found the new consumers they needed, not in France or Germany, but in Vienna. Among their specific demands, the most important was that the government purchase 1,500,000 tons of crude oil for the fueling of engines.[83] If the government acquiesced, the employers would introduce the eight-hour day within five months from the signing of a government contract.[84]

In 1910, the government assisted the workers indirectly by assisting the producers directly. Producers resented having to turn to the central government for assistance, but not enough to refuse it. MacGarvey's testimony at the 1910 oil crisis conference betrayed a sense of shame in the producers' obligation to the government: "If we had developed this industry with our own money and our own good drillers and good workers—and my experience tells me that there are none better anywhere in the world—then we would not have to turn to the government for assistance, because [the industry] would have developed naturally and such desolate conditions would not have arisen."[85] Having failed to develop the necessary infrastructure themselves, the producers were forced to admit that they had become dependent on the imperial government. Once they recognized the need for government support, producers turned their attention to acquiring it. Boasts of natural bounty were added to warnings of environmental calamity in appeals to Vienna to promote the industry. An article in the newspaper organ of the GLPV asserted that "it would be an economic crime, were we to . . . sacrifice the natural development of an industry that draws its right to exist from a bountifully available, valuable natural product."[86] The producers' own references to the Galician environment and the place of oil within it amounted to little more than economic justifications for aid to the oil industry. Nature had provided this natural wealth; it would be a sin for men to waste it—or even to fail to make use of it for their own maximum benefit.

Economic arguments did not always base themselves on calls to exploit fully the raw materials provided by nature. The economic development of Galicia was inarguably a matter of extreme importance for all of the province's residents, regardless of its source. Moreover, because Galicia was the empire's largest province and its only source of petroleum, Galician problems were Austrian problems as well. The producers called on the government to support

> the strengthening and further development of Galician petroleum production, which is forced to cover an annual demand of engines, pipes, drilling tools, and fuel worth approximately 10,160,000 crowns, employs 60,000 people, pays nearly 50 million crowns in direct and indirect taxes, contributes outstandingly to the income of the State Railways, keeps the machine factories and chemical industries of the industrial provinces busy, and is an eminent consumer of iron and therefore a source of wealth that promotes industry.

This was clearly, so argued the producers, in the government's own interest "not only from a purely economic point of view, which requires the development of all branches of industry, in particular those that have their natural basis in the wealth of the land, but also from a purely fiscal point of view. . . . We strive therefore not only in the interest of the province, so that the only industry that it possesses might bring it prosperous progress, but also in the interest of the entire state."[87] It is not surprising that Galician producers would attempt to portray their own plight as one that affected the entire empire. But would the central government agree that there was truth to their claims?

There were voices in Vienna that supported state-sponsored development of infrastructure, whatever the fiscal cost. Ernest von Koerber, prime minister from January 1900 to 1905, advocated economic development on the periphery of the empire as the only effective means of keeping it together. Through state promotion of development, Koerber hoped to rescue Parliament from the crisis into which it had been thrown by (primarily Czech) obstructionism. Although it was thus designed with political rather than purely economic motives in mind, according to Alexander Gerschenkron, Koerber's program for economic development had the potential to resuscitate the ailing empire. Koerber's main goal, Gerschenkron asserts, "was to engineer a radical shift in political emphasis away from the highly divisive nationality problem and toward a common concern that would unite, coalesce, and integrate all the nationalities of Cisleithania. That 'concern' was to be the economic interests."[88] The means that Koerber chose to promote the regional economies (and the national economy) was the expansion of the railway network (in particular, connecting Galicia directly to the Hungarian plains via the Carpathian Mountains and building a second route to Trieste, the empire's major port), as well as the construction of new inland waterways and the regulation of navigable rivers.

On Koerber's initiative, two investment bills, one relating to railways and the other to inland waterways, were passed by Parliament on 1 June 1901.[89] Both met with the enthusiastic approval of Galicia's oil producers, who viewed the high expense of delivering their product to markets outside of Galicia as one of the main obstacles to the further development of their industry. "Only waterways are suitable to enable a cheapening of transportation and an expansion of the market. . . . A transport system that is fair and serves the large interest groups of the empire can only be created through the simultaneous tapping of the—until now neglected— natural wealth of the land in the largest crownland of the Empire via a great traffic route, which connects the Russian border in the east and north . . . with the west." Galicia's producers eagerly awaited the canalization of both the Dniestr and the Vistula and at the same time the regulation of the Stryj, San, and Wisłoka rivers (which ran through the heart of oil country).[90]

Railroads had the potential to serve Galicia's producers as more than merely a means of exporting their product. Railroads could also become a main consumer of oil at a time when augmenting consumption was critical. In August 1908, the minister of railways, Juliusz Derschatta, traveled to Galicia to meet with producers and agree on a plan that would alleviate their overproduction crisis while it benefited the Austrian railway system. Derschatta offered to use oil (rather than coal) to power locomotives on all the public lines of the Austrian state railway in Galicia. At his instigation, the producers formed a syndicate, the Provincial Association of Crude Oil Producers (Landesverband der Rohöl-Produzenten, LVRP), whose members represented 80 percent of total Galician production. The LVRP quickly entered into a contract with the government. Since the production of fuel oil required the removal of gasoline, the government offered to set up a gasoline-removal refinery in Drohobycz, which it would lease to the LVRP. The LVRP promised to provide the government with 1,065,000 tons of fuel oil between 1 November 1909 and 31 December 1914, which the government promised to buy for 2.84

crowns per 100 kilograms.[91] The construction of the refinery was itself a major project. According to Viceroy Michał Bobrzyński, it was one of the "largest and most intensive constructions ever carried out in Galicia" and employed ten thousand workers, for whom special barracks and kitchens also had to be erected.[92] In order to provide and transport the necessary supplies of wood and iron to the site, a special road and railway track, as well as a water pipeline, were built. Thirty-six reservoirs were constructed by the summer of 1909, and the refinery was completed by April 1910, an oil pipeline by the end of 1910, and buildings for the residence of administrators and guards by 1911.[93] The viceroy's office, which oversaw the project, reported to the Ministry of Public Works that it had spent over 6.2 million crowns on the construction of reservoirs, roads leading to them, fire-safe stairways, warm rooms for workers, fences, gates, pipelines, guard buildings, insulation and roofing, and other infrastructure by 29 March 1911. These preliminary costs did not include the planned gardens flanking the administrative buildings, bathing houses, worker apartments, and reparations to a forester whose property was partially obstructed by the government installations.[94] Preparations and construction involved the Ministries of Commerce, Finance, Railways, Public Works, and Agriculture. Bobrzyński held the project up as a model of public work at its best.[95]

Even with the government's promise of assistance, the producers felt unable to sustain their business operations as production continued to rise, reaching its all-time peak in 1909. Always lurking in the shadows, Standard Oil saw its opportunity to gain a foothold in Galicia. Standard offered to subsidize the construction of large reservoirs, but in exchange demanded the option to purchase crude oil from local producers at a reduced price. By guaranteeing its own refinery control over Galician crude oil supply, Standard would have been able to block competing refineries from purchasing Galician crude unless they were willing to buy from Standard.[96] The Austrian government was horrified at the prospect of a Standard Oil monopoly in Galicia. To nip any emerging relationship between Standard and Galician producers in the bud, the Ministry of Finance recommended discussions with Galician producers, which led to a new agreement, revised in the producers' favor. Instead of providing the government with 1,065,000 tons of fuel oil, the LVRP was to provide it with 1,500,000 tons of crude oil, which the government would purify itself, taking over the gasoline-removing refinery it had previously leased to the LVRP. At the same time, the Ministry of Commerce introduced a new requirement that concessions be acquired to store oil or to transport it via pipelines (with the understanding that certain companies—in other words, those affiliated with Standard Oil—would find these concessions difficult to receive).[97] The government further granted itself eight million crowns to finance the construction of necessary reservoirs, pipelines, pump stations, and oil-catching devices in waterways.[98]

So eager was the government to get started on this project that it began construction even before parliamentary approval had been obtained.[99] Revealing that it had more in mind than lending a helping hand to Galician producers, the Ministry of Railways took secret steps to set freight prices such that they would be disadvantageous to Standard.[100] This move naturally aroused the fury of Standard and American diplomats in Vienna.[101] Nevertheless, it was successful both in preventing the producers from working with Standard and also in increasing prices. Prices, which had sunk to 0.80 crowns per 100 kilograms in early 1909 and recovered only to 1.20 crowns per 100 kilograms in June 1909 (before the second government action) now quickly rose to 3.50 crowns per 100 kilograms.[102]

Fear of Standard Oil was nothing new, nor was it restricted to the Austro-Hungarian Empire. Over several years, Standard had been able to seize control of large portions of the European oil industry. By the 1890s, Standard oversaw a network of European affiliates in Great Britain, Denmark, Italy, Belgium, and Holland, and by 1907 it had expanded its control to fifty-five enterprises outside of the United States, with a capitalization of approximately thirty-seven million dollars.[103] Suspicion of Standard was so exaggerated that during the 1904 oil workers' strike, Piwocki felt obligated to discount widely circulating rumors (published in *Słowo Polskie*) that Standard was financing the work stoppage.[104] The belief that independent Galician producers were a perpetual annoyance to Standard in its attempts to maximize profits in Germany was widespread and was even reflected in articles in the *New York Times*.[105] The *Hamburger Fremdenblatt* published an article in September 1909 that warned of the nasty behavior of Standard, which had driven smaller competitors in Germany out of business after doing the same thing in the United States. The outlook for independent European oil industries was not optimistic:

Attempts to escape the clutches of the Trust by promoting the Russian, Romanian, and Galician petroleum industry have met so far with little success. After protracted—and for the Russians and Romanians nearly deadly—battles, the latter reached an agreement with Standard that ultimately amounts to nothing less than their subjugation to the will of their powerful opponent. There remains only the Galician oil industry. From there we have now received confirmations of the happy news that the Galician crude oil producers . . . together with the Austro-Hungarian government, have stood up to the invasion of American petroleum.[106]

Articles such as this circulated throughout the various Austrian government ministries. Ludwig Neuwirth, the director of the Viennese great bank, the Österreichische Credit-Anstalt für Industrie und Gewerbe, blamed Standard's attempts to destroy its Austrian competition for the drop in prices and the failure to maintain an effective cartel. He speculated that the activities of the Vacuum Oil Company (a subsidiary of Standard that built a large refinery in Galicia in 1905) might have done as much damage to the industry as overproduction itself.[107]

Not only was Standard accused of trying to seize control over the Galician oil industry, it was also blamed for preventing poor Galician producers and refiners from finding any foreign markets—a serious problem for an industry plagued by overproduction.[108] Some of Standard's wrath was admittedly brought on the Austrian industry by that industry's own doings. In an attempt to find markets for annual overproduction averaging about 700,000 to 750,000 tons, Galician producers first turned to Germany. While Austrian exports to Germany dwarfed those of both Romania and Russia in 1908–1909, they were in turn dwarfed by U.S. exports to Germany.[109] In their desperate (and failed) attempt to secure a foothold in the French market, Austro-Hungarian refiners were willing to sell at a loss, with French prices less than one-sixth of their domestic prices for the same products. Ultimately they were unable to sustain this campaign.[110] Standard perceived this as a challenge to its hegemony and in retaliation had built a refinery in Limanowa with the sole purpose, according to MacGarvey, of destroying its Austro-Hungarian competitors.[111]

Standard's activities were carefully monitored. Viceroy Bobrzyński sent an enciphered telegram to the minister for public works in 1910 relaying the chief district magistrate of Drohobycz's report that three English companies had acquired thirty-four oil wells and all the private pipelines connected to them over the past four weeks. Try as he might, he was not able to discern "whether or not these purchases were not actually made on behalf of the American Standard Oil company."[112] Perhaps this constant fear of Standard Oil exacerbated the government's suspicion of foreign investment in general. As the diplomatic situation in Europe grew more tense in the first decade of the twentieth century, the government echoed Galician patriots' concern about the excessive presence (and influence) of foreigners in the oil industry. In 1901, there were fifteen joint-stock companies (of foreign and domestic origins) in the oil production and refinery industries registered in Austria, with a total share capital of 45.1 million Austrian crowns. In addition to these, there were at least sixteen foreign companies operating in Galicia without being incorporated in the Austrian Empire.[113] By 1914, the number of large foreign joint-stock companies investing in Galician oil production had grown dramatically. There were eight English companies with a total registered capital value of £4.7 million, four German companies with a total registered capital value of 44 million Austrian crowns, one American company (Vacuum) with a total registered capital value of $20 million, and nine French and Belgian companies with a total registered capital value of 60 million francs and 12 million Austrian crowns, in addition to eight Austrian companies with a total registered capital value of 90.4 million Austrian crowns.[114]

These foreign companies operated on a scale that few domestic companies could hope to match. Since its foundation in 1910, for example, the British concern Premier Oil and Pipeline Company had grown to monstrous size, swallowing numerous competitors large and small.[115] By the beginning of the war, Premier Oil was the most important foreign company in Galicia, with a nominal capital of £3,450,000.[116] It owned 2,752 acres outright, leased an additional 7,000 acres, and had exploitation rights for 8,000 acres more. It also controlled various oil properties through its subsidiaries, Central Carpathian Oil, Alpha Petroleum Company, and Rypne Syndicate, as well as diverse pipelines and refineries. During the fiscal year 1912–1913, the company produced over 262,000 tons of crude oil, almost a quarter of all Galician production, transported 678,000 tons of oil in its own pipelines, and treated 141,000 tons of crude oil in its own refineries.[117] By the war's end, its capital grew to £3,750,000, and its holdings encompassed twelve Austrian subsidiaries, 21,000 acres,

OVERPRODUCTION
— PRICE COLLAPSE
— POLLUTION

(167)

*took crisis ,
took steps
to precipitate
soviet-backed
infrastruct.
projects
railways
waterways
oil equip.*

110 oil wells, and four large refineries.[118] Stefan Bartoszewicz claimed that although Premier's nominal capital was 38,960,000 crowns, its real capital was around £4 million, or 100 million crowns.[119]

Controlled by larger groups like the Credit Anstalt (of Vienna), Premier Oil (of London), the Deutsche Bank, Deutsche Erdöl, and Standard, these large organizations struck the government as suspiciously powerful. In Russia, Minister of Finance Sergei Witte pushed through foreign investment, in particular that of the French and British, to benefit industry even when landowners opposed it.[120] In contrast, the Austrian government seemed to share the disquiet of those who cursed foreign money and foreign influence in the exploitation of a natural treasure, a disquiet that only grew as the fear of imminent European conflict increased.

environ- degradat. was a concern not for flora + fauna but mainly nearby human populations

The turn of the twentieth century was a tumultuous period for Galicia's oil industry. Convinced that the key to Galicia's prosperity was economic growth, oil producers built up a visible lobby to represent their interests in Vienna. Producers were able to direct considerable attention to what came to be known as the "crisis in the oil industry"—a crisis caused not by dwindling supply, but by an overabundance of oil. By persuasively connecting their own profits to the greater economic health of the province and thus of the empire, producers were able to solicit support from the government in saving their industry from the devastation they claimed threatened it. Together, producers and government officials guaranteed a new supply of consumers, private and public, whose increased demand would alleviate price collapse. The government provided the producers with the military assistance they needed to avoid making major concessions to an increasingly vocal and dissatisfied workforce. As long as the industry's problems remained the same—disgruntled workers, uncontrollable production, and unstable prices—the steps taken by the government and the producers to alleviate the crisis remained effective. Neither the producers nor the government that offered to rescue them were prepared for what the next few years would bring—a sudden and unexpected decrease in production and a devastating war.

helped integrate Gal. into imperial gov & its pursuits

152: fire tourism

p. 142, main argument
143, 145

Galicia - 95 companies in 1898; 310 in 1909

p. 148 - blind focus on profits; too much small + foreign investment

p. 150 - insufficient infrastructure to hold reserves
↳ attempts to remedy this "scarred the landscape" with earthen reservoirs

FIRES

p. 153 - extensive damage to environment (rivers)
p. 160 - strikers attacked infrast. → threat to life environ, & property

— 6 —

Blood of the Earth

The Crisis of War

The problem of petroleum supply was not universally recognized in 1914, but it would become one of the great lessons of the First World War—a war that taught the director of France's Comité Général du Pétrole that oil, "the blood of the earth," was also "the blood of victory."[1] In retrospect, it is clear that the great difference in fuel supply between the Entente and the Central Powers was one of the former's fundamental advantages. Everyone needed oil. Writing shortly before the outbreak of the Second World War, geologist and jurist Ferdinand Friedensburg argued that "conducting the war over an extended period without gasoline for automobiles and airplanes, without oil for lighting in dugouts and on the homeland's flat soil, without diesel oil for submarines, and without lubricating oil for the innumerable machines in industry and transportation would have been unthinkable."[2] Toward the end of the war, Georges Clemenceau claimed that a drop of oil was worth a drop of soldier's blood, but at its outbreak, he dismissed oil's significance with the (apocryphal) remark "When I want some oil, I'll find it at my grocer's."[3] As shortsighted as his attitude appears today, it was all too common among political leaders ill prepared to provide their military colleagues with the materiel they would need in the event of an extended conflict.

Austria-Hungary entered the war in a position to cover its own petroleum needs with production on its own soil. Despite greater production sums in Romania, during the war itself, the oilfields of Galicia provided approximately 60 percent of the Central Powers' petroleum supply.[4] What should have been an advantage to Austria-Hungary's war effort, however, was also a disadvantage in its preparations. The fact that Galicia was a constituent part of the empire and that its oil fields were "domestic"

173

[handwritten marginalia: "— trouble retrieving oil"]

[handwritten marginalia: "Galicia was remote from naval bases on the Adriatic"]

masked the fact that they were also terribly remote from those places in which oil would be most desperately needed during a conflict: the industrial centers of Bohemia and Lower Austria (including Vienna) and, even more important, the naval bases on the Adriatic. Austrian consumers had become confident that oil would always be available in Galicia should it be worth the trouble to retrieve it, without taking any steps to significantly reduce how much trouble retrieving it would be. In the years before the First World War, political, industrial, and military leaders alike were well aware of the problem of too much oil—the producers' desperate attempts to find consumers and prevent price collapse were well known. Overproduction had inspired a relatively early conversion to petroleum use in the empire, enabling oil to compete with coal in industry, the railroads, and the navy. The problem of too little oil, on the other hand, garnered little attention.

The crisis in the oil industry and concomitant low prices had won new consumers and encouraged those who otherwise might not have done so to consider conversion to a source of fuel that appeared to be practically free in the worst years of price collapse.[5] Much had been done to improve the appeal of petroleum for industrial heating and firing in the period of rock-bottom prices that made coal look like a luxury in comparison. Comparisons of the "calorific value" of coal and oil (i.e., how much heat or power could be generated per unit) suggested that oil and coal were equally cost-effective when oil cost 3.40 crowns per 100 kilograms.[6] If the oil price rose above that level, coal was more cost-effective; below it, oil was preferable. When the price of crude oil fell to 0.80 crowns per 100 kilograms in 1909, producers were delighted to find a new market for oil among the growing number of devotees of internal combustion engines, especially given that the market for kerosene had flattened. It is perhaps indicative of how far behind the United States the Austrian Empire was in terms of industrial use of petroleum that the GLPV could proudly predict (rather than report) in 1901 that the use of petroleum for fuel would one day surpass that of kerosene. With their eyes to the west, oil producers intended to speed up the transition to an industry fueled by cheap, plentiful petroleum and "considered it [their] task to supply the engine rooms with this surplus of oil."[7]

An entire industrial branch soon developed based on providing new-style engines to factories interested in switching from coal to petroleum fuel. The Mödling Boiler Factory argued that oil was far superior in per-

[handwritten marginalia: "much investment in oil use for consumers"]

formance and price to coal and deserved to be called "the most ideal and best fuel of our time."[8] The Leobersdorfer factory management recalled the hazards of coal dependence, pointing to the "sad example" of England, where a protracted national coal strike had brought industry to its knees in February 1912.[9] That same year, Austria's oil-powered motors represented a total of 50,000 horsepower (80,000 to 90,000 horsepower if one included Hungary), and Austria alone had eighty-two power plants providing municipal and rural electricity that were fitted with diesel motors.

Nor were industrial concerns the only ones whose interest in oil was piqued. The Galician producers' desperate search for new consumers had come at the same time that the War Ministry was trying to modernize its navy, having noticed steps taken by the English and Japanese admiralties to use oil as the fuel for warships.[10] Recognizing how valuable this new market could be for his province, Minister for Galicia Władysław Ritter von Dulęba encouraged the War Ministry's interest in a 1910 report. "The crisis in Galician production caused by the extraordinary richness of the Galician crude oil terrain (whose value not only for that province, but for the entire empire is always acknowledged) has led the imperial royal government to take steps to prevent any further waste of the crude oil treasures lying dormant under the soil." Dulęba supported his argument in favor of naval conversion with comparisons to the successful conversion of state railways from coal to fuel oil: "one of the most important steps to rehabilitating the Galician crude oil industry was the introduction of crude oil heating on the Galician state railways, which met with complete technical and economic success."[11] Similarly, he argued, it was the need for ever-increasing markets, given the bitter struggle with Standard, that had initially led the imperial Parliament to consider introducing petroleum on the ships of the Imperial and Royal Navy. It was of critical importance to the military, he continued, that the Galician oil supply did not fall into foreign hands. Here Dulęba touched on a point of weakness of the navy's fuel supply. Because domestic coal was not suited for warship use, the navy turned to Great Britain for its coal stocks. From 1897 to 1904, 98 percent of the navy's coal was purchased from British mines.[12] This reliance on foreign energy could be corrected by switching to petroleum: "it is significant, disregarding the advantages of a technical nature emphasized by experts, that crude oil is a *domestic* material, for which reason in a case of emergency the Imperial and Royal

Navy would be made independent of the need to draw fuel from abroad (Dardiff coal)." But when the navy took steps to investigate exploiting its domestic source of energy, it found that this was easier said than done.[13]

Just as low prices and concern over dependence on coal were winning new consumers, the government had taken steps to boost crude oil prices during the 1908–1909 crisis. These measures were not popular among industrialists who had stepped up to the cutting edge of fuel consumption. By 1910, domestic refiners (who refined not only Galician but also Romanian oil) represented about 500 million crowns in domestic capital, employed 18,000 to 20,000 workers, and were responsible for exports worth 60 million crowns. They argued that they, too, were punished by measures aimed at hemming Standard and were forced to work at a loss when the price of their raw material was driven up.[14] Those who had profited from the very sharp decrease in the price of oil were distressed at the prospect of rising prices buoyed by the state's large purchases (which were, after all, intended to have just that effect).[15]

The government's action was not solely responsible for the increase in prices. Just when the state refinery in Drohobycz was completed, just when the railways had been converted to fuel oil, and just when producers were eyeing their guaranteed 2.84 crowns per 100 kilograms with relief, statistics collected by the LVRP began to show that oil production was slowing. Month after month, Borysław, Tustanowice, and the basin's other villages were returning less oil. From 1909 to 1911, Galician production dropped by 58 percent.[16] Not surprisingly, at the same time, the price of crude oil steadily rose. While the government had contractually ensured itself a rate that even the producers admitted had been generous at the time, producers were easily able to sell petroleum to other purchasers for as much as 4.20 crowns per 100 kilograms in the same period.[17] The government contract, once a gesture of munificence, had become a burden, and crude oil, once cheaper than coal per calorie, was now more expensive.

From the perspective of the navy, the rise in prices caused by decreasing production was only part of the problem. The incredibly high cost of transporting the oil from where it was unearthed to where it would be burned was a greater problem still. The difficulty with this domestic supply of oil stemmed from its location. Galicia was part of the Austro-Hungarian Empire, but it could hardly have been farther away from the empire's major Adriatic seaport, Trieste, or its naval base in Pola. Prime

Minister Ernest von Koerber's ambitious plans to use government investment in infrastructure and economic development to glue together
the empire had come to naught, despite their initial enthusiastic reception. His proposed second railway route to Trieste was never constructed,
and its lack was lamented too late: only after the outbreak of war in 1914
did the strategic significance of Koerber's main railroad become clear.[18]
Nor did the proposed expansion of transportation routes out of Galicia
(the trans-Carpathian railroad and a network of navigable waterways)
ever materialize to connect Galicia directly with Austria-Hungary's industrial centers and military bases. Even in the days when the price of
the oil itself had been minimal, the cost of transporting it had been
horrendous.[19]

Under these conditions, to its immense frustration, the navy found
itself unable to win contracts with domestic refiners (outside of Trieste
and Fiume) who would agree to provide it with the necessary fuels at its
offered price. Naval Commissioner Oskar Lorenz was outraged at the
Naval Administration's inability to find an affordable source of domestic
oil. During a conference held to discuss the mineral oil industry in Austria
in 1912, he went so far as to hint that the LVRP was actually a dangerous
cartel, setting prices at unreasonable rates. "The prices [for diesel oil] are
so high that a consideration of domestic industry is not possible."[20] David
Fanto, one of Austria's most prominent refiners, explained that refineries
north of Trieste and Fiume were at a disadvantage because of the high
cost of transportation. Their cost to deliver to Pola was 3.5 crowns per
100 kilograms higher than to deliver to Oderberg.[21] His colleague, Julius
Priester, added that the freight costs from Drohobycz to Trieste for fuel
oil were as high as those for lighting oil, although the latter was still a
much more valuable product.[22]

It may therefore come as a surprise that the navy should have continued to express interest in Galician oil, especially since the conservatism
of the navy had hindered advances in the powering of its vessels in the
past.[23] Undaunted by its reputation for obsolescence, in the early twentieth century, Austria-Hungary turned its attention to building up a powerful fleet. Amid growing popular support for a strong Austrian presence
in the Mediterranean, the Austrian Navy League was founded in 1904.
Like the German Navy League upon which it was modeled, the Austrian
Navy League supported the contention, championed by the American
admiral Alfred Thayer Mahan, that only a naval power could be a great

power. In 1909, the navy proudly announced its plan to launch a new period of modernization.[24] Across Europe, naval strategists recognized that a modern navy was a petroleum-driven navy.

No country was more enthusiastic about the potential of petroleum than Great Britain. Starting with Winston Churchill's appointment as first lord of the admiralty in 1911, Great Britain's navy found itself headed by one of petroleum's most influential champions. Churchill argued that the technical advantages of oil over coal (e.g., greater speed, the more efficient employment of human labor, and the ability to refuel at sea) warranted the risks in securing a supply from foreign sources.[25] Spurred on by reports that the Germans were building ocean liners powered by oil and that the German navy had plans to experiment with internal combustion engines, Churchill sought the cooperation of the founder of Shell, Marcus Samuel. Samuel wrote to Admiral John Fisher (first sea lord from October 1904 to January 1910 and later the leader of Churchill's Royal Commission on Fuel Oil), "The development of the internal combustion engine is the greatest the world has ever seen for so surely as I write these lines it will supersede steam," an opinion Churchill himself came to share.[26] Fisher, to whom Churchill turned regularly for council,[27] wrote to Churchill, "When a cargo steamer can save 78 percent in fuel and gain 30 percent in cargo space by the adoption of internal combustion propulsion and practically get rid of stokers and engineers—it is obvious what a prodigious change is at our doors with oil!"[28] As important as gains in fuel efficiency and space were the four to five knots in increased speed that would come with a conversion to fuel oil. Fisher encouraged Churchill to "remember the recipe for jugged hare in Mrs. Glasse's Cookery Book! 'First catch your hare!' "[29] The British navy had fifty-six destroyers and seventy-four submarines that ran on petroleum even before Churchill's naval programs of 1912, 1913, and 1914 created a fleet of new petroleum-powered battleships.[30] Nor was the navy Great Britain's only military consumer of oil. Continuing investment in and expansion of a fleet of motorized vehicles enabled Great Britain to prove by the end of the First World War that reliance on railways was inferior to access to a fleet of more flexible motor vehicles.[31] Here, too, Britain took the lead. British Expeditionary Forces could take advantage of the services of 827 automobiles and 15 motorcycles at the outset of the war, but by November 1918 the British army had 56,000 trucks, 23,000 automobiles, and 34,000 motorcycles.[32]

Germany required gasoline for stationary engines, automobiles, and airplanes, as well as diesel oil for trains and ships.[33] Similarly, Austria-Hungary dramatically increased its naval dependence on oil in the last years before the war. By 1910, a dozen 110-ton coastal torpedo boats burning oil instead of coal were operational. Starting with the *Erzherzog Ferdinand Max,* all Austro-Hungarian battleships were equipped to burn oil.[34] In January 1909, the submarine station in Pola was officially opened. Several months later, in August 1909, the first Austro-Hungarian submarine, the *U4,* was put in service, proudly fueled by two petroleum motors of three hundred horsepower each.[35] By 1914, the Austro-Hungarian navy boasted six submarines, all of which required petroleum fuel or gasoline.[36] The petroleum-burning motors themselves were objects of fascination on these new boats: when the new fleet inspector visited the *U5* in October 1912, an explanation of the operation of its gasoline motor formed a prominent part of his tour.[37]

Because of the high costs of transport from Galicia, in the prewar period, the supply of fuel oil needed to run the navy was provided almost exclusively from overseas or from Romania.[38] But as Austria-Hungary's military commanders prepared for a possible European conflict, their concern about state control over industries of strategic importance grew. Just as the Ministry for Public Works preferred to have Austrian citizens control Austrian oil fields, so did the Ministry of War prefer to supply the Austro-Hungarian army and navy with Austrian oil. Despite earlier rebuttals, the Ministry of War looked with renewed interest at the oil fields of Galicia. In May 1914, the Naval Section reported to the Imperial and Royal Sea Arsenal Command in Pola that it was again considering purchasing gasoline and submarine fuel from the state refinery in Drohobycz.[39]

At the same time, the army also voiced concern over the empire's ability to secure access to oil as necessary. At the outset of the war, the army's Department 5/M demanded that "the great quantities of gasoline that the army requires in case of war must be guaranteed *within the borders of the empire*" and that depots be established throughout both halves of the empire. At the same time, it warned of the vulnerability of the Galician oil fields because of their proximity to the Russian Empire and recommended "a sufficient securing of the crude oil sources and refineries in Galicia, which find themselves in an exposed position."[40]

Some historians have argued against concentrating exclusively on the

Balkans as the fulcrum of prewar conflict and ignoring the role that Galicia played in exacerbating tensions between Austria-Hungary and Russia.[41] It was clear to both Russia and Austria-Hungary that Galicia's location would make it an important military theater in the event of a conflict between the two empires.[42] Austro-Hungarian officials, including joint finance minister Baron István Burián and Austrian prime minister Karl Count Stürgkh, recognized the strategic significance not only of Galicia's location, but also of its residents. Given that both empires shared large Polish- and Ukrainian-speaking populations, these could be—and would be—played against one another in a complicated game of preventing insurrection at home and promoting it abroad. Irredentists agitating within Galicia for an independent Poland, on the one side, and an independent Ukraine, on the other, represented a greater threat to Russia than to Austria-Hungary. If Ukrainian nationalists, free to speak and organize within the constitutional structure of Austria, were successful in separating Ukraine from the Russian Empire, Russia stood to lose 76 percent of its iron ore production, 78 percent of its coal production, and significant portions of its oil, wheat, rye, and barley production.[43] Burián, who "regarded the 'Ukrainian bogey' as far more crucial in determining Russia's attitude to the Monarchy than 'secondary' Balkan issues," sug-

Loading gasoline for war automobiles. New technologies required secure sources of oil for the military. (Reproduced by permission of the Österreichisches Staatsarchiv, Kriegsarchiv.)

gested that if Austria could guarantee an end to Polish and Ukrainian nationalism in Galicia, this might suffice to convince Russia to remain neutral in a Balkan conflict.[44]

More common within the upper echelons of the monarchy's administration, however, were plans to employ Polish and Ukrainian nationalism against their Russian rival, both before and during the war. There was no doubt in the Austrian administration's mind that Poles would be loyal to Austria over Russia in the event of a conflict between the two empires, but they were not as certain about the sentiments of the Ruthenian population. Even after the prominent Ruthenian parliamentary delegate Mykola Ritter von Vasylko assured the readers of the *Neue Freie Presse* that Ruthenians would remain loyal to Austria in the event of a Russo-Austrian war, concern that Ruthenians were vulnerable to anti-Austrian propaganda flowing out of Russia remained.

Throughout the early twentieth century, Galicia's sizeable Ruthenian population was a common target for pro-Russian propaganda. As tension between Russia and Austria-Hungary mounted in the wake of the annexation of Bosnia-Herzegovina in 1908, Austrian officials were increasingly concerned by what they feared could become widespread Russophile tendencies within the Ruthenian population. They were alarmed by "the grave security risk posed by Pan-Orthodox, Slavophile propaganda promoted by nationalist circles in Russia close to the Tsarist regime and operating amongst the Ruthene peasants of eastern Galicia."[45] Steps taken by the government to encourage Poles to grant the Ruthenians concessions in Galicia were thus not made on the basis of sympathy for the Ruthenians, but rather out of a calculated attempt to guarantee that nationalist Ukrainians would not become a fifth column working on behalf of the Russians. As Stürgkh wrote to Hungarian prime minister István Count Tisza shortly after the "Galician compromise" of January 1914, "If the situation there [in Galicia] is secure, then something has really been won for the monarchy vis-à-vis Russia and its politics."[46] From 1909 onwards, Prime Minister Stürgkh became an enthusiastic advocate of a Ukrainian university, increased subsidies for cultural and educational institutions such as the Shevchenko Society, and a reform of the curial Galician electoral system.[47] Constitutional guarantees and electoral privileges did not go unnoticed by the Russian government; Russian officials suspected that Austria not only tolerated but even encouraged nationalist agitation in Galicia at Russian expense.[48]

When the war broke out, conquering eastern Galicia became one of

Russia's primary war aims. Only control over that territory would enable it to eliminate the Ukrainian nationalism it had so fervently opposed within its own borders in what threatened to become a Ukrainian Piedmont next door.[49] Likewise, Austria encouraged its Ruthenian subjects to spread news of the pleasures and freedoms of constitutional rule among Ukrainians on the eastern side of the international border. In August 1914, the Austrians were faced with the demands of Ukrainian nationalists for autonomy within the empire. The only way to retain the support of Ukrainian nationalists would be to promise them some sort of autonomy once the war was won—a concession that would only be able to overcome Polish resistance if it were combined with a promise for an enlarged Polish province to include Congress Poland and western Galicia after a defeat of Russia.[50] Thus, within a month of the war's outbreak, Galicia and its reorganization had become central to the planning of imperial authorities who recognized the need to secure the continued loyalty of a population they had too often neglected. The division of Galicia along nationalist lines, enabling the creation of an expanded Polish national political unit, as well as a Ukrainian national political unit, became a wartime strategy designed to strengthen domestic support in Austria and, in turn, weaken it in Russia. All of these plans were based on the idea that the Central Powers would be able—with the help of the Poles—to wrest control of Congress Poland away from Russia. They would all come to naught if Russia were able instead to gain control of Galicia for itself.

Galicia's proximity to Russia made it and its oil supply particularly vulnerable to invasion. This, combined with transportation difficulties exacerbated by the outbreak of the First World War, only made Galicia seem more distant from oil's prime markets than ever before. In July 1914, during the last hours of peace, the Ministry for Public Works, which was in charge of the Imperial Royal Mineral Oil Factory in Drohobycz, suggested that in times of "deteriorating political relations"—and certainly July 1914 qualified as such—the state refinery could send fuel oil to the Adriatic via rail. Once again negotiations foundered on transportation difficulties and the Naval Department of the Ministry of War's confidence that the fuel oil needs of the navy were easily covered by current stocks.[51] According to the Sea Arsenal Headquarters in Pola, gasoline and diesel oil were cheaper from Drohobycz than from Trieste or Fiume even given high transportation costs. The problem was not primarily the cost, but rather the logistical difficulty caused by the distance.[52]

In addition, since the Ministry of War was required to purchase the same amount of refined petroleum products from Hungarian as from Austrian sources, and since the Hungarians' oil was provided in free tanks, Hungarian sources were more attractive than those in Galicia.[53] Thus the Ministry of War entered the war with the Trieste and Fiume refineries as its only prearranged sources for refined oil products, although large portions of the crude on which they were dependent came from neutral Romania.

The decision not to build a second railway line from the northern part of the empire to Trieste and the decision not to collect stocks of oil near naval bases both point to the general conviction among Austria-Hungary's war planners (as well as those of all the other belligerents) that the war would be short, a mistake that historians have long acknowledged to have been very costly.[54] This error had devastating consequences in the empire's fuel preparedness. According to one historian, "The most important prerequisite for the maintenance of the k.u.k. Navy's ability to act proved to be its sufficient supply with engine fuel. . . . The need for these materials—because of numerous new assignments which were given to the navy—increased to an unanticipated degree compared to peacetime demand. Since no one had anticipated a longer duration for the war, the stored supplies of these fuels were insufficient for longer-lasting fleet operations from the very beginning."[55]

Before the war, the annual oil consumption of the Austro-Hungarian navy was approximately 16,000 to 20,000 tons.[56] The navy had stocks of fuel and gas oil that, combined, amounted to 32,000 tons, but only 200 tons of the gasoline required by submarines and airplanes.[57] It therefore could have reasonably assumed that, at the current rate of use, its fuel and gas oil stocks would last for two years, much longer than anyone expected a war to last. So, although the naval command anticipated that war would break out, that Italy would enter the conflict on the other side, and that, in the event of war, its fuel supply needs would increase, none of this caused too much distress.[58] This same lack of concern was manifested in the provisioning of the naval port at Pola. Not only were no steps taken to ensure sufficient stocks of petroleum, but there was also no attention paid to constructing adequate docks or living quarters for navy personnel, lacks that were sorely felt when the war had commenced.[59]

Although it was Germany's experiments with oil that had initially started the naval fuel race, Germany's conversion never approached the thoroughness of that achieved by Great Britain, in part because of an anticipation of the difficulty of securing access to sufficient oil. Its High Seas Fleet remained primarily coal driven throughout the entire war. Although oil burners had been installed in forty-eight destroyers, even modernized ships were only partly adapted to the new fuel: if three boilers were installed on a cruiser, one would be petroleum fueled and the other two would use coal. Although Germany's navy may have recognized the strategic superiority of oil over coal, it did not have the luxury of allies with enormous domestic oil reserves. Germany and Austria-Hungary had airplanes, trucks, armored cars, and ships with oil-burning engines, but, compared with the Allies, they also had an acute shortage of fuel. Germany's annual consumption of oil before the war had been 1,250,000 tons, of which 77 percent came from the United States and 3 percent from Russia. This 80 percent would no longer be available after the outbreak of a European conflict. The remaining 20 percent, drawn from Romania and Galicia, did not seem to be enough to support a petroleum-based fleet.[60]

Austria-Hungary did its part to supply the German military with the oil it did need. Romania's ban on petroleum exports denied both Germany and Austria-Hungary access to Romanian oil until an agreement could be reached in December 1914.[61] Completely dependent on its ally for oil, Germany persuaded Austria-Hungary to supply mineral oil products at the request of the German government even after all other oil exports from the empire had been forbidden.[62] As the German navy grew desperate for oil to power its submarines, the occasional exception was contractually transformed into regular deliveries of 10,000 tons a month.[63] In order to meet its own petroleum needs and to fulfill its contractual obligations to Germany, the Austro-Hungarian Ministry of War was obliged to find a way to get oil out of Galicia and into its own storage tanks.

Shortly after the war broke out, the Austro-Hungarian Ministry of War became much more interested in Drohobycz. Already in the first week of August it purchased fuel oil for test runs of the new Danube monitors.[64] Four weeks later, on 3 September 1914, the navy requested another 700 cisterns (7,000 tons) of fuel oil for various ships and boats to be sent to Pola, at a rate of 300 to 400 tons a week. Neither the high price of 7.85 crowns per 100 kilograms (excluding transport costs) nor the requirement that purchasers provide their own tanks for delivery deterred the navy. Recognizing the need for a cost-effective supply of oil, the Ministry of Finance decided to allow tax-free preparation of fuel oil for naval use only for the duration of the war.[65] At the same time, the navy purchased gasoline for submarines at a cost of 37 crowns per 100 kilograms.[66] These short-term contracts bound the Ministry for Public Works to supply oil at unfavorable prices; news of imminent military disaster in Galicia drove prices up faster than contracts could be renegotiated.[67] The absence of qualified workers after mobilization and the onset of an economic depression only exacerbated producers' inability (and reluctance) to produce large quantities of oil; drilling activity nearly ceased altogether.[68] Crude oil prices threatened to rise indiscriminately. Offered the option to purchase 50,000 tons of crude oil from a Borysław producer eager to unload his stocks before being forced to evacuate the region, the Ministry of War considered the suggested price of 10 crowns per 100 kilograms exorbitant. It forwarded the offer to the Ministries of Commerce and Public Works, requesting that they "take the necessary steps to prevent the anticipated enormous price hikes" (without specifying what those steps would be).[69] Despite unfavorable prices, the Ministry of War had no choice but to negotiate.

By mid-September 1914, the military situation in the province had become urgent. Bad news from the Russian front forced the navy to speed up its attempts to secure several months' worth of petroleum from Galicia. "Since, given the current situation, the shipment of this fuel appears absolutely necessary, and the same is most urgently needed by the navy," the navy decided to purchase oil from any refinery willing to sell it rather than limiting itself to the Drohobycz state refinery.[70]

But it was too late to secure any significant stocks of oil from Galicia. The Russian army captured Drohobycz and Borysław on 6 September and the rest of the oil basin on 13 September.[71] For the next eight months, until the Central Powers ended the Russian occupation of the province by breaking through the Russian line at Gorlice in May 1915, Galicia's oil fields, pipelines, wells, and storage reservoirs were all under the control of the Russian army. The operation of the state refinery in Drohobycz ceased immediately.[72] Soon after the loss of the Galician oil fields, the government took steps to deal with an inevitable oil crisis. The Ministry of Railways demanded that all exports of petroleum products be prevented, that domestic demand be assessed, and that this demand be compared with the available supply. After collection of all the necessary information, measures would have to be taken to secure the systematic provision of the military, then other state organs (including the railways), and then private operations. This would only be feasible, the ministry argued, if all mineral oils were requisitioned, and it recommended setting up a state-controlled petroleum *Zentrale* (Exchange) to regulate its distribution, a step that was not taken until October 1916.[73]

The delay in setting up a central body to coordinate petroleum acquisition and distribution was mirrored by similar delays in other sectors. Centralization of mobilization in general was hindered by a fear that it would not be politically acceptable to Hungarians. This concern led to a tripartite administration of mobilization machinery. Following the German model, *Zentralen* should have been the spine of civilian war organization, but in many sectors of the Austrian economy, they were simply founded too late. Even when the Petroleum Exchange was founded, it was not permitted to take full responsibility for all petroleum procurement and distribution, but rather shared this task with the Ministry of War and other government agencies.[74] Because of this shared responsibility, the Ministry of War joked that the *Zentralen* should actually be called *Dezentralen*. But the decentralization of the centrals was no joking matter. The Petroleum Exchange failed to guarantee adequate supplies of materiel to the War Ministry and was not even able to prevent price hikes, since it did not have jurisdiction over all the oil fields in the monarchy.[75]

In the absence of centralized control over oil, the Ministry of War was forced to embark on a multifaceted plan to secure access to petroleum. Transport tanks had been sequestered by the government at the war's outset, and bans on exports of gasoline and heavy lubricating oil had been introduced in August 1914.[76] On 5 October 1914, a more extensive ban forbade all exports of any mineral oils (the only exception was exports to Germany).[77] In late November, the military administration requisitioned all stocks of refined petroleum products, restricting sales to civilians and private companies until after the needs of the military had been met. Shortages of kerosene affected all of the empire's cities, particularly in the cold winter of 1914–1915, when nights were long and prices for kerosene reached sixty-two crowns in Austria and ninety crowns in Hungary.[78] The mayor's office in Vienna took immediate notice of the end of the Russian occupation of Galicia and begged the Ministry of Public Works to make supplying Viennese civilians with petroleum a top priority.[79] In order to monitor availability of refined products, on 18 November 1914, all Austrian and Hungarian refineries were required to divulge their stocks of airplane gasoline, crude oil, diesel oil, and other refined products by 30 November.[80] Without access to Galician oil, however, none of these measures would prove sufficient for long. Although Austria-Hungary was finally able to reach an agreement with Romania that allowed for the export of Romanian oil in 1915, Austrian imports from Romania that year reached only 280 tons.[81]

When the Galician oil fields were recovered in May 1915 and the damage done by the Russian occupation was assessed, the Ministry of War breathed a sigh of relief. When the Russians marched into the province, they set off a chain reaction in which thousands of Galicians chose to leave their homes rather than endure the notoriously brutal treatment of Russian troops. The roads were flooded with refugees, seeking—but unlikely to find—food, work, and safety in Vienna or elsewhere in the monarchy. The refugees' fears were justified. The Russian occupying forces' policies stood in stark contrast to prewar attempts on the part of the Viennese administration to win friends in eastern Galicia by supporting Ukrainian cultural development. Eastern Galicia was officially considered a "Russian province restored to the fatherland" and became the site of an intensive Russification program, to which both Poles and Ruthenians were subjugated. Polish and Ruthenian schools were closed; only Russian-language teaching was tolerated.[82] The Russian forces' attacks on the Greek Catholic Church began the moment they occupied the city of Lviv on 22 August 1914. Eastern Orthodox clergy were sent in to convert Greek Catholic Ruthenians, and the metropolitan of the Greek Catholic Church, Count Andrei Sheptyts'kyi, was placed under house arrest and subsequently deported to Russia. Later, Greek Catholic priests, as well as members of the secular intelligentsia, were rounded up by Russian military forces and sent into exile. The total number of Galicians deported to Russia and Siberia reached into the tens of thousands.[83] The occupying administration tried to replace Polish and Ukrainian with Russian throughout the educational system.[84] According to one Ukrainian historian, Russian soldiers organized pogroms in both Drohobycz and Borysław within a fortnight of gaining control of the region.[85]

In a study of the problems surrounding Ukrainian subjects of the Russian Empire under German occupation, Geoff Eley has suggested that the war created a "demographic earthquake" because of its massive civilian casualties, epidemics of influenza and other diseases that prey on the vulnerable, and migrations that disrupted work patterns. Reflecting on the gravity of the damage done to Ruthenian and Polish subjects of the Austrian Empire who had to endure the Russian occupation of 1914–1915, Eley argues that the lasting effects of this occupation can be seen in the weakness of local regimes as they attempted, unsuccessfully, to create viable independent states in the aftermath of the war.[86]

During their retreat, the Russians took the opportunity to wreak considerable damage on large portions of the oil fields. Commandos of Russian soldiers burned down 229 out of 319 existing derricks (the vast majority of which were constructed of wood).[87] The Russians also destroyed all of the fire-extinguishing equipment in the region.[88] They set forty-two of seventy-nine productive wells in Tustanowice on fire, but did not touch a single well in Borysław.[89] Stranger still, they left most of the refineries and transfer sites undisturbed. The oil fields did not seem to have been prime targets of Russian aggression, and the wholesale destruction of the oil fields expected by their owners did not occur. During over eight months of occupation, the Russians did not dip substantially into local oil stocks.[90] When the Russian retreat began in May 1915, Galician storage tanks contained 830,000 tons of oil. Some of these were set aflame during the retreat, giving Austrian soldiers in the region the opportunity to shoot some of the more dramatic photographs in the Ministry of War's Picture Collection.[91] Nevertheless, after the Russians were gone, about 480,000 tons of crude oil remained to be reclaimed by their rightful owners.[92]

This should not imply that no damage was done. Because of a near-total cessation in production and the partial destruction of reservoirs by fire, Austria had access to an estimated one million tons of oil less than it would have had had Galicia not been lost.[93] Friedensburg suggested that the Russians could have inflicted far greater damages if they had systematically set about destroying the oil fields: "This effect would have been doubtless much greater—perhaps even decisive for the war effort—if the retreating Russian troops had burned all the stocks and thoroughly destroyed the installations. They certainly had the time and the technical possibility to do so, and the loss of at least another million tons would have been a major blow to the Central Powers."[94] Friedensburg could only explain the Russians' failure to make the most of this opportunity by positing a general ignorance of the strategic importance of petroleum fuel supply during the First World War.

The military went to great lengths to secure tighter control over Galicia and its oil fields now that they had been regained. With the breakthrough at Gorlice, a fair and competent governing of the province once again became a hot topic, and the Army High Command (AOK) increased pressure on the emperor to create a military administration of Galicia. The head of the Second Army, Field Marshal Eduard Böhm-Ermolli, submitted a request to the Military Chancellery to attend to the AOK's request promptly. In it, he wrote, "A spirit of order, justice, and fairness must rule in this land, in great part very rich in natural endowments, but very poor in reality. A spirit that, above all, thinks black-yellow Austrian and speaks Polish-Ruthenian, a spirit that is politically absolutely neutral and economically independent. Considering all of the above, it is my deepest conviction that only a k.u.k. general who is neither Pole nor Ruthene can be called upon to represent such a new spirit at the head of this sorely tried land."[95]

In advocating military control, the AOK hoped to prevent the return

Burning oil wells in Borysław. The War Ministry records damage done by the retreating Russian army. (Reproduced by permission of the Österreichisches Staatsarchiv, Kriegsarchiv.)

of Polish hegemony in the largely Ruthenian areas of eastern Galicia, thereby reducing alleged Russophile sentiments that the AOK feared would make Ruthenian subjects disloyal to Austria.[96] Fears of Russophile sentiments among Austria's Ruthenian subjects, though not well founded, were common among both civilian and military authorities within Austria-Hungary. On 3 August 1914, all of the political parties representing Ruthenians in the empire formed the general Ukrainian Council, which declared that "the victory of the Austrian-Hungarian monarchy will be our victory, and the greater the defeat of Russia, the sooner will come the hour of Ukrainian liberation."[97] Such protestations of loyalty notwithstanding, fear of Russophile tendencies remained high. In the hope that the military could gain control of the situation, the emperor approved the AOK's request, and on 19 July 1915, Viceroy Witold Korytowski resigned and was replaced by General Hermann von Colard—the first non-Pole to head the administration of Galicia in half a century.[98]

The introduction of military law was intended to reduce national tensions, but it also gave the military command closer control over the oil region and its products. The Ministry of War was confronted by demands for increased supplies of petroleum from all sides, military and civilian, including the Vienna Magistrate's Office, which reproached the Ministry of War for denying the civilian population kerosene all winter.[99] To meet its own fuel needs more efficiently, the government requisitioned all crude oil as soon as it reached the earth's surface in a decree dated 10 August 1915.[100] To ensure compliance, on 18 December 1915, the minister of commerce required that any companies that produced mineral oil products had to report their supply on 1 January 1916 and from then submit semimonthly reports of any growth or decrease in the same.[101] Refined petroleum products could only be bought or sold with permission from the Ministry of Agriculture or of Commerce. At the same time, price ceilings were set for all petroleum products.[102] On 31 May 1916, the Ministry of War took over the Limanowa refinery (previously controlled by a French company) and placed it under its own administration.[103]

These measures eliminated any financial incentive producers would have had to continue extracting oil, not to mention pursuing costly drilling or exploration activities. Galicia's military administrators tried to prevent production from dropping with threats of monetary fines and imprisonment for those who shut down their companies. Petroleum producers did not hesitate to point out that these measures forced them to produce at a loss. The government justified its decision:

For quite some time, due to the events of the war, the crude oil produced in the Galician oil region could not be made available for refining of the products . . . that are indispensable for the conduct of the war, the running of railways, industry, agriculture, and general consumption, so that a bitter shortage of more or less all mineral oil products set in. After driving out the enemy from this region, it was therefore a dictate of the most pressing necessity to take measures so that not only the crude oil stocks, but also ongoing crude oil production could be refined as quickly as possible and in the most efficient manner. . . . In order to reach the above goals under the extraordinary circumstances prevailing at the time, a measure had to be taken through which the crude oil, while completely safeguarding all entitled interests, was withdrawn from the free market and placed under the disposition of the state.[104]

Providing sufficient oil workers for Galician production companies was another part of the military's attempt to keep production going at a steady pace. The Ministry of War tried to support the oil industry by exempting oil workers from military duty, beginning in the first months of the war. From the start, the Ministry of War tried to balance its need for soldiers with the need for trained workers to keep the oil fields running. The army observed a labor shortage in Galicia after the outbreak of the war with care. The Ministry of War reported to the Front High Command on 12 August 1914:

In the interests of providing the army with gasoline, it appears necessary to maintain drilling operations in the oil region. Due to the calling up of the *Landsturm* [the Austrian reserve], many of the qualified workers serving there have departed, so that individual companies had to be shut down. This undesirable circumstance could be alleviated in that the *Landsturm* formations from Galicia and Bukovina would collect workers qualified for oil work and set up separate divisions in Cracow, Przemyśl, and Lviv that could then be used for the maintenance of these companies.[105]

The Imperial Royal Ministry of National Defense passed on the Ministry of Labor's report that it was possible that several companies in the oil districts in Galicia would close down. The Ministry of National Defense pointed out that "this measure would not only touch on a vital interest of the army leadership, but it is also easily possible that the fired workers would endanger the oil wells."[106] In order to prevent this disaster, the

Ministry of War suggested "laying claim to such operations for the purposes of the army administration, on the basis of the war production law, in order to keep them running."[107] The importance of protecting the oil fields justified maintaining five companies in the Borysław basin to guard them, even though these same soldiers were needed elsewhere.[108] When the Front High Command called the troops away, Department 5/M insisted that they be sent back immediately. In late August, the Ministry of Commerce itself intervened to ensure that 250 soldiers would be sent back to Borysław to support the 50 gendarmes and reservists still there.[109]

Maintaining order in the region became even more difficult when rumors of impending Russian victory began to circulate, leading to requests for more troops to guard the state refinery in Drohobycz and the oil depot: "The moral impression on the population due to the exposure of the refinery would also be significant. For this reason, an arming of workers for guard duty would be an insufficient measure, above all because of lack of people, as well as the unreliability of such a guard."[110] After the Russian occupation was over, the Ministry of War continued to receive requests for relief from military duty from workers in the oil industry, many of which were accepted.[111] In a further gesture of favor toward oil producers, the government took special care to ensure that they continued to have access to iron, an increasingly rare commodity.[112]

In December 1916, four months after Romania had declared war on Austria-Hungary, the German army was able to capture the Romanian oil fields. Hoping to secure access to vast quantities of Romanian oil, the Germans found that the British had set fire to the oil wells and refineries, destroying seventy refineries and eight hundred thousand tons of crude oil and refined products in a vindictive (and very effective) blaze. It took nearly half a year of recovery and reconstruction work before the oil fields could be made productive, and even then they returned only one-third of their 1914 production.[113] Dozens of oil workers and engineers from Borysław were sent to Romania to take part in the reconstruction efforts, a measure that met with the energetic resistance of the Ministry for Public Works, which claimed that "a withdrawal of even the smallest number of workers would lead to a disruption of operations, which in the case of productive drill holes would have the effect of a loss of crude oil production. This must be avoided at all costs in the interests of the conduct of the war."[114]

Despite demands that all workers, in particular skilled workers, be treated as vitally necessary, the government did not actually do everything in its power to provide the industry with the workers it needed. Apparently one concern overrode its fear of oil shortages: fear of enemy aliens in Galicia, even if they had been working in the oil industry for decades. As the Russians had marched ever deeper into Galicia in 1914, tens of thousands of Galicians had marched out, including many owners of oil companies and their employees. After the occupation was over, they wished to return to Galicia, assess the damage to their wells and installations, and take advantage of the immense demand for petroleum by continuing production. This required obtaining travel permission from the Ministry of War. Although innkeepers, secretaries, and office workers who had Austrian passports were quickly given approval to return to Galicia, those among Galicia's most prominent oilmen who held foreign passports were less fortunate.[115]

Jacob Perkins, for example, who had been born in Canada sometime around 1855, had come to Galicia in 1885, and had worked there for the following thirty years, was employed as the director of the Galician Petroleum Production Company. His sons, Herbert and Carl, were also employed in the oil industry and were each married to Austrian subjects. Like many of their colleagues, Perkins and his sons had fled the advancing Russian troops, traveling first to Zakopane and then moving on to Vienna in November 1914. Perkins was desperately needed back in Humniska by his employers, who wished to recommence production. Given the dire shortage of skilled oilmen in the province, his application for travel documents was supported not only by the Vienna Floridsdorf Mineral Oil Factory Company, but also by the Railway Ministry. The Ministry of Labor requested a recommendation from the District Mining Office in Jasło, which reported that Perkins—whose first name it spelled "Jakob"—was reliable and trustworthy. To demonstrate his loyalty, the Ministry for Public Works pointed out that Herbert volunteered at the Imperial and Royal Automobile Repair Workshop in Bielitz for the Red Cross. After due consideration of all of these factors, the Ministry of War denied Perkins's application because, born in Canada, he was a British subject.[116]

Perkins's son Carl fared little better. Despite the energetic petitions of the Carpathian Company, as well as the support of the Imperial Royal Provincial Mining Office in Cracow, the Ministry of War rejected his application "on principle."[117] His Austrian wife could offer him no assistance in this matter: according to Austrian law, female Austrians who married foreigners living in Austria were subsequently considered to be foreign, as were their children.[118] The Perkins family disappears from the records after the First World War, but one can assume that their attempts to endear themselves to the Austrian Ministry of War, prove their "reliability," and continue producing oil for the Austrian war effort would not have endeared them to the British or Canadian authorities in the war's aftermath.

Fear of enemy influence in Galicia extended beyond foreign citizens within the empire's borders. In 1916, any correspondence caught by the censor that contained offers to sell Galician oil terrain to foreigners was confiscated, because "it is not in the interest of the Galician oil industry that foreign capital of unknown origin should participate in it."[119] The discovery of English-language pamphlets promoting investment in Galician oil-bearing real estate that were sent from Copenhagen to Wacław Wolski in Lviv only deepened pervading insecurity. The pamphlets' conclusion caused particular alarm: "Should it come under Russian administration, however, then the value of this property will be practically limitless."[120] In 1917, the Ministry for Public Works decided that all intercepted letters containing offers to neutral foreigners to sell Galician oil fields should be confiscated and sent to the Ministry for Public Works in the original. No foreign interest in oil fields, not even from neutral parties, could be tolerated.[121]

In the last months of the war, the nationality of Austrian citizens had become as problematic as that of interested outsiders, leading to a public relations fiasco in the oil basin regarding Polish legionnaires. On 16 August 1914, the AOK had approved the creation of two Polish legions in Galicia (one western and one eastern), to be commanded by Austrian generals of Polish descent. In so doing, the AOK hoped to redirect Polish national patriotism to the empire and to "put an end to the Polish 'national independence movement.'" Led by Józef Piłsudski, champion of Polish independence, the western Legion's First Brigade was openly contemptuous of Austria and promoted Polish nationalism.[122] In August and September 1915, recruitment was briefly extended to Russian Poland. In July 1917, a proposal to subordinate the legions to the German army was rejected by Piłsudski, who was subsequently arrested by the Germans, marking the official end of sanctioned First Brigade activity. At that time, some members of the First Brigade were arrested, and others (including eight riflemen from Borysław) were labeled "politically suspect" and shipped off to the Italian front. Some made their escape, taking refuge in the oil fields of Borysław, where rumor had it that labor was scarce and papers not obligatory. Arriving there with nothing, they were provided with housing and an opportunity to earn their bread.[123]

A second wave of legionnaires came to the oil basin in February and March 1918. After a peace treaty between the Central Powers and the Ukrainian Council was signed at Brest-Litovsk in February 1918 that granted independence to a new Ukrainian state that would contain territory considered Polish by Polish irredentists, protests broke out throughout Galicia (including Borysław) among Poles who called this a "fourth partition of Poland."[124] In defiance of the treaty, General Józef Haller, formerly commander of the Second Brigade (the only surviving remnant of the ill-fated eastern legion), led the Polish Auxiliary Corps across the Austrian border and into independent Ukraine. Those legionnaires who were left on the Austrian side of the border, now representing a renegade paramilitary body, realized their vulnerability and sought to hide under cover. Józef Partyk, a legionnaire who had himself escaped from Russian imprisonment to Borysław, recalled many years later that the legionnaires found themselves welcomed with open arms by the population of the oil region. A committee for the protection of Polish soldiers was established to hide legionnaires until they could be brought away to safety; civilian clothes and papers were found for those who wished to stay in Borysław openly. Legionnaires easily found positions at the oil wells working for sympathetic employers.[125]

Haller's mutiny made Austria even more suspicious of the loyalty of all Poles, in particular the legionnaires. That many had turned to the oil fields did not escape notice. Oil companies suspected of employing legionnaires were searched for weapons; homes where legionnaires were given shelter were subjected to regular and violent inspections.[126] Finally, in what was considered a transparent attempt to forcefully remove the legionnaires from the oil basin, local military officials in Borysław ordered that all companies send their workers, whether Austrian or Polish subjects (i.e., Poles who had been recruited from former Russian Poland), who had been released, furloughed, or otherwise relieved from duty in the Polish Legion to Drohobycz on May 18. From there the Austrian subjects would be sent to Sambor and the Polish subjects to Żurawica for a so-called medical examination.[127] The legionnaires themselves had little doubt that this was a thinly veiled plan to search them, control their identification papers, and then force them into internment camps.[128] The Workers' Union, as well as the Drilling Technicians' Society, the Miners' Society, the Metal Workers' Society, and the Petroleum Officials' Society, all objected that the medical examination should take place in Borysław, adding that "the Polish subjects have acquired citizenship here, and it would be a serious injustice if they were to be removed from here to a dormitory in Żurawica."[129] On 16 May 1918, any oil workers who were Polish legionnaires and who had not reported to Drohobycz voluntarily were arrested by the Austrian authorities, outraging the local population and leading to the intervention of a Polish parliamentary delegate who argued that "this decree will call the normal course of work into question, injure national feeling, and heighten social conflicts."[130] The treatment of the legionnaires, who had evoked general sympathy among the local population, only alienated the residents of the oil basin further.[131] It was not only Poles whom the Austrians feared as disloyal. Ruthenians, long regarded as the "Tyrolians of the East" with unquestioning loyalty to the monarchy, were suspected of falling under the influence of Russian propaganda. They were deported into the inner portion of the monarchy by the thousands.[132] Many of them were held in prison camps at Thalerhof and Theresienstadt, where some were executed.[133]

The Ministry of National Defense cautioned that nationalist sentiment virtually assured that a malevolent attack on the oil companies was in the works. This claim was rejected by Johann Holobek, an expert on the local industry who had been writing reports on social and economic conditions in the Galician oil basin for decades. Nevertheless, the report he submitted in June 1918 on the conditions of the oil workers in Borysław was hardly optimistic. The economic element of local tension far outweighed the political element. He stressed the familiar distinction between professional, "skilled" oil workers and officials and the common "rabble." The former were mostly owners of small farms or properties in western Galicia, had a strongly developed self-consciousness, and were quick to resent treatment unworthy of them. They were "oriented to their fatherland and have kept themselves at a distance from serious disturbances of the peace and acts of violence, as the workers' movement of the past twenty years, the period of the real development of Galician oil mining, has proven."[134] The workers who enjoyed making trouble for trouble's sake, on the other hand, were day laborers, employed only in times of labor shortage. Holobek suggested that protests after Brest-Litovsk, considered so alarming by the Ministry of National Defense, were actually understandable. It was only natural, he argued, that the peace treaty with Ukraine, the imprisonment of Polish legionnaires who had sought sanctuary and occupation in Borysław, factory and house searches for weapons conducted by the military, and the decree that legionnaires who were Austrian citizens be separated from those who were formally Russian subjects aroused the indignation of the local population.

According to Holobek, the oil basin's biggest problem hit everyone equally, regardless of nationality. Food shortages had led to undernourishment. It was impossible to obtain clothing, linens, or shoes because of inflationary prices. There was too little bread and flour, and there had been no fat and no sausage for two months. Families received meat twice a week at five hundred grams per family, regardless of the number of family members. Potatoes were distributed only when they were available. Cornmeal and beans were given out to replace bread, but the beans were inedible. When food was available, prices were unpayable. The workers themselves demanded a pay increase, better housing, lighting and heating at no cost, and better schools for their children. In October 1918, anger about insufficient primary and secondary schooling for their children led four thousand oil workers to go on strike.[135] Although the AOK had responded to similar demands made by miners in the Moravian-Silesian industrial district by ordering a pay raise to avert the possibility of a strike, in this case, Holobek agreed with the GLPV's claim that raising wages would only lead to inflation.[136] Between July 1914 and April 1918, the cost of white flour had already risen 5,600 percent, the cost of rye bread 4,200 percent, the cost of onions 3,330 percent, the cost of men's clothing 1,430 percent, and the cost of shoes 1,700 percent.[137]

Borysław's social and economic balance, considered precarious before the war, had come undone. Once a mecca for adventurers and now a haven for deserters and persecuted Polish nationalists disguised as oil workers, Borysław was too chaotic to be a reliable source of materiel for the war effort. Occasionally there were lucky strikes; eruptive wells were proudly publicized by the Ministry of War, which distributed photographs of Borysław, "the submarines' larder," with its "fully operational oil wells."[138] Nevertheless, production in the Borysław oil basin was slowly but surely grinding to a halt. By December 1917, the number of skilled workers in Borysław had dropped to 192, 126 of whom were drillers—barely enough to keep the oil wells operating at all. By September 1918, the number had plummeted to 75. A lack of manpower, of water, and of fuel to run the various engines meant that the three hundred–odd wells that were in operation could not be run regularly. Borysław's annual production dropped to 48,380 tons in 1917.[139]

The signs that the flow of petroleum had clogged abounded all over the empire. Civilian complaints grew louder. In the 1917–1918 session of the Parliament, representatives from across the empire made dozens of complaints about shortages of petroleum.[140] Delegates petitioned on behalf of artisans in Tyrol, Styria, Moravia, and Bohemia who could no longer work after sunset, on behalf of the Czech-speaking glassmakers and weavers in the mountain villages of Bohemia (who insisted that their German-speaking neighbors had plenty of kerosene), and on behalf of farmers for whom going to collect their petroleum rations in distribution centers five to eight hours away was an impossible burden, especially since "one cannot use Russian prisoners" for the task.[141] Because of the desperate situation of the military, itself suffering drastic oil shortages, the complaints of farmers, artisans, and city dwellers fell on deaf ears.

"Borysław, the 'Submarines' Larder': The Oil Fields of Borisław with Derricks in Full Operation." The Ministry of War puts a positive spin on declining wartime production. (Reproduced by permission of the Österreichisches Staatsarchiv, Kriegsarchiv.)

In many ways, 1917 marked the beginning of the end for the Central Powers. The United States declared war on Germany in April and on Austria-Hungary in December. Despite the withdrawal of the Russians from the war as a consequence of the October Revolution, the weakness— above all in men and materiel—of the Central Powers vis-à-vis the Allies began to reveal itself. The year 1917 also marked the beginning of the military's real oil crisis. The Austro-Hungarian armed forces had never enjoyed a surplus of fuel, and their consumption had only grown over the course of the war because of an increasing reliance on oil-powered ships, submarines, planes, and motor vehicles. Stocks, on the other hand, were at an all-time low, as the Naval Section explained:

> For a long time the navy was singularly dependent on deliveries from the k.k. Mineral Oil Refinery in Drohobycz . . . and the peacetime stocks of fuel oil and gas oil, mostly of Romanian origin, have been significantly reduced during the war due to insufficient delivery. Our own monthly use comes to around 3,500 tons, compared with a delivery allotment of only 2,000 tons. The navy's stocks of gas oil, fuel oil, and tar oil at the end of 1914 were around 40,000 tons. At the end of 1915 they were around 26,000 tons, and due to significant deliveries from Romania they even grew in 1916 and reached 27,310 tons at the end of 1916, but over the course of the next year they were reduced and were in September of this year 15,189 tons, which means in the past nine months they were reduced by 12,100 tons.

In case the implications of these statistics remained unclear, the Naval Section spelled them out: "A further sinking of stocks must be prevented at all costs, in order to avoid endangering the responsiveness of the fleet, whose expenditure of fuel oil, gas oil, and tar oil in the near future will continue to grow, because of the present influx of new motor vehicles and submarines."[142]

Demand increased as production dropped and used stocks were not replenished. Contributing to the increased demand was the constant use of torpedo units for transport convoys and for patrols, as well as the growth of the number of German and Austro-Hungarian submarines based in the Adriatic Sea to over fifty units.[143] From January to November 1917, the Austro-Hungarian navy acquired thirteen new submarines, bringing the total number of imperial submarines that saw action during the war to twenty-seven.[144] The Austro-Hungarian Danube Flotilla, used to assist military operations of the army both by supporting its own operations and by obstructing those of the enemy, had acquired new oil-powered units, more than doubling its fuel-oil needs.[145] Naval air units also increased considerably over the course of the war, from sixty-four combat-ready planes in January 1915 to three hundred in May 1917.[146] By the end of 1917, these additional oil-consuming units led to an increased monthly oil consumption that exceeded 5,000 tons. Together, Galician and Romanian sources could only supply around 2,000 tons a month,[147] causing a fuel crisis. The Romanian oil fields reached only one-third of their prewar production in 1917,[148] leading the army's Division 5/M to conclude that "because of the devastation of the Romanian oil companies carried out by our enemies, the only available source of supply of mineral oil products for Austria-Hungary in the next months is Galician crude oil production." The army thus called on the navy to join with it in initiating drastic savings measures for gasoline and benzene, diesel oil, and lubricants. Gasoline-fueled engines should be replaced wherever possible by steam engines, water power, or electricity "without consideration for the cost."[149]

At the same time that the army was making this appeal, the navy had itself calculated that the present total production from Romania was 80,000 tons of crude oil, of which Romania was allowed to keep 10,000 tons. By treaty, Austria-Hungary could lay claim to one quarter of Romanian production, which meant that Austria-Hungary would get 17,500 tons of crude. This could be expected to produce 3,500 tons of diesel oil, far short of the military's monthly requirement.[150] Given the current supply and demand, stocks could be expected to last only to March 1918, at which point "all modern torpedo units and all submarines would have to be turned off and as a consequence the submarine war would have to be ended."[151] Desperate to squeeze every last drop of oil out of the available resources, the Austro-Hungarian military began to eye its monthly shipments to Germany. The Austro-Hungarian Ministry of War was well aware that the German navy was desperately in need of Austrian diesel oil for its submarines. Nevertheless, given the miserable oil situation, the justification for continuing to supply Germany with 10,000 tons of oil a month seemed weak.

Recognizing Austria-Hungary's dire situation, on 1 September 1917, Germany had agreed to return "the diesel oil used by German submarines in the Mediterranean," which would provide 800 tons in September and in the future 1,000 tons monthly.[152] That represented only one-tenth of the amount of oil that Austria-Hungary was still obliged to provide Germany every month. The Austro-Hungarian navy soon concluded that it would be able to avoid running out of oil completely before the war's end only by introducing drastic savings measures, which proved unpopular domestically.[153]

Even more problematic from a political and diplomatic perspective, but equally necessary, was its decision to demand a complete refund of the monthly amount of oil it had been providing to German navy units stationed in the Adriatic.[154] The Naval Section wrote to the naval attaché of the German embassy in Vienna, Commander Albrecht Freiherr von Freyberg, in an attempt to explain its inability to continue to honor its contract:

> According to the existing agreement, 10,000 tons of naval oil are to be delivered monthly to Germany from the production of the Austro-Hungarian mineral oil refineries. With the exception of the modest needs of the Danube fleet . . . the Imperial and Royal Navy is completely dependent on domestic production. This must cover the total needs of the monarchy, that is, also the absolutely indispensable needs of private industry—companies working for the army, agriculture, etc., which have already been drastically reduced. Altogether the Imperial and Royal Navy can claim 1,600 tons of gas oil. These amounts and the delivery of 400 tons of tar oil monthly—more cannot be brought in—that is, 2,000 tons of gas oil and tar oil together—cover hardly one-half of the demand, as 3,500–4,000 tons are used.

Since the navy had been reduced to receiving 1,000 tons from Drohobycz a month, it had been forced to deplete its stocks, which were now dangerously low. "We have not demanded it before, in consideration of the necessity of supplying our ally Germany sufficiently and to the furthest extent possible with gas oil, in order to carry out the *U-boot* war. Even so, in order to secure our own quick responsiveness, an agreement to provide the Imperial and Royal Navy with sufficient gas oil must be reached between the two navies."[155] The Naval Section concluded that the imperial and royal navy could afford to deliver only 2,000 tons of oil to Germany a month, leaving 4,000 tons of gas oil, naval oil, and tar oil for the Austro–Hungarian navy itself.[156] Germany rejected this request.[157]

The anticipated crisis came before March 1918 (the date the k.u.k. Fleet Commando had predicted that it would run out of oil). On 22 December

1917, the Fleet Commando in Pola reported to the Naval Section in Vienna by telegram that "stocks of fuel oil in Pola 2,632 tons, in Trieste 66 tons, of this 1,093 tons total is diesel oil, if fresh supplies not sent immediately and forcefully employed all traffic and then the war-readiness of torpedo units and submarines in both ports will cease in no later than twenty days."[158]

How much did all of this matter? The Austrian navy, often dismissed as irrelevant by military historians, was able to hold its own in the first months of conflict in the Mediterranean. To quote naval authority Arthur Marder, "In the first four months of war the Austrians, at a cost of only two submarines and a few aeroplanes, inflicted these losses on the Italian Fleet: two cruisers, a destroyer, two torpedo boats, three submarines, and two dirigibles (in addition to damaging the British light cruiser *Dublin* by torpedo). 'In four months,' wrote the [British Naval] Attaché [in Rome], 'the Austrian fleet has established a moral ascendancy in the Adriatic, and has played the part of the weaker force with conspicuous success. Not only has it succeeded in weakening the Italian fleet, but it has immobilised a force very considerably superior to itself.' "[159] One should thus resist the temptation to scoff at the idea that Austria's military—on sea as much as on land—had little to contribute to the Central Powers' efforts.

The Central Powers clearly had a host of other problems as significant as oil shortages. Nevertheless, the importance of petroleum in contributing to the outcome of this conflict was acknowledged by contemporaries, including Lord Curzon, president of the Inter-Allied Petroleum Conference and future British foreign secretary. Curzon, who seems to have had a poetic strain, claimed that "the Allied cause had floated to victory on a wave of oil." The energy crisis that dogged Austria-Hungary during the First World War was a result of a combination of circumstances that were beyond the empire's control, on the one hand, and planning decisions (or, perhaps more important, their absence) that reflected the priorities and weaknesses of the prewar administration, on the other. Austria-Hungary could boast of a domestic source of oil that was sufficient for its own energy needs at the beginning of the war. So why did Austria-Hungary have such problems with fuel supply? Could the great discrepancy in this matter between the Central Powers and the Allies have been avoided? Given the vast supplies of American, Russian, and later Persian oil, probably not. But Austrian prewar policies did nothing to alleviate their natural disadvantage.

When Churchill first suggested a conversion from coal to petroleum, skeptics in Great Britain had pointed out that they had no domestic source of oil. German blockades during the war did hinder Britain's oil supply from overseas. Nevertheless, years before the war, Churchill had boldly decided to cast aside Welsh coal in favor of petroleum, predicting that "mastery itself was the prize of the venture." Churchill recognized that flexibility was the key to guaranteeing a continued source of petroleum. "On no one quality, on no one process, on no one country, on no one route and on no one field must we be dependent. Safety and certainty in oil lie in variety and variety alone."[160] It is perhaps unfair to hold the Austrians responsible for not foreseeing some of the contingencies that led to the reduction of their oil supply during the war: the temporary loss of the Galician oil fields, Romania's export limitations at the beginning of the war, and then the extensive destruction of Romanian stocks and productive capacities in late 1916.[161] On the other hand, even leaving aside the question of relations with Romania, the Austrian authorities had done remarkably little to ensure that their Galician oil fields would remain accessible and productive. Austrian prewar policy exacerbated these problems by making even the Galician oil that was produced before and during the war less accessible to the military and civilian consumers who needed it most. Despite the warning cries of various Cassandras in the Ministries of War and Public Works, attempts to secure access to Galician oil in case of emergency had come to naught. Insufficient stocks in the empire's naval ports meant that regular shipments of oil from Galicia to the Adriatic were mandatory. The absence of a second railway to Trieste, along with the absence of completed waterways, worsened traffic delays, causing insurmountable transport problems. It was transportation difficulties rather than insufficient production that caused fuel shortages in Austria-Hungary, leading one historian to conclude that "there probably would have been no petroleum shortage at all if it were not for transportation difficulties and the tripartite organization of the distribution apparatus."[162] In the months and years before Archduke Franz Ferdinand's assassination in Sarajevo, the Austrian Ministry of War embarked on a program to reinvigorate its navy and army with new technologies that required a steady and significant flow of oil. These plans were not, however, placed alongside available statistical tables that recorded black-on-white a steady drop in Galician production, nor were they compared with telegrams reporting formidable transportation problems and high prices. There is, perhaps, a certain irony in the fact that the central government's attempt to rescue a provincial industry (by forcing up prices and encouraging private consumption) only contributed to its own subsequent inability to exploit that industry's product to the fullest.

During wartime mobilization, Galician oil fields were found to be highly inaccessible; many impossible to transport to Adriatic Sea

— occupations by enemies caused devastating losses of oil, infrastructure, and social stability

➤ Russians strangely did not totally destroy infrast. during occupation in 1914 Galicia

British in Romania did

all nations convinced by the war of the importance of petroleum

After occupation of Russians, Austrian gov't was wary of letting oil workers with foreign passports back into region to work

unlike Allies, Austro-Hungarian empire did not have allies with vast reserves

— No reserves had been saved prewar
— transportation connections had been neglected

— Production could not keep up w/ wartime demand, despite allowing oil workers to be exempt from military service; output severely diminished; landscape ravished

— 7 —

A Hotly Disputed Territory

The Struggle for Eastern Galicia

Polish-Ukrainian War

When, on 3 November 1918, the Austrian emperor Karl I agreed to an armistice with the Allies, this marked an end of hostilities for the Austro-Hungarian army. When, on 4 November, he withdrew from politics, turning Austrian affairs over to the leaders of the German-Austrian Democratic Republic along with the various newly declared governments of his non-German territories, this marked the end of the Habsburg dynasty and, with it, the end of the Austro-Hungarian Empire.[1] But for many of the emperor's former subjects, neither of these momentous transitions marked an end to the war. Despite armistices, despite negotiations in Paris, and despite even the signing of the Treaty of Saint-Germain, the war in Eastern Galicia continued unabated until 1921. One of the foremost objectives of this conflict was to gain control over the region's oil fields, which held out to new regimes the promise of financial solubility. At the same time, the Allies themselves had an interest in the stability of the oil region and in its continued accessibility. It was the intersection of local activity and influence from outside Galicia that determined the fate of Eastern Galicia and its oil fields. Just as central Viennese institutions cooperated with local and provincial powers and in many cases were even overridden by local interests, so, too, did the Allies find their ability to control the peace process in Galicia limited by their inability to control the behavior of Galicians.

After four years of taking Europe apart with the weapons of war, the Great Powers turned in 1919 to the process of taking it apart with the weapons of diplomacy: censuses, maps, and treaties. Point 10 of Woodrow Wilson's Fourteen Points asserted that "the peoples of Austria-Hungary, whose place among the nations we wish to see safeguarded and assured,

should be accorded the freest opportunity to autonomous development."
But what exactly would that mean? Throughout central Europe, the question of what kind of new states would be created, who would lead them,
who would reside within them, and what their borders would be was
debated in meetings and, in some cases, contested on battlefields. Wilson's
Point 13 specifically called for the establishment of a stable and independent Poland: "An independent Polish state should be erected which
should include the territories inhabited by indisputably Polish populations, . . . and whose political and economic independence and territorial
integrity should be guaranteed by international covenant."[2] This was a
goal that all the Allies came to share, although some with less enthusiasm
than others.[3]

There was, therefore, little controversy about the establishment of the
Polish Republic. On 11 November, General Józef Piłsudski took control
of the newly independent Polish Republic, and on 17 January 1919, Ignacy Jan Paderewski formed a coalition government with Piłsudski as
president. But little about the potentially Polish territories and their populations could be called "indisputable," and from the beginning, securing
"territorial integrity" was hampered by controversies over how to define
Polish territory. Despite the Allies' expressions of support in principle,
the fledgling republic found itself beset with structural difficulties. Andrzej
Korbonski sums up the problems that confronted the new state: "[Po-
land] really had no state territory it could claim to control . . . no well-
defined national boundaries . . . neither an army nor a police force; it had
neither its own parliamentary bodies nor a government in the conventional sense of the word. It had no judiciary and no legal system of its
own, nor did it possess a civil service."[4] In addition, Poland was confronted by immediate challenges to its sovereignty in regions that all of
its leaders agreed were core elements of the Polish state: East Prussia,
Gdańsk/Danzig, Silesia, Lithuania, and Eastern Galicia.

Poland's government demanded the immediate inclusion of all of Galicia in the new republic, but before it could make its declared sovereignty
a reality, it was challenged by a new rival: the Western Ukrainian People's
Republic (ZUNR), a state whose creation actually preceded that of the
Polish Republic itself.[5] On 31 October 1918, Ukrainian officers and Sich
riflemen peacefully disarmed Austro-Hungarian troops in Lviv and took
control of the city. The following day, Leopolitans awoke to see the
Ukrainian flag flying over Lviv city hall and posters mounted throughout

the city proclaiming that its residents were now living in the new capital of a Ukrainian state. On 9 November, the Ukrainian National Rada proclaimed the creation of the ZUNR, making it clear that there was more than one answer to the question of what should become of this territory. It could form a part of a new Polish republic, with or without some degree of autonomy. Alternately, it could become an independent state. This could potentially be joined with the newly founded Ukrainian People's Republic on the far side of the Austro-Russian border.

The problem of mixed populations and ensuing territorial debates was not unique to Eastern Galicia. Buoyed by Wilson's notion of the people's right to self-determination, every fledgling government wished to offer a happy home to each of its potential "nationals," ideally defined by borders within which they would form part of a decisive majority.[6] Of all the territorial conflicts that emerged in the territories of the former Habsburg Empire, the conflict over Eastern Galicia was one of the bitterest and longest and was not formally and officially resolved until March 1923.[7] Galicia had been created by Habsburg fiat in 1772; its political and social elite was almost entirely Polish. Nevertheless, the province was by no means homogeneous, nor was it undisputedly Polish territory. Determining what was in fact Polish territory proved to be tremendously complicated. Harvard University professor and Polish expert Robert Howard Lord[8] claimed that Poland was geographically "one of the hardest countries in the world to define. . . . Polish geographers are accustomed to treat the whole region between the Baltic, the Carpathians, the Dvina, and the Dnieper" as one geographic unit that "ought likewise to form a political unit—Poland." At the same time, "Russian scientists have demonstrated with equal ease that nearly all of the region in question is geographically a part of Russia; while the patriotic scholars of Kiev and Lemberg have proved that nature intended a great part of this same region to belong to neither Poland nor Russia, but to a *tertium quid* called the Ukraine."[9]

Nor was it easy to define Poland's borders on the basis of population. No reliable demographic data had been collected since 1910. Data from population censuses carried out after the Treaty of Riga were not only falsified, but also distorted by enormous postwar migrations and a boycott of the census by Galician Ukrainians.[10] Nevertheless, it was clear that Ukrainians formed a majority everywhere in the eastern half of the province, with the exception of the capital city of Lviv, which had a Polish majority, and some smaller cities and towns with a Jewish majority. This

clear ethnographic domination was the basis of Ukrainian expectations
that the territory should naturally become part of some Ukrainian political unit.[11]

The Ukrainian majority, however, had been politically and socially persecuted for generations.[12] Far from inspiring sympathetic attention to
Ukrainians' claims that they finally deserved their own state, the effects
of the persecution themselves were used to call into question Ukrainians'
ability to rule. Stanisław Wiktor Szczepanowski (1882–1961), son and
namesake of one of the oil industry's most famous and popular figures,
described what was often called the Ruthenian "ethnographic mass"[13] in
a typical formulation: "Ruthenians are not a real nation as such, they are
a tribe and not even a homogeneous one . . . only in the past dozen or
so years have they undertaken the attempt to create a new nation: Ukrainians."[14] The younger Szczepanowski became an oilman himself, and was
frequently consulted by representatives of the Western Allies on matters
relating to the oil industry and the local population. When asked if the
inclusion of so many "foreign elements" would not be dangerous for
Poland, Szczepanowski responded, "There are no foreign elements in the
exact sense of the word, except for the Jews. Poles, like the English, are
a mixed race made up of the tribes of historic Poland. The tribes that
gave us Kościuszko, Mickiewicz, Słowacki, Moniuszko and many others
are not foreign to us."[15] According to Sociologist Rogers Brubaker, the
resistance of Ukrainians to inclusion in the Polish ethnic polity only reinforced the desire of the Polish nationalizing project to defend the
"rights" of its core nation: "The new Polish state," he explains, "was
conceived as the state *of* and *for* the ethnolinguistically (and ethnoreli-
giously) defined Polish nation, in part because it was seen as made *by*
this nation against the resistance of Germans, Ukrainians, and Jews."[16]
Conversely, the Poles' insistence on forcing the assimilation of Ukrainians
into the Polish nation (unlike Germans, who could not be assimilated,
and Jews, who should not) only reinforced an increasingly broad-based
anti-Polish national Ukrainian consciousness.[17]

The battle for Lviv marked only the latest of hundreds of smaller struggles Ukrainians waged against their Polish landlords, schoolteachers, policemen, and administrators in Galicia. For politicized Ukrainians, the
prospect of existing as a minority population in a Polish national state
was far more repugnant than the imperial "subjugation" from which they
had just emerged. Even during the war they had loudly proclaimed to

the world that "Ukrainians will never consent to be placed under the guardianship of the Poles," warning further that "if the ignorance or malevolence of diplomats succeeds in reuniting some parts of Ukrainian territory with a future Polish kingdom, this is guaranteed to create a source of weakness for that kingdom, as well as a terrible danger for the lasting peace of eastern Europe."[18] Thus, before the armistice had officially been declared, two new rival governments had both made political claims to Eastern Galicia. Both were prepared to back up those claims with military force. As a consequence, expelling Austro-Hungarian troops proved to be only the beginning of the violent struggle for control of Eastern Galicia, not its end.

From the start of the Eastern Galician conflict, military and political action concentrated on two objects of prime importance: the capital city of Lviv and the Drohobycz-Borysław oil district. The oil fields of Eastern Galicia promised a degree of financial security to both new states, each otherwise sorely lacking in financial resources in the aftermath of a devastating war. It had become clear in the decade before the war that the real wealth of oil lay only in Eastern Galicia and was concentrated in the Drohobycz district. Western Galicia did possess large oil refineries, but these relied on the oil fields of the east for their raw material. Thus, with the fate of Eastern Galicia went the future of the oil industry.

Both states moved to seize control of the oil fields quickly. Polish sentries could be seen patrolling the whole oil basin as early as 1 November.[19] Throughout the first week of November, local political and business leaders met in Drohobycz in an attempt to reach a diplomatic—and binding—agreement on the region's immediate future. According to one Polish participant, these representatives divided roughly into four groups. Stanisław Wiktor Szczepanowski spoke for Polish nationalists, who claimed the whole region for Poland. Semyon Vityk, veteran of numerous strikes and skirmishes with both imperial and provincial authorities, spoke for Ukrainian nationalists, who countered by claiming the whole region for Ukraine. Two groups allegedly tried to maintain neutrality in what threatened to become an ethnonational struggle: socialists and Jewish businessmen. The former claimed that international solidarity among workers prevented them from joining the Polish nationalists. The latter claimed that maintaining economic security and ensuring that oil wells kept flowing and business was not interrupted took precedence over settling insignificant political disputes.[20]

These negotiations proved fruitless, and the debate was soon resolved, at least temporarily, by force. At midnight between 8 and 9 November, Polish nationalists tried to seize control of the oil basin by surprise, but found that they were outnumbered and outpowered by Ukrainians armed with machine guns, who took over the region on 9 November. Jan Włodek, chargé d'affaires of the Polish Republic in The Hague, noted the Ukrainian acquisition of the Eastern Galician oil fields with alarm. He urgently warned Charles Perkins, managing director of Premier Oil and Pipeline Company and chairman of the International Committee appointed to protect British, French, Belgian and Allies' Oil Interests in Galicia, that "should there be a struggle, there is the danger of the destruction of all oil fields."[21] He suggested a line of argument designed to provoke political support from the British Foreign Office and Allied intervention:

> A telegram from the Polish government makes it known that Poland cannot survive without the oil fields, and that the oil fields in Ruthenian hands will mean the destruction of the oil fields and the oil industry. Polish interests are identical with the interests of the Allies, for the oil industry is based on the capital of the citizens of the Allied states and the work of Polish laborers and engineers. The Ruthenian administration has neither the authority nor the personnel with the indispensable technical skill. This would be the ruin of the Allied capitalists, as well as Polish workers and engineers.[22]

Not for a moment did the Polish government consider ceding the oil fields to a new Ukrainian state.

Similarly, without this territory, the new Ukrainian republic was as good as doomed. Not only did Galician Ukrainians, exposed to the privileges and responsibilities that came with constitutional rule and universal suffrage for generations, promise to provide leadership in establishing local governance and civil service in the new state, but the assistance of the Ukrainian Galician army would be necessary in the eastern Ukrainians' struggle with Soviet Russia. The obligation to combat Poles for control of Galicia instead of focusing on the Soviets and the ultimate loss of Eastern Ukraine, according to Ivan Rudnytsky, "amounted to the destruction of the very foundations on which an independent Ukrainian state might have been built in the post–World War I period."[23] It was immediately apparent to both belligerents that the significance of control over the oil fields went beyond the convenience of Polish workers or the profits of industrialists: it could affect the outcome of the war itself. Włodek noted with alarm that the sales of petroleum to Hungary and Germany were made in exchange for ammunition and weapons that the Ukrainians were using in their war with the Poles.[24] Colonel H. H. Wade, head of the British military mission to Poland, believed that it was "only by the sale of this oil that [the Ukrainians] obtain munitions or money."[25]

While Polish nationalists in the oil basin awaited their "liberation" in vain, those held captive in Lviv were more fortunate. On 19 November, Polish troops arrived in Lviv, and three days later they expelled the Ukrainians from the city. As had the Russian occupying forces during the war, the Poles immediately arrested Metropolitan Sheptyts'kyi and placed him under house arrest until March 1920, signaling a renewed attack on what were perceived to be Ukrainian institutions. Thus, at the war's outset, the Poles controlled Lviv, but the Ukrainians had control of the oil fields. Neither side was content with half of Galicia's treasure, and the war between the two threatened to rage on indefinitely. The Allies, however, were not prepared to see the issue of Eastern Galicia settled by force.

On 18 January 1919, the Paris Peace Conference began. One of its key objectives was to settle once and for all the borders of the new Polish Republic, resolving the Eastern Galician problem. Wilson's Point 13 notwithstanding, the goal of supporting the establishment of a strong and independent Polish state emerged not only out of principle, but also because the Great Powers expected Poland to be an essential ally (and buffer) against Bolshevik Russia. Polish borders were thus a function of the Great Powers' larger aims regarding Germany and Russia as much as they were a reflection of so-called historic Polish rights.[26]

The ongoing Polish-Ukrainian war called into question the very premise of a peaceful or diplomatic solution to the dispute. The ZUNR's union with the Ukrainian People's Republic (UNR) on 22 January 1919 also contributed an additional degree of complexity by accentuating the perceived connection between Galician Ukrainians and Bolshevik Russia.[27] With the prospect of a violent military resolution of the Eastern Galician border dispute over which they would have no control looming on the eastern horizon, the Great Powers quickly resolved on 24 January 1919 that the question of the reconstitution of Poland, as well as that of the other new independent states of central and eastern Europe, should be decided by them in Paris and not on the field of battle.[28]

The stubborn prolongation of the Polish-Ukrainian war was a troublesome irritant, and the Allies labored to bring it to a speedy end, whatever the cost for the combatants. The Supreme Council made it clear that it would only settle the question of boundaries of Poland once an armistice had been reached.[29] This proved an impossibly difficult task, since, as the British were quick to point out, by settling on a preliminary demarcation line, a de facto border would be created that it would later be difficult to change.[30] General A. Carton de Wiart confessed his "doubts about a real armistice pending decision of Paris Conference on final frontiers. Both Ruthenes and Poles want oil wells, which are one of the few available sources of revenue."[31] From January to July, the Great Powers in Paris, their representatives in Poland, and delegations from Poland and Ukraine debated the merits of various borders, the San River (preferred by the Ukrainians), the Zbruch River (the former border between Austria-Hungary and Russia, preferred by the Poles), or somewhere in between. All of these discussions, theories, and proposals were bandied about against the background of an ongoing war that belied any nods in the direction of armistice.

With all of these complications, the delegates at the Paris Peace Conference faced a difficult task indeed, one that some historians believe they handled very poorly. According to historian Laurence Orzell's critical assessment, "Committed in theory to the ideal of self-determination in some form for the Ukrainian majority, but at the same time pledged to establish a viable Polish state as a bulwark against Bolshevism, the treatment of Eastern Galicia at the Peace Conference manifested a high degree of indecision stemming from an inadequate appreciation of political realities."[32] Orzell concludes that the Great Powers' aims were fundamentally contradictory and irreconcilable, and that their ultimate decisions failed to benefit Ukrainians and encouraged the Poles to resort to military action. Resolving the territorial dispute would require addressing questions that had been asked since the moment the value of oil had been discovered in the 1850s: what did it mean to own land, and what did it mean to control territory? In the 1860s and 1870s, the battle had been waged between private landowners and the state. Now the pivotal issue was not the rights accruing to private owners, but rather the process by which "nations" could lay claim to the land they considered theirs. While a synthetic presentation of the various parties' positions inevitably exaggerates their uniformity, some generalizations can be made about their overall positions, beginning with the Allies' general views on Poland and Eastern Galicia.

The position held by the delegation from the United States was defined by Wilson's views on the principle of national self-determination. In Wilson's words, at its core was "the principle of justice to all peoples and nationalities, and their right to live on equal terms of liberty and safety with one another, whether they be strong or weak." The Americans had no direct economic or geopolitical aspirations in Poland and no concrete interests in European territorial questions.[33] This lack of direct involvement applied particularly to the American position on Eastern Galicia. So removed were they from the conflict that David Hunter Miller, the legal advisor of the U.S. delegation at the Paris Peace Conference, expressed his exasperation in trying to resolve the question of what he called "the hotly disputed and very puzzling territory and population of Eastern Galicia."[34] Closer investigation had revealed to the American delegation the naïve optimism represented by Wilson's claim that his Fourteen Points were expressed "in terms too concrete to admit of any further doubt or question."

Great Britain and France, on the other hand, were more directly concerned with the outcome of the Polish border dispute. Like the Americans, the British desired the creation of a democratic Poland inhabited (mostly) by Poles. The greater the ethnic homogeneity, they argued, the stronger the new Polish state would be. At the same time, British delegates were far more distrustful of Poland's own claims than their French colleagues. While the British promoted the establishment of a strong Polish state, they also wished to grant the Ukrainians at the very least some form of autonomy, if not a state of their own. Convinced that Ukrainians could never live peacefully as a minority in a Polish national state, Lewis Namier suggested establishing an independent Ruthenian state on both sides of the Carpathians.[35] British foreign secretary Arthur James Balfour shared Namier's view that Poland should have an ethnographic frontier (that is, not one tracing the border of the historic Polish-Lithuanian Commonwealth, which would include a huge Lithuanian, Belorussian, and Ukrainian population), with a buffer zone of independent states separating it from Russia. According to British delegate Edward Hallett Carr, "the picture of Poland which was universal in Eastern Europe right down to 1925 was of a strong and potentially predatory power."[36] Whether or not this opinion was truly "universal," the delegation was concerned that

the needs of Poland's potential minority populations be carefully protected.

The French proved to be the Poles' most reliable and forceful ally, both
at the peace conference in Paris and on the ground in Eastern Galicia.
The French strongly supported a new Poland that would include all of
Eastern Galicia, arguing that Poland would suffer more than Ukrainians
from losing Eastern Galicia. Although they were willing to consider
making Eastern Galicia an autonomous, bilingual province, they insisted
that it must remain within the Polish state. A strong Poland served French
interests. With the Bolsheviks in power in the east, the French were no
longer able to turn to Russia as an ally against their German rival and
hoped to replace Russia with Poland, which made the Polish state "a
central link" in French security policy.[37]

A Polish delegation was present in Paris to represent the new republic's
demands from the very beginning, led by Paderewski and Roman
Dmowski, leader of the nationalist Polish National Democratic Party.
Dmowski insisted that all of Galicia must be incorporated into the new
Polish state, which would itself be centralized and dominated by Poles.
He exploited fears of German aggression to insist on a strong Poland—
with its own oil fields—as a guarantor of Western European security. In
Warsaw, Piłsudski argued for more extended boundaries around a fed-
eralist state.[38] Aware that his ideal boundaries might not be palatable to
the Great Powers, Piłsudski had also proposed a "national minimum,"
which would include Lviv, Kałusz (an important source of potash, a key
ingredient in fertilizer), and the oil fields, but not necessarily the rest of
Eastern Galicia. Piłsudski's close associate, Michał Sokolnicki, put together
a proposal in late 1918 in which he insisted that Lviv, Drohobycz, and
Borysław must all remain Polish, although he was willing to sacrifice
Kałusz if necessary. Dmowski's and Piłsudski's own visions of Poland were
mutually exclusive and incompatible, and their opinions on the question
of Eastern Galicia differed. Nevertheless, two immutable characteristics
linked all members of the Polish delegation and the Polish government:
Lviv and the Drohobycz-Borysław oil basin must stay on the Polish side
of the border. Here there could be no dispute.

Initially, these arguments in favor of Polish control over Galicia could
not be opposed by official representatives of the Ukrainian position. Only
the Poles had the opportunity to present their arguments to the Great
Powers in Paris. Although the Ukrainians sent numerous appeals to the

Paris Peace Conference in an attempt to secure recognition of Ukraine as an independent state containing both formerly Russian and formerly Austrian territory, it was not until March 1919 that the Great Powers finally acknowledged the Ukrainian delegation.[39] The Ukrainians' attempts to garner support were hindered by the Allies' complete lack of familiarity with either the ZUNR or the UNR, or with Ukrainian culture or language. On several occasions, representatives of the Allies actually turned to Poles with questions about what it was that the Ukrainians wanted. Wade, for example, interviewed Stanisław Wiktor Szczepanowski, who had been appointed petroleum expert to the Polish government and liaison officer to French General M. J. Berthélemy's mission, on the Ukrainians' war aims. Szczepanowski was, however, far from a reliable source on this issue. He had retained his father's patriotism, but, as far as can be judged from the documentary evidence he left behind, not his penchant for philanthropy. The younger Szczepanowski's own presentation of his views regarding Ukrainians and Jews demonstrates that he shared the prejudice of his brother-in-law, Edward Dubanowicz, a member of Dmowski's nationalist party, Narodowa Demokracja. He reduced the Ukrainians' goals to the "the expropriation of Polish property and the plundering of estates, inventories, and cities."[40] Negative propaganda about the Ukrainians also reached the British Press. In a January 1919 article about the battle for Lviv sent in by a "special correspondent," for example, the *Times* of London reported that "boys and women" were fighting in the Polish Army, while "among the Ruthenians or Ukrainians are a number of German and Austrian officers." The reporter concluded, "Freebooters as these men are, presumably their presence is not unconnected with the desire of the Ukrainian leaders to retain possession of the large oilfields which lie south of Lemberg (Lviv)."[41] News reports such as this suggest that Ukrainians had lost the publicity war long before the military conflict in Eastern Galicia was resolved.

The arguments presented by the Ukrainian and Polish delegations contained not only contradictory statistics and factual claims, but also differing views on how to define ownership of land and nationality of territory. The Ukrainian delegation could simply point to statistics indicating that a majority of Eastern Galicia's residents were Ukrainian. They also tried to demonstrate that their land was somehow naturally Ukrainian. While its natural borders might be hard for the untrained eye to distinguish, Ukraine was clearly "of a different formation than Russia and Poland by virtue of its geologic origin and volcanic eruptions."[42] In addition, the Ukrainians argued that the territory of Eastern Galicia was "ethnographically and historically a Ukrainian territory" by virtue of the "independent Ukrainian state" that had existed on the territory until the sixteenth century.[43]

The Polish delegation did not dispute that there were many Ukrainians in Eastern Galicia, although it stressed that Lviv itself was predominantly inhabited by Poles. It did not, however, concede that a mere demographic majority automatically entitled Ukrainians to the land. One of the Poles' Western defenders tried to convince the Belgian delegation that determinations based on nationality statistics were worthless. Preceded by a summary of religious and national statistics from various censuses and parish records, his assessment of the relative merits of each nation typified the Western view of gradations in inferiority as one moved further east: "only the Polish element represents civilization and education. The Ruthenian population is made up entirely of peasants who lack any intellectual culture, are totally primitive, and share their houses with beasts."[44] Polish historians quickly provided treatises demonstrating the long domination of Poles in Galicia. While Ukrainians boasted of the medieval kingdoms of Halych and Vladimir, Polish historians strove to demonstrate that Galicia had been a constituent part of the Polish-Lithuanian Commonwealth since Grand Duke Jagiello took the throne in 1386.[45]

Even more creative was the Polish delegation's defense of the Poles' right to the oil fields. It argued that the oil district had become what it was thanks to Polish talent, and the contribution of Poles in rendering the natural wealth of the oil region socially useful entitled them to a claim to the land that they themselves had transformed. The Polish economic delegation to the Paris Peace Conference argued that it was only thanks to Poles (in particular, Ignacy Łukasiewicz) that the oil industry had ever been born. Under Polish control it had flourished, despite the obstacles imposed by outsiders: the power of U.S. competition, refined petroleum smuggled in from Russia, prejudicial Austrian fiscal policy, hostile Hungarian tariffs, and the influence of the large (non-Galician) refineries. These had significantly exacerbated the insufficiency of capital and credit and the downward pressure on prices caused by overabundance. According to the economic delegation, the industry had developed in spite of all these difficulties only "thanks to the enterprising spirit of small Polish capital, the *merits of Polish technicians*, and the *vigor of Polish workers.*"[46] It even spuriously claimed that it was a Pole, Stanisław Prus Szczepanowski, who had introduced the Canadian drilling method to Galicia, although even Szczepanowski himself had credited MacGarvey with this development.[47] In western Galicia, it added, drilling had become a family trade, passed down from father to son in Polish families, leading to the formation of a nation of born oilmen: "Poles are in general *geologists and pioneers*—the entrepreneurs searching for new veins of petroleum—*Poles the directors, engineers, correspondents, surveyors, and above all, Poles the oil workers.*"[48] Simply living on top of the soil was no longer enough to lay claim to ownership: by virtue of the blood and sweat they had poured into the industry over several generations, Poles had earned control over the oil industry and thus over Eastern Galicia.

The two delegations were equally aware of the importance of the Drohobycz-Borysław oil fields, both for the economic viability of their own states and as a tool for soliciting foreign support. The Ukrainians used their current possession of the oil fields as a justification for their existence as an independent state. The Ukrainian Republic, they argued, was no romantic pipe dream but rather a realistic project for an independent state that would have the economic basis to support itself, with large deposits of "lead, coal, iron, and petroleum, as well as other riches."[49] According to the Ukrainian delegation to Paris, the economic strength that these mineral resources would provide would render doubts as to the viability of an independent Ukraine irrelevant: "In sum, the natural conditions that can favor the economic development of the Ukraine and permit it to exist as an independent state are excellent."[50]

Ukrainian representatives tried to secure allies with promises of favorable trade conditions for petroleum. After a second Hungarian revolution put Béla Kun in power in March 1919, Ukrainian delegates quickly went to Budapest to forge a petroleum trade agreement with the Hungarians, which Kun signed without reservation. They pursued a similar treaty with the new government in Prague. The Ukrainians were desperate to trade their petroleum for Czech coal, without which railway transport throughout Western Ukraine would break down. The Czechoslovaks were similarly eager to find crude oil to be processed in the numerous refineries that remained in Bohemia and Moravia.[51] The Poles were alarmed to learn that representatives of Western Ukraine and Czechoslovakia were even considering a political union, which the Polish envoy to Vienna, Marcel Szarota, ascribed to the Czechoslovak desire to secure raw oil for

their refineries.[52] On 11 April 1919, Czechoslovakia and the ZUNR agreed
that the Ukrainians would provide ninety thousand tons of crude oil at
a rate below the world average in exchange for Czechoslovak weapons
and ammunition, coal, sugar, and textiles.[53]

While the Ukrainians sought cooperative agreements with Hungary
and Czechoslovakia, the Poles set their sights further west. In this endeavor, they found their most reliable ally in Perkins's International Committee appointed to protect British, French, Belgian, and Allies' Oil Interests in Galicia, which had been founded on 22 October 1914 by oilmen
from the countries of the Entente.[54] Both Perkins and the Polish delegation tried to convince the Allied delegates in Paris that it was in their
nations' own interest to support Polish territorial claims to Eastern Galicia.

The first step was to present the magnitude of Allied involvement in
the Galician oil industry. Here figures in millions of pounds, francs, and
Austrian crowns were bandied about—each account based on slightly
different definitions of investment and Allied ownership. Perkins prepared a memorandum in which he claimed that British investments totaled 10,125,000 pounds sterling; French investments, 44,800,000 francs;
and Belgian investments, 20,000,000 francs.[55] Paderewski immediately
submitted this document to the Armistice Commission, adding that "the
figures for France and Belgium are certainly an underestimate."[56] According to a memorandum prepared for the Belgian delegation to the
Paris Peace Conference by Perkins's Belgian colleague, Paul LeGrand, Polish capital accounted for only 20 percent, while Germans and Austrians
controlled 40 percent, and British, French, and Belgian investors another
40 percent of the Galician oil industry.[57] The Crédit Lyonnais estimated
that the total value of fixed capital invested in the Galician oil industry
before the war had been 275 million francs, and that by 1919 British
companies together had issued 29.7 million francs to their shareholders,
while French and Belgian companies had together issued 47.6 million
francs to their shareholders.[58]

Certainly the amount of foreign capital invested in the Galician oil
industry was large enough to merit concern lest the investors be cut off
from the oil fields permanently. Perkins was not willing to allow that to
happen. Because he represented not only the committee to protect Allied
interests, but also one of the largest British companies, Premier Oil and
Pipe Line, his responsibility was to ensure that Premier's investments in
Galicia would not be lost by the vagaries of peace.

How could foreign investments be expected to fare after the collapse of the Austro-Hungarian Empire? According to the Crédit Lyonnais, the immediate postwar outlook was far from rosy. Without commenting on the relative merits of Polish and Ukrainian administrators, the dozens of financial studies compiled by employees of the Crédit Lyonnais (which had been collecting information on French investment in Poland since the late 1890s) show both that the bank was interested in assessing the profitability of oil and that it was not as enthusiastic about investments in Galician industry, in part because of the uncertainty of Eastern Galician borders.[59]

It was the job of the Polish delegation to convince foreign investors—and through them, the Allied delegates in Paris—that only a Polish government in charge of all of Eastern Galicia could safeguard their past investments and reward those made in the future. The new Polish government tried to establish its theoretical sovereignty over the oil district even before it fell into Polish hands. In January 1919, Professor Jerzy Michalski, head of the Cracow Agency of Congressional Work, composed a report on the settling of accounts with the former Austrian authorities. His work was later reviewed by a Petroleum Inquiry Board, leading to a subsequent report in March 1919, prepared by Dr. Alfred Kohl. Kohl's report was intended to present the official Polish policy regarding ownership of oil properties to the interested public (including, presumably, foreign investors). The report stressed that the Polish government was entitled to settle this matter even though Ukrainians (whom the document never mentions directly) currently "occupied" much of the territory in question.[60] The report served an immediate dual purpose. First, it reinforced the Polish claims that the Ukrainians were in fact "occupying" Polish property by refusing to acknowledge the legality or potential permanence of the current distribution of control. Second, it served to assure Allied petroleum interests that their investments, past and future, would be secure under the auspices of a friendly Polish government. Although all properties belonging to the Austrian state (including the large refinery in Drohobycz, as well as state oil fields, pipelines, and mines) were declared to be the sole property of the Polish state, the rights and properties of "French, Belgian, English, and Americans" would be as secure as they had been before the war, if not more so. Any rights, privileges, and exemptions to which foreign companies of the Allied states had been entitled before the war would be honored by the Polish government. The Polish government "call[ed] on foreign owners to take possession of their properties" to the mutual benefit of both parties, explaining that "this postulate is as political as it is economic, as we cannot allow a vacuum to develop in this matter."[61]

Representatives of the Polish government happily made promises of favorable treatment to investors, always stressing that they would only be able to carry out their good intentions once the oil fields were returned to them for good. The Polish delegate to the Paris Peace Conference, Władysław Grabski,[62] and the head of the Polish economic delegation, Andrzej Wierzbicki, assured Perkins that "the Polish government—as soon as it has the power to do so—is prepared to use all legal means it possesses to return to the Premier Oil and Pipe Line Company possession of those oil terrains in Galicia that were exploited before the war for the use of that company."[63] No such favors could be expected from the Ukrainians, according to Stanisław Wiktor Szczepanowski. When Major Fordham, a member of the British military mission in Poland, visited Galicia in February 1919, Szczepanowski informed him, "During the Ukrainians' invasion, Borysław production completely collapsed because no one wanted to work for them."[64] With such statements Szczepanowski hoped to dispel the notion that the oil industry could ever flourish under Ukrainian control.

This same position was promoted by the Polish economic delegation to the Paris Peace Conference. In a pamphlet it prepared for the conference on the oil industry, it presented the Ukrainian "invasion" of November 1918 as an occurrence that fundamentally threatened the very existence of the oil industry: "If this region is attributed to Poland, the petroleum industry will develop normally as it has done until now, but it is condemned to disappear entirely if this territory becomes part of Ukraine."[65] In contrast to the chaos ensured under Ukrainian control, it pointed to what it claimed was the healthy and normal development of the industry under Polish control within the framework of Austrian Galicia. Only in Poland could sizeable foreign investments thrive. It asserted that Premier had invested ninety million crowns of capital in Galician oil and noted that Galicia's major western Galician refineries were controlled by the Belgians (Krosno), the French (Limanowa and Jedlicze), the English (Maryampol and Trzebinia), and the Americans (Dziedzice). Dividing Galicia along the San River would cut off these refineries from their sources of crude oil in the east. In addition, investments would be more secure in the hands of practiced Polish statesmen than given over

Int'l Committee gave full support to Poles

to the "neophyte Ukrainian [state] whose future cannot be foreseen today."[66]

The economic delegation also argued that businessmen must bend to the sheer power of nature. Transporting Galician oil eastward into Ukraine and toward Russia—its inevitable destination if it were given over to the Ukrainians—made no sense. Since the Dniestr was not navigable (despite all the promises and proposals for canals made in the last decade before the war), oil would have to be transported by railway all the way across the length of Ukraine to regions that were much closer to Romania and therefore, presumably, represented a less favorable market for Galician oil. The "natural market" for oil from Borysław, like that for Galician wood, salt, and potash, was not to the east, but to the north: Poland. The San River was navigable; goods could easily be transported north and west to the Vistula and from there as far as Danzig.[67]

Poles threatened that under Ukr. control, oil would be sent eastward to Russia

Just as the Polish government hoped, it was rewarded for its conciliatory attitude and its image of reliability with the full support of the International Committee appointed to protect British, French, Belgian, and Allies' Oil Interests in Galicia. Perkins informed Wierzbicki that "the committee believes that the material interests of its shareholders can only be effectively secured in the case that the Peace Conference determines that all of Galicia should fall under Polish sovereignty."[68] Although much of the fear of Ukrainian control was based on lies, misinformation, and ignorance, there was some legitimate reason to worry that stability would not characterize the Ukrainian state for some time to come. One modern Ukrainian historian has described the situation in Ukraine in 1919 as utterly chaotic: "In the modern history of Europe no country experienced such complete anarchy, bitter civil strife, and total collapse of authority as did Ukraine at this time. Six different armies—those of the Ukrainians, the Bolsheviks, the Whites, the Entente, the Poles and the anarchists—operated on its territory. Kiev changed hands five times in less than a year."[69] These were not the conditions that would enable investors in Paris, Brussels, and London to sleep peacefully, dreaming of high dividends. Irrespective of the Ukrainians' ability to provide stability in Eastern Galicia, Perkins further argued against dividing the refineries of Western Galicia from the oil fields in the east, which would surely ruin those companies that owned shares in both.[70]

Perkins's activities as a lobbyist preceded the negotiations in Paris. Convinced that the Allies would be swayed by news of threats to their own citizens' holdings, he had encouraged Włodek to provide information about Ukrainian confiscations specifically of British, French, or Belgian property after the Ukrainian capture of the oil fields in November. After the conference began, his attempts at intervention became all the more frenzied. He sent persistent missives to Balfour, John Cadman (chairman of both H. M. Petroleum Executive, an advisory organ to the British government, and the Inter-Allied Petroleum Conference), and Herbert James Paton and Esme Howard (British members of the Commission for Polish Affairs [CPA]). Hoping to awaken concerns that the threat of Ukrainian control might not be the least of their fears, Perkins warned Balfour to take note of the "great weight placed on the acquisition by Germans of a controlling position in the Galician oil fields."[71]

Although the Polish economic delegation to the Paris Peace Conference acknowledged its indebtedness to the work of Perkins,[72] Perkins's protestations and demands on behalf of the Polish cause proved to be more energetic than effective. Despite the harrowing claims of impending doom for the oil industry, Poland, and foreign investors, Perkins found little sympathy from British diplomats, who were not convinced that Polish control over Eastern Galicia was in anyone's best interest, and who were suspicious of the overtly Polish bias of the French delegation. Paton informed him that in resolving the extremely delicate situation in Eastern Galicia, "there are many considerations of greater importance than the interests of British financiers." Perkins got no further with Howard, who said, "The interests of the oil co[mpanies] of E[astern] Galicia cannot of course be allowed to stand in the light of the just settlement of the question."[73] When Perkins warned Balfour that "any attempt to diminish Polish sovereignty in Eastern Galicia will jeopardise interests of seventy-five thousand British shareholders," the British Foreign Office replied that it rejected outright the "principle that rights and liberties of inhabitants of any particular country should be subordinated to real or supposed interests of foreign investors."[74] As a whole, the British delegation distrusted Perkins, calling him "a man of wrong political prejudices which he does not attempt to disguise."[75] There is even evidence of some personal dislike of Perkins: E. H. Carr, whose opinion of the Polish case became worse and worse the more exposure he had to the Polish delegation, called Perkins a swine in a letter to Colonel F. H. Kisch from the Military Section of the British delegation.[76] Perkins did not fail to notice that he was getting nowhere with Howard and Paton, reporting in a letter to John

Cadman that he found his conversations with them in Paris "disquieting."[77]

The French and Belgian delegates were subjected to a similar barrage of requests on behalf of the Poles from industrialists and from the Polish delegates themselves. Knowing the French concern with Germany, representatives of the French company Karpaty in Galicia stressed in repeated visits to Paris that in the case of a division of Galicia into western and eastern halves, the whole industry would be sure to fall into the hands of the Germans.[78] The French delegates in Paris responded more favorably to these pleas than did their British colleagues. Spurred on by requests from Dmowski, French foreign minister Stephen Pichon recommended to Clemenceau that the French take action to assist the Poles in protecting the Eastern Galician oil fields: "I would be grateful if you would inform Marshal Foch of this matter with the greatest speed, signaling its weight from a political, as well as an economic, perspective, with an eye to the numerous oil companies situated in this region in which a particularly substantial amount of French capital is invested."[79]

Given the pro-Ukrainian inclinations of the British and the pro-Polish inclinations of the French, along with the intransigence of both belligerents, reaching a compromise was very difficult. The various suggestions for an armistice proposed by a subcommission dispatched to Galicia by the CPA were as contested among the Allies in Warsaw and Paris as they were distasteful to the Ukrainians and Poles they were intended to appease. The main accusation made by the Great Powers in Paris against the proposed demarcation line was that it was egregiously biased in favor of the Poles, a factor that was blamed on the French (although Wade and de Wiart, both of whom contributed to its formulation, were British).[80] The proposed demarcation line would officially designate the oil fields, which were under Ukrainian control at the time, as a neutral zone administered by an Allied commission. This so-called neutrality was belied, however, by the fact that the oil fields would be guarded by Polish policemen. Stanisław Wiktor Szczepanowski described an early version of this proposal in detail in January 1919:

Major Fordham along with an Englishman from [Galicia] (whom I have known for several decades), Mr. George MacIntosh, composed a plan to induce the Ukrainians to withdraw with a restitution to them of 50 percent of the profits and products in the Borysław-Drohobycz basin and half of the petroleum wagons during the armistice. The Ukrainian army would have to withdraw beyond the Stryj River, the Polish army beyond the Dniestr so that the oil region would be neutral, with Polish police and Polish administrators of railways. The oil basin and all mines, refineries, and reserves, regardless of who owned them, would be given over to a commission of the Entente under the leadership of Mr. MacIntosh. The control and development of production, as well as the significant share of the costs from the Ukrainian and Polish side, would proceed under the cooperation of delegates, two from each side.[81]

The High Command of the Polish army in Eastern Galicia interpreted the proposal as placing "the Drohobycz-Borysław petroleum terrain completely in our hands under the condition that a certain contingent would be delivered [to the Ukrainians], but only in exchange for goods that we require."[82] The implications of the proposal were equally transparent to the Ukrainians. Why assent to such a plan when they themselves controlled the region? The government of the ZUNR predictably rejected it and proceeded with a renewed attack on Lviv.[83] As long as the Ukrainians controlled the oil fields, they would not agree to any temporary demarcation line east of the San River, a position to which the British were sympathetic.

Wade and Berthélemy had created a policy so entirely pro-Polish as to call the impartiality of the Inter-Allied Commission to Poland's (IAC) subcommission into doubt. By proposing a border to the east of both Lviv and the oil fields, they guaranteed that the Ukrainians would object, giving the Poles the tactical advantage of appearing more compliant. When the IAC's subcommission left Lviv on 1 March to report back to the IAC, "they left no one in doubt that they wished to give the Ukrainians the full responsibility for the depressing results of their efforts" to achieve an armistice between Poland and Ukraine.[84] Berthélemy's bias was such that he even openly favored allowing Haller's army to fight on behalf of the Poles in Eastern Galicia, leading Colonel F. H. Kisch to ask the Polish Commission pointedly "whether they wished to stop the hostilities, or to help the Poles conquer Ukrainian areas?" David Lloyd George was likewise exasperated with the Poles, whom he accused of being only after the oil, with no higher aspirations in the region than pecuniary gain.[85]

The real problem with reaching a diplomatic solution was that both sides were wary of ceding any ground during an armistice that they were not willing to cede in the final territorial settlement. No one was convinced by claims that the final settlement would not be affected by who actually controlled what territory. Therefore, the willingness of either party to accept a proposed demarcation line was affected by the current status of the war and by that party's prospects for improving its holdings in the near future. When the Poles gained the upper hand in the spring of 1919, the Allies revised their proposal and offered to grant the Poles control over Lviv only and the Ukrainians control over the oil fields. The Ukrainians, fearing that they could do no better, agreed immediately. The Poles, on the other hand, now preferred to keep fighting until they acquired control over both prizes, rightly anticipating that the oil fields would soon fall into their hands.[86] With the prospect of seizing the oil fields before them, not even neutrality of the oil fields was acceptable to the Poles. As the deputy commander of the Polish army in Eastern Galicia wrote to the deputy chief of staff: "Such an unfavorable line could even cause a revolution in our country. . . . We are not afraid of the Ukrainians, and we will take care of them ourselves. If, however, the Entente wants this to happen more quickly, then they can give us necessary materials, uniforms, weapons, etc. In conversations with Englishmen I gathered that if we stand firmly by our demands we can get something out of them."[87] According to that approach, continued military action on the part of the Poles would cost them little, but had the potential to reap great rewards indeed.

In an attempt to justify continued Polish military activity in Eastern Galicia in April 1919, despite explicit Allied instructions to cease, Paderewski portrayed it as directed against Bolsheviks, not against Ukrainians.[88] The British were not fooled. General F. J. Kernan (who, unlike his fellow American, Lord, made a concerted attempt to learn about both sides of the dispute) actually took the trouble to speak to Ukrainians directly, instead of quizzing Poles about their enemies' views. He concluded that accusations that the Ukrainians were Bolsheviks were nonsense and that the Ukrainians were misrepresented in Paris.[89] Paton tried to make this argument with the Poles, insisting that "one should not fight Galician Ukraine, for she is anti-Bolshevik; on the contrary, one should reach an agreement with her and fight together against the Bolshevik army."[90] General Louis Botha similarly argued that contrary to the Poles' claims, the Ukrainians could be useful allies in a battle against the Bolsheviks.[91] Indeed, the prospect of Soviet control of the region was hardly attractive to those Ukrainians who remembered the repression of Ukrainian language and culture and the brutal attacks on the Ukrainian population that had been part of the Russian occupation of Galicia only a few years earlier.

But the Poles' alleged fear of Bolshevism in their midst was little more than a smoke screen to mask their determination to conquer the oil fields before the Allies could grant them to the Ukrainians or take them for themselves. While the Poles did not challenge the Allies' right to settle the territorial question in Paris in principle, behind the scenes they were well aware that Allied interests and Polish interests were not, in fact, identical. First, while the Allies desired the most rapid possible attainment of peace and security in the region, the Poles would be better served by a longer conflict if it left them indisputably victorious. In Szczepanowski's report of a conversation that he had with Berthélemy in early February, he described his response to Berthélemy's request that he, as an oilman himself, should wish to find a compromise with the Ukrainians that would prevent any further destruction of oil wells. "If it comes to the destruction of wells, I am ready to see mine the first to be burned down. ... For Poland it might even be more advantageous if they destroyed as much as one-third of the wells and the remaining two-thirds fell into our hands, than if they destroyed nothing and the whole of it served as a source of strength for our enemies against us."[92] Nor did Szczepanowski's cynicism stop there. He warned that the Allies' motives were suspect: the "*capitalist spheres of these countries have ongoing plans of annexation* and make efforts to obtain the basis [for action] in that direction. The governments seek every possible means and source to *obtain their inclusion as war reparations.*" He insisted that "*oil matters* require great vigilance, for I *have a very strong fear* lest petroleum be neutralized to our great detriment in that the *English and French* would annex it *for themselves.*"[93]

Polish intransigence exasperated the Allies in Paris. Lloyd George noted in despair that eastern European "nations were going straight to perdition."[94] Since General Haller's army had been allowed to return to Poland (theoretically to fight the Bolsheviks), the Polish army's superiority over the Ukrainian forces ensured an imminent Polish victory. Capturing the oil fields remained the Poles' primary goal in the region. On 19 May, the British minister to Warsaw, Percy Wyndham, made one last attempt to convince Piłsudski to sign on to an armistice. But Piłsudski remained firm: Lviv and the Drohobycz-Borysław oil region must be Polish, even though he was prepared to leave the other Polish territorial demands to be settled by the peace conference in Paris. Aside from the oil fields, he was willing to give up large portions of Eastern Galicia in exchange for Lithuania.[95] As Wyndham and Piłsudski discussed the fate of the oil fields in Warsaw, on 19 May 1919, the Polish army marched into Borysław.[96]

The loss of the oil fields was a major economic and military setback for the Ukrainians, who were deprived of one of the few commodities they had been able to sell in exchange for arms. The Czechoslovaks were also devastated. There were seven Czech refineries left over from the empire, which were totally dependent on Eastern Galician oil. The Czechoslovak government had made arrangements with Ukraine for a trade profitable to both parties when the Ukrainians had controlled the oil region.[97] Now they were afraid that Polish control would cut off their supply, and with good reason, since the conclusion of an agreement with the Polish government was out of the question.[98] As the Czechoslovaks feared, the Poles were not eager to honor any contractual obligations into which the Ukrainians had entered before losing the oil fields. The Czechoslovak minister of public works, F. Staňka, requested that President Edvard Beneš intervene with the Great Powers in order to achieve the neutralization and international (including Czechoslovak) control of the Borysław region. In addition, he asked that the Poles be forced to recognize the Czech-Ukrainian petroleum agreement.[99] Although the Czechoslovaks found sympathy with the French delegate to Poland, Eugène Pralon, he was unable to sway the Poles. When Pralon asked the Polish minister of foreign affairs to honor the Czechoslovak demand that ninety thousand tons of oil they had purchased from the Ukrainians be delivered, the minister replied that "we do not take over any Ukrainian obligations. Besides which, our nation knows that, in exchange for oil, the Czechs paid ammunition, which was then used against us."[100] The Poles believed that the Czechoslovaks even planned a direct attack on Borysław to remove it from Polish hands (and presumably return it to the Ukrainians, who were more agreeable).[101]

Outdone and exhausted, the Ukrainians succumbed to the overwhelming strength of the Polish forces and signed an armistice on 16 June that ceded Lviv and the oil fields, but it was repudiated by Dr. Jevhen Petrushevich, who led a renewed Ukrainian attack.[102] On 25 June, the Council of Four decided that the Bolshevik threat and increased Bolshevik activity in Ukraine mandated Polish military occupation of Eastern Galicia for the time being, claiming that this would not affect its final decision on the fate of the territory. This claim came as no consolation to the Ukrainian delegation, which immediately appreciated the gravity of its loss.[103] Ukrainian troops were forced to withdraw east of the Zbruch River.[104] On 28 June 1919, a treaty with Poland announced that Eastern Galician borders would be determined at a later date.[105] In July 1919, the Polish-Ukrainian war came to a close, leaving fifteen thousand Ukrainians and ten thousand Poles dead.[106] Only on 4 September 1919 did the Poles and Ukrainians reach a final armistice, the Ukrainians having accepted the Zbruch River as the Polish frontier.[107] As Ukrainian politicians had feared all along, with Polish control of Eastern Galicia came measures designed to deny the Ukrainians even those cultural and social benefits they had achieved under Habsburg rule: Ukrainian chairs at Lviv University were abolished, Ukrainian professors were dismissed, and Ukrainian students were denied admission unless they could demonstrate

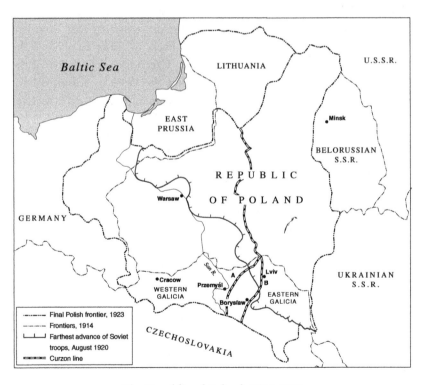

The Republic of Poland, 1914–1923

that they had served in the Polish army during the Polish-Ukrainian war; Ukrainians were removed from government positions, use of the Ukrainian language was restricted, and the term "Ukrainian" was banned.[108]

Ultimately, despite the work of the various committees and commissions, it was the military activities of the Poles and Ukrainians that decided the fate of the oil fields, not the diplomacy of the Allies. For some, the results of the Paris Peace Conference's attempts to bring peace to Eastern Galicia had been a travesty of international diplomacy. Even one of Poland's greatest advocates, Lord, had to admit that its fate had been settled "*vi et armis,* without the Conference and at times to the lively displeasure of the Conference," and that it had "been denounced as a craven surrender in the face of a *fait accompli,* a betrayal of principle, the sacrifice of three and a half million Ukrainians to the ravenous Polish imperialists."[109]

Still, the Poles' de facto control over Eastern Galicia was not secured until it had been awarded de jure as well. Some diplomats continued to tinker with the borders throughout the fall of 1919 and into the 1920s. The British delegation, in particular, still favored some sort of self-determination for the Ukrainians. Lord Curzon, who replaced Balfour as British foreign secretary, insisted "that under no circumstances should E. Galicia be annexed to Poland," thereby separating Galician Ukrainians "from their racial fellows" east of the Zbruch River.[110] Under pressure from the British, on 19 September the Council of Heads of Delegations examined the CPA's statute on Eastern Galicia, in which it again recommended a frontier that would leave Lviv and the oil fields part of an autonomous territory connected to but outside of Poland proper.[111] Even when the British succumbed in November and decided to grant Poland administration of Eastern Galicia, they added the caveat that the current settlement would last twenty-five years, after which time the League of Nations could reconsider.[112]

This temporary settlement naturally made the Poles nervous. Paderewski was not impressed and insisted that the provisional nature of the proposal made it impossible for the Poles to accept. Arguing that it was the Polish state that would provide the main source of funds for the reconstruction of Eastern Galicia, "especially in the oil districts where much Allied capital had been invested," Paderewski asked, "If at the end of the temporary period . . . Galicia be snatched from Poland, from what source would Poland draw its reimbursement?"[113] Grabski pointed out that "Galicia's resources in petroleum would not suffice to amortize the numerous sums which would have to be advanced if its economic rehabilitation were to be made possible."[114] Investments would not be secure if investors could not be sure with what government they would have to negotiate for favorable business terms in the future.

Given the lack of finality in all of these decisions and the continuing resistance of the British, it was very important for the Polish administration to be able to demonstrate that it had complete control over the province. If protecting investments had been a motivation for the Great Powers to cede control of the basin to the Poles, this decision might be reconsidered if the Poles did not live up to their claims to be competent administrators. But forcing the Ukrainian army to retreat from the oil basin was only the beginning of the struggle to restore peace and order and enable the resuscitation of the oil industry. So in August 1919, when tensions mounted between workers and their employers, it was a matter of great concern to the Drohobycz chief district magistrate, who called on the governor's office to provide "six to eight mature, well-paid," and "qualified, energetic police agents" to restore control to the oil basin and prevent a general strike of oil workers.[115] Throughout the fall, the chief district magistrate's fears were realized as the situation in the Drohobycz district worsened both politically and economically. After a large demonstration protesting food distribution in late October and rumors of impending oil workers' demands for a 100 percent pay increase, the chief district magistrate was concerned that local Ukrainians would plan an uprising on 1 November, and also that a socialist movement was becoming stronger in the Borysław basin and was perhaps even tending in the direction of Bolshevism.[116] Drohobycz, after all, had been the site of the only significant Communist uprising in the Western Ukrainian People's Republic, in April 1919. The Ukrainians, he deduced, were trying to bring their maltreatment at the hands of the Polish government to the attention of the world. The oil basin needed to be protected if it was to retain its value: "In order to secure the priceless treasures in the shape of the oil reserves in Borysław basin today as in the future, I obtained from the military authorities an intensification of military personnel, which I assigned quarters in Drohobycz and in the closest regions of the oil basin."[117] Aside from close military supervision, the chief district magistrate recommended that the best means of countering Bolshevism was to make sure that the oil workers were well fed, and he recommended taking energetic measures to ensure this, predicting that the moment the food distribution problem was solved, the Bolsheviks would lose their appeal.

As the weather turned colder and worker anger increased, the employers became incensed at the lack of police protection.[118] Equipment that was irreplaceable in a time of economic trouble was being stolen from under their noses, and there were not enough police to stop the thefts. Hitting the Polish government in Warsaw where it really hurt, they asserted that "because of this, the oil industry sustains incalculable damage, diminishes, and is today on a significantly lower level of development, in spite of the opening of fresh oil-bearing fields, than it was under the Austrian government."[119] As the employers predicted, the winter of 1919–1920 was a time of trial for the oil basin's residents. On 10 December 1919, ten thousand workers and clerks in the oil mines of Borysław-Tustanowice went on strike, demanding that the government live up to promises to improve the food situation it had made during earlier disturbances through the late fall. Their strike was successful to a certain degree: the State Oil Office provided the Committee for Food Distribution with twenty-five hundred tons of refined oil products to trade for food. This measure secured enough bread, flour, legumes, salt, and cheap jam for the near future and appeased the workers, who returned to work.[120]

The workers' action and the miserable conditions that provoked it came to the attention of the British ambassador, Sir Horace Rumbold. He sent numerous complaints to the Ministry of Foreign Affairs recounting a long list of disturbing reports emerging from the oil basin. He insisted that it was the fault of bad management of food distribution that the workers engaged in "disquieting behavior." He demanded the rescinding of a decree that forbade transfer of food from one district of Galicia to another, as well as the removal of corrupt administrators. Scandalous accounts of officials taking bribes to redirect food "naturally have a strong effect on the starving population." Such miserable conditions made the residents vulnerable to extremism—perhaps even Bolshevism, he warned. Inflation had led to an increase in workers' wages of 700 percent since the beginning of the war, but prices had risen 2,000 percent during the same period. Workers complained not only of employers' maltreatment, but also of government abuse. The ambassador suggested that if the government took the lead in providing assistance, then perhaps the employers would be swayed to make larger contributions to providing adequate housing, still a pressing problem. The local police, young men recruited from Poland (i.e., not from Galicia), appeared to be totally corrupt; it had been proven that many acts of theft were carried out with the knowledge of the police. Jews and Ukrainians were the main victims of illegal police confiscation of food. Hunger and malnutrition had led to an outbreak of a typhoid fever epidemic in the region.[121]

The ambassador's complaints created a flurry of activity that stretched from Warsaw to the oil basin. The minister of foreign affairs, greatly embarrassed, turned in exasperation to the prime minister and the minister of the interior in Warsaw for help:

> This letter from the British ambassador seems to point to a strong interest on the part of the British in the domestic affairs of our country. There is no doubt that nothing damages us in the eyes of the British as much as poor administration. Opinions shaped in this regard today will become decisive in the moment of the resolution of the question of the Polish eastern territories, in particular Eastern Galicia. . . . I ask you, Mr. President, to direct this matter to the appropriate parties and apply pressure in the direction of examining and improving the conditions in the Borysław district.[122]

A Committee for Fighting Typhoid Fever was created, which sent a letter to the director of state railways, again referring to the ambassador's memorandum. The ambassador had suggested that the ubiquitous bugs and vermin infesting the trains into and out of Borysław were partially responsible for the spread of typhoid fever, and the committee ordered that they be cleaned regularly.[123]

After himself warning of Bolshevism, famine, and worker strikes, the chief district magistrate now tried to defend the local situation and his own administration. None of these problems was unique to Borysław, he argued. The entire republic suffered from food demands that exceeded available supply. He adamantly denied that any local officials were corrupt. On the contrary, the government was actually favoring oil workers: by selling oil to buy them food, the state had taken on a large burden of expense to the workers' benefit, which made them better off than other citizens of Poland. Local chaos and crime were remnants of the Ukrainian "invasion" that the Polish authorities had not yet had the opportunity to repair. The chief district magistrate had recently been able to arrange for better security in the region: a new investigative unit would be stationed in Borysław equipped with fingerprinting and photographic equipment, police dogs, and other hallmarks of modern crime prevention.

However, it was not only the political insecurity of the region that caused the trouble. The chief district magistrate reported that it was also peculiarly vulnerable to the whims of nature, in particular devastating floods:

> It is hard to blame the Polish government that over the course of a few months it has not built housing for 10,000 families! The fault here must be ascribed in first measure to the owners of the mines and particularly the conviction that Borysław and the entire basin is only temporary, that water covers and will soon cover the entire oil terrain. Thanks to this provisional quality, not only have no houses been built, but in general no lasting construction has been carried out in the town itself— no communication networks have been created nor have any of the constructions that are common in industrial centers been undertaken.[124]

As for confiscations, they only affected known speculators and were totally legal. The typhoid fever epidemic had been reduced by the energetic activities of the local doctor. In conclusion, he called the British ambassador's accusations a "tendentious and malicious representation of the situation in the petroleum basin."[125]

The district police commissioner in Przemyśl and the food distribution inspector for the region were also called upon to respond to the ambassador's accusations. The police commissioner admitted that the food situation remained dire, particularly for married workers, and that the influence of Communist agitators on the workers was obvious. Nevertheless, he had been unable to uncover any evidence of wrongdoing by the police. Just to be safe, he had fired any suspicious individuals throughout the Przemyśl district.[126] The food distribution inspector likewise reported steady improvements.[127] Despite all their efforts, throughout 1920 and 1921 strikes were a regular feature of the Borysław calendar, to the consternation of the minister of the interior. Most of the strikes in the oil basin centered around insufficient food and stimulated the chief district magistrate to make renewed demands for better food distribution in the area, the only way to fend off political radicalization.[128]

That Poland continued to feel insecure about its hold over the oil basin, and the rest of Eastern Galicia, for that matter, is further demonstrated by the attention given to rumors of imminent Ukrainian attack as late as

1921. The Head Command of the Polish army's General Staff reported in January 1921 that Ukrainians were planning an upcoming attack on Eastern Galicia, basing this claim on information provided by a "reliable Viennese source." According to this source, the foreign branch of the Communist Party (Bolshevik) of Ukraine (KP[b]U) had held a conference in Vienna in November 1920.[129] There, according to the informant, it discussed plans to launch a new offensive against the reactionary Polish state in the spring. Eastern Galicia was the most important region. It agreed to send 1 million Polish marks to Lviv to support agitation, 200,000 of which were to be spent in the Drohobycz-Borysław oil region.[130] The concern that this news provoked signals the Polish military's nervousness about the retention of the oil fields. While the Ukrainians did not launch a renewed attack on Eastern Galicia, a war did break out between Poland and Soviet Russia on 25 April. At first the Soviets appeared to overpower the Polish army, but with extensive military equipment from France, the Poles were able to emerge victorious on 12 October.

The French military and political support that assisted the Poles in their victory against Russia came at a cost, as was revealed by the terms of the Petroleum Convention signed by the two states. On 19 February 1921, a Polish-French treaty for "mutual aid and military cooperation" set the groundwork for the Petroleum Convention, which was negotiated one year later[131] and was later ratified by the Polish Sejm on 12 May 1922. According to Polish historian Zofia Zaks, the terms of the Petroleum Convention were very unfavorable for Poland. Poland was forced to grant the French the right to duty-free exports of petroleum and its refined products in excess of the quota designated for domestic production. The French also received preferential treatment regarding taxes, including an exemption from property taxes and forced loans of French capital placed in petroleum companies in the future. Zaks concludes that "with the help of the convention, France secured itself definitively a controlling position in the Galician oil industry."[132]

The French had every reason to be pleased with their progress in securing control over the Galician oil industry. The First World War had convinced France, like all the other belligerents, of the significance of petroleum. Throughout the 1920s, the French took steps to ensure that in the event of another European conflict, their supply of petroleum would be secure. Galicia played an important role in this endeavor, as the detailed studies and investigations made by the Crédit Lyonnais reveal. A certain Jean Chanove approached the bank in July 1922 with plans to create a corporation in response to the French government's concern that France was "currently completely at the mercy of foreign (English or American) suppliers [of petroleum], and in case of war, its situation would be very serious as a consequence." Chanove was in a position to ensure control of a company that owned pits in Borysław and other villages in Eastern Galicia, as well as pits in Romania and Mexico, and wished to know if the Crédit Lyonnais would like to participate in this venture.[133]

Although there is no evidence that the Crédit Lyonnais chose to become directly involved in the Polish oil industry at that time, French involvement in the oil industry was unquestionably increasing (as it was throughout the various branches of Polish industry, mostly at the expense of the Germans).[134] Since the San Remo Convention of 1920, during which Great Britain and France had agreed to divide control over the Galician oil fields between themselves,[135] British interest had progressively diminished, making room for French domination.[136] Contemporary analysts compiled figures demonstrating that the French owned 55 percent of the Polish oil industry by 1920 and 75 percent by 1923.[137] French companies that had begun to get involved before the First World War redoubled their efforts at expansion. Foremost among these was the Société des Pétroles de Dabrowa (Lille). It gained control over the descendants of the companies founded by MacGarvey and Szczepanowski in the 1880s. In 1920, it increased its capital from 13 to 50 million francs (by creating 74,000 new shares) and in 1921 to 138 million francs (by creating 176,000 new shares). By the end of 1922, it could proudly proclaim to its shareholders that it had "taken a very important place in Poland, in the refining industry and in the market for products refined from petroleum."[138] Dabrowa alone controlled 25 percent of the total oil production of Galicia. Its holdings covered over 13,000 hectares and included more than 350 productive wells and another 80 in exploration. In 1922, it was responsible for 12,000 meters of drilling. Its reservoirs could hold 300,000 tons, and the six refineries under its control (three in Poland and one each in Czechoslovakia, Austria, and Hungary) had a refining capacity of 300,000 tons. Its pipelines covered 400 kilometers, and it owned 1,000 railway transport cisterns and one boat cistern of 600 tons. Its commercial subsidiaries included seventy-seven points of retail sale. It employed 6,600 people. Dabrowa looked forward to a future that held only happy prospects for the Polish oil industry and for its own shareholders:

> At the moment when the young Polish state, emerging itself from the thankless period of its reconstitution, shows itself disposed to favor the expansion of its great national industry, the Société des Pétroles de Dabrowa ... is ready to respond to its appeal and contribute in a large measure to the rapid development of the natural riches of this country. [The company] finds itself in a state of prosperity paralleling its industrial development, the legitimate recompense for its reasoned confidence and its perseverant efforts.[139]

When Eastern Galicia was formally given to Poland in March 1923, the political situation appeared to have been stabilized. The territory was officially Polish, even if many of its residents did not feel themselves to be. Local administrators and businessmen could go about their work with the security that came from knowing that they fell under the jurisdiction of the government in Warsaw. But as French investors congratulated themselves on their ability to wrest control of the industry from the Germans and the British, and the Polish government celebrated the beginning of the Second Republic, the real meaning of the steady decline in production over the preceding decade became impossible to ignore. The Polish (as opposed to Austrian or Galician) oil industry had been born, but the oil supply that was to provide its lifeblood was in terminal decline.

[handwritten annotations:]

source base: Paris peace Conf. records

— This cpt, & the book as a whole, reveals the major demographic challenges of a region created by fiat and with very little demographic homogeneity

217 — what did it mean to own land, and what did it mean to control territory?
↳ no longer private vs. public control, but which "nations" could lay claim to land considered theirs?

— Boryslaw oil fields (and Lviv) were the subject of a tug-of-war between Polish + Ukrainian nationalists following World War 1

235 — Petroleum Convention — French + Poles - ceded very lopsided oil export terms for French in exch for arms against soviets

Conclusion

terminal decline

1923 →

By 1923, no one could deny that the history of the Austrian oil industry in Galicia had come to a close. Nevertheless, many hoped that the history of the Polish oil industry had just begun, and that it would be blessed with production and profits previously unknown to poor Galicia. In the 1920s, a Polish geologist estimated that 30 million tons of oil had been extracted from Polish soil, and that 120 to 160 million tons remained.[1] This estimate was quickly taken up by the American-Polish Chamber of Commerce as proof that with only 7 percent of its existing oil reserves exploited, the industry deserved considerable investment.[2] At the same time, the Bankers Trust Company pointed out that Galicia still possessed the third-largest oil reserves in Europe, and that the Drohobycz refinery was the largest on the continent.[3] Even in the late 1930s, many continued to place their hopes on the potential for increased production in Galicia, now called "Little Poland." As in the earlier period of expansion, it was not only Poles who hoped to benefit from Poland's natural resources; interested parties appeared from the West and the East, with plans based on varying predictions of voluntary cooperation from the Polish government. French companies' investment in Galician oil fields continued to increase throughout the early 1920s. According to one historian, at the beginning of the Second World War, "Soviet experts were unanimous in asserting that the recovery of oil could be substantially increased in the part of the Ukraine seized from Poland, that is, in Galicia."[4] In the face of such stubborn optimism, it took decades before the suspicions of a few became the conviction of many: oil would not play a significant role in resuscitating the Polish economy, nor would it provide the pathway to economic development of the region. Polish, French, and Soviet hopes

many hopes

alike were to prove unsubstantiated, and by the last years of the Second World War, an American expert reporting to the Petroleum Industry War Council asserted that "oil [was] truly ammunition in World War II" and simultaneously dismissed Poland's oil industry as insignificant and unworthy of attention. "Poland's negligible oil industry," he reasoned, "enemy-occupied and Nazi-dominated, has doubtless been mulcted to the limit."[5]

Why did it take so long to notice a decline that, with hindsight, can clearly be seen to have begun in 1910? Drops in Galician production had indeed been noted by contemporaries, but past experience had proven to the optimistic that downward trends were often reversible. After all, periodic declines were known not only in Galicia, but also in the gigantic and incontestably thriving oil industry of the United States.[6] A year or two of stagnating or declining production was not considered a sign of irreversible decline and doom. Since 1910, oil production had periodically fallen, then risen again—from 1921 to 1925 as much as 10 percent—giving industry experts cause to believe as late as 1928 that "the decline in production is thus not yet an unhesitating and hopeless decrease."[7]

When French companies took over the industry in the aftermath of the First World War, they found that the amount of investment required to extract oil had become too great to merit further production. French investments had been based on two optimistic assumptions, both of which were to prove false. First, widespread hopes that the export of refined products to France would be profitable were not realized. Second, the anticipated discovery of new oil fields and increases in production after several years of consistent decline remained elusive. The continued decrease in production led to a massive reassessment of the Polish oil industry's value to the French. By 1926, Germany was again the main importer of Polish oil, followed by Austria, Czechoslovakia, Scandinavia, and Hungary. France imported only 1.5 percent of Polish oil.[8] In 1938, Poland produced 501,300 tons of crude, compared with over 2 million tons in 1909.[9]

Declining oil production challenges claims of the importance of human agency. At first glance, it would appear that the real cause for the long-term failure of the Galician and later the Polish oil industry had a lot to do with geological givens that were unrelated to foreign capital investment, tariffs, labor relations, or railroads. After a few brief years of devastating overproduction, the "immeasurable quantities of oil"[10] buried in

Anthropocene quote

Galician soil had petered out just as their availability became critical to the Central Powers' wartime strategy. This supports the contention that "geography and geology are themselves givens—variable across time—that affect the course of economic history, and this is particularly the case with oil."[11] Men certainly cannot create oil where there is none, a problem that plagued the Central Powers in the First World War and Germany again in the Second and threatens to create chaos in states that have come to depend on fossil fuels to drive their entire economies.

Nevertheless, human activity does profoundly affect how much oil finds its way from the belly of the earth to the bottom of a barrel. On the one hand, human technology has won access to subterranean regions of once unimaginable depths. By the Second World War, a proud industry expert could claim that "in the first few minutes of a drilling operation, the fishtail bit has often penetrated antiquity more remote than recorded human history."[12] Even in the three decades before the First World War, the average depth of wells sunk in Galicia increased dramatically. In the 1860s, the deepest wells were 120–150 feet deep, and in the early 1870s, a well that reached 350 feet still raised eyebrows.[13] By the 1880s, both of these figures had been dwarfed by wells sunk down to 1,000 feet with the help of MacGarvey's drilling technology.

On the other hand, producers can rob themselves of access to oil that does in fact exist, and whose location is even known. Thus one can argue that the practice and methodology of extraction do affect the amount of petroleum ultimately available for human consumption. In 1925, one oil expert expressed concern about "a quick exhaustion"[14] and explained how much precious oil was lost to wasteful human extraction: "Every drilling means predatory mining. It has been proven that a drilling can only remove one-fifth to one-third of the petroleum in an oil bed. The remainder remains in the stone like moisture in an only slightly squeezed sponge. Many probes were given up as exhausted, when in reality they were not, and thus became victims of watering down."[15] It is possible that the recklessness with which wells were sunk, drained, and abandoned in the early years of the Galician oil industry negatively affected the amount of oil that could be extracted. As engineers warned, hastily and thus carelessly dug pits were more vulnerable to collapse, water breaks, and premature abandonment. But oilmen must wrest every possible drop of oil from each of their producing wells in order to cover their losses in wells that remain dry, since producing oil from an existing well is much less costly than digging a new well.[16] Premature collapse not only meant less oil, but also substantially less profit. This was the lasting legacy of private ownership of mineral rights, of the wild years of the 1860s and 1870s, and of the race to reach oil "before the neighbors" throughout the nineteenth century.

Much of the excitement and glamour of the early oil industry surrounded the wildcatters and their heated race to discover oil. Even when oil was found, it still had to be coaxed from its resting place and up to the surface. The key ingredient in this process was gas. Tapping into a reserve of gas would cause it to rush toward the surface, carrying along with it the oil trapped underground. Inevitably, where there was oil, there was gas; the question was, how much? Too much gas would cause a gusher, a spectacular and disastrous occurrence. It was impossible to gain control of a gusher until the gas itself was spent, which brought the operator back to the problem of too little gas. Without the aid of gas, extracting oil was a much more laborious process, requiring the slow and expensive pumping of oil that would otherwise rise up of its own accord. Rarely did pumping pay for itself; more rarely still could a pumped well turn a profit.

The problem of gas, along with similar problems caused by water, which would fill up wells dug poorly, too quickly, or without appropriate reinforcements, and by earth, which would cause poorly reinforced wells to cave in, meant that the oil industry was not amenable to a learn-as-you-go style of industrial development. Austria did not, after all, possess "immeasurable quantities of oil" in Galicia. The process of exploring rashly and foolishly could make precious oil inaccessible to later operators, who knew how to do it correctly, just as the work of an inexperienced archaeologist not only may fail to uncover traces of civilizations past, but also may render potentially effective work by later generations impossible. Allowing producers to run roughshod over Galician oil terrain, with the desire to beat competitors to the goods as their primary concern, carried with it serious consequences for the later development of the industry. In this way, social structure and legal policies made in reflection of that structure did indeed change the lay of the land and its potential to produce wealth.

Galicia suffered from the juxtaposition of an economy that was widely considered to lag behind industrializing Europe and the early discovery of a natural resource that predated its discovery just about anywhere else.

Many Polish scholars have stressed that the 1853 delivery of lamps and lighting oil to the Lviv General Hospital preceded the internationally recognized birthday of the oil industry, Colonel Edwin L. Drake's August 1859 success in drilling for oil in Titusville, Pennsylvania. The "Polish" oil industry, they claim, was therefore the oldest.[17] The producers, legislators, drillers, distributors, and administrators who created the Galician oil industry did not have the opportunity to learn from the mistakes others had already made. In the 1870s, oilmen expected that their only continental competition might come from what appeared to be promising oil fields in Italy.[18] Significant Russian oil exploration did not begin until the Nobel brothers founded their Baku-based joint-stock company in 1879.[19] There were no established state-controlled industries to emulate, and the consequences of the wildcatter system in the United States were mitigated there by an entirely different social and economic pattern. In addition, the Americans were able to abandon the ravaged oil fields of Pennsylvania when they began to run dry and head south to Texas, where supply again seemed unlimited. During an 1874 legislative debate over mineral rights, the president of the Galician Sejm suggested following the best model for mining regulations available at that time: those of neighboring Prussia.[20] Prussia boasted a rapidly developing economy, it is true, but it had no oil.

Nonetheless, while a slower, more rational method of extraction might have slowed the decline, it could not have stopped it. The significance of the oil lost to water, mud, and greed pales in comparison with the industry's greater problem: not only was there too little oil in Galicia, but there was too much oil elsewhere. The scale of world oil production was a factor completely out of the control of the Polish government and Polish industrialists. Global oil production skyrocketed after the First World War, while Polish production could, at the very best, hope to stay constant. Although Polish production recovered somewhat from 1921 to 1925, as a percentage of world production it continued its inexorable decline. Global oil production was around 500 million barrels in 1917; by 1940, the United States alone produced 1.7 billion barrels a year.[21] As oil became cheaper and cheaper elsewhere, extraction in Poland became comparatively unaffordable.[22] Stanisław Wiktor Szczepanowski argued that the First World War had proven "the value of the Polish petroleum Subcarpathians as one of the most important strategic points of Europe." Yet he had to acknowledge that the world's need for oil had been transformed since the days when Galicia could satisfy the entire domestic consumption of one of Europe's largest states: when the Germans moved to regain Galicia from Russian occupation, "they were not interested in kerosene for lamps, but rather in railway lines dependent on lubrication, in military automobiles and the entire air force, dependent on gasoline, in the power of nautical submarine weapons driven by Polish oils."[23] If the consumers of oil had changed since the nineteenth century, so had its producers. The modern machine-made world, driven by the fuel combustion engine, was also a world in which petroleum could be found in locations as diverse as Mexico, Indonesia, the Middle East, and South America and in quantities that made Galicia look remote indeed. In 1909, Galicia ranked third among the world's top ten leaders in oil production, behind only the United States and the Russian Empire, and accounted for 5 percent of world production. Its nearest competitors were Romania, British India, Mexico, and Japan.[24] By 1925, Galicia squeaked in at number ten with only 0.54 percent, behind the United States (71.2 percent), Mexico (10.7 percent), the Soviet Union (5 percent), Persia (3.1 percent), Dutch East India (2 percent), Venezuela (1.9 percent), Romania (1.5 percent), Peru (1 percent), and British India (0.75 percent). Global oil production totaled in one year five times the amount that Galicia had produced in the sixty-eight years from 1857 to 1925.[25] The future of oil production did not appear to lie within Europe, even if it did lie under the influence of European powers.

The statistical significance of the Galician oil fields did not survive the Second World War. Derricks grew fewer, and the hustle and bustle of the Borysław (now Boryslav) basin became a thing of the past. Still, some reminders of the excitement and promise of the oil industry—as well as its victims and its misery—remain even today. After the territorial issue of Eastern Galicia had been resolved, and after Austrian companies and bureaucrats had been forced out of the region and replaced by Polish officials (sometimes the same individuals with different uniforms and titles), both German Austrians and Poles turned to the process of memorializing the industry that was no more—in the former case, as part of a nostalgic program of commemorating the monarchy itself, in the latter case as part of an optimistic program to buoy an important national industry with a glorious national past.

The year 1928 marked the seventy-fifth anniversary of Łukasiewicz's invention of the petroleum lamp, an occasion that did not pass unnoticed in Polish circles. Commemorations were multiple. The Committee for the Commemoration of Ignacy Łukasiewicz dedicated a monument to Łukasiewicz as part of the greater Monument of Great Discoverers in Krosno in 1928.[26] The pages of the trade journal *Przemysł Naftowy* (The Oil Industry) were filled with notices of celebrations and articles recording the great deeds of the local hero, as were those of national papers such as *Ilustrowany Kurjer Codzienny* (Illustrated Daily Courier), *Czas* (Time), and *Kurjer Polski* (Polish Courier).[27] Solemn ceremonies were held in his honor at the academy named after him in Krosno. Łukasiewicz's example suggested that Poland, too long derided as an eastern European backwater, had more in common with Great Britain than was often recognized: "This industry—not only in our country, but also elsewhere—had as its pioneers and creators people bringing to it idealistic elements, people whose thoughts stretched across wide horizons, who had great ideas for the creation of the nation-state. That is how it was here, and that is how it was in England."[28]

Journalists also congratulated other great national pioneers of Polish industry, like Stanisław Prus Szczepanowski. Thanks to the elder Szcze-

Borysław in 1936. Polish street signs claim the town for the Polish Republic. (Reproduced by permission of the Österreichische Nationalbibliothek, Vienna.)

panowski, one engineer and freelance writer wrote, "The previously poor Carpathian foothills began to come to life. On the slopes of the Carpathian Mountains, where until then the silence of forests had ruled, the earth began to rumble under the impact of drills." He reminded readers that this was truly a Polish industry—if oil could not be used to boost the Polish economy, at least it could be used to boost Polish national pride. The Borysław basin, even if it was the site of much foreign investment, was created by the "Polish ingenuity" of Władysław Długosz and Władysław Szujski.[29] Długosz himself was proud to note the importance of Borysław as the cradle not only of the oil industry, but of Polish engineering: "Borysław was a school for Polish technology from which grew an entire host of resourceful engineers, who guide that industry to further development for the good of the Fatherland."[30] The emphasis on the importance of Poland's "human resources" in creating the oil industry was thus not only an expedient line of argument created during the 1919–1920 negotiations over Poland's borders, but also a matter of conviction for Polish patriots. The importance of the human—and Polish—contribution to the "natural utility" of the region continued to be stressed, further proof that the republic's southeastern region must remain Polish.

Throughout the 1920s and 1930s, *Przemysł Naftowy* published historical articles lauding Polish engineers and industrialists of times gone by. These articles served to emphasize the Polish nature of the industry, downplaying the influence of Ukrainian workers, Jews, and foreign entrepreneurs (with the occasional exception of MacGarvey). Academics proudly demonstrated the incontrovertible claim that the Polish oil industry was actually the world's oldest, despite Colonel Drake's greater name recognition.[31] Short memoirs of numerous oilmen recounted their entry into the industry and bragged of their personal connection to local legends such as Szczepanowski, MacGarvey, and others.[32]

Galicia and its oil industry came to symbolize something else in German-language literature. References to the province's poverty and misery abounded in the interwar years, as well as during the life of the monarchy itself. References to the oil industry, though relatively rare, demonstrate that the Borysław basin was not entirely forgotten and still attracted eminent visitors. In 1924, Alfred Döblin, a Stettin-born German writer, traveled through Poland and devoted an entire chapter of his account of that journey to the oil basin. Seen through Döblin's eyes, this was an industrial wasteland in the midst of fertile farmland. "I ride across a rich plain filled with arable land. Meadows come, stubble fields, huge herds of black and dappled cattle, horses run free with young chestnut colts. White spots in the green, moving, craning necks and yellow beaks, shrieking: geese."[33] Entering the Drohobycz petroleum refinery, Döblin confronted "a different world"—a clean, modern world of pipes, conveyor belts and typewriters. And in Borysław itself? "The smoke puffs densely from the ground, by the derricks. Slender, wooden, house-high pyramids–they already stand here, next to the highway, singly, in groups; but on the mountains, they stand in bevies, in the middle of the green, amid tree stumps. All the trees around them are polled."[34] A few years later, in 1928, Joseph Roth made a similar pilgrimage to Borysław as a correspondent for the German newspaper *Die Frankfurter Zeitung*. Where Döblin had seen only "mutilated forests," Roth suggested that nature was able to hold its own against the encroachments of industry. "The oil derricks here in Borysław . . . although they number in the thousands, are not the only vegetation of the land. There are still forests that only hesitantly give way to the towers and appear rather to surround them peacefully than to flee them with hostility."[35]

But if Roth and Döblin were both impressed by the relatively harmonious intermingling of oil derricks and oak trees, their portrayals of the social landscape were not as forgiving. Both authors painted a similarly miserable picture of the living conditions that continued to characterize "Austrian El Dorado" long after Polish independence. Döblin described Drohobycz: "Anyone who hasn't seen these alleys and 'houses' doesn't know what poverty is. These aren't houses, these are remnants of houses, shacks, sheds, huts."[36] The housing fared no better in Roth's description: "Only once in a while a larger house of brick, whitewashed and with a stony face, interrupts the sad row of the slanted, decaying, and crumbling dwellings. . . . Not a single one of these hurried homes looks designed to accommodate sleeping people, but rather to agitate sleeplessness and to strengthen it." Roth suggested that the very earth under those houses threatened to swallow them whole: "Right next to the houses runs a wooden walkway, held up by short stumpy posts. It would be impossible to build a paved sidewalk, because pipes carrying oil to the train station run under the street. The difference between the level of the walkway and that of the street, but also that of the small houses is considerable, and the pedestrian reaches or towers over the roofs of the houses and looks down diagonally through the windows."[37] The misery of "Galician

Sodom" and "Galician Inferno" outlasted the excitement of "Galician California."

Intrigue and conspiracy also found their place in literary memorials to the Galician oil industry. Galicia appears only peripherally in Robert Musil's unfinished novel *The Man without Qualities,* written in the 1930s. It is, for example, the birthplace of a Jewish chambermaid and a potent symbol of dirty and unpleasant travel—both images that are typical for the memory of Galicia. But the careful reader will be surprised to find that Galicia plays a central role in some of the main characters' motivations and strategies. The novel is set in 1913, and focuses on the plans for the seventieth anniversary of Francis Joseph's reign (which would have occurred in 1918 had the emperor lived that long). To the delight of some of the event's planners, and to the consternation of others, a Prussian industrialist (Arnheim) appears strangely interested in participating in the preparations. The novel's hero (if a man without qualities can be referred to as such), Ulrich, uncovers Arnheim's true motivation and confronts the Ministry of War's delegate to the planning committee with his suspicions:

> "Of course you're involved with the oilfields!" Ulrich burst out, suddenly seeing the light. "It's a problem that concerns your naval branch because it needs fuel for its ships, and if Arnheim wants the drilling fields, he'll have to concede a favorable price for you. Besides, Galicia is deployment territory and a buffer against Russia, so you have to provide special safeguards in case of war for the oil supply he wants to develop there. So his munitions works will supply you with the cannons you want! Why didn't I see this before! You're positively born for each other!"[38]

The motives and crises of the Austrian military during the First World War are thus retained not only in the archives of the Ministry of War, but on the pages of one of twentieth-century Austria's greatest literary masterpieces. Musil captured an image of Galicia that was preserved in literature not only as the birthplace of fleas and poor Jewish refugees, but also of petroleum-fueled intrigue.

Since the Second World War, commemorating the history of the Boryslav oil basin has been taken up with the greatest energy by Ukrainian historians and park planners. At the center of many of these memorials stands Ivan Franko. Franko has been physically memorialized in statues throughout western Ukraine—in Drohobycz, where he went to high school, in Nahuievychi, where he was born, and elsewhere. In Lviv, where he studied, the university now bears his name, as does the city of Ivano-Frankivsk, formerly Stanisławów (Stanyslaviv). Franko is, at least within Ukraine, one of the greatest symbols of the region's Ukrainian past.

In 1956, the hundredth anniversary of Franko's birth, the Ukrainian literary magazine *Zhovten'* (October) published a special issue in his honor that included an interview of a Ukrainian who claimed to have met Franko personally. He recounted a tale about Franko that he had heard from a friend of his father's. His story unwittingly reproduces the plot of Franko's novella *Boryslav Is Laughing,* only substituting Franko himself for the novel's fictional hero, Bened'o. Now it is Franko who came to Borysław and taught the workers how to organize and form a strike committee and gave their leader "a book by Karl Marx in German."[39] The creation of a Borysław mythology of proletarians, get-rich-quick schemes, and patrimonial land lost by naïve Ukrainian peasants to predatory foreigners reveals the impact of the oil industry on Galician culture and cultural memory.

In the 1980s and 1990s, Galicia became a popular object of the fantasy of authors who escort readers through a country that no longer exists as a single administrative or geographic unit. Imaginary travel guides lead one through the province, from Martin Pollack's *Nach Galizien* (To Galicia) to Stanisław Grodziski's *Wzdłuż Wisły, Dniestru i Zbrucza* (Along the Vistula, Dniestr, and Zbruch Rivers).[40] Stephan Vajda's *Reisen Anno 1900: Ein Führer durch die Länder der k.u.k. Monarchie* (Travel in the year 1900: A Guide through the Lands of the k.u.k. Monarch) finds traces of the oil industry in Gorlice.[41] Everywhere one finds something quaint, something long gone:

> The eastern Galician earth is black and juicy and always looks a bit sleepy, like a huge fat cow that stands there and good-naturedly allows itself to be milked. In this way the eastern Galician earth gratefully gives back a thousandfold everything that one puts into it, without having to flatter her with fertilizers and chemicals. Eastern Galician earth is wasteful and rich. It has fat oil, yellow tobacco, grains heavy like lead, old dreamy woods and rivers and lakes, and above all, beautiful, healthy people: Ukrainians, Poles, Jews.[42]

Literary compilations trace the province's multiethnic past in poems, short stories, and essays translated from German, Polish, Ukrainian, and Yiddish.[43]

While these compilations, memoirs, and wanderings trace the effects of the oil industry on imagined Galicia—or, in some cases, try to reinvent Galicia for readers who have no imagined vision of it at all—they do not explain more physical remnants of the oil industry in today's Ukraine. Three-quarters of a century after Roth's and Döblin's visits to the region, the trees they described as "hesitantly" giving way to oil derricks have regained control over the hills surrounding Boryslav. A few lone pumps stand amid pastures and gardens. There are monuments to oilmen, and statues and schools have been named in their honor, but is the region any richer for having stored this natural wealth? Not discernibly. Do the grandchildren of oilmen study in better schools or reach Lviv by more efficient roads and railways because of a lasting contribution made by oil revenues to local infrastructure? Certainly not. Is the air more polluted and the water poorer in fish today because of oil spills and gasoline leaks in decades gone by? Quite possibly, although it would require the research of an ecologist to be certain. To the naked eye, the industry seems to have left almost no trace at all.

The relationship between oil and human society has evolved considerably over the past 150 years. What was once a curious, messy, and dangerous substance has become our constant companion—at times visibly, as when we fuel our own cars, and at times invisibly, as when we store our left-overs in plastic containers or apply moisturizers to our chapped lips. The centrality of petroleum and its by-products in our own lives can blind us to the nature of our predecessors' relationship with it. In the nineteenth century, the most profitable use for oil was as a source of light, and kerosene was its most valuable by-product. Gasoline, on the other hand, was discarded as useless.[44] The first men to concern themselves with oil were not speculators, entrepreneurs, or industrialists, but "mad" scientists who alienated themselves from their neighbors in the process. In the first regions where petroleum was exploited, and where, consequently, law-makers could not learn from the mistakes of predecessors, this affected the way oil laws were set up. In Austrian Galicia in the 1850s, no one had any experience with petroleum, and no one could predict just how valuable it would become. Legislators, lawyers, pharmacists, and land-owners who oversaw the infancy of the "oil industry" in the mid-nineteenth century—whether in Pennsylvania or Galicia—had little idea of the long-term significance of the decisions they made. The difference between the two cases is that in the United States, the mistakes made in Pennsylvania in the 1850s and 1860s could be used to make the wildcatters of Texas smarter because the Texas oil industry was, in effect, a different one and was regulated by a different set of state laws. Texan wildcatters had the chance to start over on fresh territory. But in Galicia there was no moving and starting over. Laws, even when amended, remained at the most basic level the same. Regulations, even when they became more strict, were subject to the weight of long-established traditions and expectations embedded within the local culture.

The world our protagonists inhabited is a difficult one to re-create. Its heroes not only had different expectations about oil, but also moved in conceptual circles that no longer exist and that call up identities that seem contradictory or nonsensical to modern sensibilities. If the development of the Galician oil industry contributed to Polish and Ukrainian nation-building—and the rhetoric of its leaders, as well as its financial and even military centrality in the 1910s and 1920s, suggests that it did—its heroes do not fit nicely into the typical narrative of national awakening. Even where drillers, industrialists, and investors did intend to support nation-

Boryslav in June 2000. Where derricks once dominated the skyline, trees and gardens now flourish. (Photograph by author.)

building, their lives, relationships, loyalties, interests, and business activities crossed over national boundaries. Szczepanowski was a Polish expert on India who immigrated to Austria with a British passport. MacGarvey and many other early drillers who could not replicate his leap to entrepreneurship were North Americans searching primarily for adventure and profit. While these North Americans had little interest in national development, their very actions contributed to it.

As individuals, the work of Galicia's most prominent oil pioneers lasted only as long as their reputations—and, in most cases, these have been unable to survive the nationalizing impulses of the twentieth century. Szczepanowski's reputation was irrevocably tarnished by his trial and the scandal it aroused. But even without it, the combination of his Polish patriotism and his commitment to working within the structure of the Austrian Empire made him a complicated example of Polish heroism and has kept him out of Polish biographical dictionaries. MacGarvey, who died in Vienna during the Russian occupation of his oil fields in the first months of the First World War, built an oil empire that was destroyed by the reconfiguration of European space with no room for grand industrialists from Canada. The legacies of these two great "Galicians" remind us that whom we choose to commemorate is more a reflection of ourselves and our current values than of the actual accomplishments or contemporary contributions of our predecessors. Although MacGarvey is uncelebrated in Poland, he was inducted into the Canadian Petroleum Hall of Fame in 2000.

If Galicia's multinational population of oil pioneers defies easy categorization, the motivations of the industry's workers are equally difficult to pigeonhole. Their behavior does not fit nicely into the typologies we have inherited from the theories of the nineteenth and twentieth centuries. Oil workers had multiple identities that confuse Marxists and students of nationalism, but that did not confuse the workers themselves. They were workers, but also peasants—and young bachelors, and alcoholics, and Roman Catholics, or Greek Catholics, or Jews, and, in some cases, but not all, Poles or Ukrainians. Although contemporary politicians and modern historians alike look for worker interest in nationality, class consciousness, political freedoms, and physical safety, the evidence suggests that workers' daily concerns actually revolved around passing their few idle hours as pleasantly as possible, earning money as quickly as possible, and spending it as they saw fit and not as their "betters" thought they should. Hence a requirement to invest in accident insurance or to provide for one's widow with a mandatory life insurance policy aroused enough anger to cause a strike, but layoffs combined with free railway passes home or (in some cases) to America were greeted with quiet acceptance.

Equally offensive to modern sensibilities is the relatively lackadaisical attitude to oil during the First World War. The complete lack of foresight that characterized the Ministry of War's energy policy in the early 1910s suggests a degree of incompetence that it is hard for the modern observer to forgive. Scattered statements by contemporaries recognizing the centrality of petroleum both to industry and to waging war make the failure to solve the problem of transporting oil from Galicia to the Adriatic all the more puzzling. We must, however, be careful not to interpret those scattered remarks as universal conviction or even general knowledge. Hindsight, as they say, is 20/20, and in retrospect, Churchill's decision to convert the British navy from coal to petroleum seems ingenious. But only slowly did military and civilian leaders become aware of the importance of oil during the First World War. A comparison of the fate of the Galician oil fields in 1915 and the Romanian oil fields in 1917 makes this all the more clear. The story of the British destruction of the Romanian oilfields in anticipation of their capture by the Germans is well known. How did the Russians behave, though, when they retreated from Galicia and left its oil fields to the Central Powers? For all the plundering, raping, and pillaging that the Russian troops engaged in, they left the oil fields remarkably intact. Austrians were surprised at the limited extent of the damage. The Russians, themselves suffering from an inability to get oil from where it was produced to where it was needed, did not even exploit the Galician oil fields fully during the period of occupation.[45] When the outbreak of the Second World War loomed, a historian looking back on the First could say with a degree of consternation, "In any case, the course of the World War 1914–1918 as it relates to oil supply shows us that a recognition of the importance of economic strength to the waging of war was completely absent. One needs only to imagine how a general would incorporate into his plans objects of such value as the two great oil regions [of Galicia and Romania] and with what effort one would fight over them in a war today in order to measure the change in perspective over the past two decades."[46]

Of course, it did not take long for military planners to learn from the mistakes and oversights of the First World War. In the interwar period, Lord Curzon's conviction that the Allies rode to victory on a wave of oil was widely shared and became a matter of pressing concern for politicians and generals in every European state without its own domestic source of oil. Not convinced that they enjoyed "peace for our time," France and Germany, in particular, were keen to find a solution to the problem of how to secure petroleum should another conflict follow upon the "war to end all wars." The conviction that reliable sources of petroleum needed to be secured helped inspire the French to invest heavily in the Polish industry, but also explains their concern that Polish oil was neither secure enough nor available in large enough quantities to satisfy their needs completely. As one historian has concluded, "it was not reason and argument that prevailed" in determining the fate of Eastern Galicia, but rather "the obsessive fear of the Allied and Associated Powers of Bolshevism" combined with the French and American bias favor of historic Poland.[47]

Hitler, too, devoted considerable time and money to the problem of oil production. In 1939, 65 percent of Germany's oil consumption needed to be imported from outside the Reich, a problem that German leaders knew would become acute should hostilities break out with France and Russia. Hitler's awareness of the need to develop a domestic supply of petroleum that could not be cut off by Germany's neighbors led to his interest in synthetic oil production—a project that received considerable investments during the 1930s. Hitler went so far as to impose a duty of 170 Reichsmarks per ton on petroleum imports (amounting to approximately 500 percent of its value) in order to encourage the production of synthetic fuel.[48]

Whether as a source of light or as engine fuel, oil had a lot to offer in the late nineteenth and early twentieth centuries. Then, as now, oil could mean great financial success, industrialization fueled by the internal combustion engine, economic development, and military might. In central Europe, oil could also mean national legitimacy—a key factor in the prolongation of hostilities in Eastern Galicia in 1919. For the nascent Western Ukrainian People's Republic, the exploitation of oil offered much more than personal financial gain—oil was the ticket to Ukraine's very existence as a state. Likewise, for Polish combatants, control over the oil fields both provided and was justified by the call for much-needed continuity. If the men who were the first inventors, pioneers, and investors in the industry were Polish, then, it was argued, the Polish nation had a rightful claim to the industry its sons had built. If it was Poles who had invested the land with its value, then they deserved to control it. Even after the Polish-Ukrainian war ended in victory for the Poles, this line of reasoning continued to inspire countless histories of the "Polish" oil industry. Poles' claim to have the world's oldest oil industry, preceding even Colonel Drake's inauguration of the oil era in the United States, became a matter not only of national pride but of national justification.

If the history of Galicia's oil industry has a slogan, it is "disaggregate." Historians must create categories and make generalizations—without them, history is only a chaotic conglomeration of infinite actions, statements, births, and deaths. But our desire to make sense out of the past by simplifying it has to be moderated by a commitment to reproducing its complexity. This means acknowledging how incomplete national groups and national identities were. It also means underscoring that even the most coherent groups are only adequately described when they are disaggregated. Oilmen were not all alike—some controlled large companies, some small. Some profited from strikes and production stoppages, some were undone by them. The mixed motives of oil producers explain the failure of cartels in Galicia, but also the general inability to work together with "united strength" for the benefit of the industry as a whole. This only becomes clear when oil producers are not treated as a single unit. Likewise, oil workers existed as a coherent group only in the minds of those who tried to use them to further their own agendas. They were divided into skilled and unskilled, Catholic and Jew, west Galician and east Galician, aboveground and belowground, men and (a very few) women. The closer one looks, the less surprised one can be by a lack of worker "solidarity."

The political structures in which decisions about the oil industry were made also deserve to be treated severally. The oil industry provides a classic example of an industry affected by the global economy, international commerce, imperial (or "national") consumption patterns, provincial laws, local behaviors, and geological conditions that vary by the meter. Here we see an imperial government that did not impose its own, oppressive, "colonial" interests on hapless local businessmen, but rather an imperial government that largely ceded control of an entire industry— an industry whose development was imperative for the economic health of the empire at large—to provincial authorities. Imperial interference in the oil industry came only "on request," in deference to the specific desires of the oil industry's local representatives. Ironically, by rescuing the Galician oil producers from price collapse in the first decade of the twentieth century, the imperial government actually exacerbated the oil shortage that proved fateful during the Great War. Here too, then, the only accurate analysis of the politics of oil in Austria-Hungary is one that acknowledges the diversity of platforms on which political activity was performed—from the most local to the imperial and beyond.

In considering the postarmistice (one cannot really say postwar) fate of the Galician oil fields, diversity again becomes the key. Not only did different Polish political actors have different visions of the new, re-created Polish state, but so, too, did Ukrainian politicians, west and east, and the Allies. To explain why and how Eastern Galicia ended up in Polish hands, one must understand not only the course of negotiations in Paris, but also the changing fortunes of the belligerents on the battlefields of Galicia itself. The outcomes of battles between Polish and Ukrainian forces were affected by help they received or did not receive from the western Allies, but so, too, were the Allies' negotiations constrained by their inability to impose decisions made in Paris on soldiers and civilians in Galicia.

Finally, the rise and particularly the fall of the Galician oil industry remind us of the plurality of landscapes that can characterize one place: pastoral, industrial, bleak, verdant, ravaged by warfare, abandoned by industry. In the oil fields of Galicia we see no progression from the characteristically "traditional" to the stereotypically industrial/modern. There is no progression, only movement—the repetitive rise and fall of the grasshopper pump mirrors the circular rise and fall of production, of vegetation, of population.

As the landscape changed, so did the problems faced by its inhabitants—and when problems change, solutions must either be flexible or risk not being real solutions for long. Galicia and, for that matter, Austria-Hungary would have benefited from this perspective in the early twentieth century. Oil producers based their strategies on the premise that they had more oil than they could possibly use, but they would soon learn that great wealth in a particular commodity does not translate into wealth for its producers unless they are very smart and very lucky. Too many producers were more concerned with their own short-term profits than with creating long-term prosperity, greater integration of the industry, and superior infrastructure in the province that was their home. Even those whose sights were set higher than company profitability could not overcome the incompatibility of their desire for Galician autonomy with the industry's need for economic integration with the rest of Austria. For the Galician oil industry, it was too much autonomy, not too little, that proved catastrophic.

Appendix

Notes

Archival and Primary Sources

Index

Appendix: Data on Oil Production

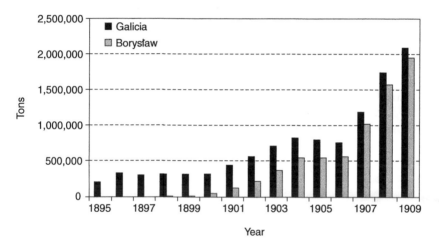

Galician crude oil production, 1895–1909. *Note:* Figures for Borysław here also include production in the villages of Tustanowice and Wolanka (incorporated into the city of Borysław/Boryslav in 1919). Borysław and Tustanowice together accounted for 65.97 percent of all Galician production in 1904 and 95.3 percent of all Galician production in 1908. *Source:* Joseph Mendel and Robert Schwarz, eds., *Internationale Petroleumstatistik,* vol. 2, *Österreich-Ungarn* (Vienna: Verlag für Fachliteratur, 1912), 10.

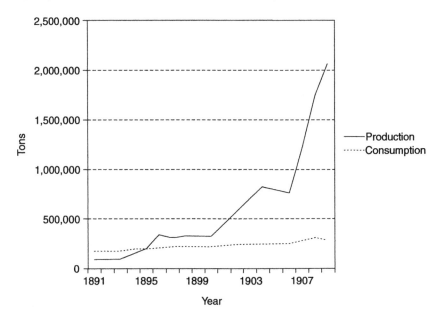

Austro-Hungarian oil production versus consumption, 1891–1909. *Source:*
Joseph Mendel and Robert Schwarz, eds., *Internationale Petroleumstatistik,* vol.
2, *Österreich-Ungarn* (Vienna: Verlag für Fachliteratur, 1912), 10.

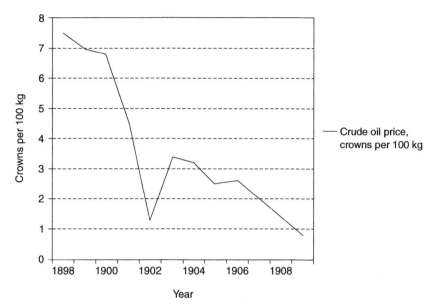

Average price of crude in Galicia, 1898–1909. *Sources:* 1898–1907: Report prepared by the Chamber of Commerce and Trade in Lviv for the viceroy's office, 22 May 1908, TsDIAUL 146.4.3419: 72. 1908: "Volkswirthschaft und kaufmännische Interessen: Die Sanierungsaktion in der Rohölindustrie von Dr. S. Segil," *Zeit,* 14 May 1908. 1909: Sigmund Brosche, "Enquête über die Krise in der Mineralölindustrie," MföA F. 664 Z. 1079 XIV 1910.

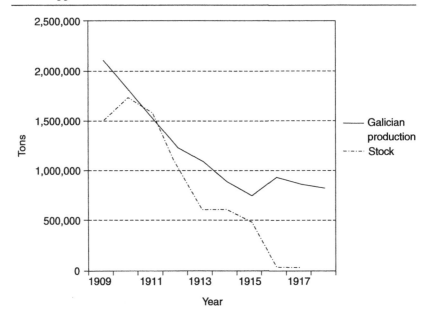

Galician oil production and oil stocks, 1908–1918. *Source:* Robert Schwarz, *Petroleum-Vademecum: Tafeln für die Erdölindustrie und den Mineralölhandel,* 6th ed. (Berlin: Verlag für Fachliteratur, 1929), 178–179; ÖSTA KM MS II GG 1917.

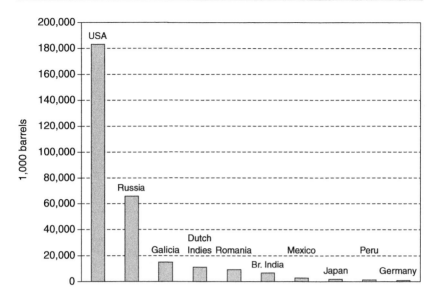

Global oil production, 1909. *Source:* Robert Schwarz, *Petroleum-Vademecum: International Petroleum Tables,* 7th ed. (Berlin: Verlag für Fachliteratur, 1930), 4–6.

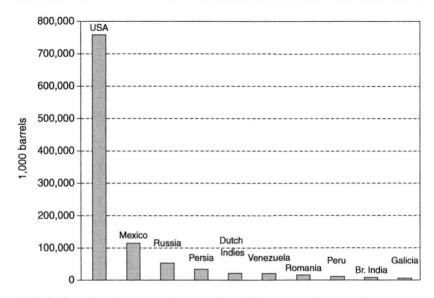

Global oil production, 1925. *Source:* Robert Schwarz, *Petroleum-Vademecum: International Petroleum Tables,* 7th ed. (Berlin: Verlag für Fachliteratur, 1930), 4–6.

Notes

Introduction

1. Fernand Braudel, "On a Concept of Social History," in *On History*, trans. Sarah Matthews (Chicago: University of Chicago Press, 1980), 131.
2. L. von Neuendahl, *Das Vorkommen des Petroleums in Galizien und dessen Gewinnung* (Vienna: Gerold, 1865), 4–6; Ladislaus Szajnocha, "Über die Entstehung des karpathischen Erdöls," *Naphta* 7, no. 1 (15 January 1899): 5–7; Carl Diener, Rudolf Hoernes, Franz E. Suess, and Victor Uhlig, *Bau und Bild Österreichs* (Vienna: Tempsky, 1903), 823.
3. Georg Engelbert Graf, *Erdöl, Erdölkapitalismus und Erdölpolitik* (Jena: Urania Verlag, 1925), 29.
4. Daniel Yergin, *The Prize: The Epic Quest for Oil, Money, and Power* (New York: Simon and Schuster, 1991), 14.
5. Robert Schwarz, *Petroleum-Vademecum: Tafeln für die Erdölindustrie und den Mineralölhandel,* 6th ed. (Berlin: Verlag für Fachliteratur, 1929), 2–5.
6. Robert Schwarz, *Petroleum-Vademecum: Tafeln für die Erdölindustrie und den Mineralölhandel,* 7th ed. (Berlin: Verlag für Fachliteratur, 1930), 18–19. The top four producers were the United States, Russia, the Dutch Indies, and Mexico.
7. Gary Cohen, "Neither Absolutism nor Anarchy: New Narratives on Society and Government in Late Imperial Austria," *Austrian History Yearbook* 29, no. 1 (1998): 49.
8. John W. Boyer, "Religion and Political Development in Central Europe around 1900: A View from Vienna," *Austrian History Yearbook* 25 (1994): 32–34.
9. P. H. Frankel, *Essentials of Petroleum: A Key to Oil Economics* (New York: Kelley, 1969), 21.
10. Ibid., 82, 70.

11. Edith Penrose, "Oil and the International Economy: Multinational Aspects," in *Oil in the World Economy*, ed. R. Ferrier and A. Fursenko (London: Routledge, 1989), 9.

12. Frankel, *Essentials of Petroleum*, 31–32.

13. Penrose, "Oil and the International Economy," 9.

14. Ibid., 5.

15. This statistic is based on calculations made by Stanisław Szczepanowski in his classic work *Nędza Galicyi w cyfrach i program energicznego rozwoju gospodarstwa krajowego* (Lviv: author, 1888), 28–29. Ever since its original publication, it has been cited (often without attribution) by historians wishing to demonstrate the miserable economic conditions in which Galicians lived (see, for example, Ivan L. Rudnytsky, "The Ukrainians in Galicia under Austrian Rule," in *Nationbuilding and the Politics of Nationalism*, ed. Andrei S. Markovits and Frank E. Sysyn [Cambridge, MA: Harvard University Press, 1982], 52, or Raphael Mahler, "The Economic Background of Jewish Emigration from Galicia to the United States," *YIVO Annual of Jewish Social Science* 7 [1952]: 257). Even those contemporaries who agreed with his basic conclusions viewed some of Szczepanowski's statistics skeptically. See, for example, Ivan Franko's favorable but skeptical review, "Zlydni Halychyny v tsyfrakh," in *Zibrannia tvoriv u p'iatdesiaty tomakh*, vol. 44, no. 2 (Kiev: Naukova Dumka, 1985), 11–35.

16. Paul Robert Magocsi, *Galicia: A Historical Survey and Bibliographic Guide* (Toronto: University of Toronto Press, 1983), 138; Mahler, "Economic Background," 255.

17. William Alexander Jenks, *The Austrian Electoral Reform of 1907* (New York: Columbia University Press, 1950; New York: Octagon Books, 1974), 71. Citations are to the 1974 edition.

18. Magocsi, *Galicia*, 139.

19. Heinrich-Eduard Gintl, *Die Concurrenzfähigkeit des galizischen Petroleums mit Rücksicht auf die neuen Oelgruben in Sloboda-Rungurska nächst Kolomea* (Vienna: Spielhagen und Schurich, 1885), 27.

20. Ladislaus [Stanisław] Szajnocha, *Die Petroleumindustrie Galiziens*, 2nd ed. (Cracow: Verlag des Galizischen Landesausschusses, 1905), 4.

21. Joseph Roth, "Reise durch Galizien," *Frankfurter Zeitung* (20 and 22 November 1924).

22. C. F. Eduard Schmidt, *Die Erdöl-Reichthümer Galiziens: Eine technologisch-volkswirthschaftliche Studie* (Vienna: Carl Gerold's Sohn, 1865), 4.

23. "Ausserordentliche Generalversammlung des galiz. Landes Petroleum Vereines," *Naphta* 7, no. 1 (15 January 1899): 5.

24. Szczepanowski, *Nędza Galicyi*, xvii.

25. Rudnytsky, "Ukrainians in Galicia," 52.

26. Ivan Franko, "Der galizische Bauer," *Die Zeit* (Vienna), 21 August 1897, in Ivan Franko, *Beiträge zur Geschichte und Kultur der Ukraine: Ausgewählte deutsche Schriften des revolutionären Demokraten*, ed. E. Winter and P. Kirchner (Berlin: Akademie-Verlag, 1963): 348–399.

27. Szczepanowski, *Nędza Galicyi*, xiii.

28. Theodore Bohdan Ciuciura, "Ukrainian Deputies in the Old Austrian Parliament," *Mitteilungen der Arbeits- und Förderungsgemeinschaft der Ukrainischen Wissenschaften* (Munich) 14 (1997): 44–45.

29. See, for example, Rudnytsky, "Ukrainians in Galicia," 38–42; Ivan Rudnytsky, "Polish-Ukrainian Relations: The Burden of History," in Ivan Rudnytsky, *Essays in Modern Ukrainian History* (Edmonton, Alberta: Canadian Institute of Ukrainian Studies), 49–76; Yaroslav Hrytsak, "A Ukrainian Answer to the Galician Ethnic Triangle: The Case of Ivan Franko," in *Polin: Studies in Polish Jewry*, vol. 12, *Focusing on Galicia: Jews, Poles, and Ukrainians, 1772–1918*, ed. Israel Bartal and Antony Polonsky (London: Littman Library of Jewish Civilization, 1999), 142; John-Paul Himka, "Dimensions of a Triangle: Polish–Ukrainian–Jewish Relations in Austrian Galicia," in Bartal and Polonsky, *Polin*, 28–29.

30. Ivan Franko, "Drei Riesen im Kampfe um einen Zwerg," *Die Zeit* (Vienna), 29 June 1907, in Franko, *Beiträge*, 435.

31. John-Paul Himka, *Socialism in Galicia: The Emergence of Polish Social Democracy and Ukrainian Radicalism, 1860–1890* (Cambridge, MA: Harvard University Press, 1983), 177.

32. Neuendahl, 3.

33. Franz Pošepny, "Die Anwendung des amerikanischen Verfahrens der Petroleum-Gewinnung auf Galizien," *Österreichische Zeitschrift für Berg- und Hüttenwesen* 13, no. 39 (25 September 1865): 309.

34. *Die österreichische-ungarische Monarchie in Wort und Bild*, vol. 11, *Galizien* (Vienna: k.k. Hof- und Staatsdruckerei, 1898), 857.

35. Stanisław Szczepanowski, *Nafta i praca, złoto i błoto* (Lviv: author, 1886), 40.

36. H. Wachtel, "Die Naphta und deren Industrie in Ostgalizien vom Standpunkte des Bergregals," *Österreichische Zeitung für Berg- und Hüttenwesen* 8, no. 16 (16 April 1860): 131.

37. Iván Berend and György Ránki, *Economic Development in East-Central Europe in the 19th and 20th Centuries* (New York: Columbia University Press, 1974), 166.

38. Yergin, *Prize*, 249–252.

39. Letter from Ivan Franko to Mykhailo Pavlyk, 12 November 1882, in *Zibrannia tvoriv u p'iatdesiaty tomakh*, vol. 48 (Kiev: Naukova Dumka, 1986), 325.

40. Charters Wynn, *Workers, Strikes, and Pogroms: The Donbass-Dnepr Bend in Late Imperial Russia, 1870–1905* (Princeton, NJ: Princeton University Press, 1992), 4, 37; Douglas Holmes, *Cultural Disenchantments: Worker Peasantries in Northeast Italy* (Princeton, NJ: Princeton University Press, 1989), 56; Ronald Grigor Suny, *The Baku Commune, 1917–1918: Class and Nationality in the Russian Revolution* (Princeton, NJ: Princeton University Press, 1972), 10.

41. Diener et al., *Bau und Bild Österreichs*, 826.

1. The Land Where Salt and Oil Flowed

1. Ignacy Daszyński, *Pamiętniki*, vol. 1, (Cracow, 1925–1926; repr., Warsaw: Książka i Wiedza, 1957), 32.

2. "Programm für die Allerhöchste Reise Sr. Majestät des Kaisers nach Olmütz, ferner durch Galizien und die Bukowina, endlich nach Czegléd und Fünfkirchen vom 29. August bis 23. September 1880": telegram from Feldmarschall-Lieutenant Freiherr von Mondel to Obersthofmeister Feldmarschall-Lieutenant Fürst zu Hohenlohe Schillingfürst, 18 September 1880; Obersthofmeisteramts-officier Loebenstein, "Bericht über die Vorfallenheiten während der Reise S.M. des Kaisers vom 29. August bis 1. September d.J.," in "Geheime Berichte." Each of these files is in ÖHHSA, Neue Zeremonialakten. A. R. XV. Hofreisen etc. 1880, No. 640–661: Galizien und Ungarn.

3. "Kantata zur Feier des Allerhöchsten Hoflagers Seiner Apostolischen Majestät in der königlichen Freistadt Sambor." ÖHHSA, "Sambor," Neue Zeremonialakten. A. R. XV. Hofreisen etc. 1880, No. 640–661: Galizien und Ungarn.

4. Alexander Gerschenkron, *An Economic Spurt That Failed: Four Lectures in Austrian History* (Princeton, NJ: Princeton University Press, 1977), 60.

5. Francis Joseph's motto. *Souvenir de la Visite de S.M. I. & R. Apost. l'Empereur d'Autriche à l'Exploitation de la Société Française de Cire Minérale et Pétrole à Boryslaw-Wolanka le 18 Septembre 1880* (n.p., n.d.).

6. Aleksander Nowolecki, *Pamiątka podróży Cesarza Franciszka Józefa I. po Galicyi i dwudziesto-dniowego pobytu Jego w tym kraju* (Cracow: Wydawnictwo Czytclni Ludowcj Nowoleckicj, 1881), 209–210.

7. For more on the 1851 imperial inspection tour as an expression of power, see Daniel Unowsky, "Reasserting Empire: Habsburg Imperial Celebrations after the Revolutions of 1848–1849," in *Staging the Past: The Politics of Commemoration in Habsburg Central Europe, 1848 to the Present*, ed. Maria Bucur and Nancy Wingfield (West Lafayette, IN: Purdue University Press, 2001), 27–34.

8. For a complete account of the causes and course of all three partitions, to which this summary is heavily indebted, see Jerzy Lukowski, *The Partitions of Poland, 1772, 1793, 1795* (New York: Longman, 1999).

9. Ibid., 89.

10. Today's Republic of Austria is 83,894 square kilometers in size.

11. Christoph Freiherr Marschall von Bieberstein, *Freiheit in der Unfreiheit: Die nationale Autonomie der Polen in Galizien nach dem österreichisch-ungarischen Ausgleich von 1867* (Wiesbaden: Harrassowitz, 1993), 29.

12. Tadeusz Wiśniowski, "Przyczynek do geologii Karpat," in *Sprawozdanie dyrekcyi c.k. wyższego gimnazyum w Kołomyi* (Kołomyja: Fundusz szkolny, 1897), 2.

13. *Sceneries and People of Austria: Described by Order of the Imperial Royal Ministry of Railways* (Vienna: O. Maass' Sons, [1904]), 5; Patrice Dabrowski, "Mountains and Mountaineers in Polish Consciousness: An Examination of the Carpathian Borderlands" (paper presented at the sixth annual convention of the Association for the Study of Nationalities, Columbia University, New York, 5–7 April 2001).

14. A[lexander] Guttry, *Galizien: Land und Leute* (Munich: Georg Müller, 1916), 45.

15. V. F. Klun, ed. *Statistik von Oesterreich-Ungarn* (Vienna: Wilhelm Braumüller, 1876), 328.

16. Guttry, *Galizien*, 121, 126; Klun, *Statistik*, 328.

17. Ivan Franko, "Der galizische Bauer," *Die Zeit* (Vienna), 21 August 1897, in Franko, *Beiträge zur Geschichte und Kultur der Ukraine: Ausgewählte deutsche Schriften des revolutionären Demokraten*, ed. E. Winter and P. Kirchner (Berlin: Akademie-Verlag, 1963), 350; Stanisław Szczepanowski, *Nędza Galicyi w cyfrach i program energicznego rozwoju gospodarstwa krajowego* (Lviv: author, 1888), 2.

18. Wilhelm Feldman, *Stan ekonomiczny Galicyi: Cyfry i fakta* (Lviv: Nakładem Stanisława Urody, 1900), 18, 23.

19. *Bericht der k.k. Gewerbe-Inspektoren über ihre Amtsthätigkeit im Jahre 1884.* (Vienna: k.k. Hof- und Staatsdruckerei, 1885), 238.

20. Klun, *Statistik*, 329.

21. From 1881 to 1910, Austrian emigration statistics recorded the departure of 605,136 Polish speakers (including Jews) and 251,615 Ukrainian speakers from Galicia. Rudolf A. Mark, *Galizien unter österreichischer Herrschaft: Verwaltung, Kirche, Bevölkerung* (Marburg: Herder-Institut, 1994), 77–78; Robert A. Kann, *A History of the Habsburg Empire, 1526–1918* (Berkeley: University of California Press, 1974), 606; David Good, *The Economic Rise of the Habsburg Empire, 1750–1914* (Berkeley: University of California Press, 1984), 121.

22. Klun, *Statistik*, 327; Mark, *Galizien unter österreichischer Herrschaft*, 76.
23. Szczepanowski, *Nędza Galicyi*, 1, 25–26. Szczepanowski restricted his comparison to countries "with a temperate climate."
24. See the Note on Translation for a discussion of the political implications of this terminology. See John-Paul Himka, *Religion and Nationality in Western Ukraine: The Greek Catholic Church and the Ruthenian National Movement in Galicia, 1867–1900* (Montreal: McGill-Queen's University Press, 1999), 5–8 for more background on the Greek Catholic Church.
25. Andrzej Walicki, "From Sarmatianism to Romanticism," in *Poland between East and West: The Controversies over Self-Definition and Modernization in Partitioned Poland*, Harvard Papers in Ukrainian Studies (Cambridge, MA: Harvard Ukrainian Research Institute, 1994), 9–10.
26. Roman Szporluk, "Polish-Ukrainian Relations in 1918: Notes for Discussion," in *The Reconstruction of Poland, 1914–1923*, ed. Paul Latawski (London: Macmillan, 1992), 42.
27. Lukowski, *Partitions of Poland*, 2–3. Piotr Wandycz estimates that nobles made up between 8 and 10 percent of the commonwealth's population. Piotr Wandycz, *The Lands of Partitioned Poland, 1795–1918* (Seattle: University of Washington Press, 1974), 5.
28. A few Poles did appreciate the necessity of including the Mazurian masses within the Polish nation even in the eighteenth century, foremost among them Tadeusz Kościuszko, who wrote in his émigré pamphlet *Czy Polacy mogą się wybić na niepodległość?*, "We must awaken love of our country among those who hitherto have not even known that they have a country." The pamphlet, first published in Paris in 1800, has been reprinted with an introduction by Emanuel Halicz (Warsaw: Wydawnictwo Ministerstwa Obrony Narodowej, 1967).
29. Leila Everett, "The Rise of Jewish National Politics in Galicia, 1905–1907," in *Nationbuilding and the Politics of Nationalism*, ed. Andrei S. Markovits and Frank E. Sysyn (Cambridge, MA: Harvard University Press, 1982), 149.
30. As cited in Jerzy Lukowski, *Liberty's Folly: The Polish-Lithuanian Commonwealth in the Eighteenth Century, 1697–1795* (New York: Routledge, 1991), 9.
31. Keely Stauter-Halsted, "From Serf to Citizen: Peasant Political Organizations in Galician Poland, 1848–1895" (Ph.D. diss., University of Michigan, 1993), 9. For an analysis of the development of broad-based Polish national identity, see Keely Stauter-Halsted, *The Nation in the Village: The Genesis of Peasant National Identity in Austrian Poland, 1848–1914* (Ithaca, NY: Cornell University Press, 2001).
32. As translated by Percival Cundy and cited in Antony Polonsky, "The Revolutionary Crisis of 1846–1849 and Its Place in the Development of

Nineteenth-Century Galicia," in *Cultures and Nations of Central and Eastern Europe: Essays in Honor of Roman Szporluk*, ed. Zvi Gitleman, Lubomyr Hajda, John-Paul Himka, and Roman Solchanyk (Cambridge, MA: Harvard University Press, 2000), 443.

33. Karl Marx, "Speech on Poland (22 February 1848)," in *The Revolutions of 1848: Political Writings*, vol. 1, ed. David Fernbach (London: Penguin, 1973), 105.

34. John-Paul Himka, *Socialism in Galicia: The Emergence of Polish Social Democracy and Ukrainian Radicalism, 1860–1890* (Cambridge, MA: Harvard University Press, 1983), 111–115.

35. Balthasar Hacquet, *Neueste physikalisch-politische Reisen in den Jahren 1791, 92 und 93*, vol. 3, *Die Dacischen und Sarmatischen oder Nördlichen Karpathen* (Nürnberg: Verlag der Naspeschen Buchhandlung, 1794), 7. Hacquet's accusations have been echoed by modern historians. See Samuel Myorich, "Josephism at its Boundaries: Nobles, Peasants, Priests, and Jews in Galicia, 1772–1790" (PhD diss., Indiana University, 1994).

36. J[oham] G[eorg] Kohl, *Reisen im Inneren von Rußland und Polen*, vol. 3, *Die Bukowina, Krakau, und Mähren* (Dresden: Arnoldische Buchhandlung, 1841), 133–40.

37. Franz Szabo, "Austrian First Impressions of Ethnic Relations in Galicia: The Case of Governor Anton von Pergen," in *Polin: Studies in Polish Jewry*, vol. 12, *Focusing on Galicia: Jews, Poles, and Ukrainians, 1772–1918*, ed. Israel Bartal and Antony Polonsky (London: Littman Library of Jewish Civilization, 1999), 53.

38. Ibid., 54–59. Quotations are Szabo's translations of Pergen's reports.

39. Wandycz, *Lands of Partitioned Poland*, 12.

40. Stanisław Grodziski, "Zur politischen Karriere von Polen in Österreich (1860–1914)," in *Polen-Österreich: Aus der Geschichte einer Nachbarschaft*, ed. Walter Leitsch and Maria Wawrykowa (Vienna: Österreichischer Bundesverlag 1988), 182.

41. Mark, *Galizien unter österreichischer Herrschaft*, 71.

42. Kann, *History of the Habsburg Empire*, 329.

43. Stanisław Grodziski, *Sejm krajowy galicyjski, 1861–1914* (Warsaw: Wydawnictwo Sejmowe, 1993), 1:83.

44. Andrzej Walicki, "Organic Work and Civilizational Options," in *Poland between East and West: The Controversies over Self-Definition and Modernization in Partitioned Poland*, Harvard Papers in Ukrainian Studies (Cambridge, MA: Harvard Ukrainian Research Institute, 1994), 26–42.

45. A. J. P. Taylor, *The Habsburg Monarchy, 1809–1918: A History of the Austrian Empire and Austria-Hungary* (Chicago: University of Chicago Press, 1948), 138–139.

46. Bieberstein, *Freiheit in der Unfreiheit*, 37.

47. Ibid., 50.

48. Piotr Wandycz has pointed to the great privileges that Poles expected—and demanded—in exchange for their expression of loyalty as proof that the address was not "an act of unilateral submission," although he would disagree with my claim that the Poles ran the province relatively undisturbed by Vienna. Wandycz concludes that the willingness of Poles to keep to their side of the bargain after the "Austrian side failed to satisfy Polish conditions" made their cooperation self-defeating. Wandycz, *Lands of Partitioned Poland*, 218.

49. Stanisław Witkiewicz (1908), as cited in Bieberstein, *Freiheit in der Unfreiheit*, 279.

50. Józef Buszko, "Das autonome Galizien als Zentrum der polnischen Unabhängigkeitsbewegung," in *Galizien um die Jahrhundertwende: Politische, soziale und kulturelle Verbindungen mit Österreich*, ed. Karlheinz Mack (Vienna: Verlag für Geschichte und Politik, 1990), 27–34.

51. Gustav Kohn, ed., *Von Goluchowski bis Taaffe: Tausend Redefragmente* (Vienna: Moritz Perles, 1888), 36.

52. Bieberstein, *Freiheit in der Unfreiheit*, 64, 66, 89, 266, 271. For a comparison of the rights and privileges won by Czechs, Slovenes, Hungarians, Croatians, Ruthenians, Serbs, and Romanians—but not, incidentally, Poles—see Robert A. Kann and Zdeněk David, *The Peoples of the Eastern Habsburg Lands, 1526–1918* (Seattle: University of Washington Press, 1984).

53. Roman Szporluk, "Thoughts about Change: Ernest Gellner and the History of Nationalism," in *The State of the Nation: Ernest Gellner and the Theory of Nationalism*, ed. John A. Hall (Cambridge: Cambridge University Press, 1998), 28.

54. David Blackbourn, "Progress and Piety: Liberals, Catholics and the State in Bismarck's Germany," in *Populists and Patricians: Essays in Modern German History* (London: Allen and Unwin, 1987), 143.

55. Lech Trzeciakowski, *The Kulturkampf in Prussian Poland*, transl. Katarzyna Kretkowska (New York: Columbia University Press, 1990), 115.

56. Ibid., 123–133 (school system), 134–135 (judiciary and administration), 136 (Germanization of names).

57. Wandycz, *Lands of Partitioned Poland*, 195–196 (Russia), 235–236 (Prussia).

58. Trzeciakowski, *Kulturkampf*, 117.

59. Raimund Löw, " 'Separatisten': Nationalitätenkonflikte in der Sozialdemokratie," in *Die ersten 100 Jahre: Österreichische Sozialdemokratie, 1888–1988*, ed. Helene Maimann (Vienna: Christian Brandstätter, 1988), 186.

60. "Wahlreform contra Coalition," *Die Zeit* (Vienna), 29 December 1894, 195.

61. M. Gross, ed., *Illustrirtes österreichisches Reichsraths-Album* (Vienna: Leo Fein, 1876), 61.

62. Grodziski, "Zur politischen Karriere," 196; Bieberstein, *Freiheit in der Unfreiheit*, 337.

63. Adam Wandruszka and Peter Urbanitsch, eds., *Die Habsburgermonarchie, 1848–1918*, vol. 7, *Verfassung und Parlamentarismus*, ed. Helmut Rumpler and Peter Urbanitsch (Vienna: Österreichische Akademie der Wissenschaften, 2000), 2:1393–1394 (hereafter cited as Rumpler and Urbanitsch, *Verfassung and Parlamentarismus*).

64. Without negating the importance of this reform, which gave landless men the opportunity to vote for the first time, it should be noted that proportional representation remained grossly unfavorable to fifth-curia voters. Rumpler and Urbanitsch, *Verfassung und Parlamentarismus*, 1:1242, 1247.

65. For a detailed presentation of the development of imperial electoral laws, see William Alexander Jenks, *The Austrian Electoral Reform of 1907* (New York: Columbia University Press, 1950; New York: Octagon Books, 1974).

66. Grodziski, *Sejm krajowy galicyjski*, 1:47–53.

67. Jan Stapiński, 15 July 1904, TsDIAUL 146.4.3775: 9–11.

68. Stefan Kieniewicz, *The Emancipation of the Polish Peasantry* (Chicago: University of Chicago Press, 1969), 207.

69. John Leslie, "The Antecedents of Austria-Hungary's War Aims: Policies and Policy-Makers in Vienna and Budapest before and during 1914," *Wiener Beiträge zur Geschichte der Neuzeit* 20 (1993): 354; Rumpler and Urbanitsch, *Verfassung und Parlamentarismus* 2:1338.

70. Krzysztof Dunin-Wąsowicz, "Die sozialen und politischen Bewegungen der polnischen Bauern in Galizien am Ende des 19. und zu Beginn des 20. Jahrhunderts," in *Galizien um die Jahrhundertwende: Politische, soziale und kulturelle Verbindungen mit Österreich*, ed. Karlheinz Mack (Vienna: Verlag für Geschichte und Politik, 1990), 51.

71. Dunin-Wąsowicz, "Sozialen und politischen Bewegungen," 51; Kieniewicz, *Emancipation*, 207.

72. A formulation for which I thank Roman Szporluk.

73. Ks. Andrzej Gołda, *Środki ku zaradzeniu nędzy stanu włościańskiego w Galicyi i Ks. Krakowskiem* (Crakow: Gebethner, 1880), 5.

74. Rumpler and Urbanitsch, *Verfassung und Parlamentarismus*, 2:1387–1388.

75. Ibid., 208.

76. Stapiński, 15 July 1904, TsDIAUL 146.4.3775: 13–14.

77. Himka, *Religion and Nationality*, 128–129. Sheptyts'kyi was born Roman Szeptycki. His brother, Stanisław Szeptycki, was a prominent Polish general and preferred the Polish spelling of their name. See Philipp Ther, "War versus Peace: Interethnic Relations in Lviv during the First Half of the Twen-

tieth Century," in "Lviv: A City in the Crosscurrents of Culture," ed. John Czaplicka, special issue, *Harvard Ukrainian Studies* 24 (2000): 253. Because of Andrei Sheptyts'kyi's conversion to the Greek Catholic rite, his service as metropolitan of that church for over four decades (1901–1944), and his dedicated defense of the Ukrainian nation, however, I have chosen to use the Ukrainian version of his name.

78. John-Paul Himka, "Dimensions of a Triangle: Polish-Ukrainian-Jewish Relations in Austrian Galicia," in *Polin: Studies in Polish Jewry*, vol. 12, *Focusing on Galicia: Jews, Poles, and Ukrainians, 1772–1918*, ed. Israel Bartal and Antony Polonsky (London: Littman Library of Jewish Civilisation, 1999), 41fn35.

79. As cited in and translated by Andrii Krawchuk, *Christian Social Ethics in Ukraine: The Legacy of Andrei Sheptytsky* (Edmonton: Canadian Institute of Ukrainian Studies Press, 1997), 4, 5.

80. As cited in and translated by Krawchuk, *Christian Social Ethics*, 63. For an analysis of Sheptyts'kyi's positive influence on the development of Ukrainian nationalism, see John-Paul Himka, "The Greek Catholic Church and the Ukrainian Nation in Galicia," *Religious Compromise, Political Salvation: The Greek Catholic Church and Nation-building in Eastern Europe*, ed. James Niessen, The Carl Beck Papers in Russian and East European Studies 1003 (Pittsburgh: The Center for Russian and East European Studies, University of Pittsburgh, 1993), 14–16.

81. Franko's articles on Galician electoral abuses include several aimed at a German-language readership. See, for example, "Die jüngste galizische Wahl," (*Die Zeit*, 1895), "Polen und Ruthenen," (*Die Zeit*, 1897), "Die neueste Wahlkomödie in Galizien," (*Die Zeit*, and *Neue Freie Presse*, 1898), and "Die jüngsten galizischen Landtagswahlen" (*Die Zeit*, 1901), all collected in Ivan Franko, *Beiträge zur Geschichte und Kultur der Ukraine: Ausgewählte deutsche Schriften des revolutionären Demokraten*, ed. E. Winter and P. Kirchner (Berlin: Akademie-Verlag, 1963).

82. "Introduction," *Ukraine's Claim to Freedom: An Appeal for Justice on Behalf of 35 Millions* (New York: Ukrainian National Association and the Ruthenian National Union, 1915); Yaroslav Hrytsak, "A Ukrainian Answer to the Galician Ethnic Triangle: The Case of Ivan Franko," in *Polin: Studies in Polish Jewry*, vol. 12, *Focusing on Galicia: Jews, Poles, and Ukrainians, 1772–1918*, ed. Israel Bartal and Antony Polonsky (London: Littman Library of Jewish Civilisation, 1999), 142.

83. Józef Buszko, "The Consequences of Galician Autonomy after 1867," in *Polin: Studies in Polish Jewry*, vol. 12, *Focusing on Galicia: Jews, Poles, and Ukrainians, 1772–1918*, 97.

84. Ivan Franko, "Die erste Session des galizischen Landtags" (*Die Zeit*, 1896), in Franko, *Beiträge*, 313–319.

85. Ibid. According to Yaroslav Hrytsak, nine people were killed, twenty-nine wounded, and eight hundred arrested during the "bloody elections" of 1897. Hrytsak, "Ukrainian Answer," 142.

86. "A Galician Governor," *Ukrainische Rundschau* 4 (1908), as reprinted and translated in *Ukraine's Claim to Freedom*, 90.

87. Simon Pollock, "The Misrule of the Polish Aristocracy," in *Ukraine's Claim to Freedom*, 65–85.

88. See, for example, Pollock, "The Misrule of the Polish Aristocracy," and "A Galician Governor" in *Ukraine's Claim to Freedom*. For an impassioned argument in defense of Potocki, see Stanislaus Zielinski, *Die Ermordung des Statthalters Grafen Andreas Potocki: Materialen zur Beurteilung des Ukrainischen Terrorismus in Galizien* (Vienna: C. W. Stern, 1908).

89. Ivan Franko, "Die Folter in Galizien" (*Die Zeit*, 1900), in Franko, *Beiträge*, 372–375.

90. Ivan Franko, "Ein Triumph der österreichischen Idee in Galizien" (*Die Wage*, 1898), in Franko, *Beiträge*, 364. For a brief biography of Vakhnianyn, see Ihor Chornovol, *Ukraïns'ka Fraktsiia Halyts'koho Kraiovoho Seimu, 1861–1901* (Lviv: Natsional'na Akademiia Nauk Ukraïny Institut ukraïnoznavstva im. I. Kryp'iakerycha, 2002), 238.

91. Ibid., 365.

92. Gross, *Illustrirtes österreichisches Reichsraths-Album*, 65.

93. Ivan Franko, "Polen und Ruthenen," (*Die Zeit*, 1897) and "Unmögliches in dem Lande der Unmöglichkeiten" (*Die Zeit*, 1899), in Franko, *Beiträge*, 332–343 and 370–372.

94. Karl Markus Gauß and Martin Pollack, eds., *Das reiche Land der armen Leute: Literarische Wanderungen durch Galizien* (Vienna: Jugend und Volk Dachs Verlag, 1992), 18.

95. Charles Ingrao, *The Habsburg Monarchy, 1618–1815* (Cambridge: Cambridge University Press, 1994), 201–202.

96. Kieniewicz, *Emancipation*, 37. Kieniewicz's study forms the basis for information on the development of landholding patterns in the paragraphs that follow.

97. Taylor, *Habsburg Monarchy*, 18.

98. Kieniewicz, *Emancipation* 135; Wandycz, *Lands of Partitioned Poland*, 144.

99. For a more extensive explanation of the servitudes controversy, see John-Paul Himka, *Galician Villagers and the Ukrainian National Movement in the Nineteenth Century* (New York: St. Martin's Press, 1988), 36–40.

100. Kieniewicz, *Emancipation*, 135–39.

101. Dunin-Wąsowicz, "Sozialen und politischen Bewegungen," 53, 203.

102. Kieniewicz, *Emancipation*, 204.

103. Ivan Franko, "Der galizische Bauer," *Die Zeit* (Vienna), 21 August 1897, in Franko, *Beiträge*, 348–449.

104. Adam Wandruszka and Peter Urbanitsch, eds., *Die Habsburgermonarchie, 1848–1918*, vol. 1, *Die wirtschaftliche Entwicklung*, ed. Alois Brusatti (Vienna: Österreichische Akademie der Wissenschaften, 1973), 423, citing Stefan Surzycki, *Die landwirtschaftlichen Betriebsmittel in ihrem Einfluß auf den Zustand und die Entwicklung des Großgrundbesitzes sowie der Bauernwirtschaft in Galizien* (Leipzig, 1896), 112.

105. Kieniewicz, *Emancipation*, 204.

106. Szczepanowski, *Nędza Galicyi*, 26.

107. Feldman, *Stan ekonomiczny Galicyi*, 2.

108. Rumpler and Urbanitsch, *Verfassung und Parlamentarismus*, 2:1395.

109. Paul Robert Magocsi, *Galicia: A Historical Survey and Bibliographic Guide* (Toronto: University of Toronto Press, 1983), 140.

110. Good, *Habsburg Empire*, 122.

111. Feldman, *Stan ekonomiczny Galicyi*, 13.

112. Franko, "Galizische Bauer," 348–349.

113. Stephan Vajda, *Reisen Anno 1900: Ein Führer durch die Länder der k.u.k. Monarchie* (Vienna: Ueberreuter, 1981), 9.

114. *Neue Freie Presse* (Vienna), 2 October 1899, M, 3.

115. Ivan Franko, "Partseliatsiia bil'shoï zemel'noi vlasnosti," in *Zibrannia tvoriv u p'iatdesiaty tomakh*, vol. 44, pt. 2, *Ekonomichni pratsi (1888–1907)* (Kiev: Naukova Dumka, 1985), 38.

116. Kieniewicz, *Emancipation*, 204.

117. Szczepanowski, *Nędza Galicyi*, 28–29 (see Introduction, n. 14).

118. Ivan Franko, "Die Auswanderung der galizischen Bauern," *Arbeiter Zeitung* 43 (21 October 1892), in Franko, *Beiträge*, 278.

119. Klun, *Statistik von Oesterreich-Ungarn*, 329.

120. Ibid.

121. Leonid Rudnytzky, "The Image of Austria in the Works of Ivan Franko," in *Nationbuilding and the Politics of Nationalism*, ed. Andrei S. Markovits and Frank E. Sysyn (Cambridge, MA: Harvard University Press, 1982), 252.

122. Franko, "Galizische Bauer," 350–351.

123. Raphael Mahler, "The Economic Background of Jewish Emigration from Galicia to the United States," *YIVO Annual of Jewish Social Science* 7 (1952): 256.

124. Dunin-Wąsowicz, "Sozialen und politischen Bewegungen," 52.

125. Magocsi, *Galicia*, 139.

126. Leslie Kool, "Economic Development on the Periphery: A Case Study of East Galicia" (Ph.D. diss., Temple University, 1994).

127. Aleksander Borucki, *Nasze Góry: Malownicze opisanie Karpat i Tatr, oraz ich mieszkańców*, vol. 1, *Karpaty* (Cieszyn: Edward Feitzinger, 1888), 29.

2. Galician California

1. For a vivid description of the landscape of Pennsylvania oil country, see Brian Black, *Petrolia: The Landscape of America's First Oil Boom* (Baltimore, MD: Johns Hopkins University Press, 2000).
2. See, for example, Stefan Kovaliv, *Obrazki z Halyts'koi Kalifornii* (Lviv: Naukove Tovarystvo im. Shevchenka, 1913); Alexander Heksch and Wladimir Kowszewicz, eds., *Illustrirter Führer durch die ungarischen Ostkarpathen, Galizien, Bukowina und Rumänien: Handbuch für Touristen und Geschäfts-Reisende* (Vienna: Hartlebens Verlag, 1882), 121; and Ivan Krevets'skyi, "Stefan Kovaliv: Pokhresnyk y ynshi opovidannia," draft review for the Ukrainian newspaper *Dilo* (Lviv), 1909, TsDIAUL 779.1.97.
3. David Blackbourn, *The Fontana History of Germany, 1780–1918: The Long Nineteenth Century* (London: Fontana, 1997), 177.
4. Jakob Scheließnigg, "Bemerkungen und Wünsche hinsichtlich der Brennstoff-Frage," *Österreichische Zeitschrift für Berg- und Hüttenwesen* 6, no. 22 (31 May 1858): 172–173.
5. Ladislaus Szajnocha, *Die Petroleumindustrie Galiziens*, 2nd ed. (Cracow: Verlag des Galizischen Landesausschusses, 1905), 4.
6. George A. Hill Jr., *Trends in the Oil Industry in 1944 (Including United States Foreign Oil Policy): As presented to the Petroleum Industry War Council, January 12, 1944* (Washington, DC: Petroleum Industry War Council, 1944), 1.
7. Genesis 6:14.
8. C. E. Eduard Schmidt, *Die Erdöl-Reichthümer Galiziens: Eine technologisch-volkswirthschaftliche Studie* (Vienna: Carl Gerold's Sohn, 1865), 1–2.
9. Ivan Franko, *Boryslav smiiet'sia. Boa Constrictor. Povisti* (Kiev: Vydavnytstvo Khudozhn'oï Literatury "Dnipro," 1981), 302. Originally published in 1878 in the journal *Hromads'kyi Druh*.
10. Ibid., 302.
11. Richard Wagner, *Organisationsfragen aus der Petroleumindustrie mit besonderer Berücksichtigung Österreichs* ([Vienna?], [1915?]), 26.
12. Roger Olien and Diana Davids Olien, *Wildcatters: Texas Independent Oilmen* (Austin: Texas Monthly, 1984), 2; Sally Helgesen, *Wildcatters: A Story of Texans, Oil, and Money* (Garden City, NY: Doubleday, 1981), 13, 33. In fact, absolute ownership of mineral rights was not granted to landowners everywhere in the United States. Samuel Glassmire, *Law of Oil and Gas Leases and Royalties: A Practical Legal Treatise on Petroleum Rights Accruing by Virtue of Mineral Deeds and Oil and Gas Leases* (Saint Louis: Thomas Law Book Company, 1935), 104.
13. Oscar Jaszi, *The Dissolution of the Habsburg Monarchy* (Chicago: University of Chicago Press, 1929) 220, 451.

14. See, for example, David Good, *The Economic Rise of the Habsburg Empire, 1750—1914* (Berkeley: University of California Press, 1984); Richard Rudolph, *Banking and Industrialization in Austria-Hungary: The Role of Banks in the Industrialization of the Czech Crownlands, 1873–1914* (Cambridge: Cambridge University Press, 1976); John Komlos, *Economic Development in the Habsburg Monarchy in the Nineteenth Century* (Boulder: East European Monographs, 1983); Komlos, *The Habsburg Monarchy as a Customs Union: Economic Development in Austria-Hungary in the Nineteenth Century* (Princeton, NJ: Princeton University Press, 1983); Herbert Matis, ed., *The Economic Development of Austria since 1870* (Brookfield: Elgar, 1994); Matis, *Österreichs Wirtschaft, 1848–1913: Konjunkturelle Dynamik und gesellschaftlicher Wandel im Zeitalter Franz Josephs I* (Berlin: Duncker und Humblot, 1972); Scott Eddie, "Economic Policy and Economic Development in Austria-Hungary," in *The Cambridge Economic History of Europe*, vol. 8, ed. Peter Mathias and Sidney Pollard (Cambridge: Cambridge University Press, 1989), 814–886; Max-Stephan Schulze, "Patterns of Growth and Stagnation in the Late Nineteenth Century Habsburg Economy," *European Review of Economic History* 4, no. 3 (2000): 311–340.

15. Gustav von Gränzenstein, *Das allgemeine österreichische Berggesetz vom 23. Mai 1854 und die Verordnungen über die Bergwerksabgaben vom 4. Oktober 1854* (Vienna: Friedrich Manz, 1855), 82.

16. "Ozokerit-Gewinnung im Großen," *Österreichische Zeitschrift für Berg- und Hüttenwesen* 2, no. 17 (24 April 1854): 135.

17. Gränzenstein, *Allgemeine österreichische Berggesetz*, 83.

18. *Allgemeines Berggesetz für das Kaiserthum Oesterreich vom 23. Mai 1854: Amtliche Handausgabe* (Vienna: k.k. Hof- und Staatsdruckerei, 1854), 9–10.

19. Joseph Berlinerblau, *Das Erdwachs: Ozokerit und Ceresin; Geschichte, Vorkommen, Gewinnung und Verarbeitung* (Braunschweig: Friedrich Vieweg und Sohn, 1897), 6.

20. Jan Zeh, "Pierwsze objawy przemysłu naftowego w Galicyi," *Czasopismo Towarzystwa Aptékarskiego* 18, no. 12 (18 June 1889): 201–205.

21. J. Hecker, *Das Bergöl in Galizien* (1820), cited in Tadeusz Mikucki, "Nafta w Polsce do połowy XIX w.," *Przemysł Naftowy* 13, no. 17 (10 September 1938): 469; Szajnocha, *Petroleumindustrie Galiziens*, 13; Zygmunt Bielski, "W sprawie starzeństwa przemysłu naftowego," *Przemysł Naftowy* 7, no. 4 (25 February 1932): 89–90; Heinrich E. Gintl, *Die Concurrenzfähigkeit des galizischen Petroleums mit Rücksicht auf die neuen Oelgruben in Sloboda-Rungurska nächst Kolomea* (Vienna: Spielhagen und Schurich, 1885), 6.

22. W. J. Klimkiewicz, "The Polish Petroleum Industry from Its Inception to 1909," in *Studies in Polish Civilization*, ed. D. S. Wandycz (New York: In-

stitute on East Central Europe, Columbia University, and Polish Institute of Arts and Sciences in America, 1969), 4.

23. Hofkammer Z. 11 967, 27 October 1838; Fr. Emler, "Der Bergtheer in Galizien vom Standpunkte des Bergregals," *Österreichische Zeitschrift für Berg- und Hüttenwesen* 8, no. 29 (16 July 1860): 238.

24. Berlinerblau, *Erdwachs*, 6.

25. Zeh, "Pierwsze objawy przemysłu naftowego," 201.

26. Ibid., 202, 205.

27. *Bericht der Handels- und Gewerbekammer in Lemberg an das hohe k.k. Ministerium für Handel, Gewerbe und öffentliche Bauten über die Zustände des Handels und der Industrie in ihrem Kammerbezirke in den Jahren 1854, 1855 und 1856* (Lviv: Winiarz, 1859), 110.

28. Polish and Ukrainian historians disagree over the correct assessment of Łukasiewicz's role in the development of the new distillate. While Łukasiewicz is generally credited with the discovery in Polish historiography, Ukrainians counter that the imperial patent granted for the purification process was issued in Zeh's name only (Lev Monchak and Heorhii Boiko "L'viv—batkivshyna naftovoï osvitliuval'noï lampy," *Halyts'ka Brama* 1 [January 1997], 12.)

29. Zeh, "Pierwsze objawy przemysłu naftowego," 203.

30. *Die Großindustrie Österreichs: Festgabe zum glorreichen Fünfzigjährigen Regierungs-Jubiläum seiner Majestät des Kaisers Franz Joseph I.* (Vienna: Leopold Weiss, 1898), 329; *Die ersten fünfzig Jahre der Kaiser Ferdinands-Nordbahn, 1836–1886* (Vienna: Verlag der k.k. pr. Kaiser Ferdinands-Nordbahn, n.d), 92; Gintl, *Concurrenzfähigkeit*, 7.

31. *Bericht der Handels- und Gewerbekammer in Lemberg*, 110.

32. *Naphta* 6 no. 10 (30 May 1898), 97.

33. Z. Bielski, "Ueber das Alter der Erdölindustrie," *Allgemeine österreichische Chemiker- und Techniker-Zeitung* 50, no. 2 (15 January 1932), 12.

34. Schmidt, *Erdöl-Reichthümer Galiziens*, 1.

35. *Allgemeines Berggesetz für das Kaiserthum Oesterreich vom 23. Mai 1854*, 9–10.

36. Berlinerblau, *Erdwachs*, 4.

37. HM file 573/74, TsDIAUL 146.55.11: 10.

38. Stefan Kieniewicz, *The Emancipation of the Polish Peasantry* (Chicago: University of Chicago Press, 1969), 37–40.

39. Tadeusz Porembalski, *Wspomnienia nafciarza* (Warsaw: Panstwowe Wydawnictwo Naukowe, 1978), 25. For more detail on early production methods, see Felicjan Łodziński, "Jak dawniej kopano i wiercono za ropą," *Przemysł Naftowy* 3, no. 17 (1928): 460–463; no. 18: 499–501; no. 20: 560–561; no. 21: 598–600; no. 23: 660–663.

40. Adolf Lipp, *Verkehrs- und Handels-Verhältnisse Galiziens* (Prague: Hunger, 1870), 102.

41. Emil Schieffer, *Bericht über das Nafta führende Terrain West-Galiziens* (Vienna: Verlag des Gründungs-Comité's der Hamburg-Galizischen Petroleum-Actien Gesellschaft, 1865), 6.

42. Ibid.; *Sprawozdanie stenograficzne z rozpraw galicyjskiego Sejmu krajowego* (Lviv), 23. posiedzenie 4. sesyi 3. peryodu Sejmu galicyjskiego, 16 January 1874, 12.

43. Wilhelm Jičinský, "Das Vorkommen und die Gewinnung des Bergöles und Bergwachses zu Borislaw bei Drohobicz in Ostgalizien," *Österreichische Zeitschrift für Berg- und Hüttenwesen* 13, no. 52 (25 December 1865): 414.

44. Kraiova zemel'no-podatkova komisiia Ministerstva Zemlerobstva ta ahrarnykh reform, m. L'viv, "Podvirni ta zvedenyi opysy zemel'noho maita m. Boryslava Sambiirs'koho okruhu," TsDIAUL f. 186.1.4393; "Wykaz przedsiębiorstw górniczych," TsDIAUL f. 146.7.4371: 3–5.

45. *Großindustrie Österreichs*, 324.

46. Mining Commissioner Edward Windakiewicz's untitled report was published by the Ministry of Agriculture in *Berg- und Hüttenmännisches Jahrbuch der k.k. Bergacademien zu Leoben und Przibram* 23, no. 1 (1875).

47. Marian Bernhard Leopold, "Über die Rohölgruben in Borysław," *Naphta* 9, no. 5 (15 March 1901): 84.

48. Lipp, *Verkehrs- und Handels-Verhältnisse Galiziens*, 101–102; 1 *Klafter* = 1 fathom = 1.8965 meters.

49. Ivan Franko, *Poluika i yn'shi Boryslavs'ki opovidania* (Lviv: Ukraïns'ka-Rus'ka Vydavnycha Spilka, 1899); "Erdwachsgruben in Galizien und die neuen Bergpolizeilichen Vorschriften der k.k. Berghauptmannschaft in Krakau von 16. September 1897," *Naphta* 6, no. 2 (8 February 1898): 14.

50. Lipp, *Verkehrs- und Handels-Verhältnisse Galiziens*, 102.

51. Berlinerblau, *Erdwachs*, 8.

52. TsDIAUL f. 146.4.3414: 6.

53. TsDIAUL f. 146.55.59, 61, 62, 69, 70, 71, 73, 74, 88, 97.

54. TsDIAUL f. 146.4.3853; Mieczysław Orlowicz and Roman Kordys, *Illustrierter Führer durch Galizien: Mit einem Anhang: Ost-Schlesien* (Vienna: Hartlebens Verlag, 1914), 240.

55. Józef Rogosz, *W piekle galicyjskiem: Obraz z życia* (Gródek: J. Czaiński, 1896), 10.

56. Report from the viceroy's office to the IM, 17 December 1874, TsDIAUL f. 146.4.3411: 187.

57. Ibid.; Memo from AM to IM, 2 October 1874, TsDIAUL 146.4.3411: 183.

58. Carl Ritter von Schmedes, *Geographisch-statistische Uebersicht Galiziens und*

der Bukowina, nach amtlichen Quellen bearbeitet, 2nd ed. (Lviv: k.k. galizische Aerarial-Staats-Druckerei, 1869), 285.

59. Berlinerblau, *Erdwachs,* 10.

60. Julius Noth, *Oesterreichische Zeitschrift für Berg- und Hüttenwesen* 24 (1876): 420.

61. Ibid.

62. Ibid.

63. Gränzenstein, *Allgemeine österreichische Berggesetz,* 79.

64. H. Wachtel, "Die Naphta und deren Industrie in Ostgalizien vom Standpunkte des Bergregals," *Österreichische Zeitung für Berg- und Hüttenwesen* 8, no. 16 (16 April 1860): 131.

65. Ibid. Gränzenstein, *Allgemeine österreichische Berggesetz,* expressed the same concern in his 1855 analysis of the mining laws, as did Windakiewicz years later in his unpublished 1875 report.

66. Jičinský, "Vorkommen," 414.

67. H. Perutz, *Industrie der Mineralöle, des Petroleums, Paraffins und der Harze, nebst sämmtlichen damit zusammenhängenden Industriezweigen,* vol. 1 (Vienna: Carl Gerold's Sohn, 1868), 25.

68. Borysław, Wolanka, Mrażnica, and Schodnica. The statistics that follow are derived from *Przegląd stanu kopalń nafty i wosku ziemnego w Galicyi, w drugiem półroczu 1881* (Gorlice: Towarzystwo Naftowe, 1882), 32–55.

69. A regulation American football field is 110 meters by 49 meters, or 5,390 square meters.

70. *Die Bergwerks-Inspektion in Österreich: Berichte der k.k. Bergbehörden über ihre Thätigkeit im Jahre 1898 bei Handhabung der Bergpolizei und Beaufsichtigung der Bergarbeiterverhältnisse* (Vienna: k.k. Hof- und Staatsdruckerei, 1901), 643.

71. Stanisław Szczepanowski, *Nafta i praca, złoto i błoto* (Lviv: author, 1886), 33–34.

72. Edward Dzwonkowski, *Sprawozdanie stenograficzne,* 16 January 1874, 14.

73. Vasyl' Koval's'kyi, ibid., 16.

74. Mykola Antonevych, ibid., 22.

75. Ferdynand Weigel, ibid., 13.

76. Noth, 420.

77. *Sprawozdanie stenograficzne z rozpraw galicyjskiego Sejmu krajowego* (Lviv), 21. posiedzenie, 17 October 1881, 466, TsDIAUL f. 146.4.3414: 7b; "Bericht des Montanausschusses über die Petition des Landesvereins zum Schutz und zur Hebung des Bergbaues und der Petroleum-Industrie in Galizien," submitted to the Minister of Agriculture, L. Z. 264/1881, TsDIAUL f. 146.4.3414: 9–14.

78. "Gesetz vom 11. Mai 1884, Nr. 71 R.G.Bl., womit im Königreiche Galizien

und Lodomerien samt dem Großherzogtume Krakau und im Herzogtume Bukowina das Rechts zur Gewinnung der wegen ihres Gehaltes an Erdharz benützbaren Mineralien geregelt wird," in *Das Recht der Rohölgewinnung in Oesterreich: Die das Gebiet der Rohölgewinnung regelnden Gesetze und Verordnungen sowie die hierauf bezughabenden oberst- und verwaltungsgerichtlichen Entscheidungen,* ed. Josef Blauhorn, vol. 1, *Die Gesetze und Ministerial-Verordnungen* (Berlin: Verlag für Fachliteratur, 1910), 1–5.

79. "Verordnung des Justizministers vom 15. Juni 1885 L.G.Bl. f. Galizien Nr. 36 ex 1886 betreffend die Anlegung und Führung von Naphthabüchern, auf Grund des Reichsgesetzes vom 11. Mai 1884, Nr. 71 R.G.Bl., und des galizischen Landesgesetzes vom 17. Dezember 1884, Nr. 35 L.G.Bl. vom Jahre 1886," in Blauhorn, *Recht,* 120–122.

80. "Gesetz vom 21. Juni 1884 Nr. 115 R.G.Bl., über die Beschäftigung von jugendlichen Arbeitern und Frauenspersonen, dann über die tägliche Arbeitsdauer und die Sonntagsruhe beim Bergbau," in Blauhorn, *Recht,* 146–148.

81. "Gesetz vom 11. Mai 1884," in Blauhorn, *Recht,* 5.

82. Andrei S. Markovits and Frank E. Sysyn, eds., *Nationbuilding and the Politics of Nationalism* (Cambridge, MA: Harvard University Press, 1982), 7.

83. Gary Cohen, "Neither Absolutism nor Anarchy: New Narratives on Society and Government in Late Imperial Austria," *Austrian History Yearbook* 29, no. 1 (1998): 53.

3. Petroleum Fever

1. Ignaz Leichner, *Erdöl und Erdwachs: Ein Bild galizischer Industrie,* Sozialpolitische Flugschriften (Vienna: Ignaz Brand, 1898), 2.

2. Robert Musil, *The Man without Qualities,* vol. 1, transl. Sophie Wilkins (New York: Vintage, 1996), 406.

3. Józef Rogosz, *W piekle galicyjskiem: Obraz z Życia* (Gródek: J. Czaiński, 1896), 14.

4. Alexander F. Heksch and Wladimir Kowszewicz, eds., *Illustrirter Führer durch die ungarischen Ostkarpathen, Galizien, Bukowina und Rumänien: Handbuch für Touristen und Geschäfts-Reisende* (Vienna: Hartlebens Verlag, 1882), 121–22.

5. *Tygodnik Samborsko-Drohobycki,* cited in Martin Pollack, *Nach Galizien: Von Chassiden, Huzulen, Polen und Ruthenen; Eine imaginäre Reise durch die verschwundene Welt Ostgaliziens und der Bukowina* (Vienna: Edition Christian Brandstätter, 1984), 34.

6. Mieczysław Orlowicz and Roman Kordys, *Illustrierter Führer durch Galizien:*

Mit einem Anhang: Ost-Schlesien (Vienna: Hartlebens Verlag, 1914), 242–243; K. k. statistische Central-Commission, *Orts-Reportorium des Königreiches Galizien und Lodomerien mit dem Grossherzogthume Krakau* (Vienna: Carl Gerold's Sohn, 1874), 58. By 1910, Drohobycz, with 34,665 residents, was Galicia's sixth-largest city. Rudolf A. Mark, *Galizien unter österreichischer Herrschaft: Verwaltung, Kirche, Bevölkerung* (Marburg: Herder-Institut, 1994), 97, 101–102.

7. *Przegląd stanu kopalń nafty i wosku ziemnego w Galicyi, w drugiem półroczu 1881* (Gorlice: Towarzystwo Naftowe, 1882), 33–55.

8. *Bericht der k.k. Gewerbe-Inspektoren über ihre Amtsthätigkeit im Jahre 1884* (Vienna: k.k. Hof- und Staatsdruckerei, 1885), 238.

9. ÖSTA, FM, VI Pra. S. 20/2 1883 Z. 5822/624 Nr. 5264 Fasz 8/5 Reg. II.

10. Otto Hausner, "Promemoria über den Nothstand der galizischen Petroleumindustrie und einige Mittel der Abhilfe," unpublished report, ÖSTA, k.k. FM, VI Pra. S. 10/5 1883 Z. 15302/1683.

11. Joseph Mendel and Robert Schwarz, eds., *Internationale Petroleumstatistik*, vol. 2, *Österreich-Ungarn* (Vienna: Verlag für Fachlitnatur, 1912), 25.

12. Alfred Buresch, "Memorandum in der Angelegenheit der Zulassung der ausländischen Petroleum-Actien-Unternehmungen zum Geschäftsbetriebe in Galizien und in der Bukowina," *Naphta* 7, no. 18 (30 September 1899): 255.

13. Stanisław Szczepanowski, "Die Entwicklung der Petroleum-Industrie in Galizien," in *Die Großindustrie Österreichs* (Vienna: Leopold Weiss, 1898), 324.

14. Ivan Franko, "Zlydni Halychyny v tsyfrakh," in *Zibrannia tvoriv u p'iatdesiaty tomakh*, vol. 44, pt. 2 (Kiev: Naukova Dumka, 1985), 12.

15. S. W. Sweet, *Report on Coal* (Albany: State of New York, Senate No. 71, 1865), 90–92, in Ernest Miller, ed., *This Was Early Oil: Contemporary Accounts of the Growing Petroleum Industry, 1848–1885* (Harrisburg: Pennsylvania Historical and Museum Commission, 1968), 88–89.

16. Harold Williamson and Arnold Daum, *The American Petroleum Industry*, vol. 1, *The Age of Illumination, 1859–1899* (Evanston, IL: Northwestern University Press, 1959), 137.

17. Szczepanowski, "Entwicklung," 332; *Nachrichten über Industrie, Handel und Verkehr aus dem statistischen Departement im k.k. Handelsministerium*, vol. 38, *Statistik der Oesterreichischen Industrie nach dem Stande vom Jahre 1885* (Vienna: k.k. Hof- und Staatsdruckerei, 1889), 243.

18. Marian Bernhard Leopold, "Über die Rohölgruben in Borysław," *Naphta* 9, no. 5 (15 March 1901): 83.

19. Ladislaus Szajnocha, *Die Petroleumindustrie Galiziens*, 2nd ed. (Cracow: Verlag des Galizischen Landesausschusses, 1905), 16.

20. *Beiträge zur Statistik der Oesterreichischen Industrie: Erzeugnisse aus nicht metallischen Mineralien und chemischen Industrie* (Vienna: k.k. Hof- und Staatsdruckerei, 1876), 296.

21. Leichner, *Erdöl und Erdwachs,* 22; H. Perutz, *Industrie der Mineralöle, des Petroleums, Paraffins und der Harze, nebst sämmtlichen damit zusammenhängenden Industriezweigen,* vol. 1 (Vienna: Carl Gerold's Sohn, 1868), 25. On women: *Bericht der k.k. Gewerbe-Inspektoren über ihre Amtsthätigkeit im Jahre 1884* (Vienna: k.k. Hof- und Staatsdruckerei, 1885), 250; 1885 (Vienna, 1886), 371.

22. This process was described in detail by Ivan Franko in several of his short stories, including "Poluika" (The Bonus), in *Poluika i yn'shi Boryslavs'ki opovidania* (Lviv: Ukraïns'ka-Rus'ka Vydavnycha Spilka, 1899), 3–29.

23. Szajnocha, *Petroleumindustrie Galiziens,* 17–19.

24. Perutz, *Industrie,* 25–26.

25. Penalties levied against oil companies and individuals, TsDIAUL f.146.55.61.

26. Obituary of Efroim Hersch Schreier, *Naphta* 6, no. 2 (8 February 1898), 20.

27. Leszek Kuberski, *Stanisław Szczepanowski, 1846–1900: Przemysłowiec, Polityk, Publicysta* (Opole: Uniwersytet Opolski, 1997), 39.

28. Stanisław Szczepanowski, *Nędza Galicyi w cyfrach i program energicznego rozwoju gospodarstwa krajowego* (Lviv: author, 1888), xix.

29. "Zarys życia i prac Stanisława Prus Szczepanowskiego," in Stanisław Szczepanowski, *Myśli o odrodzeniu narodowym,* vol. 1, *Pisma i przemówienia,* 3rd ed. (Lviv: Tow. Nauczycieli Szkół Wyższych, 1923), 9.

30. Alexander Wójcik, *Mowa wygłoszona przez O. Aleksandra Wójcika, gwardyana z Przeworska w czasie Żałobnego Nabożeństwa we Lwowie za dusze ś. p. Stanisława Szczepanowskiego i Kazimierza Odrzywolskiego* (Cracow: Anczycz i Spólki, 1900), 3.

31. Szczepanowski, *Nędza Galicyi,* xx. Szczepanowski's European tour is described in more detail in Kuberski, *Stanisław Szczepanowski,* 29–37.

32. Kuberski, *Stanisław Szczepanowski,* 33.

33. Stanisław Szczepanowski, *O samodzielność kraju: Sprawy poselskie lata 1887–1891,* vol. 3, *Pisma i przemówienia* (Lviv: Gubrynowicz, 1912), 450.

34. Szczepanowski, *Myśli o odrodzeniu narodowym,* 8.

35. Szczepanowski, *Nędza Galicyi,* xxi.

36. Stanislaus Blejwas, *Realism in Polish Politics: Warsaw Positivism and National Survival in Nineteenth Century Poland* (New Haven, CT: Yale Concilium on International and Area Studies, 1984), 190.

37. Andrzej Walicki, *Poland between East and West: The Controversies over Self-Definition and Modernization in Partition Poland,* Harvard Papers in Ukrainian Studies (Cambridge, MA: Harvard Ukrainian Research Institute, 1994), 28.

38. Stanisław Szczepanowski, *Nafta i praca, złoto i błoto* (Lviv: author, 1886), 3.

39. Szczepanowski, *Nędza Galicyi*, xvii.

40. Szczepanowski's testimony, *Neue Freie Presse* (Vienna), 10 October 1899, A, 3.

41. Kuberski, *Stanisław Szczepanowski*, 44; *Compass: Jahrbuch der österreichischen Industrie*, ed. Rudolf Hanel (Vienna: Compassverlag, 1916), s.v. "S. Szczepanowski and Company.'"

42. Another contemporary claimed that Szczepanowski's Słoboda Rungurska wells produced fifteen to twenty-five tons a day once the initial explosion of oil had passed (Szajnocha, *Petroleumindustrie Galiziens*, 19). Articles about Wanda appeared in multiple trade and regional papers, including the *Gazeta Lwowska*, and are summarized in Kuberski, *Stanisław Szczepanowski*, 44–45.

43. Szczepanowski, *Nafta i praca*, 25.

44. *Neue Freie Presse*, 10 October 1899, A, 3, and 11 October 1899, M, 7.

45. *Neue Freie Presse*, 11 October 1899, M, 7.

46. Kuberski, *Stanisław Szczepanowski*, 33.

47. Wójcik, *Mowa wygłoszona*, 5.

48. Stanisław Borzym, "Idea polska Stanisława Szczepanowskiego," in *Idea Polska: Wybór pism*, by Stanisław Szczepanowski (Warsaw: Panstwowy Instytut Wydawniczy, 1988), 15.

49. Szczepanowski's testimony, *Neue Freie Presse*. 11 October 1899, M, 7.

50. Szczepanowski, *Nędza Galicyi*, xix.

51. Ibid., xi, xii–xiii.

52. Stefan Sulimirski, "Stanisław Szczepanowski, Życiorys," *Przemysł Naftowy* 4, no. 11 (June 1929): 324–326; Szczepanowski, *Nafta i praca, złoto i błoto*.

53. "Der Proceß der Galizischen Sparkasse," *Neue Freie Presse*, 2 October 1899, 3–4.

54. Szczepanowski, *Nędza Galicyi*, v, vi.

55. John M. Carland, "Enterprise and Empire: Officials, Entrepreneurs, and the Search for Petroleum in Southern Nigeria, 1906–1914," *International History Review* 4, no.2 (May 1982): 192.

56. Bergheim's obituary, *The Times* (London), 11 September 1912, 9.

57. W. H. MacGarvey, introduction to *Oil Fields of the Empire: A Survey of British Imperial Petroleum Questions and a Comprehensive Technical Description of the Oil Fields of Trinidad and Newfoundland*, by J. D. Henry (London: Bradbury, Agnew and Co., 1910), vii.

58. Gary May, *Hard Oiler! The Story of Early Canadians' Quest for Oil at Home and Abroad* (Toronto: Dundurn Press, 1998), 136.

59. Franciszek Żychliński, "Z przeszłości przemysłu Naftowego w powiecie gorlickim," *Przemysł Naftowy* 4, no. 11 (1929): 337.

60. *Petroleum* 9, no. 10 (18 February 1914).

61. Leopold, "Über die Rohölgruben," 83.
62. MacGarvey, introduction to *Oil Fields of the Empire*, vii.
63. Szajnocha, *Petroleumindustrie Galiziens*, 17–19.
64. May, *Hard Oiler!* 126, 138.
65. As late as 1873, experts were impressed by wells dug to depths of 350 feet (about 106 meters). J. T. Henry, *The Early and Later History of Petroleum* (Philadelphia: Jas. B. Rodgers Co., 1873), 150.
66. Leopold, "Über die Rohölgruben," 84.
67. "Galizische Karpathen-Petroleum-Actien-Gesellschaft vormals Bergheim & MacGarvey, Gorlice" in *Die Großindustrie Österreichs* (Vienna: Leopold Weiss, 1898) 332–333.; Leon Rymar, *Galicyjski przemysł naftowy* (Cracow: Skład główny w księgarni G. Gebethner, 1915), 28–29; Robert Schwarz, *Petroleum-Vademecum: Tafeln für die Erdölindustrie und den Mineralölhandel*, 6th ed. (Berlin: Verlag für Fachliteratur, 1929), 178; *Ergebnisse der vom k.k. Ackerbauministerium im Jahre 1903 eingesetzten Kommission zur Untersuchung der Betriebsverhältnisse des Erdölbergbaues in Galizien* (Vienna: k.k. Hof- und Staatsdruckerei, 1904), 33; Julian Fabiański, "Rozwój polskiego wiertnictwa i wydobywania ropy i gazu," *Przemysł Naftowy* 4, no. 11 (1929): 326–329; Piotr Franaszek, *Myśl techniczna w Galicyjskim wiertnictwie naftowym w latach 1860–1918* (Cracow: Uniwersytet Jagielloński, 1991); Franaszek, "Przesłanki Rozwoju Górnictwa Naftowego w Galicji," *Zeszyty Naukowe Uniwersytetu Jagiellońskiego, Prace Historyczne* 121 (1997): 173–201.
68. Władysław Szajnok, *Skorowidz polskiego i austrjackiego przemysłu naftowego 1919* (Lviv: Wydawnictwo Polskie, 1920).
69. Letter from the IM to the Presidium of the Viceroy's office, TsDIAUL f. 146.55.97: 5a–5b.
70. "Enquête über die Krise in der Mineralölindustrie," ÖSTA MföA F. 664 Z. 1079 xiv 1910: 15.
71. TsDIAUL f. 242.1.32, 88, 90, 91, 92, 93, 95–113; ÖSTA MföA F. 664.1079: 83; "Neue Petroleum Bohr-Unternehmungen im Jahre 1900," *Naphta* 9, no. 6 (31 March 1901): 107; "Galizische Karpathen-Petroleum-Actien-Gesellschaft," 332.
72. Leopold, "Über die Rohölgruben," 85.
73. Contract No. 15.573, 20 March 1903, TsDIAUL f. 242.1.33: 22–33.
74. "Notizen: Aus galizischen Erdölgruben," *Naphta* 9, no. 2 (1 February 1901): 32.
75. Carpathian Company advertisement, in MacGarvey, "Introduction," xxv. For more on the western Galician oil industry, see Żychliński, "Z przeszłości przemysłu naftowego," 336–42.
76. "Pologne: Note sur la Situation Financière." Archives historiques du Crédit

Lyonnais (henceforth CL) DEEF 73294. Its capital continued to grow until it reached 18 million crowns in 1916 (CL DEEF 73294).

77. Galizische Karpathen Petroleum AG vormals Bergheim & MacGarvey, *Geschäftsbericht für das Geschäftsjahr 1895/1896: Erstattet durch den Verwaltungsrat in der ersten ordentlichen Versammlung der Actionäre am 15. Juni 1896* (Gorlice: Verlag der Galizischen Karpathen-Petroleum AG vormals Bergheim & MacGarvey, 1896).

78. *Compass*, 1916, s.v. Galizische Karpathen-Petroleum Actien-Gesellschaft; Szajnok, *Skorowidz*.

79. "Dividences des Principales Sociétés de Pétrole," CL DEEF 30167, File 303.2 #11.

80. May, *Hard Oiler!*, 135, 141–143; MacGarvey, "Introduction," viii.

81. *Bericht der k.k. Gewerbe-Inspektoren über ihre Amtsthätigkeit im Jahre 1886* (Vienna: k.k. Hof- und Staatsdruckerei, 1887), 404.

82. "Statistik der Petroleum-Industrie in Galizien im Jahre 1900," *Naphta* 9, no. 6 (31 March 1901): 107.

83. Mendel and Schwarz, *Internationale Petroleumstatistik*, 2.

84. *Verhandlungen der vom k.k. Handelsministerium veranstalteten Kartellenquete*, vol. 3, *Mineralölindustrie*, 26 and 27 March 1912 (Vienna: k.k. Hof- und Staatsdruckerei, 1912), 146.

85. Felix Somary, *Die Aktiengesellschaften in Österreich* (Vienna: Manz, 1902), 55.

86. According to the mining inspector, Jakób's output remained at seven hundred tons of oil a day even after the initial outburst had passed. *Bericht der k.k. Gewerbe-Inspektoren über ihre Amtsthätigkeit im Jahre 1895* (Vienna: k.k. Hof- und Staatsdruckerei, 1896), 381. Even when its productivity sank to around thirty tons a day a few months later, Jakób continued to be one of the province's most productive wells. *Die österreichische-ungarische Monarchie in Wort und Bild*, vol. 11, *Galizien* (Vienna: k.k. Hof- und Staatsdruckerei, 1898), 856; Carl Morawitz, *Fünfzig Jahre Geschichte einer Wiener Bank: Vortrag gehalten in der Gesellschaft österreichischer Volkswirte anläßlich des 50jährigen Jubiläums der Anglo-Oesterreichischen Bank* (Vienna: J. R. Vernay, 1913), 47.

87. Szajnocha, *Petroleumindustrie Galiziens*, 19.

88. *Berichte der k.k. Bergbehörden über ihre Thätigkeit im Jahre 1895 bei Handhabung der Bergpolizei und Beaufsichtigung der Bergarbeiterverhältnisse* (Vienna: k.k. Hof- und Staatsdruckerei, 1897), 370–371.

89. Joseph Berlinerblau, *Der Erdwachs: Ozokerit und Ceresin; Geschichte, Vorkommen, Gewinnung und Verarbeitung* (Braunschweig: Friedrich Vieweg und Sohn), 13.

90. See Ivan Franko, *Boryslavs'ki opovidannia* (Kiev: Vydavnytstvo Khudozhn'oï

Literatury "Dnipro," 1966); and Stefan Kovaliv, *Obrazki z Halyts'koi Kalifornii* (Lviv: Naukove Tovarystvo im. Shevchenka, 1913).

91. Myrna Santiago, "Huasteca Crude: Indians, Ecology, and Labor in the Mexican Oil Industry, Northern Veracruz, 1900–1938" (PhD. diss., University of California at Berkeley, 1997), 142–143.

92. May, *Hard Oiler!* 140.

93. Ibid., 127, 138–139, 153, 159.

94. Obituary of Robert Waldeck, *Naphta* 9, no. 12 (30 June 1901).

95. Franciszek Brzezowski, *Środki zaradcze w celu uzdrowienia przemysłu naftowego w Borysławiu i zmniejszenia niebiezpieczeństw właściwych temu przemysłowi* (Cieszyn: author, 1903), 125–126; A. Fauck, "Zur Lage der galizischen Naphta-Industrie," *Naphta* 9, no. 4 (28 February 1901), 63–65.

96. *Bericht der k.k. Gewerbe-Inspektoren über ihre Amtsthätigkeit im Jahre 1885* (Vienna: k.k. Hof- und Staatsdruckerei, 1886), 365.

97. *Österreichisches Biographisches Lexikon, 1815–1950*, vol. 7, ed. Eva Obermayer-Marnach (Vienna: Verlag der österreichischen Akademie der Wissenschaften, 1978), s.v. "Odrzywolski, Kazimierz."

98. Stefan Bartoszewicz, *Wspomnienia z przemysłu naftowego, 1897–1930* (Lviv: Piller-Neumann, 1934), 4.

99. Julius Noth, *Oesterreichische Zeitschrift für Berg- und Hüttenwesen* 24 (1876): 420.

100. "Die Industrie der bituminösen Stoffe (Erdöl, Petroleum, Nafta, Erdwachs, Asfalt, u.s.w.) im östlichen Europa," unpublished report of Oberbergcommissär Heinrich Walter, 1 November 1882, ÖSTA FM, VI Pra. S. 20/2 1883 Z. 5822/624. Nr. 5264, Faszikel 8/5 Reg. II.

101. *Bericht der k.k. Gewerbe-Inspektoren über ihre Amtsthätigkeit im Jahre 1886* (Vienna: k.k. Hof- und Staatsdruckerei, 1887), 404; TsDIAUL 146.62.99.

102. Bartoszewicz, *Wspomnienia*, 1.

103. See correspondence between the management of the Administration of the Societé des Pétroles d'Iwonicz and Count Andrzej Lubomirski, TsDIAUL 835.1.502.

104. 'Notices,' *Naphta* 6 no. 7 (15 April 1898): 66.

105. Bartoszewicz, Wspomnienia, 1.

106. *Bericht der k.k. Gewerbe-Inspektoren über ihre Amtsthätigkeit im Jahre 1885*, 365.

107. Ibid., 383; " 'Schodnica' Actien-Gesellschaft für Petroleum-Industrie, Wien," in *Die Großindustrie Österrichs* (Vienna: Leopold Weiss, (1898), 336.

108. Borzym, "Idea polska Stanisława Szczepanowskiego," 15.

109. *Österreichisches Biographisches Lexikon*, s.v. "Odrzywolski, Kazimierz."

110. "Statistik des Naphthabetriebes in Galizien," in *Statistisches Jahrbuch des k.k.*

Ackerbau-Ministeriums für 1888, pt. 3, *Der Bergwerksbetrieb Österreichs im Jahre 1888,* 2nd ed. (Vienna: k.k. Hof- und Staatsdruckerei, 1889).

111. Ibid., 83.

112. This phenomenon has been documented in France and Great Britain. See Donald Reid, "Schools and the Paternalist Project at Le Creusot, 1850–1914," *Journal of Social History* 27, no. 1 (1993): 129–143; and Marilyn Cohen, "Paternalism and Poverty: Contradictions in the Schooling of Working-Class Children in Tullyish, County Down, 1825–1914," *History of Education* 21, no. 3 (1992): 291–306.

113. *Neue Freie Presse,* 2 October 1899, M, 3.

114. Borzym, "Idea Polska Stanisława Szczepanowskiego," 6.

115. *Neue Freie Presse,* 2 October 1899, M, 4.

116. Ibid.

117. Ibid., 3–4.

118. The term "Stańczyk" referred to the Cracow conservatives. See Piotr Wandycz, *The Lands of Partitioned Poland, 1795–1918* (Seattle: University of Washington Press, 1974), 216.

119. Borzym, "Idea Polska Stanisława Szczepanowskiego," 8.

120. *Neue Freie Presse,* 11 October 1899, M, 3, 7.

121. *Neue Freie Presse,* 2 October 1899, M, 4.

122. *Neue Freie Presse,* 11 October 1899, M, 8. Badeni became prime minister of Austria in October 1895.

123. "Gisements Pétrolifères de Schodnica (Galicie): Concessions de Messieurs Wolski et Odrzywolski," 30 March 1898, CL DEEF 25245.

124. *Neue Freie Presse,* 11 October 1899, M, 8.

125. *Neue Freie Presse,* 2 October 1899, M, 4.

126. Walicki, *Poland between East and West,* 34.

127. *Neue Freie Presse,* 10 October 1899, A, 3.

128. *Neue Freie Presse,* 12 October 1899, M, 4.

129. *Neue Freie Presse,* 11 October 1899, M, 7.

130. *Neue Freie Presse,* 10 November 1899, M, 7; Bartoszewicz, *Wspomnienia,* 4.

131. Bartoszewicz, *Wspomnienia,* 4.

132. Ibid., 4.

133. Zygmunt Bielski, "Wspomnienie ze Schodnicy," *Przemysł Naftowy* 4, no. 11 (June 1929): 333.

134. Borzym, "Idea polska Stanisława Szczepanowskiego," 8.

135. Wójcik, *Mowa wygłoszona,* 2, 5.

136. Ibid., 4.

137. *Kraj,* no. 50 (1899), as cited in Borzym, "Idea polska Stanisława Szczepanowskiego," 9.

138. Borzym, "Idea polska Stanisława Szczepanowskiego," 8–9.
139. *Czas*, no. 269 (2 November 1900), as cited in Borzym, "Idea polska Stanisława Szczepanowskiego," 16.
140. [Edmund Wengraf], *Das hohe Haus: Parlamentsbilder aus Oesterreich* (Vienna: Verlag der "Neuen Revue," 1896), 67–69.

4. The Boys Don't Sleep at Home

1. Joseph Mendel and Robert Schwarz, eds., *Internationale Petroleumstatistik*, vol. 2, Österreich-Ungarn (Vienna: Verlag für Fachliteratur, 1812), 2; "Statistik des Naphtabetriebes in Galizien," in *Statistisches Jahrbuch des k.k. Ackerbau-Ministeriums für 1886*, pt. 3, *Der Bergwerksbetrieb Österreichs im Jahre 1886* (Vienna: k.k. Hof- und Staatsdruckerei, 1887), 136. According to statistics compiled by Ukrainian historians working in the Soviet era, there were 10,500 oil workers in Borysław in 1875. D. Nyzovyi and Ia. Sadovyi, "Boryslav—Misto Oblasnoho Pidnoriadkuvannia," in *Istoriia mist i sil Ukraïns'koï RSR: L'vivs'ka Oblast'*, ed. V. Iu. Malanchuk (Kiev: Holovna Redaktsiia Ukraïns'koï Radians'koï Entsyklopediï AN URSR, 1968), 102.
2. Wages for Drohobycz district, 1906–1909. Mendel and Schwarz, *Internationale Petroleumstatistik*, 8.
3. Arnulf Nawratil, in *Bericht der k.k. Gewerbe-Inspektoren über ihre Amtsthätigkeit im Jahre 1885* (Vienna: k.k. Hof- und Staatsdruckerei, 1886), 385.
4. Eric J. Hobsbawm, *The Age of Empire, 1875–1914* (New York: Vintage, 1989), 113–114.
5. Eric R. Wolf, *Europe and the People without History* (Berkeley: University of California Press, 1982), 354.
6. Orlando Figes, *A People's Tragedy: The Russian Revolution, 1891–1924* (New York: Penguin, 1996), 138.
7. Vernon Lidtke, *The Outlawed Party: Social Democracy in Germany, 1878–1890* (Princeton, NJ: Princeton University Press, 1966), 67, 77–81, 252–253.
8. Vernon Lidtke, *The Alternative Culture: Socialist Labor in Imperial Germany* (New York: Oxford University Press, 1985), 50–74.
9. Robert Wistrich, *Socialism and the Jews: The Dilemmas of Assimilation in Germany and Austria-Hungary* (Rutherford, NJ: Fairleigh Dickinson University Press, 1982), 300.
10. Otto Bauer, *Die Nationalitätenfrage und die Sozialdemokratie* (Vienna: Wiener Volksbuchhandlung, 1924), 108.
11. Piotr Wandycz, *The Lands of Partitioned Poland, 1795–1918* (Seattle: University of Washington Press, 1974), 227–228; Wistrich, *Socialism and the Jews*, 300.

12. Karl Marx, "Speech on Poland (22 February 1848)," in Karl Marx, *The Revolutions of 1848, vol. 1, Political Writings, vol. 1*, ed. David Fernbach (London: Penguin, 1973), 104–105; Timothy Snyder, *Nationalism, Marxism, and Modern Central Europe: A Biography of Kazimierz Kelles-Krauz (1872–1905)* (Cambridge, MA: Harvard University Press, 1997), 205.

13. Leonid Rudnytzky, "The Image of Austria in the Works of Ivan Franko," in *Nationbuilding and the Politics of Nationalism: Essays on Austrian Galicia*, ed. Andrei S. Markovits and Frank E. Sysyn (Cambridge, MA: Harvard University Press, 1982), 244.

14. *Der Arbeter*, (Journal of the Jewish Labor Party, founded in 1892), as cited in Jonathan Frankel, *Prophecy and Politics: Socialism, Nationalism, and the Russian Jews, 1862–1917* (Cambridge: Cambridge University Press, 1981), 177.

15. On Galician populists: Wandycz, *Lands of Partitioned Poland*, 295; on Germany and France: Hobsbawm, *Age of Empire*, 137.

16. Wandycz, *Lands of Partitioned Poland*, 227.

17. *Bericht der k.k. Gewerbe-Inspektoren über ihre Amtsthätigkeit im Jahre 1884* (Vienna: k.k. Hof- und Staatsdruckerei, 1885), 238.

18. Charters Wynn, *Workers, Strikes, and Pogroms: The Donbass-Dnepr Bend in Late Imperial Russia, 1870–1905* (Princeton, NJ: Princeton University Press, 1992), 4.

19. Douglas Holmes, *Cultural Disenchantments: Worker Peasantries in Northeast Italy* (Princeton, NJ: Princeton University Press, 1989), 56.

20. Ibid.

21. Adrian Hall, *Fenland Worker-Peasants: The Economy of Smallholders at Rippingdale, Lincolnshire, 1791–1871* (Aberdeen: British Agricultural History Society, 1992), 18–21.

22. Richard Charles Murphy, *Guestworkers in the German Reich: A Polish Community in Wilhelmian Germany* (Boulder, CO: East Europe Monographs, 1983), 65.

23. John Kulczycki, *The Polish Coal Miners' Union and the German Labor Movement in the Ruhr, 1902–1934: National and Social Solidarity* (Oxford: Berg, 1997), 9.

24. Ronald Grigor Suny, *The Baku Commune, 1917–1918: Class and Nationality in the Russian Revolution* (Princeton, NJ: Princeton University Press, 1972), 10.

25. As cited in Wynn, *Workers, Strikes, and Pogroms*, 37.

26. Suny, *Baku Commune*, 30.

27. *Bericht der k.k. Gewerbe-Inspektoren über ihre Amtsthätigkeit im Jahre 1884*, 240–243.

28. *Die Bergwerks-Inspection in Österreich: Berichte der k.k. Bergbehörden über ihre Thätigkeit im Jahre 1892 bei Handhabung der Bergpolizei und Beauf-*

sichtigung der Bergarbeiterverhältnisse (Vienna: k.k. Hof- und Staatsdruckerei, 1894), 163.

29. Nyzovyi and Sadovyi, "Boryslav," 103.

30. Saul Raphael Landau, *Unter jüdischen Proletariern: Reiseschilderungen aus Ostgalizien und Rußland* (Vienna: Rosner, 1898), 30–31.

31. John-Paul Himka, *Socialism in Galicia: The Emergence of Polish Social Democracy and Ukrainian Radicalism, 1860–1890* (Cambridge, MA: Harvard University Press, 1983), 39. In Germany, too, skilled artisans formed a large portion of the working classes. Wolf, *Europe and the People Without History,* 358.

32. *Die Bergwerks-Inspection in Österreich* (1892), 196.

33. Ignaz Leichner, *Erdöl und Erdwachs: Ein Bild galizischer Industrie,* Sozialpolitische Flugschriften (Vienna: Commissions-Verlag der Ersten Wiener Volksbuchhandlung, Ignaz Brand, 1898), 1.

34. I. I. Bass and A. A. Kaspruk, *Ivan Franko, zhyttevyi i tvorchyi shliakh* (Kiev: Naukova Dumka, 1983), 18.

35. Ivan Franko, "Meine jüdischen Bekannten," in *Beiträge zur Geschichte und Kultur der Ukraine: Ausgewählte deutsche Schriften des revolutionären Demokraten, 1882—1915,* by Ivan Franko, ed., E. Winter and P. Kirchner (Berlin: Akademie-Verlag, 1963), 57.

36. Ivan Franko, "Autobiographie, geschrieben in Form eines Briefes an die Redaktion *Herders Konversations-Lexikon,*" in Franko, *Beiträge,* 35–37.

37. Ignacy Daszyński, *Pamiętniki,* vol. 1 (Cracow, 1925–1926; repr., Warsaw: Książka i Wiedza, 1957), 37.

38. Ibid., 38.

39. Franko, "Autobiographie," 37.

40. Letter from Ivan Franko to Mykhailo Pavlyk, 12 November 1882, in *Zibrannia tvoriv u p'iatdesiaty tomakh,* vol. 48 (Kiev: Naukova Dumka, 1986), 325.

41. Cited in Himka, *Socialism in Galicia,* 116.

42. For a closer examination of the development of Franko's political views, see Yaroslav Hrytsak, "A Ukrainian Answer to the Galician Ethnic Triangle: The Case of Ivan Franko," in *Polin: Studies in Polish Jewry,* vol. 12, *Focusing on Galicia: Jews, Poles, and Ukrainians, 1772–1918,* ed. Israel Bartal and Antony Polonsky (London: Littman Library of Jewish Civilization, 1999), 137–146.

43. Files on the Polish socialists in Drohobycz, the Social Democratic Party, and individual socialists, TsDIAUL 387.1.41, 146.7.4686, and 146.6.1152.

44. Police files on May Day celebrations in 1890, 1897, 1899, and 1900, TsDIAUL 146.4.3615, 3621, 3622, and 3623.

45. *Bericht der k.k. Gewerbe-Inspektoren über ihre Amtsthätigkeit im Jahre 1885,* 351–352.

46. Ibid., 371.

47. TsDIAUL 146.55.61 and 62 each contain hundreds of objections to fines for violations of safety precautions made by the workers.

48. Among wax workers, 213 deaths and 326 serious injuries; among oil workers, 48 deaths and 270 injuries. M. V. Bryk, O. M. Horpynko, Ia. D. Isayevych, V. F. Nadim'ianov, Iu. I. Palkin, Ia. S. Khonigsman, A. M. Chernenko, "Drohobych," *Istoriă mist i sil Ukraïns' koï PCP: L'vivs'ka Oblast'*, ed. V. Iu. Malanchuk (Kiev: Holovna Redaktsiia Ukraïns'koï Radians'koï Entsyklopediï AN URSR, 1968), 267.

49. *Times* (London), 2 September 1890.

50. In 1885, for example, Nawratil heard of 152 accidents, but only 73 were reported to him officially by courts, hospitals, and chief district magistrates. The rest he learned of "privately." *Bericht der k.k. Gewerbe-Inspektoren über ihre Amtsthätigkeit im Jahre 1885*, 370.

51. Tom Bottomore, ed., *A Dictionary of Marxist Thought* (Cambridge, MA: Harvard University Press, 1983), 79.

52. Karl Marx, "The Metaphysics of Political Economy," in *The Poverty of Philosophy* (New York: International Publishers, 1963), 173.

53. Karl Marx and Friedrich Engels, "Manifesto of the Communist Party," in Karl Marx, *The Revolutions of 1848: Political Writings*, vol. 1, ed. David Fernbach (London: Penguin, 1973), 76.

54. *Die Bergwerks-Inspection in Österreich: Berichte der k.k. Bergbehörden über ihre Thätigkeit im Jahre 1896* (Vienna: k.k. Hof- und Staatsdruckerei, 1898), 503.

55. Ivan Franko, *Narys istoriï ukraïns'ko-rus'koï literatury do 1890 r.* (Lviv, 1910), 261, cited in Yaroslav Hrytsak, "Istorychna osnova povisti I. Franka 'Boryslav smiiet'sia,' " in *Ukraïns'ke literaturoznavstvo: Ivan Franko; Statti ta materialy*, vol. 44 (Lviv: 1985), 3.

56. See, for example, Nyzovyi and Sadovyi, "Boryslav," 103; and V. Makaiev, *Robitnychyi klas Halychyny v ostannii tretyni XIX st.* (Lviv, 1968), 82, cited in Himka, *Socialism in Galicia*, 117. For a criticism of these histories, see Hrytsak, "Istorychna osnova."

57. Absence of proof is not proof of absence, but this author's inability to find any evidence, combined with Yaroslav Hrytsak's insistence that there is none, leads her to make this claim with confidence. Hrytsak, "Istorychna osnova."

58. Debates in the provincial diet, reports from the Drohobycz chief district magistrate, and the findings of a special commission to investigate the fire are in TsDIAUL 146.4.3411.

59. Landau, *Unter jüdischen Proletariern*, 37.

60. *Die Bergwerks-Inspection in Österreich: Berichte der k.k. Bergbehörden über*

ihre Thätigkeit im Jahre 1904 (Vienna: k.k. Hof- und Staatsdruckerei, 1907), 407, 414.

61. *Bericht der k.k. Gewerbe-Inspektoren über ihre Amtsthätigkeit im Jahre 1885,* 384, and Leichner, *Erdöl und Erdwachs,* 11.

62. Leichner, *Erdöl und Erdwachs,* 11.

63. *Die Bergwerks-Inspection in Österreich: Berichte der k.k. Bergbehörden über ihre Thätigkeit im Jahre 1893* (Vienna: k.k. Hof- und Staatsdruckerei, 1896), 271.

64. Landau, *Unter jüdischen Proletariern,* 39.

65. Leichner, *Erdöl und Erdwachs,* 12, 18.

66. *Die Bergwerks-Inspection in Österreich* (1892), 195–196.

67. Hobsbawm, *Age of Empire,* 115. For specific examples of communities characterized by constant inward and outward migration, see James Harvey Jackson, *Migration and Urbanization in the Ruhr Valley, 1821–1914* (Atlantic Highlands, NJ: Humanities Press, 1997); Elke Hauschildt, *Polnische Arbeitsmigranten in Wilhelmsburg bei Hamburg während des Kaiserreichs und der Weimarer Republik* (Dortmund: Forschungstelle Ostmitteleuropa, 1986); and David Crew, *Town in the Ruhr: A Social History of Bochum, 1860–1914* (New York: Columbia University Press, 1979).

68. Ivan Franko, "Deshcho pro Boryslav," in *Znadoby do vychennia movy i etnohrafiï ukraïns'koho narodu,* in *Zibrannia tvoriv u p'iatdesiaty tomakh,* vol. 50 (Kiev: Vydavnytstvo Naukova Dumka, 1986), 192–193; Franko, "Der Schafhirt," *Ukrainische Rundschau* 5 (1907): 27–33, reprinted in Franko, *Beiträge,* 220.

69. *Die Bergwerks-Inspection in Österreich* (1896), 462.

70. Franko, "Deshcho," 193.

71. Ivan Franko, "Vivchar," in *Poluika i yn'shi Boryslavs'ki opovidania* (Lviv: Ukraïns'ka-Rus'ka Vydavnycha Spilka, 1899), 89–96.

72. Johann Holobek, "Bericht," in *Die Bergwerks-Inspection in Österreich: Berichte der k.k. Bergbehörden im Jahre 1898* (Vienna: k.k. Hof- und Staatsdruckerei, 1901), 638.

73. Ivan Franko, "Bauernstreiks in Ostgalizien," *Die Zeit,* no. 27 (23 October 1902): 3–4, reprinted in Franko, *Beiträge,* 413.

74. *Die Bergwerks-Inspection in Österreich: Berichte der k.k. Bergbehörden über ihre Thätigkeit im Jahre 1900* (Vienna: k.k. Hof- und Staatsdruckerei, 1903), 567; Marian Bernhard Leopold, "Über die Rohölgruben in Borysław: Schluss," *Naphta* 9, no. 8 (30 April 1901): 148; TsDIAUL 146.7.4689; Leichner, *Erdöl und Erdwachs,* 18.

75. Landau, *Unter jüdischen Proletariern,* 33.

76. *Die Bergwerks-Inspection in Österreich* (1892), 193, 198.

77. *Die Bergwerks-Inspection in Österreich: Berichte der k.k. Bergbehörden über*

ihre Thätigkeit im Jahre 1895 (Vienna: k.k. Hof- und Staatsdruckerei, 1897), 388; *Die Bergwerks-Inspection in Österreich* (1892), 195; and *Die Bergwerks-Inspection in Österreich: Berichte der k.k. Bergbehörden über ihre Thätigkeit im Jahre 1901* (Vienna: k.k Hof- und Staatsdruckerei, 1904), 427.

78. Wynn, *Workers, Strikes, and Pogroms,* 7.
79. The Lviv daily newspaper *Gazeta Lwowska* estimated 3,800 Jewish workers; the anti-Semitic Drohobycz biweekly newspaper *Gazeta Naddniestrzańska* estimated as many as 5,000. "Zaburzenie w Borysławie," *Gazeta Lwowska* 175 (30 July 1884): 3; "Morderstwa w Boryslawiu," *Gazeta Naddniestrzańska* 12 (1 August 1884): 4–5.
80. Himka, *Socialism in Galicia,* 118.
81. This was part of a larger trend of the displacement of Jews from Galician industry in the late nineteenth century, described in Raphael Mahler, "The Economic Background of Jewish Emigration from Galicia to the United States," *YIVO Annual of Jewish Social Science* 7 (1952): 261.
82. *Bericht der k.k. Gewerbe-Inspektoren über ihre Amtsthätigkeit im Jahre 1884,* 251.
83. Leichner, *Erdöl und Erdwachs,* 19.
84. Wistrich, *Socialism and the Jews,* 181.
85. John Boyer, *Political Radicalism in Late Imperial Vienna: Origins of the Christian Social Movement, 1848–1897* (Chicago: University of Chicago Press, 1981), 77.
86. Wistrich, *Socialism and the Jews,* 283.
87. Victor Adler, 1889, cited in Wistrich, *Socialism and the Jews,* 242.
88. Wistrich, *Socialism and the Jews,* 186.
89. Abraham Korkis, "Zur Bewegung der jüdischen Bevölkerung in Galizien," in *Jüdische Statistik,* ed. Alfred Nossig (Berlin: Jüdischer Verlag, 1903), 311.
90. Mahler, "Economic Background," 261.
91. David Blackbourn, "The Mittelstand in German Society and Politics, 1871–1914," *Social History* 4 (January 1977): 430; Hobsbawm, *Age of Empire,* 131.
92. Report from Drohobycz Chief District Magistrate Napadiewicz to the Presidium of the viceroy's office, TsDIAUL 146.7.4689: 10–14.
93. TsDIAUL 146.7.4689: 51–56.
94. Report from the Drohobycz Chief District Magistrate, TsDIAUL 146.7.4689: 13.
95. Ibid.
96. *Die Bergwerks-Inspection in Österreich* (1900), 543, 569.
97. The sale of spirits was at this time still overwhelmingly in the hands of Jews and would remain so until Jews were banned from selling alcoholic beverages in 1910 (Wistrich, *Socialism and the Jews,* 311).
98. See, for example, Ivan Franko, "Na roboti" (At Work) and "Ripnyk" (The

Oil Worker), both originally published in 1877, reprinted in Ivan Franko, *Boryslavs'ki opovidannia* (Kiev: Vydavnytstvo Khudozhn'oï Literatury "Dnipro," 1966).

99. Wynn, *Workers, Strikes, and Pogroms,* 195.
100. *Die Bergwerks-Inspection in Österreich* (1900), 543, 569.
101. Tadeusz Bobrzyński's 10 June 1901 report to the Presidium, TsDIAUL 146.8.62. In contemporary documents, Wityk's given name was alternately spelled Semen, Zeman, or Semyon and his surname Wityk, Wittyk, Wittek, or Witek. I have chosen to write his name as if it were transliterated from Ukrainian. He was later elected as a representative in the imperial Parliament after the introduction of universal suffrage in 1907.
102. Snyder, *Nationalism,* 189.
103. Bobrzyński's 19 June 1901 report to the Presidium, TsDIAUL 146.8.62.
104. Various reports, TsDIAUL 146.8.62.
105. *Die Bergwerks-Inspection in Österreich: Berichte der k.k. Bergbehörden über ihre Thätigkeit im Jahre 1899* (Vienna: k.k. Hof- und Staatsdruckerei, 1901), 524.
106. Prince Adam Sapieha (1828–1903) was a member of one of Galicia's most prominent families. He was an active member (and from 1875 president) of the Galician Agricultural Society, a representative in the Provincial Diet, and a member of the Austrian House of Lords. A railroad financier, magnate, philanthropist, and publicist, he was also elected to be an arbiter of the Galician Provincial Petroleum Society (GLPV).
107. Biblioteka Stefanyka, f. Sap[ieha], Sprava 824 V b, folder 9: 229–232.
108. Ibid., 231.
109. *Die Bergwerks-Inspection in Österreich* (1899), 509.
110. Ibid., 520–521.
111. Ibid., 524–525. Departure for the United States was a popular solution to the economic troubles of Jewish Galicians, whose rates of emigration surpassed those of non-Jewish Galicians, as well as Jewish Russians. Mahler, "Economic Background," 255, 266; Korkis, "Zur Bewegung," 314.
112. TsDIAUL 146.4.3765, 146.4.3766, 146.4.3771, 146.4.3772, 146.4.3773, 146.4.3774, 146.4.3775, 146.8.62, and 146.8.345.
113. Bobrzyński's report to Presidium, 23 June 1904, TsDIAUL 146.4.3772.
114. Daszyński, *Pamiętniki,* 1:27.
115. As cited in and translated by Snyder, *Nationalism,* 204.

5. Oil City

1. "Enquête über die Krise in der Mineralölindustrie," ÖSTA MföA F. 664 Z. 1079 XIV 1910; Joseph Mendel and Robert Schwarz, eds., *Internationale*

Petroleumstatistik, vol. 2, *Österreich-Ungarn* (Vienna: Verlag für Fachliteratur, 1912), 12–13.

2. Ladislaus Szajnocha, *Die Petroleumindustrie Galiziens,* 2nd ed. (Krakow: Verlag des Galizischen Landesausschusses, 1905), 20.

3. "Enquête über die Krise in der Mineralölindustrie," 14; "Ist die galizische Rohölproduktion in der Lage den Bedarf der Monarchie zu decken?," *Naphta* 6, no. 9 (15 May 1898), 82.

4. Daniel Yergin, *The Prize: The Epic Quest for Oil, Money, and Power* (New York: Simon and Schuster, 1991), 79; "Die Besteuerung des Naphta-Bergbaues," *Oleum* 1, no. 2 (9 March 1912): 20.

5. Szczepanowski's testimony, *Neue Freie Presse,* 11 October 1899, M, 7.

6. Heinrich Walter, "Gutachten über das Vorkommen von Erdöl auf den Gütern Korczyn und Kruszelnica Seiner Durchlaucht des Fürsten Andreas Lubomirski, Juli 1891," TsDIAUL f. 835.1.495:5.

7. This is an adaptation of a phrase by Richard White, referring to the salmon in the Columbia River. Richard White, *The Organic Machine: The Remaking of the Columbia River* (New York: Hill and Wang, 1995), 16.

8. "Enquête über die Krise in der Mineralölindustrie," 13.

9. Michał Bobrzyński, *Z moich pamiętników* (Wrocław: Wydawnictwo Zakładu imienia Ossolińskich, 1957), 45.

10. "Ein Überblick über die Petroleum Industrie im verflossenen Jahre," *Naphta* 9, no. 1 (15 January 1901): 6.

11. Szajnocha, *Petroleumindustrie Galiziens,* 3.

12. A. A. Fursenko, "The Oil Industry," in *International Banking 1870–1914,* ed. Rondo Cameron and V. I. Bovykin (New York: Oxford University Press, 1991), 449.

13. Mendel and Schwarz, *Internationale Petroleumstatistik,* 17.

14. "Pologne Autrichienne," CL DEEF 73294: 12.

15. 16 July 1904, TsDIAUL f. 146.4.3773: 26–27.

16. "Gisements Pétrolifères de Schodnica (Galicie): Concession de M. Gartenberg et Cie.," May 1897, and "Gisements Pétrolifères de Schodnica (Galicie): Concessions de Messieurs Wolski et Odrzywolski," 30 March 1898, CL DEEF 25245.

17. *Gründungsakt und Statuten der Petroleum und Ozokerit Gewerkschaft "Niebyłów"* (Drohobycz: Verlag der Petroleum und Ozokerit Gewerkschaft "Niebyłów," 1906); citation from *Niebyłów: Neues grosses Naphta u. Erdwachsgebiet in Ostgalizien* (Lviv: W. A. Szyjkowski, 1905), 7 (spelling, emphasis, and punctuation as in original).

18. "Enquête über die Krise in der Mineralölindustrie," 61.

19. Mendel and Schwarz, *Internationale Petroleumstatistik,* 1, 4.

20. Siegfried Fleischer, "Enquête über die Lage der jüdischen Bevölkerung Gal-

iziens," in *Jüdische Statistik*, ed. Alfred Nossig (Berlin: Jüdischer Verlag, 1903), 209–231.

21. Lubomirski family file, TsDIAUL f. 835.1 (1586–1939). For a defense of the nobility's role in the oil industry, see Stefan Bartoszewicz, *Wspomnienia z przemysłu naftowego, 1897–1930* (Lviv: Piller-Neumann, 1934), 6.

22. "Enquête über die Krise in der Mineralölindustrie," 67.

23. Ibid. Refineries, of course, benefit from low crude oil prices.

24. "Berichterstattung der Bergbau Commission in Angelegenheit der seitens der Gemeinden Drohobycz und Boryslaw an den galizischen Landtag gerichteten Petition in Sachen der k.k. Berghauptmannschaft in Krakau unter dem 13. September 1897 Nr. 65 LGB erlassenen polizeilichen Vorschriften," *Naphta* 6, no. 4 (8 March 1898): 32.

25. Marian Bernhard Leopold, "Über die Rohölgruben in Borysław: Schluss," *Naphta* 9, no. 8 (30 April 1901): 149.

26. Wilhelm Feldman, *Stan ekonomiczny Galicyi: Cyfry i fakta* (Lviv: Nakładem Stanisława Urody, 1900), 19.

27. "Die Lage der galizischen Naphta-Industrie," *Naphta* 9, no. 3 (15 February 1901): 43.

28. "Aus der Technik der Gründungen," *Oleum* 1, nos. 6 and 7 (13 April 1912): 86. See also "Oil Trust of Galicia," *Oleum* 1, no. 3 (16 March 1912): 35–36; "Oil Trust of Galicia II," *Oleum* 1, no. 5 (30 March 1912): 65.

29. "Enquête über die Krise in der Mineralölindustrie," 61.

30. Wolski's remark: "What surprises me the most is to have heard this comment from Mr. MacGarvey, who came to us as a foreigner himself." Ibid., 67.

31. *Bericht der k.k. Gewerbe-Inspektoren über ihre Amtsthätigkait im Jahre 1884* (Vienna: k.k. Hof- und Staatsdruckerei, 1885), 241.

32. Complete data on production are available in Mendel and Schwarz, *Internationale Petroleumstatistik*.

33. Bobrzyński, *Z moich pamiętników*, 46.

34. "Der galizische Petroleum-Ring," *Naphta* 9, no. 23 (15 December 1901): 449.

35. *Die Gross-Industrie Österreichs: Festgabe zum glorreichen Sechzigjährigen Regierungs-Jubiläum seiner Majestät des Kaisers Franz Joseph I* (Vienna: Leopold Weiss, 1908), 22.

36. [Hermann] D[iamand], "Brand im Boryslawer Petroleumgebiet," *Arbeiter-Zeitung*, 22 September 1909, Biblioteka Stefanyka, f. 44 (Diamand).

37. *Die Bergwerks-Inspection in Österreich. Bericht der k.k. Bergbehörden über ihre Thätigkeit im Jahre 1908* (Vienna: k.k. Hof- u. Staatsdruckerei, 1912), 465.

38. 13 October 1909, TsDIAUL 146.4.3420: 62.

39. D[iamand], "Brand."

40. *New York Times*, 6 July 1908, 4; "Fire in the Galician Oilfields," *Times* (London), 6 July 1908.

41. *Die Bergwerks-Inspection in Österreich* (1908), 467.

42. Mieczysław Orlowicz and Roman Kordys, *Illustrierter Führer durch Galizien: Mit einem Anhang: Ost-Schlesien* (Vienna: A. Hartlebens Verlag, 1914), 243.

43. *Die Bergwerks-Inspection in Österreich* (1908), 468.

44. Orlowicz and Kordys, *Illustrierter Führer durch Galizien*, 243.

45. "Bericht des k.k. Statthalters in Galizien von 23. Mai 1909," TsDIAUL f. 146.4.3420: 12–24.

46. *Die Bergwerks-Inspection in Österreich. Bericht der k.k. Bergbehörden über ihre Thätigkeit im Jahre 1892* (Vienna: k.k. Hof- und Staatsdruckerei, 1894), 176.

47. "Bericht des k.k. Statthalters in Galizien von 23. Mai 1909," TsDIAUL f. 146.4.3420: 12–24.

48. Bobrzyński, *Z moich pamiętników*, 46.

49. "Prix de Revient du Pétrole Raffiné en Galicie," in "Gisements Pétrolifères de Schodnica (Galicie): Concessions de Messieurs Wolski et Odrzywolski," 30 March 1898, CL DEEF 25245.

50. Ignacy Łukasiewicz, "Bericht," 10 May 1898, unpublished report, TsDIAUL f. 146.55.40:16b (1863 and 1868 prices); Sigmund Brosche, opening remarks, "Enquête über die Krise in der Mineralölindustrie" (1909 price).

51. Marian Bernhard Leopold, "Über die Rohölgruben in Borysław," *Naphta* 9 no. 5 (15 March 1901): 83; CL DEEF 30167, Etude No. 303.2: 7.

52. TsDIAUL f. 146.4.3772: 46.

53. TsDIAUL f. 146.4.3773: 144.

54. TsDIAUL f. 146.4.3772: 35–40 146.4; 3773: 1, 42–43.

55. TsDIAUL f. 146.4.3772: 44, 52, 53, 64–68; Ignacy Daszyński, *Pamiętniki* vol. 1 (Cracow, 1925–1926; repr., Warsaw: Książka i Wiedza), 208.

56. TsDIAUL f. 146.4.3773: 8–9.

57. TsDIAUL f. 146.4.3772: 71, 107.

58. Mykhailo Demkovych-Dobryans'kyi, *Potots'kyi i Bobzhyns'kyi: Tsisars'ki namisnyky Halychyny, 1903–1913* (Rome: Vydannya Ukraïns'koho katolyts'koho universytetu sv. Klymenta Papy, 1987), 121.

59. Encoded telegram, TsDIAUL f. 146.4.3773: 8–9.

60. Alexander Gerschenkron, *An Economic Spurt That Failed: Four Lectures in Austrian History* (Princeton, NJ: Princeton University Press), 1977), 31–32.

61. TsDIAUL f. 146.4.3773: 4; TsDIAUL f. 146.4.3772.

62. Wolaniecki, *Po strajku w Borysławiu! Z doświadczeń i rozmyślań Wolanieckego* (Wolanka: Edward Oczosalski, 1904), 5.

63. TsDIAUL f. 146.4.3773: 45.

64. Ibid., 24–25. The large companies to which Piwocki was referring were the Carpathian Company, Borysław Syndicate, Nafta Joint Stock Company, Perkins, and Freund.
65. TsDIAUL f. 146.4.3773: 31–38.
66. TsDIAUL f. 146.4.3772: 105.
67. Ibid., 5–12, 52, 53, 64–68, 77, 92–96, 99.
68. Ibid., 94, 103.
69. Ibid., 125–127, 85–87.
70. TsDIAUL f. 146.4.3775: 31, 82.
71. TsDIAUL f. 146.4.3773: 71.
72. TsDIAUL f. 146.8.345: 1–17.
73. TsDIAUL f. 146.4.3773: 31–38, 84, 90.
74. TsDIAUL f. 146.4.3772: 42, 131.
75. TsDIAUL f. 146.4.3773: 51–55, 57, 133–134, 147.
76. CL DEEF 49083, Table 3281; CL DEEF 30167.303.2.
77. TsDIAUL f. 146.4.3773: 18–20.
78. TsDIAUL f. 146.4.3772: 142.
79. TsDIAUL f. 146.4.3773: 156–157, 162, 185.
80. Ibid., 26–27.
81. MföA F. 661 Z. 206 XIV/1910.
82. TsDIAUL f. 146.4.3771, 3765, and 3766.
83. 11 December 1910, TsDIAUL 146.4.3766: 10.
84. *Die Bergwerks-Inspection in Österreich. Bericht der k.k. Bergbehörden über ihre Thätigkeit im Jahre 1910* (Vienna: k.k. Hof- und Staatsdruckerei, 1913), 458. The eight-hour day was introduced for long-term workers in 1911. *Die Bergwerks-Inspection in Österreich. Bericht der k.k. Bergbehörden über ihre Thätigkeit im Jahre 1911* (Vienna: k.k. Hof- und Staatsdruckerei, 1914), 507.
85. "Enquête über die Krise in der Mineralölindustrie," 62.
86. "Sind die beabsichtigten Wirkungen der Zollerhöhung auf galizisches Rohöl eingetreten und haben die Forderungen nach einer Erhaltung dieser Massregel ihre volle Berechtigung oder nicht?" *Naphta* 9, no. 10 (31 May 1901): 191.
87. Ibid., 190.
88. Gerschenkron, *Economic Spurt*, 23, 58.
89. Ibid., 71.
90. "Das Projekt der Wasserwege vom Standpunkte der gal. Petroleum-Production," *Naphta* 9, no. 12 (30 June 1901): 227. The 1901 Canal Act was all but revoked by the 1911 Bill to Supplement. Gerschenkron, *Economic Spurt*, 125–27.
91. TsDIAUL f. 146.4.3420; CL DEEF 30167; Sigmund Brosche, opening remarks, "Enquête über die Krise in der Mineralölindustrie."

92. Bobrzyński, *Z moich pamiętników*, 47–49.
93. Ibid.; ÖSTA MföA F. 663 X 1909–1918, 258.
94. ÖSTA MföA F. 663 Z. 21/230 to Z. 21/238.
95. Bobrzyński, *Z moich pamiętników*, 49.
96. Brosche, opening remarks, "Enquête über die Krise in der Mineralölindustrie."
97. Decree of the Ministry of Commerce, 16 September 1909; Brosche, opening remarks, "Enquête über die Krise in der Mineralölindustrie."
98. To put this in perspective, the government spent 96 million crowns on the construction of various canals and regulation of waterways as part of the Canal Act of 1901 between 1904 and 1918. The total state budget for 1901 was 1.6 billion crowns. Gerschenkron, *Economic Spurt*, 71, 125.
99. ÖSTA MföA F. 664 Z. 704/2-XIV ex 09, 1 July 1909, 29. The question of funding was first brought before the imperial Parliament on 6 July 1909. Since the legislative session closed before the issue was settled, it was brought up again in the twentieth session (October 1909–March 1910).
100. "Tarifmaßnahmen zur Unterstützung der heimischen Petroleumindustrie," ÖSTA MföA F. 664, 30 Mai 1910.
101. Notes from U.S. Ambassador R. C. Kerens to Foreign Ministry, 13 and 15 July 1910, ÖSTA MföA F. 664 Z. 874.
102. "Enquête über die Krise in der Mineralölindustrie," 9.
103. Fursenko, "Oil Industry," 449.
104. Letter from Piwocki to Potocki, 16 July 1904, TsDIAUL 146.4.3773: 24–25.
105. "Galician Oil Wells Wanted—So the Standard Oil Company Has Set About Getting Them—Owners Want $10,000,000," *New York Times*, 2 February 1903, 2.
106. Clipping from the *Hamburger Fremdenblatt*, no. 210 (8 September 1909), in MföA F. 664 Z. 937.
107. Untitled article clipping, 5 March 1910, MföA F. 664 Z. 354.
108. "Enquête über die Krise in der Mineralölindustrie," 15.
109. "Autriche-Hongrie, Importations et Exportations de Pétroles par Pays pour l'année 1907," CL DEEF 30167; Mendel and Schwarz, *Internationale Petroleumstatistik*, 33–34.
110. CL DEEF 30167, Etude No 303.2: 11.
111. "Enquête über die Krise in der Mineralölindustrie," 15; "The Oil Question Abroad," *New York Times*, 22 April 1895, 5.
112. TsDIAUL f. 146.6.1338, 845.
113. Felix Somary, *Die Aktiengesellschaften in Österreich* (Vienna: Manz, 1902), 55; Alfred Buresch, "Memorandum in der Angelegenheit der Zulassung der ausländischen Petroleum-Actien-Unternehmungen zum Geschäftsbetriebe

in Galizien und in der Bukowina," *Naphta* 7, no. 18 (30 September 1899): 256.

114. CL DEEF 30167, tables 1–5.
115. TsDIAUL 255.1.1–8.
116. "La Pologne. Note de février 1919," CL DEEF 73294: 28.
117. "Pétroles de Galicie: III. Groupes Anglaises," CL DEEF 30166: 3–5.
118. Memorandum on Premier Oil and Pipe Line regarding German holdings (5 July 1919), in *Rola nafty w kształtowanie stosunku państw zachodnich do sprawy Galicji wschodniej (1918–1919)*, ed. Barbara Ratyńska (Warsaw: Polski Instytut Spraw Międzynarodowych), Doc. 20: 84–5.
119. Stefan Bartoszewicz, "Memoriał o udziale kapitału austriackiego, niemieckiego i węgierskiego w przedsiębiorstwach naftowych w Galicji wschodnej," in Ratyńska, *Rola nafty*, Doc. 14: 72–73.
120. Fursenko, "Oil Industry," 451.

6. Blood of the Earth

1. Daniel Yergin, *The Prize: The Epic Quest for Oil, Money, and Power* (New York: Simon and Schuster, 1991), 183.
2. Ferdinand Friedensburg, "Das Erdöl auf dem Gebiet des galizischen und rumänischen Kriegsschauplatzes, 1914—1918," *Militärwissenschaftliche Mitteilungen* 70 (1939): 435.
3. Blood: Ferdinand Friedensburg, *Das Erdöl im Weltkrieg* (Stuttgart: Ferdinand Enke, 1939), iii; grocer's: as quoted in Yergin, *Prize*, 189.
4. Friedensburg, *Erdöl im Weltkrieg*, 21.
5. "Ein Überblick über die Petroleum Industrie im verflossenen Jahre," *Naphta* 9, no. 1 (15 January 1901): 7.
6. *Verhandlungen der vom k.k. Handelsministerium veranstalteten Kartellenquete*, vol. 3, *Mineralölindustrie*, 26 and 27 March 1912 (Vienna: k.k. Hof- und Staatsdruckerei, 1912), 16 (hereafter cites as *Mineralölindustrie*).
7. Ibid., 13.
8. Röhrenkessel Fabrik Mödling AG Brochure, ÖSTA MföA F. 664 Z. 809 (30–31 July 1909).
9. *Mineralölindustrie*, 387.
10. ÖSTA MföA F. 664 Z. 1053 XIV 1910. Petroleum had been used to replace coal in the merchant marine as early as 1900. "Überblick über die Petroleum Industrie im verflossenen Jahre," 7.
11. ÖSTA F. 664 Z. 1053 XIV 1910.
12. Lawrence Sondhaus, *The Naval Policy of Austria-Hungary, 1867–1918: Navalism, Industrial Development, and the Politics of Dualism* (West Lafayette, IN: Purdue University Press, 1994), 159.

13. ÖSTA MföA F. 664 Z. 1053 XIV 1910 (citation); ÖSTA KM MS II GG 1914 8A6/103, 12 June 1914.

14. Brosche's remarks, "Enquête über die Krise in der Mineralölindustrie," ÖSTA MföA F. 664 Z. 1079 XIV 1910: 9.

15. ÖSTA MföA F. 664 Z. 809 (30–31 July 1909); *Mineralölindustrie*, 387–388.

16. *Mineralölindustrie*, 146.

17. Ibid., 11–12, 175–176.

18. Alexander Gerschenkron, *An Economic Spurt That Failed: Four Lectures in Austrian History* (Princeton, NJ: Princeton University Press, 1977), 61.

19. "Enquête über die Krise in der Mineralölindustrie," ÖSTA MföA F. 664 Z. 1079 XIV 1910: 62.

20. *Mineralölindustrie*, 79.

21. Austrian Oderberg (today's Bohumin) lies within the Czech Republic, near the border with Poland. It was an important railway juncture, from which Galician goods could be taken northwest to Dresden or southwest to Vienna.

22. *Mineralölindustrie*, 79. Fanto and Priester both participated in the conference as representatives of the Cartel of Austrian Mineral Oil Refineries in Vienna.

23. Anthony Sokol, *The Imperial and Royal Austro-Hungarian Navy* (Annapolis, MD: United States Naval Institute, 1968), 58.

24. Milan Vego, *Austro-Hungarian Naval Policy, 1904–1914* (London: Frank Cass, 1996), xiv; Hans Hugo Sokol, *Geschichte der k.u.k. Kriegsmarine*, vol. 3, *Des Kaisers Seemacht: Die k.k. österreichische Kriegsmarine 1848–1914* (Vienna: Amalthea, 1980), 204ff; Sondhaus, *Naval Policy*, 191–204.

25. Arthur Marder, *From the Dreadnought to Scapa Flow: The Royal Navy in the Fisher Era, 1904–1919*, vol. 1 (London: Oxford University Press, 1961), 269–270.

26. Yergin, *Prize*, 154–155.

27. Marder, *From the Dreadnought to Scapa Flow*, 1:264–265.

28. Yergin, *Prize*, 155.

29. As cited in Marder, *From the Dreadnought to Scapa Flow*, 1:269.

30. Yergin, *Prize*, 155–156, 173.

31. A. A. Fursenko, *The Battle for Oil: The Economics and Politics of International Corporate Conflict over Petroleum, 1860–1930*, trans. and ed. Gregory Freeze (Greenwich, CT: JAI Press, 1990), 179.

32. Yergin, *Prize*, 171. According to John Singleton, British forces had 507 assorted motor vehicles at the war's outbreak and 57,000 trucks and tractors, 23,000 cars and vans, and 7,000 motor ambulances at the time of the armistice. John Singleton, "Britain's Military use of Horses, 1914–1918," *Past and Present* 139 (1993): 194.

33. Joseph Mendel, *Die Entwicklung der internationalen Erdölwirtschaft in den letzten Jahren* (Leipzig: K. F. Koehler, 1922), 7. On Austria-Hungary's fleet of naval airplanes, see Hans Hugo Sokol, *Des Kaisers Seemacht*, 232–233. According to W. G. Jensen, the German army was accompanied by 70,000 motor vehicles during its march in France in 1914 and mustered 384 airplanes and 30 zeppelins that same year—a number that was to increase to over 14,000 aircraft produced in 1918 (although never more than 4,000 airplanes were used at a time). W. G. Jensen, "The Importance of Energy in the First and Second World Wars," *Historical Journal* 11, no. 3 (1968): 538, 542–543.

34. Sondhaus, *Naval Policy*, 181, 211.

35. Wladimir Aichelburg, *Die Unterseeboote Österreich-Ungarns* (Graz: Akademische Druck- und Verlagsanstalt, 1981), 41, 55, 262.

36. The illness of sailors succumbing to gasoline poisoning later drove submarines to be converted to diesel fuel. Ibid., 210.

37. Horst Friedrich Mayer and Dieter Winkler, *Als die Schiffe tauchen lernten: Die Geschichte der k.u.k. Unterseeboot-Waffe* (Vienna: Österreichische Staatsdruckerei, 1997), 54.

38. Karl Fanta, *Die österreichisch-ungarische Kriegsmarine im Ersten Weltkrieg: Eine logistische Untersuchung* (Vienna: n.p., 1997), 157.

39. ÖSTA KM MS II GG 1914 8A4/5894, 9 May 1914.

40. ÖSTA KM 1914 Abt 5/M, 34–4/211.

41. Klaus Bachmann, *Ein Herd der Feindschaft gegen Rußland: Galizien als Krisenherd in den Beziehungen der Donaumonarchie mit Rußland (1907–1914)* (Vienna: Verlag für Geschichte und Politik, 2001); Wolfdieter Bihl, "Die Beziehungen zwischen Österreich-Ungarn und Rußland in Bezug auf die galizische Frage, 1908–1914," in *Galizien um die Jahrhundertwende: Politische, soziale und kulturelle Verbindungen mit Österreich*, ed. Karlheinz Mack (Vienna: Verlag für Geschichte und Politik, 1990), 35–50; John Leslie, "The Antecedents of Austria-Hungary's War Aims: Policies and Policy-Makers in Vienna and Budapest before and during 1914," *Wiener Beiträge zur Geschichte der Neuzeit* 20 (1993): 307–394; and A[rmin] Mitter, "Galizien— Krisenherd in den Beziehungen zwischen Österreich-Ungarn und Rußland (1910—1914)," *Jahrbuch für Geschichte der sozialistischen Länder Europas* 28 (1984): 207.

42. Mitter, "Galizien," 208.

43. Bachmann, *Herd der Feindschaft*, 259.

44. Leslie, "Antecedents," 339.

45. Ibid., 352.

46. Ibid., 354.

47. Ibid., 350.

48. Bachmann, *Herd der Feindschaft*, 260.

49. Roman Szporluk, "Polish-Ukrainian Relations in 1918: Notes for Discussion," in *The Reconstruction of Poland, 1914–1923*, ed. Paul Latawski (London: Macmillan, 1992), 47.

50. Leslie, "Antecedents," 359.

51. ÖSTA KM MS II GG 1914 8A6/140, 31 July 1914.

52. ÖSTA KM MS II GG 1914 8A4/Z5894.

53. OSTA KM MS II GG 1914 8A4/Z8200, 28 July 1914.

54. Robert Wegs, *Die österreichische Kriegswirtschaft, 1914–1918* (Vienna: Schendl, 1979), 25.

55. Fanta, *Österreichisch-ungarische Kriegsmarine*, 628.

56. ÖSTA KM MS II GG 1913 8A6/103, 12 June 1914,; ÖSTA KM MS II GG 1914 8A4/5894.

57. Fanta, *Österreichisch-ungarische Kriegsmarine*, 632.

58. ÖSTA KM MS II GG 1914 8A6/140; Hans Hugo Sokol, *Des Kaisers Seemacht*, 280.

59. Aichelburg, *Unterseeboote*, 67–68.

60. Fursenko, *Battle for Oil*, 120, 179.

61. ÖSTA KM 1914 Abt 5/M 34–26; Robert Dressler, *Die Entwicklung der galizischen Erdölindustrie* (Vienna: Richards, 1933), 43.

62. ÖSTA MföA F. 665 Z. 4353 ex 1915.

63. ÖSTA KM MS II GG 1917 8A2/101; KM MS II GG 1917 8A2/4.

64. ÖSTA KM MS II GG 1914 8A6/146.

65. ÖSTA KM MS II GG 1914 8A6/162, 163.

66. ÖSTA KM MS II GG 1914 8A4/Z.15163.

67. ÖSTA KM MS II GG 1914 8A4/Z.19035 and 19555.

68. ÖSTA KM 1914 Abt 5/M 34–26. Labor shortages also threatened coal production. Zdeněk Jindra, "Der wirtschaftliche Zerfall Österreich-Ungarns (nach den Berichten der reichsdeutschen Bevollmächtigten in Wien, 1916–1938)," in *Österreich und die Tschechoslowakei, 1918–1938: Die wirtschaftliche Neuordnung in Zentraleuropa in der Zwischenkriegszeit*, ed. Alice Teichova and Herbert Matis (Vienna: Böhlau, 1996), 26–27.

69. ÖSTA KM 1914 Abt 5/M 34–26, official's note of 3 September 1914.

70. Fanta, *Österreichisch-ungarische Kriegsmarine*, 185; ÖSTA KM MS II GG 1914 8A6/171; ÖSTA KM MS II GG 1917 8D6/61–63, 65, 66, 72.

71. Jakov Khonigsman, *600 Let i Dva Goda (Istorija Jevreev Drogobycha i Borislava)* (Lviv: Bnej-Brit "Leopolis," 1997), 24; Fanta, *Österreichisch-ungarische Kriegsmarine*, 160; Walter Kleindel, *Der Erste Weltkrieg: Daten—Zahlen—Fakten* (Vienna: Österreichischer Bundesverlag, 1989), 49.

72. ÖSTA KM MS II G. G. 1914 8A6/177.

73. ÖSTA MföA F. 665, k. k. Eisenbahnministerium Z 5414/21a; Fanta,

Österreichisch-ungarische Kriegsmarine, 185. For a discussion of the short-comings of *Zentralen* in other industries, see Maureen Healy, *Vienna and the Fall of the Habsburg Empire: Total War and Everyday Life in World War I* (Cambridge: Cambridge University Press, 2004), 45–46.

74. See the excellent analysis of Austria-Hungary's *Zentralen* in Wegs, *Österreichische Kriegswirtschaft*, 26–29.

75. Ibid., 131.

76. ÖSTA MföA F. 665 Z. 4353 ex 1915.

77. Dressler, *Entwicklung der galizischen Erdölindustrie*, 42.

78. Ibid., 43. Presumably prices are per 100 kilograms.

79. ÖSTA MföA F. 665 Z. 31317, 31 May 1915.

80. ÖSTA KM 1914 Abt 5/M 34–11/7(17).

81. Dressler, *Entwicklung der galizischen Erdölindustrie*, 52.

82. Piotr Wandycz, *The Lands of Partitioned Poland, 1795–1918.* (Seattle: University of Washington Press, 1974), 337, 339.

83. Andrii Krawchuk, *Christian Social Ethics in Ukraine: The Legacy of Andrei Sheptytsky* (Edmonton: Canadian Institute of Ukrainian Studies Press, 1997), 47–48, 70–71.

84. Orest Subtelny, *Ukraine: A History*, 2nd ed. (Toronto: University of Toronto Press, 1994), 341.

85. Khonigsman, *600 Let i Dva Goda*, 25.

86. Geoff Eley, "Remapping the Nation: War, Revolutionary Upheaval and State Formation in Eastern Europe, 1914–1923," in *Ukrainian-Jewish Relations in Historical Perspective*, ed. Howard Aster and Peter Potichnyj, 2nd ed. (Edmonton: Canadian Institute of Ukrainian Studies, 1990), 207, 217–218.

87. Fanta, *Österreichisch-ungarische Kriegsmarine*, 161.

88. *Stenographische Protokolle des Hauses der Abgeordneten des österreichischen Reichsrates*, 23. Sitzung der XXII. Session am 26. September 1917 (Vienna: k.k. Hof- und Staatsdruckerei, 1917), 803/I.

89. Alfred Pfaff, "Die Entwicklung des Boryslaw-Tustanowicer Erdölrevieres seit seiner Befreiung von russisch. Herrschaft," *Petroleum: Zeitschrift für die gesamten Interessen der Petroleum-Industrie und des Petroleum-Handels* 19 (1916): 982–989.

90. Józef Metzis, "Przyczynek do historji przemysłu naft[owego] w Polsce: Przemysł rafineryjny w okręgu Drohobycz-Borysław," *Przemysł Naftowy* 5, no. 23 (1930): 511.

91. ÖSTA KM BS 1.WK Album 335.

92. Fanta, *Österreichisch-ungarische Kriegsmarine*, 161.

93. Ibid.

94. Friedensburg, "Erdöl auf dem Gebiet," 440.

95. Cited in Christoph Führ, *Das k.u.k Armeeoberkommando und die Innen-politik in Österreich, 1914–1917* (Graz: Hermann Böhlau, 1968), 68.

96. Ibid., 69.

97. As cited in Subtelny, *Ukraine*, 340.

98. Führ, *K.u.k. Armeeoberkommando*, 70.

99. ÖSTA MföA F. 665 Z. 31317.

100. Kaiserliche Verordnung vom 10. August 1915, Reichsgesetzblatt (R.G.Bl.) 239, § 1.

101. R.G.Bl. 377, ÖSTA MföA f. 665.

102. R.G.Bl. 378, ÖSTA MföA f. 665.

103. *Stenographische Protokolle des Hauses der Abgeordneten des österreichischen Reichsrates*, 52. Sitzung der XXII. Session am 20. Dezember 1917 (Vienna: k.k. Hof- und Staatsdruckerei, 1917), 1843/I; Alfred Kohl, *Nasz przemysł naftowy w rozrachunku z Austryą: Referat dla Biura Prac Kongresowych* (Krakow: Drukarnia Przemysłowa, 1919), 20–21.

104. "100 der Beil. Reg. Kais. Ver. vom 10 August 1915 R.G.Bl. Nr 239 betreffend die Beschlagnahme des Rohöls (Erdöls): Erläuternde Bemerkungen," *Beilagen zu den Stenographischen Protokollen des Hauses der Abgeordneten des österreichischen Reichsrates im Jahre 1917*, XXII Session. I. Band (Vienna: k.k. Hof- und Staatsdruckerei, 1917).

105. ÖSTA KM 1914 Abt 5/M 34–15/3, 12 August 1914.

106. ÖSTA KM 1914 Abt 5/M, 34–15, 5 August 1914.

107. Ibid.

108. ÖSTA KM 1914 Abt 5/M, 34–15/2.

109. ÖSTA KM 1914 Abt 5/M, 34–15/5–3, undated telegram from Abteilung 5/M to Etappenoberkommando; ÖSTA KM 1914 Abt 5/M 34–15/5–5, 27 August 1914.

110. ÖSTA KM 1914 Abt 5/M 34–15/5–4, 23 August 1914.

111. ÖSTA MföA f. 662, 1909–1918.

112. "Versorgung der galizischen Erdölbergbaue mit Eisenmaterial," MföA f. 666.

113. Yergin, *Prize*, 181.

114. ÖSTA MföA F. 666, 7 July 1917.

115. ÖSTA MföA 665 Z. 52557, 65882, 61652, and 61106.

116. ÖSTA MföA F. 665 Z. 32479, 9–21 June 1915.

117. ÖSTA MföA F. 665 Z. 34917, Z. 36133, Z. 39821, 21 June–10 July 1915.

118. *Österreichische Statistik*, vol. 32, pt. 5, *Die Ausländer in den im Reichsrathe vertretenen Königreiche und Länder, sowie die Angehörigen dieser letzteren im Auslande* (Vienna: k.k. Hof- und Staatsdruckerei, 1895). For a discussion of women's citizenship in wartime Austria, see Healy, *Vienna*, chapter 4.

119. ÖSTA MföA F. 665 Z. 34370/XIV de 1916.

120. ÖSTA MföA F. 665 Z. 75609, 21 January 1919.
121. ÖSTA MföA F. 666 Z. 93459.
122. Wandycz, *Lands of Partitioned Poland*, 334, 338.
123. Johann Holobek, "Bericht über die Verhältnisse der Erdölarbeiter in Boryslaw-Tustanowice," MföA f. 666 Z. 36082, 1 June 1918.
124. *Borysław w walce o Niepodległość: Wspomnienia* (Borysław: Drukarnia Naftowa T.S.L. Koło-Borysław, 1932), 21, 22.
125. Wandycz, *Lands of Partitioned Poland*, 334; Józef Partyk, "Wspomnienia z 1918 roku: Co się działo w Borysławiu po pokoju brzeskim?" in *Borysław w walce*, 66.
126. Holobek, "Bericht über die Verhältnisse der Erdölarbeiter."
127. "Musterung der bei den Erdölbetrieben in Boryslaw-Tustanowice beschäftigten polnischen Legionäre," MföA F. 666 Z. 31876.
128. Holobek, "Bericht über die Verhältnisse der Erdölarbeiter."
129. ÖSTA MföA F. 666 Z. 31876.
130. ÖSTA MföA F. 666 Z. 34111, 24 May 1918.
131. Holobek, "Bericht über die Verhältnisse der Erdölarbeiter."
132. Führ, *K.u.k. Armeeoberkommando*, 63–64. Tyrolians were proverbially the Habsburgs' most loyal subjects.
133. Krawchuk, *Christian Social Ethics*, 77.
134. Holobek, "Bericht über die Verhältnisse der Erdölarbeiter."
135. TsDIAUL f. 146.4.4900.
136. Führ, *K.u.k. Armeeoberkommando*, 125.
137. Holobek, "Bericht über die Verhältnisse der Erdölarbeiter."
138. ÖSTA KM BS 1.WK Galizien 026.
139. ÖSTA MföA F. 666 Z. 146652 and 70361.
140. *S.P.A.*, XXII Session, 30 May 1917–12 November 1918, vol.1, 1. bis 21. Sitzung (Vienna: k.k. Hof- und Staatsdruckerei, 1917).
141. *S.P.A.*, XXII. Session (Vienna: k.k. Hof- und Staatsdruckerei, 1917), 14 July 1917, 690/I, 20 November 1917, 1444/I, and 3 December 1917, 1636/I.
142. ÖSTA KM MS II GG 1917 8A2, 19 October 1917.
143. Fanta, *Österreichisch-ungarische Kriegsmarine*, 632.
144. Mayer and Winkler, *Als die Schiffe tauchen lernten*, 95, 105, 157–158.
145. Olaf Richard Wulff, *Die österreichische-ungarische Donauflotille im Weltkriege, 1914–1918* (Vienna: Wilhelm Braumüller, 1934), 11, 234.
146. Anthony Sokol, *Imperial and Royal Austro-Hungarian Navy*, 113.
147. Fanta, *Österreichisch-ungarische Kriegsmarine*, 633.
148. Yergin, *Prize*, 181.
149. ÖSTA KM MS II GG 1917 8A2/10 Z. 7227.
150. ÖSTA KM MS II GG 1917 8A2.
151. ÖSTA KM MS II GG 1917 8A2/7, 28 November 1917.

152. ÖSTA KM MS II GG 1917 8A2.
153. ÖSTA KM MS II GG 1917 8A2/10 Z. 7227.
154. ÖSTA KM MS II GG 1917 8A2.
155. ÖSTA KM MS II GG 1917 8A2/4 Z. 41145, 6 November 1917.
156. Ibid.
157. ÖSTA KM MS II GG 1917 8A2/6 Z. 45046, 24 November 1917.
158. ÖSTA KM MS II GG 1917 8A2/8.
159. Arthur J. Marder, *From the Dreadnought to Scapa Flow: The Royal Navy in the Fisher Era, 1904–1919*, vol. 2, *The War Years: To the Eve of Jutland* (London: Oxford University Press, 1965), 332.
160. Ibid., 12, 156, 160.
161. Fanta, *Österreichisch-ungarische Kriegsmarine*, 632.
162. Wegs, *Österreichisch-ungarische Kriegswirtschaft*, 92.

7. A Hotly Disputed Territory

1. Walter Kleindel, *Der Erste Weltkrieg: Daten—Zahlen—Fakten* (Vienna: Österreichischer Bundesverlag, 1989), 256–263; Joseph Held, ed., *The Columbia History of Eastern Europe in the Twentieth Century* (New York: Columbia University Press, 1992), xi.
2. Woodrow Wilson Foundation, *Official Documents Issued during the Two World Wars* (New York: Woodrow Wilson Foundation, 1944).
3. Laurence J. Orzell, "A 'Hotly Disputed' Issue: Eastern Galicia at the Paris Peace Conference," *Polish Review* 25, no. 1 (1980): 50.
4. Andrzej Korbonski, "Poland: 1918–1990," in Held, *Columbia History of Eastern Europe*, 231.
5. Tadeusz Jędruszczak, "Powstanie II Rzeczypospolitej (rządy i terytorium)," *Dzieje Najnowsze* 10, no. 4 (1978): 42–58; *Les Documents les plus importants de la République Ukrainienne de l'Ouest* (Vienna: Engel, 1918); Orest Subtelny, *Ukraine: A History*, 2nd ed. (Toronto: University of Toronto Press, 1994), 367.
6. Rogers Brubaker, *Nationalism Reframed: Nationhood and the National Question in the New Europe* (Cambridge: Cambridge University Press, 1996), 83–84.
7. Przemysław Piotr Żurawski vel Grajewski, *Sprawa Ukraińska na Konferencji Pokojowej w Paryżu w Roku 1919* (Warsaw: Semper, 1995), 79–80; Zofia Zaks, "Galicja Wschodnia w Polskiej Polityce Zagranicznej (1921–1923)," *Z dziejów stosunków polsko-radzieckich: Studia i materiały* 8 (1971): 3–36.
8. Lord also served as an American delegate in the Inter-Allied Commission's Polish Mission. His strong bias in favor of Poland was revealed in his many writings, in which he argued that Poles were "socially, economically, and intellectually the strongest element" in Eastern Galicia. As cited in Leonid

Sonevytsky, "The Ukrainian Question in R. H. Lord's Writings on the Paris Peace Conference," *Annals of the Ukrainian Academy of Arts and Sciences in the United States* 10, nos. 1–2 (1962–1963): 77.

9. As cited ibid., 67.

10. Janusz Radziejowski, *The Communist Party of Western Ukraine, 1919–1929*, transl. Alan Rutkowski (Edmonton: Canadian Institute of Ukrainian Studies, 1983), 1. The Treaty of Riga (signed on 18 March 1921) ended the Polish-Soviet war and resolved temporarily the question of Poland's eastern borders. The treaty was not sanctioned by the Western powers until March 1923. Stefan Ripetskyj, *Ukrainian-Polish Diplomatic Struggle, 1918–1923* (Chicago: Ukrainian Research and Information Institute, 1963), 23–24.

11. Roman Szporluk, "Polish-Ukrainian Relations in 1918: Notes for Discussion," in *The Reconstruction of Poland, 1914–1923*, ed. Paul Latawski (London: Macmillan, 1992), 46.

12. Ivan Rudnytsky, "Polish-Ukrainian Relations: The Burden of History," in *Essays in Modern Ukrainian History* (Edmonton: Canadian Institute of Ukrainian Studies, 1987), 49–76.

13. Jerzy Tomaszewski, "The National Question in Poland in the Twentieth Century," in *The National Question in Historical Context*, ed. Mikuláš Teich and Roy Porter (Cambridge: Cambridge University Press, 1993), 309.

14. Taras Hunczak, ed., *Ukraine and Poland in Documents, 1918–1922*, vol. 1 (New York: Shevchenko Scientific Society, 1983), Doc. 8: 62.

15. Ibid., Doc. 8: 64.

16. Brubaker, *Nationalism Reframed*, 85.

17. Ibid., 98–100.

18. Bureau Ukrainien en Suisse, *Revendications ukrainiennes: Memorandum présenté aux pays neutres et belligérants* (Lausanne: Imprimeries réunies, 1917), 37.

19. K. Schodnicki, *Borysław postanowił o sobie!* (Cracow: Gebethner i Wolf, 1919), 3–9.

20. Ibid. Schodnicki was himself strongly inclined to the Polish position. His description of the Jewish position was tinged with overt disappointment that Jews did not declare their unreserved support of the Polish cause.

21. 18 November 1918, in Barbara Ratyńska, ed., *Rola nafty w kształtowaniu stosunku państw zachodnich do sprawy Galicji wschodniej (1918–1919)* (Warsaw: Polski Instytut Spraw Międzynarodowych, 1957), Doc. 1.2: 22; PRO FO 371 / 3906, folder 48975, file 28011 (1919), 3–4.

22. 30 November 1918, in Ratyńska, *Rola nafty*, Doc. 1.4: 23.

23. Rudnytsky, "Polish-Ukrainian Relations," 67.

24. Ratyńska, *Rola nafty*, Doc. 1.7: 27.

25. PRO FO 371 / 3906, folder 28011, file 30572.

26. Arno Mayer, *Politics and Diplomacy of Peacemaking: Containment and Counterrevolution at Versailles, 1918–1919* (New York: Knopf, 1967), 9–10, 22, 286. Kay Lundgreen-Nielsen, *The Polish Problem at the Paris Peace Conference: A Study of the Policies of the Great Powers and the Poles, 1918–1919*, trans. Alison Borch-Johnson (Odense: Odense University Press, 1979).

27. The UNR had been created on 20 November 1917 as an independent Ukrainian state on the territory of the former Russian Empire. Ivan Rudnytsky, "The Fourth Universal and Its Ideological Antecedents," in *Essays in Modern Ukrainian History* (Edmonton: Canadian Institute of Ukrainian Studies, 1987), 389; Zofia Zaks, "Galicja Wschodnia w polityce Zachodno-Ukraińskiej Republiki Ludowej i Ukraińskiej Republiki Ludowej w drugiej połowie 1919 r.," in *Historia dziewietnastego i dwudziestego wieku: Studia i Szkice*, ed. Andrzej Garlicki, Jozef Ryszard Szaflik, and Marian Wojciechowski (Wrocław: Zakład Narodowy im. Ossolinskich, 1979), 387–405.

28. Lundgreen-Nielsen, *Polish Problem*, 165.

29. Orzell, " 'Hotly Disputed' Issue," 57.

30. Lundgreen-Nielsen, *Polish Problem*, 184.

31. As cited in Orzell, " 'Hotly Disputed' Issue," 52.

32. Ibid., 49.

33. Lundgreen-Nielsen, *Polish Problem*, 90.

34. As cited in Orzell, " 'Hotly Disputed' Issue," 51.

35. Mark Baker, "Lewis Namier and the Problem of Eastern Galicia," *Journal of Ukrainian Studies* 23, no. 2 (1998): 59–104, and Taras Hunczak, "Sir Lewis Namier and the Struggle for Eastern Galicia, 1918–1920," *Harvard Ukrainian Studies* 1, no. 2 (June 1977): 198–210.

36. Lundgreen-Nielsen, *Polish Problem*, 61, 67; quotation as cited in Jonathan Haslam, *The Vices of Integrity: E. H. Carr, 1892–1982* (London: Verso, 1999), 29.

37. Lundgreen-Nielsen, *Polish Problem*, 75, 90.

38. See ibid., 32–57; Leo Haczynski, "The Problem of Eastern Galicia at the Paris Peace Conference: A Re-examination in the Light of American Materials in the Archives of the United States" (PhD diss., Fordham University, 1971), 131–132.

39. 10 February 1919, in *Notes présentées par la Délégation de la République Ukrainienne à la Conférence de la Paix à Paris*, vol. 1 (Paris: Robinet-Houtain, February—April 1919), 5–7; Baker, "Lewis Namier," 84.

40. Hunczak, *Ukraine and Poland*, vol. 1, Doc. 8: 62.

41. "Poland as Ally: Paderewski's Appeal to Britain: Help Needed Against Anarchy," *Times* (London), 22 January 1919, 8.

42. *Mémoire sur l'indépendance de l'Ukraine présenté à la Conférence de la Paix*

par la délégation de la République Ukrainienne (Paris: Robinet-Houtain, 1919), 11.

43. Vladimir Temnitsky and Joseph Burachinsky, *Polish Atrocities in Ukrainian Galicia: A Telegraphic Note to M. Georges Clemenceau, President of the Peace Conference* (New York: Ukrainian National Committee of the United States, 1919), 3–4.

44. Memorandum prepared by Paul LeGrand, Belgian oil industrialist (19 July 1919), in Ratyńska, *Rola nafty,* Doc. 23: 104–105.

45. The Polish-Lithuanian Commonwealth was actually founded in 1569. The marriage of the Lithuanian grand duke Jagiello and the Polish princess Jadwiga in 1386 created a dynastic union between the two principalities. Oskar Halecki, *Polens Ostgrenze im Lichte der Geschichte Ostgaliziens, des Chelmer Landes und Podlachiens* (Vienna: Moritz Perles, 1918), reprinted in *Irredentist and Nationalist Questions in Central Europe, 1913–1939: Poland,* vol. 1, Seeds of Conflict Series 1 (Nendeln: Kraus Reprint, 1973), 21, 42.

46. Délégation Polonaise à la Conférence de la Paix, Délégation Économique, *L'Industrie du pétrole en Galicie* (Paris: [Imp. Levé], March 1919), 5.

47. "Galizische Karpathen-Petroleum-Actien-Gesellschaft vormals Bergheim & MacGarvey, Gorlice," in *Die Großindustrie Österreichs* (Vienna: Leopold Weiss, 1898), 332.

48. Délégation Polonaise, *L'Industrie du pétrole en Galicie,* 5, 6.

49. *Notes présentées par la Délégation de la République Ukrainienne,* 8.

50. *Mémoire sur l'indépendance,* 87.

51. Zofia Zaks, "Walka dyplomatyczna o naftę wschodniogalicyjska, 1918–1923," *Z dziejów stosunków polsko-radzieckich: Studia i materiały* 4 (1969): 45.

52. 1 May 1919, in Ratyńska, *Rola nafty,* Doc. 12: 58.

53. Krzysztof Lewandowski, *Sprawa ukraińska w polityce zagranicznej Czechosłowacji w latach 1918–1932* (Wrocław: Zakład Narodowy Imienia Ossolińskich, 1974), 93.

54. Zaks, "Walka dyplomatyczna," 39.

55. As cited ibid., 38.

56. David Hunter Miller, *My Diary at the Conference of Paris* vol. 10 (New York, 1924), 348, as cited in Orzell, " 'Hotly Disputed' Issue," 51.

57. Ratyńska, *Rola nafty,* Doc. 23: 102.

58. CL DEEF 73294: 15, 35.

59. "Intérêts Français en Pologne," CL DEEF 25255; "Pologne Autrichienne," CL DEEF 73294.

60. Alfred Kohl, *Nasz przemysł naftowy w rozrachunku z Austryą: Referat dla Biura Prac Kongresowych* (Cracow: Drukarnia Przemysłowa, 1919), 7.

61. Ibid., 12–13.

62. Grabski was an economist and National Democrat, the minister of agriculture, and a member of the Polish economic delegation to the Peace Conference in Paris.

63. 4 June 1919, in Ratyńska, *Rola nafty*, Doc. 19: 82.

64. Szczepanowski's report, 2 February 1919, in Hunczak, *Ukraine and Poland*, 1:67.

65. Délégation Polonaise, *L'Industrie du pétrole en Galicie*, 4.

66. Ibid., 6–8.

67. Ibid., 7.

68. 18 June 1919, in Ratyńska, *Rola nafty*, Doc. 23: 94.

69. Subtelny, *Ukraine*, 359.

70. 24 April 1919, in Ratyńska, *Rola nafty*, Doc. 10: 50.

71. 28 March 1919, in Ratyńska, *Rola nafty*, Doc. 9: 48.

72. 21 February 1919, in Ratyńska, *Rola nafty*, Doc. 6: 38.

73. As cited in Lundgreen-Nielsen, *Polish Problem*, 536n147.

74. Joachim Bartoszewicz, Secretary-General of the Polish Delegation, to Balfour, 29 August 1919, in *Documents on British Foreign Policy, 1919–1939*, 1st ser. (London: His Majesty's Stationery office, 1949), 3:884–885, and Balfour to Perkins, 27 August 1919, ibid., 3:885.

75. As cited in Lundgreen-Nielsen, *Polish Problem*, 536n147.

76. Ibid., 576n175; Haslam,*Vices of Integrity*, 27–30.

77. 24 April 1919, in Ratyńska, *Rola nafty*, Doc. 10: 51.

78. 5 February 1919, in Ratyńska, *Rola nafty*, Doc. 3: 30–1.

79. 12 January 1919, in Ratyńska, *Rola nafty*, Doc. 2: 28.

80. Lundgreen-Nielsen, *Polish Problem*, 186. Readers interested in a detailed account of British and American suspicions of French bias and their causes are directed to Lundgreen-Nielsen's extensive monograph and Orzell's more succinct " 'Hotly Disputed' Issue" on the subject.

81. Hunczak, *Ukraine and Poland*, vol. 1, Doc. 8: 67.

82. 28 February 1919, Hunczak, *Ukraine and Poland*, vol. 1, Doc. 17: 87.

83. Orzell, " 'Hotly Disputed' Issue," 52; Hunczak, *Ukraine and Poland*, vol. 1, Doc. 20: 93.

84. Lundgreen-Nielsen, *Polish Problem*, 183–185.

85. Ibid., 217, 220.

86. Orzell, " 'Hotly Disputed' Issue," 54.

87. Hunczak, *Ukraine and Poland*, vol. 1, Doc. 26: 110.

88. Lundgreen-Nielsen, *Polish Problem*, 277.

89. Sonevytsky, "Ukrainian Question," 81.

90. 21 May 1919, in Ratyńska, *Rola nafty*, Doc. 16: 76.

91. Lundgreen-Nielsen, *Polish Problem*, 322. Botha (1862–1919) was the first prime minister of the South African Union and a member of the British

imperial delegation to the Paris Peace Conference, as well as chair of the Inter-Allied Commission for a Polish-Ukrainian Armistice.

92. 5 February 1919, in Ratyńska, *Rola nafty,* Doc. 5: 36.
93. 13 March 1919, in Ratyńska, *Rola nafty,* Doc. 8: 41.
94. As cited in Orzell, " 'Hotly Disputed' Issue," 57.
95. Lundgreen-Nielsen, *Polish Problem,* 318.
96. TsDIAUL 146.8.2999: 10.
97. Zaks, "Walka dyplomatyczna," 45.
98. Ibid., 51–52; Zofia Zaks, "Problem Galicji Wschodniej w czasie Wojny Polsko-Radzieckiej," *Studia z dziejów ZSRR i Europy Środkowej* 8 (1972): 89–92.
99. Lewandowski, *Sprawa ukraińska,* 103–104.
100. 13 June 1919, in Ratyńska, *Rola nafty,* Doc. 21: 93; Lewandowski, *Spawa ukraińska,* 104n123.
101. As cited in Zaks, "Walka dyplomatyczna," 52.
102. Orzell, " 'Hotly Disputed' Issue," 60.
103. *Notes présentées par la Délégation de la République Ukrainienne à la Conférence de la Paix à Paris,* vol. 2 (Paris: Robinet-Houtain, April–July 1919), 31.
104. *The Bloody Book: Returns Concerning the Invasion of the Poles into the Ukrainian Territory of East-Galicia, in 1918/19* (Vienna: Government of the West Ukrainian Republic, 1919), reprinted in *Irredentist and Nationalist Questions in Central Europe, 1913–1939: Poland,* 1:4.
105. Orzell, " 'Hotly Disputed' Issue," 60.
106. Subtelny, *Ukraine,* 370.
107. Orzell, " 'Hotly Disputed' Issue," 62.
108. Radziejowski, *Communist Party of Western Ukraine,* 4–7.
109. As cited in Sonevytsky, "Ukrainian Question," 73.
110. As cited in Orzell, " 'Hotly Disputed' Issue," 64.
111. Ibid., 62.
112. Baker, "Lewis Namier," 33; Orzell, " 'Hotly Disputed' Issue," 65.
113. As cited in Orzell, " 'Hotly Disputed' Issue," 63.
114. As cited ibid., 66.
115. TsDIAUL 146.8.2999: 1.
116. Ibid., 3; Roman Solchanyk, "The Foundation of the Communist Movement in Eastern Galicia, 1919–1921," *Slavic Review* 30, no. 4 (December 1971): 781.
117. 28 October 1919, TsDIAUL 146.8.2999: 4.
118. Ibid., 6–7.
119. Ibid., 10–11.
120. TsDIAUL 146.8.4084: 3, 14, 23.
121. Ibid., 3.

122. Ibid., 1, 2.
123. Ibid., 13.
124. Ibid., 15.
125. Ibid., 16.
126. Ibid., 23.
127. Ibid., 24–27.
128. TsDIAUL 146.4.4902: 4–6.
129. The KP(b)U was founded in July 1918 as an integral part of the Russian Bolshevik Party based in Moscow. Subtelny, *Ukraine,* 364.
130. Hunczak, *Ukraine and Poland,* vol. 2 (New York: Shevchenko Scientific Society, 1983) Doc. 87: 308–310.
131. Bronisław Goldmann, *Die Erdölwirtschaft nach der Zerstörung der österreichischen-ungarischen Monarchie* (Vienna: Verlag für Fachliteratur, 1936), 13.
132. Zaks, "Walka dyplomatyczna," 56.
133. 25 July 1922, CL DAF 00040.3043.
134. Iván Berend and György Ránki, *Economic Development in East-Central Europe in the 19th and 20th Centuries* (New York: Columbia University Press, 1974), 233.
135. "Memorandum of Agreement between M. Philippe Berthelot, Directeur des Affaires politiques et commerciales au Ministère des Affaires Étrangères, and Professor Sir John Cadman, K.C.M.G., Director in Charge of His Majesty's Petroleum Department (September 1921)," in *Documents of the American Association for International Conciliation* (New York: American Association for International Conciliation, [1922]).
136. Joseph Mendel, *Die Entwicklung der internationalen Erdölwirtschaft in den letzten Jahren* (Leipzig: K. F. Koehler, 1922), 165.
137. Karl Krüger and G. R. Poschardt, *Die Erdöl-Wirtschaft der Welt* (Stuttgart: Schweizerbart'sche Verlagsbuchhandlung, 1926), 311; Goldmann, *Erdölwirtschaft,* 13.
138. Sociétés des Pétroles de Dabrowa, *État des Propriétés et Participations en Europe Centrale* (Paris: n.p., 1922), 7.
139. Ibid., 44, 49.

Conclusion

1. Stefan Bartoszewicz, "Rozwój przemysłu naftowego w Polsce i jego przyszłość," *Przemyśl Naftowy* 3, no. 19 (10 October 1928): 534. The vast majority of Polish oil production (in 1938, 72 percent) took place on land that would become part of the Ukrainian Socialist People's Republic after the Second World War (and of the Republic of Ukraine in the 1990s). Kurt

Wessely, "Hundert Jahre Erdöl im Donauraum," *Donau-Raum: Zeitschrift des Forschungsinstitutes für Fragen des Donauraumes* 3, no. 3, Sonderdruck (1958): 171.

2. American-Polish Chamber of Commerce and Industry, *Poland 1927: The Story of a Memorable Year* (New York: American-Polish Chamber of Commerce and Industry, 1928), 15.

3. Bankers Trust Company, *The Sixth Country in Europe* (New York: Bankers Trust Company, 1927), 10.

4. Alexander Nazaroff, "The Soviet Oil Industry," *Russian Review* 1, no. 1 (November 1941): 82.

5. George A. Hill Jr., *Trends in the Oil Industry in 1944 (Including United States Foreign Oil Policy): As Presented to the Petroleum Industry War Council, January 12, 1994* (Washington, DC: Petroleum Industry War Council, 1944), 10.

6. "Abnahme der amerikanischen Petroleumproduktion," *Naphta* 7, no. 1 (15 January 1899): 12–13.

7. Bartoszewicz, "Rozwój," 533.

8. Karl Krüger and G. Poschardt, *Die Erdöl-Wirtschaft der Welt* (Stuttgart: Schweizerbart'sche Verlagsbuchhandlung, 1926), 298.

9. Wessely, "Hundart Jahre Erdöl," 171.

10. C. F. Eduard Schmidt, *Die Erdöl-Reichthümer Galiziens: Eine technologisch-volkswirthschaftliche Studie* (Vienna: Carl Gerold's Sohn, 1865), 4.

11. Étienne Dalemont and Jean Carrié, *Histoire du pétrole* (Paris: Presses Universitaires du France, 1993), 5–6.

12. Hill, *Trends*, 1.

13. L. von Neuendahl, *Das Vorkommen des Petroleums in Galizien und dessen Gewinnung* (Vienna: Gerold, 1865), 6; J. T. Henry, *The Early and Later History of Petroleum* (Philadelphia: Jas. B. Rodgers Co., 1873), 150.

14. Georg Engelbert Graf, *Erdöl, Erdölkapitalismus und Erdölpolitik* 15.

15. Ibid., 36–37.

16. P. H. Frankel, *Essentials of Petroleum: A Key to Oil Economics* (New York: Kelley, 1969), 18.

17. See, for example, Zygmunt Bielski, "W sprawie starszeństwa przemysłu naftowego," *Przemyśl Naftowy* 7, no. 4 (25 February 1932): 89–91, and Tadeusz Mikucki, "Nafta w Polsce do połowy XIX w.," *Przemyśl Naftowy* 13, no. 17 (10 September 1938): 462–469.

18. *Sprawozdanie stenograficzne*, 16 January 1874, 14, TsDIAUL f. 146.4.3411: 96.

19. A. A. Fursenko, *The Battle For Oil: The Economics and Politics of International Corporate Conflict over Petroleum, 1860–1930*, trans. and ed. Gregory Freeze (Greenwich, CT: & JAI Press, 1990), 8.

20. *Sprawozdanie stenograficzne*, 16 January 1874: 14, TsDIAUL f. 146.4.3411: 91.
21. Daniel Yergin, *The Prize: The Epic Quest for Oil, Money, and Power* (New York: Simon and Schuster, 1991), 178, 379.
22. Bartoszewicz, "Rozwój," 534.
23. S. Szczepanowski [son], "Na naftowem Podkarpaciu," *Przemysł Naftowy* 4, no. 11 (June 1929): 333.
24. Leon Rymar, *Galicyjski przemsł naftowy* (Cracow: Skład główny w Księgarni G. Gebethner, 1915), 29; Robert Schwarz, *Petroleum-Vademecum: International Petroleum Tables*, 7th ed. (Berlin: Verlag für Fachliteratur, 1930), 4–6.
25. Schwarz, *Petroleum-Vademecum*, 4–6.
26. "Kronika bieżąca," *Przemyśl Naftowy* 3, no. 18 (26 September 1928): 499; "Uroczysty obchód ku czci Ignacego Łukasiewicza w Krośnie," *Przemyśl Naftowy* 3, no. 19 (10 October 1928): 535–539.
27. "Polska prasa o Łukasiewicza," *Przemyśl Naftowy* 3, no. 19 (10 October 1928): 532–533.
28. Bartoszewicz, "Rozwój," 529.
29. Ibid., 530 (quotation), 531.
30. Władysław Długosz, "Wspomnienia z Borysławia," *Przemyśl Naftowy* 4, no. 11 (June 1929): 332.
31. Bielski, "W sprawie starzeństwa," 89–91.
32. Kazimierz Gąsiorowski, "Moje przeżycia naftowe," *Przemyśl Naftowy* 11, no. 1 (1936): 12–16; 11, no. 2 (1936): 44–49; 11, no. 4 (1936): 120–123; Ferdynand Jastrzębski, "Fragmenty z pamiętników starych nafciarzy," *Przemyśl Naftowy* 8, no. 12 (1933): 337–342; 8, no. 13 (1933): 370–375; 8, no. 14 (1933): 396–398; 8, no. 15 (1933): 420–423; Długosz, "Wspomnienia," 329–332; Zygmunt Bielski, "Wspomnienie ze Schodnicy," *Przemyśl Naftowy* 4, no. 11 (June 1929): 332–333; Wit Sulimirski, "Kilka wspomnień z dawnych lat," *Przemyśl Naftowy* 4, no. 11 (June 1929): 330–331.
33. Alfred Döblin, "The Petroleum District," in *Journey to Poland*, trans. Joachim Neugroschel (New York: Paragon, 1991), 174.
34. Ibid., 177.
35. Joseph Roth, "Brief aus Polen," in *Panoptikum: Gestalten und Kulissen* (Munich: Knorr und Hirth, 1930); reprinted in *Werke*, vol. 3 (Amsterdam: Verlag Allert de Lange, 1976), 614.
36. Döblin, "Petroleum District," 176.
37. Döblin, "Petroleum District," 179: Roth, "Brief aus Polen," 615.
38. Robert Musil, *The Man without Qualities*, vol. 2, transl. Sophie Wilkins (New York: Vintage, 1995), 841.
39. Osyp Petrash, manuscript copy of interview of O. M. Soliuk, recounting tale

told by Petro Tsybuls'kyi. My thanks to Yaroslav Hrytsak for providing me with a copy of this interview.

40. Martin Pollack, *Nach Galizien: Von Chassiden, Huzulen, Polen und Ruthenen; Eine imaginäre Reise durch die verschwundene Welt Ostgaliziens und der Bukowina* (Vienna: Edition Christian Brandstätter, 1984); Stanisław Grodziski, *Wzdłuż Wisły, Dniestru i Zbrucza: Wędrówki po Galicji dyliżansem, koleją, samochodem* (Cracow: Grell, 1998).

41. Stephan Vajda, *Reisen Anno 1900: Ein Führer durch die Länder der k.u.k. Monarchie* (Vienna: Ueberreuter, 1981).

42. Alexander Granach, "Ich komme aus Wierzbowce/Werbowitz/Werbiwizi," in *Da geht ein Mensch* (Munich: F. A. Herbig, [1945]), as cited in Karl Markus Gauß and Martin Pollack, *Das reiche Land der armen Leute: Literarische Wanderungen durch Galizien* (Vienna: Jugend und Volk Dachs Verlag, 1992), 168.

43. See, for example, Gauß and Pollack, *Reiche Land*, and Stefan Simonek and Alois Woldan, eds., *Europa Erlesen: Galizien* (Klagenfurt: Wieser, 1998).

44. Yergin, *Prize*, 14.

45. Ferdinand Friedensburg, *Das Erdöl im Weltkrieg* (Stuttgart: Ferdinand Enke, 1939), 22.

46. Ibid., 19.

47. Leo Haczynski, "The Problem of Eastern Galicia at the Paris Peace Conference in the Light of American Materials in the Archives of the United States" (PhD diss., Fordham University, 1971), 256.

48. W. G. Jensen, "The Importance of Energy in the First and Second World Wars," *Historical Journal* 11, no. 3 (1968): 548–549.

Archival and Primary Sources

Archival Sources

Archives Historiques du Crédit Lyonnais, Paris
    DAF, Direction générale–Affaires financières
    DEEF, Direction des études economiques et financières
    98 AH, Siège social–Administration

L'vivs'ka Naukova Biblioteka im. V. Stefanyka, Lviv
    F. 44, Diamand, Hermann. Papers
    F. 103, Sapieha, Adam Stanisław. Papers

Public Record Office, London
    Foreign Office 371, Political Departments: General Correspondence
    from 1906

Österreichisches Staatsarchiv, Vienna
    Allgemeneines Verwaltungsarchiv
        Finanzministerium
        Handelsministerium
        Innenministerium, Präsidialakten
        Ministerium für öffentliche Arbeiten
            F. 661: 1909–1918
            F. 662: 1909–1918
            F. 663: Erdölreservoirs
            F. 664: diverses, 1909–1914
            F. 665: diverses, 1915–1916
            F. 666: diverses, 1917–1918

Haus-, Hof- und Staatsarchiv
Zeremonialakten. Hofreisen.
Kriegsarchiv
   Abteilung 5/M
   Bildersammlung, 1. Weltkrieg
   Marinesektion

Tsentral'nyi Derzhavnyi Istorychnyi Arkhiv Ukraïny, m. L'viv, Lviv
   F. 146, Halyts'ke namisnytstvo, Galician Viceroy's Office
   F. 150, Viis'kovyi Sud, High Court
   F. 152, Kraiovyi Sud, District Court
   F. 207, Landespetroleum Verein
   F. 186, Kraiova Zemel'no-podatkova komisiia, Provincial Land-Tax
   Commission
   F. 225, Małopolska
   F. 228, Fanto
   F. 238, Nafta
   F. 242, Galizische Karpathische Petroleum AG vormals Bergheim &
   MacGarvey
   F. 249, Petrolea
   F. 255, Premier Oil
   F. 275, Trzebinia
   F. 276, Jan Zeitleben
   F. 278, Dąbrowa
   F. 309, Shevchenko Scientific Society
   F. 387, Volodymyr Levyns'kyi
   F. 517, Wit Sulimirski
   F. 779, Stefan Kovaliv
   F. 835, Lubomirski family

Newspapers and Periodicals

Allgemeine österreichische Chemiker- und Techniker Zeitung (Vienna)
Compass: Jahrbuch der österreichischen Industrie (Vienna)
Czas (Cracow)
Czasopismo Towarzystwa Aptékarskiego (Lviv)
Dinglers Polytechnisches Journal (Augsburg)
Gazeta Lwowska

Gazeta Naddniestrzańska (Drohobycz)
Górnik (Gorlice)
Naphta and *Nafta* (Lviv)
Neue Freie Presse (Vienna)
New York Times
Oesterreichische Zeitschrift für Berg- und Hüttenwesen (Vienna)
Oleum (Drohobycz)
Petroleum (Berlin and Vienna)
Przemyśl Naftowy (Lviv)
Słowo Polskie (Lviv)
Times (London)
Die Zeit (Vienna)

Select Books, Pamphlets, and Essays

Allgemeines Berggesetz für das Kaiserthum Oesterreich vom 23. Mai 1854: Amtliche Handausgabe. Vienna: k.k. Hof- und Staatsdruckerei, 1854.

Bartoszewicz, Stefan. *Przemysł Naftowy w Polsce: Odbitka z "Polski Gospodarczej."* Warsaw: Sobczyński, n.d.

———. *Wspomnienia z przemysłu naftowego, 1897–1930.* Lviv: Piller-Neumann, 1934.

Bauer, Otto. *Die Nationalitätenfrage und die Sozialdemokratie.* Vienna: Wiener Volksbuchhandlung, 1924.

Beiträge zur Statistik der Oesterreichischen Industrie: Erzeugnisse aus nicht metallischen Mineralien und chemischen Industrie. Vienna: k.k. Hof- und Staatsdruckerei, 1876.

Bergpolizei-Vorschriften für die Erdölbetriebe in Galizien. Cracow: Verlag der k.k. Berghauptmannschaft, 1904.

Die Bergwerks-Inspektion in Österreich: Berichte der k.k. Bergbehörden über ihre Thätigkeit im Jahre [1892–1913] bei Handhabung der Bergpolizei und Beaufsichtigung der Bergarbeiterverhältnisse. Veröffentlicht vom k.k. Ackerbauministerium. Vienna: k.k. Hof- und Staatsdruckerei, [1894–1913].

Bericht der Handels- und Gewerbekammer in Lemberg an das hohe k.k. Ministerium für Handel, Gewerbe und öffentliche Bauten über die Zustände des Handels und der Industrie in ihrem Kammerbezirke, in den Jahren 1854, 1855 und 1856. Lviv: E. Winiarz, 1859.

Bericht der k.k. Gewerbe-Inspektoren über ihre Amtsthätigkeit im Jahre [1884–1914]. Vienna: k.k. Hof- und Staatsdruckerei, [1885–1916].

Berichterstattung des galizischen Landes Petroleum-Vereines für das Jahr 1897. Lviv: Auflage des galizischen Landes Petroleum-Vereines, 1898.

Berlinerblau, Joseph. *Das Erdwachs: Ozokerit und Ceresin: Geschichte, Vorkommen, Gewinnung und Verarbeitung.* Braunschweig: Friedrich Vieweg und Sohn, 1897.

Blauhorn, Josef, ed. *Das Recht der Rohölgewinnung in Oesterreich: Die das Gebiet der Rohölgewinnung regelnden Gesetze und Verordnungen sowie die hierauf bezughabenden oberst- und verwaltungsgerichtlichen Entscheidungen.* Vol. 1, *Die Gesetze und Ministerial-Verordnungen.* Berlin: Verlag für Fachliteratur, 1910.

Bobrzyński, Michał. *Z moich pamiętników.* Wrocław: Wydawnictwo Zakładu imienia Ossolińskich, 1957.

Bodyński, Maximilian, and Jarosław Michałowski. *Statistische Karte Galiziens und der Bukowina. Die allgemein politisch-administrativen, die Communications-, die Bodencultur- und insbesondere die Industrieverhältnisse umfassend.* (n.p.: n.p., 1878).

Borucki, Aleksander. *Nasze Góry: Malownicze opisanie Karpat i Tatr, oraz ich mieszkańców.* Vol. 1, *Karpaty.* Cieszyn: Edward Feitzinger, 1888.

Borysław w walce o niepodległość: Wspomnienia, wydane z okazji 20-tej rocznicy rozbudzenia w Borysławiu idei Związku Strzeleckiego oraz 10-tej rocznicy założenia Związku Legjonistów. Borysław: Drukarnia Naftowa T. S. L. Koło-Borysław, 1932.

Brackel, O and J. Leis. *Der dreißigjährige Petroleumkrieg.* Berlin: 1903.

Brzezowski, Franciszek. *Środki zaradcze w celu uzdrowienia przemysłu naftowego w Borysławiu i zmniejszenia niebezpieczeństw właściwych temu przemysłowi.* Cieszyn: author, 1903.

Bureau Ukrainien en Suisse. *Revendications ukrainiennes: Memorandum présenté aux pays neutres et belligérants.* Lausanne: Imprimeries réunies, 1917.

Chłędowski, Kazimierz. *Pamiętniki.* Vol. 2, *Wiedeń, 1881–1901.* Wrocław: Zakład Narodowy im. Ossolinskich, 1951.

Daszyński, Ignacy. *Pamiętniki.* 2 vols. Cracow, 1925–1926. Repr., Warsaw: Książka i Wiedza, 1957.

Délégation Polonaise à la Conférence de la Paix, Délégation Économique. *L'Industrie du pétrole en Galicie.* Paris: n.p., March 1919.

Diener, Carl, Rudolf Hoernes, Franz E. Suess, und Victor Uhlig. *Bau und Bild Österreichs.* With an introduction by Eduard Suess. Vienna: Verlag von F. Tempsky, 1903.

Döblin, Alfred. *Journey to Poland.* Translated by Joachim Neugroschel. New York: Paragon, 1991.

Les Documents les plus importants de la République Ukrainienne de l'Ouest. Vienna: Engel, 1918.

Ergebnisse der vom k.k. Ackerbauministerium im Jahre 1902 eingesetzten Kommission zur Untersuchung der Betriebsverhältnisse des Erdwachsbergbaues in Galizien. Vienna: k.k. Hof- und Staatsdrückerei, 1903.

Ergebnisse der vom k.k. Ackerbauministerium im Jahre 1903 eingesetzten Kommission zur Untersuchung der Betriebsverhältnisse des Erdölbergbaues in Galizien. Vienna: k.k. Hof- und Staatsdrückerei, 1904.

Die ersten fünfzig Jahre der Kaiser Ferdinands-Nordbahn, 1836–1886. Vienna: Verlag der k.k. pr. Kaiser Ferdinands-Nordbahn, n.d.

Feldman, Wilhelm. *Stan ekonomiczny Galicyi: Cyfry i fakta.* Lviv: Nakładem Stanisława Urody, 1900.

Fleischer, Siegfried. "Enquête über die Lage der jüdischen Bevölkerung Galiziens." In *Jüdische Statistik,* edited by Alfred Nossig, 209–231. Berlin: Jüdischer Verlag, 1903.

Franko, Ivan. *Beiträge zur Geschichte und Kultur der Ukraine: Ausgewählte deutsche Schriften des revolutionären Demokraten, 1882–1915.* Edited by E. Winter and P. Kirchner. Berlin: Akademie-Verlag, 1963.

———. *Boryslav smiiet'sia. Boa Constrictor. Povisti.* Kiev: Vydavnytstvo Khudozhn'oi Literatury "Dnipro," 1981.

———. *Boryslavs'ki opovidannia.* Kiev: Vydavnytstvo Khudozhn'ai Literatury "Dnipro," 1966.

———. *Poluyka i yn'shi Boryslavs'ki opovidania.* Lviv: Ukraïns'ka-Rus'ka Vydavnycha Spilka, 1899.

———. *Vybrani statti pro narodnu tvorchist'.* Kiev: Vydavnytstvo Akademï Nauk Ukraïns'koï RSR, 1955.

———. *Zibrannia tvoriv u p'iatdesiaty tomakh.* 50 vols. Kiev: Naukova Dumka, 1985.

Galizische Karpathen Petroleum AG vormals Bergheim & MacGarvey. *Geschäftsbericht für das Geschäftsjahr 1895/1896: Erstattet durch den Verwaltungsrat in der ersten ordentlichen Versammlung der Actionäre am 15. Juni 1896.* Gorlice: Verlag der Galizischen Karpathen-Petroleum AG vormals Bergheim & MacGarvey, 1896.

Geographische Skizze der Karpaten in der österreichischen-ungarischen Monarchie. Als Manuskript gedruckt. Weisskirchen: n.p., 1897.

Gintl, Heinrich-Eduard. *Die Concurrenzfähigkeit des galizischen Petroleums mit Rücksicht auf die neuen Oelgruben in Sloboda-Rungurska nächst Kolomea.* Vienna: Spielhagen und Schurich, 1885.

———. *Wykaz udziału Galicyi i wielkiego księztwa Krakowskiego na powszechnej wystawie 1873 w Wiedniu.* Vienna: Nakładem reprezentacyi wiedeńskiej galicyjskich komisyj wystawowych, 1873.

Glassmire, Samuel. *Law of Oil and Gas Leases and Royalties: A Practical Legal Treatise on Petroleum Rights Accruing by Virtue of Mineral Deeds and Oil and Gas Leases.* Saint Louis: Thomas Law Book Company, 1935.

Gołda, Ks. Andrzej. *Środki ku zaradzeniu nędzy stanu włościańskiego w Galicyi i Ks. Krakowskiem.* Cracow: Gebethner, 1880.

Graf, Georg Engelbert. *Erdöl, Erdölkapitalismus und Erdölpolitik.* Jena: Urania Verlag, 1925.

Granach, Alexander. *Da geht ein Mensch.* Munich: F. A. Herbig, [1945].

Gränzenstein, Gustav von. *Das allgemeine österreichische Berggesetz vom 23. Mai 1854 und die Verordnungen über die Bergwerksabgaben vom 4. Oktober 1854.* Vienna: Friedrich Manz, 1855.

Gross, M., ed. *Illustrirtes österreichisches Reichsraths-Album.* Vienna: Leo Fein, 1876.

Die Großindustrie Österreichs: Festgabe zum glorreichen Fünfzigjährigen Regierungs-Jubiläum seiner Majestät des Kaisers Franz Joseph I. Vienna: Leopold Weiss, 1898.

Die Gross-Industrie Österreichs: Festgabe zum glorreichen Sechzigjährigen Regierungs-Jubiläum seiner Majestät des Kaisers Franz Joseph I. Vienna: Leopold Weiss, 1908.

Gründungsakt und Statuten der Petroleum und Ozokerit Gewerkschaft "Niebyłów." Drohobycz: Verlag der Petroleum und Ozokerit Gewerkschaft "Niebyłów", 1906.

Guttry, A[lexander]. *Galizien: Land und Leute.* Munich: Georg Müller, 1916.

Hacquet, Balthasar. "Hacquets Autobiographie und Testament." In Belsazar Hacquet, *Physikalisch-Politische Reise aus den dinarischen durch die julischen, carnischen, rhätischen in die norischen Alpen,* edited by Hedwig Rüber and Axel Straßer, 409–427. Munich: Bruckmann, 1898.

———. *Neueste physikalisch-politische Reisen in den Jahren 1791, 92 und 93.* Vol. 3, *Die Dacischen und Sarmatischen oder Nördlichen Karpathen.* Nürnberg: Verlag der Naspeschen Buchhandlung, 1794.

Haus der Abgeordneten des österreichischen Reichsrates. *Stenographische Protokolle über die Sitzungen des Hauses der Abgeordneten des Reichsrates.* XXII Session, 30 Mai 1917–12 November 1918 (Vienna: Haus der österreichischen Staatsdruckerei, 1920).

Heksch, Alexander F., and Wladimir Kowszewicz, eds. *Illustrirter Führer durch die ungarischen Ostkarpathen, Galizien, Bukowina und Rumänien: Handbuch für Touristen und Geschäfts-Reisende.* Vienna: Hartlebens Verlag, 1882.

Henry, J. T. *The Early and Later History of Petroleum.* Philadelphia: Jas. B. Rodgers Co., 1873.

Hill, George A., Jr. *Trends in the Oil Industry in 1944 (Including United States Foreign Oil Policy): As presented to the Petroleum Industry War Council, January 12, 1944.* Washington, DC: Petroleum Industry War Council, 1944.

Holobek, Johann. *Die Schlagwetterexplosion in dem Erdwachsbergbaue "Gruppe I" in Borysław am 2. Juni 1902.* Separat-Ausdruck aus der Österreichischen Zeitschrift für Berg- und Hüttenwesen. Vienna: Manzsche k.u.k. Hof-Verlags- und Universitäts-Buchhandlung, 1903.

Hunczak, Taras, ed. *Ukraine and Poland in Documents, 1918–1922*. 2 vols. New York: Shevchenko Scientific Society, 1983.

Irredentist and Nationalist Questions in Central Europe, 1913–1939: Poland. Vol. 1. Seeds of Conflict Series 1. Nendeln: Kraus Reprint, 1973.

Klun, V. F., ed. *Statistik von Oesterreich-Ungarn*. Vienna: Wilhelm Braumüller, 1876.

Kohl, Alfred. *Nasz przemysł naftowy w rozrachunku z Austryą: Referat dla Biura Prac Kongresowych*. (Photocopy.) Cracow: Drukarnia Przemysłowa, 1919.

Kohl, J[ohann] G[eorg]. *Reisen im Inneren von Rußland und Polen*. Vol. 3, *Die Bukowina, Krakau, und Mähren*. Dresden: Arnoldische Buchhandlung, 1841.

Kohn, Gustav, ed. *Von Goluchowski bis Taaffe: Tausend Redefragmente*. Vienna: Moritz Perles, 1888.

Korkis, Abraham. "Zur Bewegung der jüdischen Bevölkerung in Galizien." In *Jüdische Statistik*, edited by Alfred Nossig, 311–315. Berlin: Jüdischer Verlag, 1903.

Kovaliv, Stefan [Stefan Pjatka]. *Hromadski promislovci*. Lviv: n.p., 1899.

———. *Obrazki z Halyts'koi Kalifornii*. Lviv: Naukove Tovarystvo im. Shevchenka, 1913.

Krüger, Karl, and G. R. Poschardt. *Die Erdöl-Wirtschaft der Welt*. Stuttgart: Schweizerbart'sche Verlagsbuchhandlung, 1926.

Landau, Saul Raphael. *Unter jüdischen Proletariern: Reiseschilderungen aus Ostgalizien und Rußland*. Vienna: Rosner, 1898.

Lehman, Arnold, ed. *Kriegwirtschaftliche Verordnungen betreffend den Wirkungskreis des kk. Handelsministeriums*. Vienna: Manzsche k.u.k. Hof, Verlags, u. Universitätsbuchhandlung, 1918.

Leichner, Ignaz. *Erdöl und Erdwachs: Ein Bild galizischer Industrie*. Sozialpolitische Flugschriften. Vienna: Ignaz Brand, 1898.

Leńczewski, Józef. *Tragedia polskiego kopalnictwa naftowego*. Lviv: Praca Polska, 1939.

Lewicky, Eugen. *Galizien: Informativer Ueberblick über nationale, wirtschaftliche, soziale und kulturelle Zustände des Landes*. Vienna: Verlag zur Befreiung der Ukraine, 1916.

Lipp, Adolf. *Verkehrs- und Handels-Verhältnisse Galiziens*. Prague: C. H. Hunger, 1870.

Lipszyc, Marya Amélie. *Wirtschaftliche Studien über Galizien, unter besonderer Rücksichtsnahme auf die gewerbliche Arbeiterfrage*. Zürich: Hans Fischer vorm. A. Diggelmann, 1901.

MacGarvey, W. H. Introduction to *Oil Fields of the Empire: A Survey of British Imperial Petroleum Questions and a Comprehensive Technical Description of the Oil Fields of Trinidad and Newfoundland*, by J. D. Henry. London: Bradbury, Agnew and Co., 1910.

Marx, Karl. *The Poverty of Philosophy*. New York: International Publishers, 1963.

———. *The Revolutions of 1848: Political Writings. Volume I*. Edited by David Fernbach. London: Penguin, 1973.

Mayer, Ferdinand. *Weltatlas Erdöl und Erdgas*. Braunschweig: Georg Westermann Verlag, 1976.

Mémoire sur l'indépendance de l'Ukraine présenté à la Conférence de la Paix par la délégation de la République Ukrainienne. Paris: Robinet-Houtain, 1919.

"Memorandum of Agreement between M. Philippe Berthelot, Directeur des Affaires politiques et commerciales au Ministère des Affaires Étrangères, and Professor Sir John Cadman, K. C. M. G., Director in Charge of His Majesty's Petroleum Department (September 1921)." In *Documents of the American Association for International Conciliation*. New York: American Association for International Conciliation [1921].

Mendel, Joseph. *Die Entwicklung der internationalen Erdölwirtschaft in den letzten Jahren*. Leipzig: K. F. Koehler, 1922.

Mendel, Joseph, and Robert Schwarz, eds. *Internationale Petroleumstatistik*. Vol. 2, *Österreich-Ungarn*. Vienna: Verlag für Fachliteratur, 1912.

Morawitz, Carl. *Fünfzig Jahre Geschichte einer Wiener Bank: Vortrag gehalten in der Gesellschaft österreichischer Volkswirte anläßlich des 50jährigen Jubiläums der Anglo-Oesterreichischen Bank*. [Vienna: J. R. Vernay, 1913].

Mściwujewski, Mścisław. *Królewske wolne miasto Drohobycz*. Lviv: Piller-Neumann, 1929.

———. *Z Dziejów Drohobycza*. Vol. 1. Drohobycz: Księgarnia Ludowa, 1935.

Musil, Robert. *The Man without Qualities*. Translated by Sophie Wilkins. New York: Vintage, 1995.

Nachrichten über Industrie, Handel und Verkehr aus dem statistischen Departement im k.k. Handelsministerium. Vol. 38, *Statistik der Oesterreichischen Industrie nach dem Stande vom Jahre 1885*. Vienna: k.k. Hof- und Staatsdruckerei, 1889.

Neuendahl, L. von. *Das Vorkommen des Petroleums in Galizien und dessen Gewinnung*. Vienna: Gerold, 1865.

Niebyłów: Neues grosses Naphta u. Erdwachsgebiet in Ostgalizien; Nowy wielki teren naftowy i woskowy we Wschodniej Galicyi; A Prominent New Petroleum and Ozokerit District in Eastern Galicia. Lviv: W. A. Szyjkowski, 1905.

Notes présentées par la Délégation de la République Ukrainienne à la Conférence de la Paix à Paris. Paris: Robinet-Houtain, 1919.

Nowolecki, Aleksander. *Pamiątka podróży Cesarza Franciszka Józefa I. po Galicyi i dwudziesto-dniowego pobytu Jego w tym kraju*. Cracow: Wydawnictwo Czytelni Ludowej Nowoleckiej, 1881.

Olszewski, Stanisław. *Mapa Górnictwo-Przemysłowa Galicyi z Objaśnieniami*. Lviv: author, 1911.

Orlowicz, Mieczysław, and Roman Kordys. *Illustrierter Führer durch Galizien: Mit einem Anhang: Ost-Schlesien*. Vienna: Hartlebens Verlag, 1914.

Pappenheim, Bertha, and Sara Rabinotwisch. *Zur Lage der jüdischen Bevölkerung in Galizien: Reise-Eindrücke und Vorschläge zur Besserung der Verhältnisse*. Frankfurt am Main: Neuer Frankfurter Verlag, 1904.

Pawlewski, Bronisław. *Technologia nafty i wosku ziemnego*. Lviv: Nakładem Wydziału Krajowego, 1891.

Perutz, H. *Industrie der Mineralöle, des Petroleums, Paraffins und der Harze, nebst sämmtlichen damit zusammenhängenden Industriezweigen*. Vol. 1. Vienna: Carl Gerold's Sohn, 1868.

Pfaff, Alfred. "Die Entwicklung des Boryslaw-Tustanowicer Erdölrevieres seit seiner Befreiung von russisch. Herrschaft." *Petroleum: Zeitschrift für die gesamten Interessen der Petroleum-Industrie und des Petroleum-Handels* 19 (1916): 982–989.

Porembalski, Tadeusz. *Wspomnienia nafciarza*. Warsaw: Panstwowe Wydawnictwo Naukowe, 1978.

Przegląd stanu kopalń nafty i wosku ziemnego w Galicyi, w drugiem półroczu 1881. Gorlice: Towarzystwo naftowe, 1882.

Ratyńska, Barbara, ed. *Rola nafty w kształtowaniu stosunku państw zachodnich do sprawy Galicji wschodniej (1918–1919)*. Warsaw: Polski Instytut Spraw Międzynarodowych, 1957.

Rogosz, Józef. *W piekle galicyjskiem: Obraz z życia*. Gródek: J. Czaiński, 1896.

Roth, Joseph. *Joseph Roth. Leben und Werk. Ein Gedächtnisbuch*. Edited by Hermann Linden. Cologne: Gustav Kiepenheuer, 1949.

———. "Das polnische Kalifornien." *Frankfurter Zeitung* 29 June 1928. Reprinted as "Brief aus Polen." In *Panoptikum: Gestalten und Kulissen*. Munich: Knorr u'nd Hirth, 1930. Reprinted in *Werke*. Vol. 3. Amsterdam: Verlag Allert de Lange, 1976.

———. "Der Segen der Erde: Naphtha, Kali, Gift." In *Der Antichrist*. Amsterdam: Allert de Lange, 1934. Reprinted in *Werke*. Vol. 3. Amsterdam: Verlag Allert de Lange, 1976.

Rymar, Leon. *Galicyjski przemysł naftowy*. Cracow: Skład główny w Księgarni G. Gebethnera, 1915.

Sceneries and People of Austria: Described by Order of the Imperial Royal Ministry of Railways. Vienna: O. Maass' Sons, 1904.

Schieffer, Emil. *Bericht über das Nafta führende Terrain West-Galziens*. Vienna: Verlag des Gründungs-Comité's der Hamburg-Galizischen Petroleum-Actien-Gesellschaft, 1865.

Schmedes, Carl Ritter von. *Geographisch-statistische Uebersicht Galiziens und der Bukowina, nach amtlichen Quellen bearbeitet*. 2nd ed. Lviv: k.k. Galiz. Aerarial-Staats-Druckerei, 1869.

Schmidt, C. F. Eduard. *Die Erdöl-Reichthümer Galiziens: Eine technologisch-volkswirthschaftliche Studie.* Vienna: Carl Gerold's Sohn, 1865.

Schodnicki, K. *Bordsław postanowił o sobie!* Cracow: Gebethner i Wolf, 1919.

Schwarz, Robert. *Petroleum-Vademecum: International Petroleum Tables.* 7th ed. Berlin: Verlag für Fachliteratur, 1930.

———. *Petroleum-Vademecum: Tafeln für die Erdölindustrie und den Mineralölhandel.* 6th ed. Berlin: Verlag für Fachliteratur, 1929.

Sociétés des Pétroles de Dabrowa. *État des propriétés et participations en Europe Centrale.* Paris: n.p., 1922.

Somary, Felix. *Die Aktiengesellschaften in Österreich.* Vienna: Manz, 1902.

Souvenir de la Visite de S. M. I. & R. Apost. l'Empereur d'Autriche à l'Exploitation de la Société Française de Cire Minérale et Pétrole à Boryslaw-Wolanka le 18 Septembre 1880. N.p., n.d.

Spyra, Jan. *Kwalifikacya prawna kontraktów naftowych.* Lviv: Drukarni Słowa Polskiego, 1905.

k.k. Statistische Central-Commission, *Orts-Reportorium des Königreiches Galizien und Lodomerien mit dem Grossherzogthume Krakau: Auf Grundlage der Volkszählung vom Jahre 1869 bearbeitet.* Vienna: Carl Gerold's Sohn, 1874.

k.k. Statistische Central-Commission, *Österreichische Statistik.* Vol. 32, *Die Ergebnisse der Volkszählung vom 31. Dezember 1890 in den im Reichsrathe vertretenen Königreichen und Ländern.* Part 5, *Die Ausländer in den im Reichsrathe vertretenen Königreichen und Ländern sowie die Angehörigen dieser letzteren im Auslande.* Vienna: k.k. Hof- und Staatsdruckerei, 1895.

Die österreichisch-ungarische Monarchie in Wort und Bild. Vol. 11, *Galizien.* Auf Anregung und unter Mitwirkung weiland Seiner kaiserl. und königl. Hoheit des durchlauchtigsten Kronprinzen Erzherzog Rudolf begonnen, fortgesetzt unter dem Protectorate Ihrer kaiserl. und königl. Hoheit der durchlauchtigsten Frau Kronprinzen-Witwe Erzherzogin Stephanie. Vienna: Druck und Verlag der k.k. Hof- und Staatsdruckerei, 1898.

Statistik der Oesterreichischen Industrie vom Jahre 1880. Vienna: 1884.

"Statistik des Naphthabetriebes in Galizien." In *Statistisches Jahrbuch des k.k. Ackerbau-Ministeriums für 1888.* Pt. 3, *Der Bergwerksbetrieb Österreichs im Jahre 1888.* 2nd ed. Vienna: k.k. Hofs und Staatsdruckerei, 1889.

Sulimirski, Filip, Bronisław Chlebowski, and Władysław Walewski. *Słownik geograficzny Królestwa Polskiego i innych krajów słowiańskich.* Vol. 1. Warsaw: Druk Wieku, 1880.

Sweet, S. W. *Report on Coal.* Albany: State of New York, Senate No. 71, 1865. In *This Was Early Oil: Contemporary Accounts of the Growing Petroleum Industry, 1848–1885,* edited by Ernest Miller, 88–89. Harrisburg: Pennsylvania Historical and Museum Commission, 1968.

Szajnocha, Ladislaus [Stanisław]. *Die Petroleumindustrie Galiziens*. 2nd ed.
Cracow: Verlag des Galizischen Landesausschusses, 1905.

Szajnok, Władysław. *Skorowidz polskiego i austrjackiego przemysłu naftowego 1919*. Lviv: Wydawnictwo Polskie, 1920.

Szczepanowski, Stanisław. *Idea Polska: Wybór pism*. Edited by Stanisław Borzym. Warsaw: Panstwowy Instytut Wydawniczy, 1988.

———. *Myśli o odrodzeniu narodowym: Pisma i przemówienia*. Vol. 1. 3rd ed. Lviv: Tow. Nauczycieli Szkół Wyższych, 1923.

———. *Nafta i praca, złoto i błoto*. Lviv: author, 1886.

———. *Nędza Galicyi w cyfrach i program energicznego rozwoju gospodarstwa krajowego*. Lviv: author, 1888.

———. *O samodzielność kraju: Sprawy poselskie lata 1887–1891*. Vol. 3. *Pisma i przemówienia*. Lviv: Gubrynowicz, 1912.

Szujski, Wlad. Ritter v. *Die galizische Rohölindustrie: Ihre Gegenwart und ihre Zukunft*. Berlin: Berliner Union Verlagsgesellschaft, 1908.

Temnitsky, Vladimir, and Joseph Burachinsky. *Polish Atrocities in Ukrainian Galicia: A Telegraphic Note to M. Georges Clemenceau, President of the Peace Conference*. New York: Ukrainian National Committee of the United States, 1919.

Ukraine's Claim to Freedom: An Appeal for Justice on Behalf of 35 Millions. New York: Ukrainian National Association and the Ruthenian National Union, 1915.

Verhandlungen der vom k.k. Handelsministerium veranstalteten Kartellenquete. Vol. 3, *Mineralölindustrie*. 26 and 27 March 1912. Vienna: k.k. Hof- und Staatsdruckerei, 1912.

Wagner, Richard. *Organisationsfragen aus der Petroleumindustrie mit besonderer Berücksichtigung Österreichs*. [Vienna?]: [1915?].

[Wengraf, Edmund]. *Das hohe Haus: Parlamentsbilder aus Österreich*. Vienna: Verlag der "Neuen Revue," 1896.

Windakiewicz, Edward. *Olej i wosk ziemny w Galicji*. Lviv: Administracyja Gazety Lwowskiej, 1875.

Wiśniowski, Tadeusz. "Przyczynek do geologii Karpat." In *Sprawozdanie dyrekcyi c. k. wyższego gimnazyum w Kołomyi za rok szkolny 1897*. Kołomyja: Fundusz szkolny, 1897.

Wójcik, Alexander. *Mowa wygłoszona przez O. Aleksandra Wójcika, gwardyana z Przeworska w czasie Żałobnego Nabożeństwa we Lwowie za dusze ś. p. Stanisława Szczepanowskiego i Kazimierza Odrzywolskiego*. Cracow: Anczyc i Spólki, 1900.

Wolaniecki. *Po strajku w Borysławiu! Z doświadczeń i rozmyślań Wolanieckego*. Wolanka: Edward Oczosalski, 1904.

Woodrow Wilson Foundation. *Official Documents Issued during the Two World Wars*. New York: Woodrow Wilson Foundation, 1944.

Zielinski, Stanislaus. *Die Ermordung des Statthalters Grafen Andreas Potocki: Materialen zur Beurteilung des Ukrainischen Terrorismus in Galizien*. Vienna: C. W. Stern, 1908.

Zoll, Fryderyk. *Reforma Prawa Naftowego*. Cracow: Czas, 1905.

Zuber, Rudolf. *Karte der Petroleum-Gebiete in Galizien mit Erläuterungen bearbeitet*. Lviv: Verlag des Verfassers, 1897.

Index